Survivor-Centred Justice

This volume interrogates global perspectives and issues that constitute and characterize survivor-centred justice, exploring the conceptual and theoretical issues surrounding the definition of a 'survivor', practical considerations of what constitutes a survivor-centred approach to justice and the avenues to justice that are available to survivors of mass atrocities.

In the first part of the book, survivor-centred justice is explored at the level of the International Criminal Court. The second part evaluates developments taking place at the local and domestic level where traditional, customary or local justice mechanisms find affinity with survivors in their quest for justice. The third part focuses on advocacy-based approaches being utilized specifically by non-governmental organizations and multilateral and regional institutions, such as the United Nations and the African Union, in support of survivors. In the final part of the book future prospects for survivors in the promotion of peacebuilding and atrocity prevention are discussed.

The discussions in this volume will be of particular value and importance to international and transitional justice scholars, including legal and development practitioners interested in survivor-centred approaches to mass atrocity crimes Most importantly it aims to be of value to survivors, survivor communities and survivor-centred networks.

Ingrid Roestenburg-Morgan is a Senior Research Fellow at the Institute for Justice and Reconciliation. She is both a legal practitioner and a scholar and specializes in international human rights, international criminal law and transitional justice. She has previously held positions at the International Criminal Court, the United Nations International Criminal Tribunal for the former Yugoslavia and ActionAid International.

Tim Murithi heads the Justice and Peacebuilding Program at the Institute for Justice and Reconciliation in Cape Town, South Africa. He is also Extraordinary Professor of African Studies at the Centre for African Studies, University of Free State, South Africa.

Europa Perspectives in Transitional Justice

The Europa Perspectives in Transitional Justice series from Routledge, edited by Professor Tim Murithi, provides a platform for innovative research and analysis of concepts, strategies and approaches to dealing with the past in deeply divided societies worldwide. The series encourages multidisciplinary scholarship on issues relating to reconciliation and how it is enhanced by efforts to promote redress and achieve socio-economic justice. The series aims to provide an invaluable resource for academics, policymakers, peace practitioners, researchers and all those interested in issues relating to addressing the deep-seated divisions within countries and communities. It also aims to propose forward-looking recommendations on how to achieve societal transformation.

The series comprises individual and edited volumes which provide analysis of transitions taking place at the global, regional and country levels, as well as engaging with thematic issues in the broad field of transitional justice and reconciliation.

Tim Murithi is Extraordinary Professor of African Studies at the Centre for African Studies, University of the Free State, and also Head of the Justice and Reconciliation in Africa Programme at the Institute for Justice and Reconciliation in Cape Town, South Africa. He has more than 21 years of experience in the fields of peacebuilding, governance, international justice and security in Africa. He sits on editorial boards and advisory panels for the *Journal of Peacebuilding and Development*, *African Journal of Conflict Resolution*, the *Africa Peace and Conflict Journal* and the journal *Peacebuilding*. He is author and editor of eight books; in addition he has authored more than 75 journal articles, book chapters and policy papers.

In the Shadow of Transitional Justice
Cross-national Perspectives on the Transformative Potential of Remembrance
Edited by Guy Elcheroth and Neloufer de Mel

Elections, Violence and Transitional Justice in Africa
Edited by Elias O. Opongo and Tim Murithi

Survivor-Centred Justice
Global Perspectives and Issues
Edited by Ingrid Roestenburg-Morgan and Tim Murithi

For more information about this series, please visit: www.routledge.com/Europa-Perspectives-in-Transitional-Justice/book-series/ECPTJ.

Survivor-Centred Justice

Global Perspectives and Issues

Edited by
Ingrid Roestenburg-Morgan and Tim Murithi

Routledge
Taylor & Francis Group
LONDON AND NEW YORK

Designed cover image: © Shutterstock

First published 2025
by Routledge
4 Park Square, Milton Park, Abingdon, Oxon OX14 4RN

and by Routledge
605 Third Avenue, New York, NY 10158

Routledge is an imprint of the Taylor & Francis Group, an informa business

British Library Cataloguing in Publication Data
A catalogue record for this book is available from the British Library

Library of Congress Cataloging-in-Publication Data
A catalog record has been requested for this book

ISBN: 9781032079899 (hbk)
ISBN: 9781032079950 (pbk)
ISBN: 9781003212409 (ebk)

DOI: 10.4324/9781003212409

Typeset in Times New Roman
by Taylor & Francis Books

Contents

Tables

The Editors and Contributors

Ingrid Roestenburg-Morgan is a Senior Research Fellow at the Institute for Justice and Reconciliation. She is both a legal practitioner and a scholar and specializes in international human rights, international criminal law and transitional justice. She has previously held positions at the International Criminal Court (ICC), the United Nations International Criminal Tribunal for the former Yugoslavia and ActionAid International. Her educational background includes the completion of a PhD and an LLM in International Criminal Law and Human Rights at the Netherlands Institute for Human Rights, Utrecht University, an LLB at the University of South Africa, specializing in Criminal Law, and a BA specializing in Sociology and Politics at the University of the Witwatersrand in Johannesburg, South Africa. Ingrid is particularly interested in the interplay between international criminal law, human rights and transitional justice including the intersections between mass violence, peace and security processes, the role of international criminal courts, international prosecutions, and traditional/local justice mechanisms within the African context.

Tim Murithi heads the Justice and Peacebuilding Program at the Institute for Justice and Reconciliation in Cape Town, South Africa. He is also Extraordinary Professor of African Studies, at the Centre for African Studies, University of Free State, South Africa. He has over 20 years' experience in the fields of peacebuilding, governance, international justice and security in Africa and has held posts in the Department of Peace Studies, University of Bradford, United Kingdom; the Institute for Security Studies in Addis Ababa, Ethiopia; and the United Nations Institute for Training and Research in Geneva, Switzerland. He has also served as an adviser to the African Union and the United Nations Development Programme (UNDP).

Mohammed Elgizoly Adam is a Sudanese Dutch national. He received his LLM from Utrecht University, specializing in Human Rights, and an LLB from Tilburg Law School in the Netherlands. He obtained his first BA degree from Juba University, South Sudan. Through his studies, he has monitored global issues and policies that influence peace and justice issues, specifically in Sudan, resulting in the publication of numerous research papers and policy reports.

Kuben David holds a BA in Fine Art and an MA in Media and Cultural Studies. He is currently undertaking a DPhil in Virtual and Augmented Reality. Based in Johannesburg, South Africa, he currently lectures in creative multimedia and consults as an art/creative Technology Director on projects. Kuben's area of interest is broad, encompassing the intersection of creativity, innovation and technology, which includes the merging of art, graphic design, storytelling, film, animation, non-linear interactivity and information design to create engaging user experiences (UX) for effective transfer of information.

Camila Fernandes Thomaz works as a Programme Manager at the Dr. Denis Mukwege Foundation in The Hague, Netherlands, supporting the Global Network of Victims and Survivors to End Sexual Violence in Conflict (SEMA) and enhancing the growth of the network. She has over five years of experience in movement building, sexual and gender-based violence prevention and response, gender equality and gender mainstreaming. She is particularly interested in post-conflict rebuilding, women and child protection, trauma-informed care and advocating for justice for victims of conflict-related sexual violence.

Monica Ingber is a Senior Lecturer in Law at Birmingham City University, UK. She has a PhD in Politics and International Relations from Keele University (2013) and an LLM in International Development Law and Human Rights from the University of Warwick (2017). Monica's monograph, *The Politics of Conflict: Transubstantiatory Violence in Iraq*, was published by McGill-Queen's University Press in 2015 and was nominated for the C.B. Macpherson Book Prize in 2016. Monica's research interests broadly include topics in international criminal law, gender justice and human rights.

Rozafa Kelmendi has over a decade of experience in journalism and project management, with a focus on gender issues and transitional justice. Since 2011 she has contributed to various projects for prominent organizations such as the Global Fund, UNDP and UN Women. In 2017 Rozafa joined UN Women, focusing on initiatives in integrating gender perspectives into transitional justice frameworks.

Emily Kenney is a Policy Specialist on Rule of Law and Transitional Justice at UN Women headquarters, where she works in the Peace, Security and Resilience Section on women's access to justice in conflict-affected countries and accountability for conflict-related sexual and gender-based violence. Emily holds a JD from NYU School of Law, USA, an MPhil from the University of Cape Town in Justice & Transformation Studies, and a BA from Tufts University, USA.

Malini Laxminarayan currently works for the Netherlands Helsinki Committee as a Programme Officer on topics related to criminal justice reform, including victim rights. She obtained her PhD in Law from Tilburg University, Netherlands, in the field of Victimology, following her MA in Criminology from the Catholic University Leuven. For the last 15 years Malini has worked for a number of organizations (NGOs, think tanks and universities), both in researcher and programme management roles. Her work has focused on themes around sexual violence in conflict (network building and survivor-centred advocacy globally but also including Bosnia, Kosovo and Ukraine), restorative justice, transitional justice and victim rights.

Michael Raila Odhiambo is a human rights expert currently based in the South Kivu province of the Democratic Republic of the Congo. He trained as a lawyer in the UK and the Netherlands and holds a PhD from the University of Cologne, Germany. He currently works for the German NGO Eirene International, supporting the organization Femmes Artisans de Paix as an adviser in the field of gender-sensitive conflict transformation. He was most recently a visiting lecturer at the University of Rwanda and the Université libre de Kigali.

Elias O. Opongo is a senior lecturer at Hekima Institute of Peace Studies and International Relations (HIPSIR), Hekima University College, Kenya, and the Director of the Centre for Research, Training and Publications at the same university. He holds a PhD in Peace Studies from the University of Bradford, UK, and an MA in International Peace Studies from the University of Notre Dame, USA. He is a peace, security and conflict researcher, resilience expert and conflict resolution practitioner. He is a transitional justice expert and post-conflict reconstructions analyst. He also researches on climate change impact, extractive industries and small-scale mining, and the impact of the proliferation of small arms and light weapons on state fragility.

Mariana Pena is a human rights lawyer with expertise in international justice. Over the past 20 years, she has focused primarily on access to justice for victims of mass atrocities and civil society-led accountability initiatives. She is currently the Director of Litigation Outreach at the Open Society Justice Initiative. Prior to joining the Open Society Foundations in 2015, she was a consultant in the non-profit sector. She previously worked in the representation of victims before the ICC and was the International Federation for Human Rights' Permanent Representative to the ICC.

Anusharani Sewchurran is an emerging scholar at the Centre for General Education, Durban University of Technology, South Africa. Her research interests include political economy of media, digital humanities and transformative pedagogy. She coordinates the DUT institutional modules, Cornerstone and Equality and Diversity. She is a member of the South African Society for Critical Theory and the Isigqi Sobuntu Organisation, a community development organization based at the Ezakhaleni informal Settlement, Umlazi.

Foreword

Esperande Bigirimana Survivor

In 2017 I participated in a series of international survivor retreats facilitated by the Dr. Denis Mukwege Foundation, uniting survivors of sexual violence from more than 15 countries. Afterwards it became clear that I was meant to act as agent of change and, together with a group of other survivors, I helped to create the Global Network of Victims and Survivors to End Wartime Sexual Violence (SEMA). Today, the SEMA network brings together survivors who work with frontline organizations supporting them on their healing and advocacy journeys. I am one of the oldest and most active members of this network and I have participated in numerous capacity-building training and advocacy events around the world. In 2018, with the necessary support and mentorship, I received the #ChangeTheCulture award for helping to change the culture of violence against girls and women and speaking out on the needs of survivors of sexual violence. As a result, a number of survivors established a global survivors' network bringing a unified voice in addressing sexual violence and in amplifying survivors' voices around the world. The network advocates that all duty bearers be held accountable in their obligation to ensure access to justice for all survivors.

As a survivor and while working with other survivors, I came to learn that rape during war or conflict is the only crime in which the victim becomes the accused. Justice from my perspective therefore entails that my story is believed and treated with respect. It means that like other survivors I should receive the recognition that a crime has been committed against me. Furthermore, it means that I should receive an apology from my government and be helped and supported in rebuilding my life. If this does not happen, then the crime remains unaddressed and unfinished business. The longer it takes to address the issue of accountability by governments, the longer survivors continue to suffer from the crime of rape and other heinous crimes committed during conflict.

In order to understand what a survivor is it is important that there is clarification on the distinction between the terms 'victim' and 'survivor'. From my perspective, the term 'victim' suggests a person who undergoes a physical incident resulting in an offender taking something meaningful from that person. It is also a technical term meant to define a person who has suffered as a result of a particular crime committed under the law. The term 'survivor', on the other hand, means surviving an incident whereby power is used in a wrongful way by one person against another to disempower the other. I define myself as survivor because although there are many people who have been violated or robbed of their power by perpetrators resulting in situations where victims have met their demise or continue to suffer emotionally or are depressed I have managed to survive against all the odds. The term 'survivor' gives me the courage and hope to speak out against the evil of abusing women's bodies through rape and using it as a weapon of war against innocent people.

It is therefore very important for survivors to be aware of and to know their rights. The only way that one can know one's rights is to meaningfully engage with and immerse oneself in the knowledgeable resources that are available on the topic such as the relevant books, stakeholder's views, workshops and information sessions. This is the start of a very good foundation in becoming empowered. My advice to all survivors is also to read up on your rights according to the Constitution of your relevant countries and to benefit from reading literature and books such as this one, which deal with the topic of survivors. This book advises survivors and associated stakeholders meaningfully on the various issues that could be of relevance and of benefit to survivors as well as those associated stakeholders and advocates of justice for survivors. It is a welcome and timely contribution, as the topic of survivor-centred justice is one that on many levels requires research and input from various stakeholders who are engaged on the topic.

Sexual violence, including conflict-related sexual violence, is undeniably a violation of human rights and it is one of the cruellest and steadily growing crimes in the world. It is not just a physical and violent act committed against one or more persons but it is a violation of the wider community and against humanity at large. Victims, survivors and their families suffer not only from the physical harm but have to deal with the enduring and devastating emotional and psychological effects of sexual violence that destabilize their lives forever. As survivors and citizens of humanity we need to work together to put an end to this inhumane and evil crime and all the other associated and heinous mass atrocity crimes that are committed during wartime.

April 2024

Acknowledgements

This book is dedicated to all those survivors who have run with endurance and overcome the obstacles and tribulations of this world with confidence and optimism onto victory. We would also like to thank all the contributors for their diligent efforts in compiling their chapters.

Introduction

Ingrid Roestenburg-Morgan

Background to the Conceptual and Theoretical Issues Underpinning Survivor-Centred Justice

Mass atrocities and atrocity crimes have been carried out throughout history and countless civilians have been murdered or left struggling to survive in the aftermath of conflict.[1] During the 20th century atrocity crimes multiplied fourfold and the gravity and severity of such crimes continue to be felt in the 21st century.[2] Within the framework of these developments the centrality of victims and survivors has become pivotal in the field of transitional justice.[3] Survivors of mass atrocities are increasingly placed centre stage through an elevation of certain human rights and a pronounced obligation on the international community to take collective action when states cannot do so on their behalf.[4] Through the conduit of various processes and avenues such as political and legal processes, survivors and those working on their behalf seek some measure of justice or redress that is meaningful. Such processes include advocacy-led processes and reconciliatory or holistic justice processes involving international, regional, domestic and local courts or tribunals. It is argued that through these relevant justice and human rights mechanisms the dignity of the survivor is upheld. In essence these political, legal and advocacy-led processes provide a conduit for survivors to tell their stories and, where possible, to meaningfully engage with others. However, the degree to which such processes are deemed to be meaningful and empowering to survivors remains a relative assessment and the question that arises is: to what extent can justice be adequately and effectively secured for survivors of mass atrocities given that each distinct category of process is unique and specific to survivors in their own right?

Thus, underpinning the rationale of survivor-centred justice is an unpacking of the meaning of justice while remaining cognizant of the victim–perpetrator dichotomy especially when one considers those affected by mass conflict or violence. In this regard one needs to consider the interchangeable roles that victims and perpetrators wield in conflict situations. Opinions vary on this topic; for example, at one end of the spectrum scholars purport that the notion of international criminal justice is purely symbolic or performative and does

DOI: 10.4324/9781003212409-1

not address the main issues driving mass violence.[5] Mahmood Mamdani, a leading commentor in this field has posited that survivor's justice should be seen as the process whereby victims transition to survivors as a result of successful political reform.[6] In other words, it is only through successful political processes underlying effective transition that justice for survivors and reconciliation can be achieved. On the other hand, some scholars have suggested that criminal prosecutions against perpetrators of mass atrocities weaken the effectiveness of the justice process especially if no measure of restoration between victim and perpetrator exists.[7] Thus, simply put, prosecution in its exclusivity diminishes the centrality of victims in the justice process and impairs any type of reconciliation that could ensue between victim and perpetrator and ultimately undermines reconciliation within the community as well. Similarly, an alternative argument is made on the premise that restorative justice applied exclusively undermines the justice process especially if no prosecutorial options to exact accountability for mass crimes are made available.[8] This is particularly the case where the scale, nature and the manner of commission of acts of mass violence indicate a diminished sense of personal, moral and legal responsibility on the part of the perpetrator, thereby making it impossible for states and survivors to forego retribution.[9] Arguably, therefore, the value of international criminal justice through prosecution remains a vital necessity within the framework of transitional justice especially if and when a customary duty to prosecute exists. The duty of prosecution is owed to all victims and survivors of mass atrocities.

What Are Mass Atrocities and Atrocity Crimes?

For the purposes of this book it is important to pinpoint and specify the particular group of survivors that the authors' contributions will pay heed to. In essence, this volume predominantly deals with survivors of mass atrocities or atrocity crimes. Currently mass atrocities and atrocity crimes understood to pertain to 'any large-scale brutality' are often deliberately directed against innocent civilians.[10] These attacks and crimes include genocide, crimes against humanity, war crimes and the crime of aggression, which are best understood and enunciated under international criminal law.[11] It can be seen that a clear correlation exists between mass atrocities and armed conflict. However, it is important to emphasize that not all armed conflicts can lead to mass atrocities. Since an alternative to this nexus also exists outside this accepted framework it may be plausible to conclude that mass atrocities can also occur outside the context of armed conflict and indeed even in peacetime.[12] Such occurrences take place when there is a violent change of government, when communal violence is orchestrated by non-state armed groups, and finally in the immediate aftermath of armed conflict when post-war retribution against former enemy groups are the order of the day.[13]

The severity of some of the atrocity crimes that have taken place over the course of history is best comprehended through an analysis of the number of civilians who have been murdered over the centuries and also through the nature of the carnage inflicted on innocent civilians who have been the victims of mass killings. It is estimated that between 30 BCE and 1900 CE as many as 40,457,000 civilians were killed.[14] Take, for example, the Christian Crusades, when some 70,000 civilians were slaughtered.[15] During the European colonization of the Americas it is estimated that around 15 million Native Americans living in both North and South America perished.[16] Similarly, the African slave trade that was spearheaded by the Europeans saw the latter claim the lives of an estimated 17 million Africans.[17] These grave examples are just a few examples of mass killings that took place during this particular era.

Current Challenges Pertaining to Mass Atrocities in the 21st Century

As mentioned earlier, during the 20th century the incidence of atrocity crimes multiplied fourfold and began to increase in severity, with the number of civilian deaths totalling a shocking 170 million.[18] Examples of such atrocities include the Armenian genocide, the Holocaust, the Khmer Rouge, the Iraq War, the civil wars in Liberia and Sierra Leone, the Bosnian War and the Rwanda genocide.[19] Sadly, in today's modern world such atrocities continue to persist and are ongoing such as in the Democratic Republic of the Congo and the Syrian Arab Republic where countless individuals have lost their lives and continue to endure harrowing circumstances and ruthless carnage on a daily basis. Factors fuelling modern-day conflicts and by implication acting as a catalyst for mass atrocity include migration, terrorism and the proliferation of arms and drugs.[20] Furthermore, modern-day conflict has become so much more complex than in the 20th century that it has come to 'represent highly complex internal disputes often involving non-state actors and armed groups who are not so easy recognizable as belligerents anymore'.[21]

This has dire implications for civilians caught up in conflicts in that the rules of war as promulgated under the auspices of International Humanitarian Law (IHL) that were intended to provide adequate protection for civilians are not respected as a result of the blurring of lines under IHL and consequently have resulted in innocent civilians being targeted. Such individuals fall prey to particularly heinous crimes such as sexual crimes, mutilations, forced killings and child soldier recruitment.[22]

State Responsibility to Protect and Provide Justice and Other Rights for Survivors

In the light of these developments there is broad consensus and a desire to protect people from acts of genocide, aggression, war crimes and crimes against humanity in the belief that these crimes have no place in the civilized world.[23] As a result, the Responsibility to Protect (R2P) concept was borne out of such consensus at the United Nations (UN) World Summit in 2005, and has come to form part of the international community's response mass atrocities and the killing of innocent civilians.[24] The R2P encourages states to prevent the incitement of mass atrocities and to protect their populations from genocide, war crimes, ethnic cleansing and crimes against humanity.[25] In addition, the international community is obliged to take collective action in the event that a state is unable to provide manifest protection to its population.[26]

Aside from the R2P doctrine, states are also burdened with the responsibility of ensuring justice after mass atrocities have taken place, and to steer their countries from conflict to peace.[27] This is how the discourse of transitional justice has developed. Aptly defined transitional justice refers to the 'full set of processes and mechanisms associated with a society's attempts to come to terms with a legacy of large scale abuse in order to ensure accountability, serve justice and receive reconciliation'.[28] A range of processes have been developed to help countries to make an effective transition such as justice processes, truth processes and institutional reform processes; however, in order to successfully realize transitional justice, both judicial and non-judicial processes may be employed. Within this framework tenets of retributive justice and restorative justice may also feature.[29]

The need for restorative justice within the transitional justice framework is pivotal for peace building with reconciliation as a final goal, in that it addresses both the societal and the individual needs of survivors of mass conflicts.[30] Similarly, retributive justice in the form of prosecution also serves an adjacent goal in many post-conflict societies, in that it advances political transition, deepens democratic cultures and offers human rights protection.[31] Furthermore, prosecutions are necessary because they have a deterrent effect; in addition, because mass atrocity crimes are so inhumane and heinous they demand accountability as part of a moral and legal obligation that the state in question owes to survivors of such atrocities.[32] Survivors who have been deeply scarred both physically and psychologically through the cruelty that typically is inflicted during incidents of mass violence require the assurance that such crimes will not take place again.[33] Thus, redress or reparations may be afforded to survivors by the state on two main grounds: it is the responsibility of the state to accord survivors reparations for the damage caused; and it is the responsibility of the state to prosecute those who are criminally responsible for the crimes committed.[34]

Thus, increasingly the centrality of victims and survivors has become pivotal within the discourse surrounding transitional justice and a growing consensus attests to the belief that certain rights need to be accorded to the victims and survivors of mass atrocities.[35]

Structure of the Book

With this related background and framework in mind this book will attempt to interrogate global perspectives and/or issues that constitute and characterize survivor-centred justice. The book will explore the conceptual and theoretical issues relating to survivor-centred justice that currently are under-investigated and under-reported. Take, for example, the frequent blurring of the terms 'victim' and 'survivor'. These terms are often employed interchangeably in the literature within international circles despite their multilayered meaning and connotations, which are often deliberately and politically utilized by proponents. Therefore, it is crucial to unpack these terms in order to gain a clearer understanding of what constitutes a 'survivor'. Relatedly, the book will by extension underpin current human rights arguments that support a survivor-centred approach to justice and which highlight pivotal human rights that are owed and imparted to victims and survivors of mass atrocities.

The book is divided into three parts, which will investigate and examine the way in which survivor-centred justice is usually administered at a practical level. In Part I an analysis of survivor-centred justice will be explored at the level of the International Criminal Court based in The Hague, Netherlands, which currently places victims and, arguably, survivors centre stage by allowing them to participate in all stages of the criminal proceedings.

Part II of this book looks at the innovative developments taking place at the domestic level where the administration of survivor-centred justice has found an affinity with traditional, customary or local justice mechanisms, which, because of their restorative nature, ensures that victims and survivors are provided with a space in which to meaningfully engage with others. Whether these mechanisms are indeed meaningful and useful to survivors of mass conflict will be explored in more detail in this part of the book.

Part III continues the investigation into the way survivor-centred justice is administered but with an emphasis on advocacy-based approaches and processes. In this regard the spotlight will focus on how non-governmental organizations (NGOs) and regional or multilateral institutions such as the UN and the African Union (AU) obtain and promote justice for survivors through the various initiatives they develop and propagate.

Finally, Part IV of this book considers new innovations and future prospects for survivors. This part dedicates itself to an examination of the prospects for survivors, which may only be made possible through the attainment of peace and security. In this regard the link between peacebuilding and atrocity prevention will come under scrutiny. Practical solutions available to post-conflict societies, such as restoring the human dignity of survivors through modern technology, including considering challenging the stereotypes of perpetrators, victims and survivors, will be explored for the benefit of survivors of mass conflict.

Theoretical and Conceptual Debates

Why 'Survivor' instead of 'Victim'?

As mentioned earlier it has become commonplace to often use the terms 'victim' and 'survivor' interchangeably. It is therefore important to clarify the meaning of these terms within the framework of this book. An attempt will be made to unpack the meaning of these definitions in more detail.

It is clear that both terms are multilayered and multifaceted and although at first glance they seem subtly similar they have different meanings and connotations. The term 'victim' usually refers to an individual who has suffered harm as a result of criminal conduct.[36] Many international laws, treaties and international organizations use the term 'victim' to denote a particular legal standing or status within the criminal justice system and also quite often within the transitional justice discourse.[37] Furthermore, on closer consideration and scrutiny some maintain that the term 'victim' may carry with it the connotation of passivity and helplessness, as well as of defeat or subjugation. Generally, the term is understood to refer to those who have been injured or killed during mass atrocities or those who have been subjugated to the types of crimes committed against them, leaving them defenceless and helpless during and after the commission of such crimes. In other words the term connotes a kind of 'passivity that robs an individual of their agency and their ability to fight back'.[38]

The term 'survivor', on the other hand, holds different connotations for those who have been caught up in mass atrocities and survived. From an activist and feminist position it implies that such individuals emerge victorious and triumphant regardless of their circumstances. It demonstrates an 'individual's ability to take action in the face of immense obstacles and the day to day work of surviving despite immense trauma', thereby suggesting tenacity and perseverance in the face of extreme and appalling circumstances.[39] The term 'survivor' therefore best depicts the 'trajectory of recovery' for individuals who consider themselves survivors of mass violence.[40] In essence the terminology is reflective of the way in which the individual positions themselves within their wider context. Therefore, the use of the term 'victim' or 'survivor' is ultimately a personal choice for a protagonist because it reflects the personal circumstances and ideologies of the person involved.

Feminists, for example, argue that the term 'survivor' is politically loaded as it confers agency upon women, which empowers them, and unlike the term 'victim' it is not a 'strategic construct used to win over public sympathy'.[41] In the latter instance it is common for activists to employ the term 'victim' in order to rally both government and public support for their causes but to the detriment of an individual or a woman's agency.[42] There are, however, others who also maintain that the term 'survivor' does not accurately sum up an individual's experience and that it is a misleading term in that it 'sugarcoats' the reality of an individual's trauma or experiences.[43] Furthermore, it vilifies victimhood by placing blame and shame on the individual concerned without putting focus on the perpetrator who actually should be the one in the public spotlight.[44] This argument therefore supports the notion that using the term 'victim' might not necessarily be devoid of agency if one considers mobilization and advocacy surrounding the term to the benefit of the individual and affected populations. Thus, it comes as no surprise that a further argument is posited, namely that the terms can be used interchangeably, chiefly because it is possible to be both a victim and a survivor depending on the circumstances and context that a protagonist finds themselves in.[45]

Arguments which prefer the term 'survivor' are quite often convincingly based on the goal to empower individuals and communities through the creation of agency. It is necessary for survivors to seek redress for past injustices by developing their capacity to pursue their own human dignity and peace.[46] While this book seeks to emphasize the role of survivors and by extension 'perpetrators' its aim is to ensure that both are beneficiaries of political, social and economic justice. Essentially, this book is mindful of the need to seek accountability and redress for the injustices suffered by those who have survived mass violence. This book thus intends to emphasize the need to provide justice for survivors through the various conduits available to them and which, if viewed holistically, could contribute to a survivor-centred approach.[47] Arguably, therefore, the term 'survivor' may be a more preferable choice because it falls in line with two basic human rights, namely restoring human dignity and ensuring justice to individuals and communities alike.

Arguments that support a survivor-centred approach to justice rely heavily on a number of human rights that should rightfully accrue to survivors of mass atrocities. For example, according to the UN Basic Guidelines on the Right to Remedy and Reparations for Victims of Gross Violations of International Humanitarian Law, victims and survivors have the right to justice, truth and reparations.[48] Therefore, the aforementioned rights are undoubtedly pivotal and form part of a larger network of rights that ought to accrue to survivors of mass atrocities. Let us consider briefly what kind of impact they have on survivors and their need for justice.

The Right to Justice

Justice means different things to different people and societies. Thus, the concept of justice is open to change and critique.[49] Arguably, from a predominantly Western perspective the term 'justice' has come to represent morality, ethics, rationality, law, religion, equity and fairness.[50] The right to justice as currently understood basically suggests the ability to have effective access to justice, which forms a fundamental part of the rule of law.[51] When access to justice is not readily available, victims or survivors are at a disadvantage, because they cannot exercise their rights or effectively challenge any type of discrimination. In other words there generally exists a presumption that justice can best be secured primarily through a retributive/court model of justice advocating for prosecution.[52] Part of accessing the court system would mean that it should be accessible to all and that it should lead to results that are individually and socially just.[53] However, given the political complexity of post-conflict societies, it is a difficult and Herculean task to ensure that all victims of mass atrocities are able to access justice.[54]

For this reason more holistic approaches to justice are advocated for which include bottom-up approaches to reconciliation. These include traditional or alternative justice systems such as truth commissions as well as community or traditional justice systems, which arguably are better equipped to address large-scale justice needs, keeping cost-effectiveness and reconciliation in mind.[55] Furthermore, more holistic approaches to justice facilitate effective victim and survivor participation, thereby meaningfully empowering victims and survivors and enhancing the legitimacy of the criminal justice systems in place.[56]

While victim participation at the international level is generally poor in most criminal proceedings and trials, the benefits of victim participation are increasingly being acknowledged and have been equated with restoring the dignity of the victim or survivor.[57] The most innovative development in this regard has been at the level of the International Criminal Court (ICC) where victims may participate in all stages of the criminal proceedings, subject to permission from the chamber in question.[58] Thus, victim participation remains at the discretion of the court, so that the defendant's rights must be balanced against the victim's rights in any determination concerned.[59]

While the ICC has certainly made enormous strides in encouraging victims to participate in the criminal justice process, victim participation also finds a very strong affinity with traditional, alternative or local justice mechanisms which are considered more restorative in nature because of their ability to place the victim or survivor at the centre of the justice process concerned and because much of the time these justice systems are accessible to the public.[60] Many of these mechanisms ensure that victims are able to tell their stories in a way that is culturally and psychologically meaningful. Such expressions are important because they are healing, empowering and cathartic, while at the same time affording accessible justice to all.[61]

It should be noted, however, that traditional or local justice mechanisms are only deemed accountable and legitimate at the international level and thus at the ICC, subject to modification, part of which would include having a prosecutorial option at hand, as well as due process standards in place.[62] Thus, certain aspects of retributive justice such as prosecution and punishment are important, including due process standards, as well as a genuine intention of the state concerned to try those accused, if such mechanism are to qualify in accordance with international standards.[63] Two mechanisms that may serve as blueprints in this regard, both of which arguably could be qualified at the international level, are Rwanda's Gacaca Courts as well as the South African Truth and Reconciliation Commission (TRC).[64] It should be noted, however, that the strength of the aforementioned mechanisms essentially has been qualified based on their holistic nature and accessibility to justice. Not only does this endow them with greater legitimacy but also, and more importantly, ensures an adequate degree of participation for victims and survivors, including perpetrators.[65]

The Right to Truth

The right to truth is based on the premise that victims and survivors of serious human rights abuses, as well as their families, have the right to know the truth to the fullest extent possible.[66] Part of this right also extends to the identity of the perpetrators, the causes, circumstances and facts surrounding violations, and ultimately the fate and whereabouts of victims in the case of forced disappearances.[67] While the right to truth has not been explicitly mentioned in any particular multilateral treaty it has emerged through applicable jurisprudence and applicable case law of the Inter-American System and Human Rights Commission which has emphasized a state's obligation to reveal the truth about disappeared persons as well as gross violations of human rights, such as extrajudicial executions and torture.[68]

According to the Inter-American Court, 'victims and their families have the right to obtain clarification of the facts through judicial investigation and adjudication'.[69] In other words, there appears to be a direct link between the right to justice and truth through judicial adjudication and thus formally through the courts. Other legal instruments that articulate the right truth include Protocol 1 of the Geneva Conventions and the UN Convention on the Protection of All Persons from Forced Disappearance, both of which place obligations on states to uncover the truth. While national and international criminal justice proceedings may not be the 'most effective avenues to uncover the truth' they do prioritize accountability for victims and survivors and also have a therapeutic effect for victims and survivors.[70] In this regard, arguably the most effective mechanism in unravelling the truth in a specific context was the TRC, which not only incorporated a thorough truth-telling process, but also ensured that a historical record was kept of the events that took place during apartheid and contributed to restoring the rights of victims and survivors by providing reparations and rehabilitation to such persons.[71]

The Right to Reparations

The provision of support for victims and survivors also includes the right to reparations, which is intended to recognize the losses and pain suffered by victims and survivors as well as providing actual benefits to the latter whether material or symbolic or a combination of both in an attempt to assist them out of dire poverty or suffering caused by mass violence.[72]

Offending states are obliged to provide reparations by way of restitution, compensation or satisfaction as a result of the violations suffered by such persons.[73] Reparations may also be claimed at the level of the ICC for atrocity crimes, including the commission of war crimes, crimes against humanity and the crime of aggression, under the Rome Statute by victims, either directly or indirectly by their representative family members who have suffered as a result of such a victims loss.[74]

The Rome Statute and the ICC's Rules of Procedure and Evidence lays down the rights available to victims who must first qualify as ICC victims before reparations may be granted. Pursuant to Article 75 of the Rome Statute, the ICC may provide reparations to victims in the form of restitution, indemnification and rehabilitation and has the option of granting individual or collective reparations in this regard.[75] Such reparations are dispensed from the court's Trust Fund for Victims, which is an independent initiative. The Trust Fund has a 'two fold mandate, namely to implement Court-ordered reparations and … to provide physical, psychological, and material support to victims and their families'.[76]

Reparations are valuable in that they help to restore the dignity of the victim by serving as a public acknowledgement of the commitment that the state in question has made to acknowledge past wrongs as well as to avoid such wrongs in the future.[77] Ensuring reparations for victims elevates their standing and places their needs more centrally by addressing them directly. This is invaluable because it helps to build trust in the state and is a means of securing sustainable peace for the future.[78] Reparations may therefore be seen as providing a measure of justice to victims and ultimately to survivors, and is thus also linked to the right to justice by 'offering victims a future that may alleviate to some extent, the suffering that they have endured'.[79]

This book will therefore critically engage on these and other related conceptual and theoretical debates in much more detail in order to provide a deeper understanding of the rights that survivors are entitled to.

Administering Survivor-Centred Justice

The administration of justice for survivors of mass atrocities clearly is not confined to criminal or retributive justice but transcends the boundaries of black letter law. Here various processes and advocacy at both the international and national level can provide a measure of justice for survivors. In order to understand how justice for survivors may be meaningfully employed or administered Parts I, II and III of this book will interrogate the various avenues to justice that are available to survivors of mass atrocities.

Part I: An Analysis of the International Criminal Court in the Administration of Survivor-Centred Justice

Often believed to be the foremost or predominant avenue to justice for survivors of mass atrocity is the criminal and human rights machinery of the state and the international community. In this regard both domestic and international courts can function in tandem to prosecute crimes of mass atrocity to the benefit of the survivor. Part I of this book will therefore look at how the international criminal court practically administers justice for survivors. A central focus will be on the ICC as the first international court to give victims and arguably survivors the opportunity to participate in legal proceedings.[80] By affording such actors the opportunity to voice their concerns during the various stages of legal proceedings the court has taken innovative steps.[81] Based on the lessons learnt from other international criminal tribunals the ICC has now placed the rights of victims' centre stage and more on par with those the accused. In this way it may be argued that the court has incorporated both the retributive and restorative aspects (through reparations) of justice as a holistic approach towards justice in dealing with mass atrocity crimes and has taken the lead in international criminal justice by advancing and prioritizing the experiences of victims and survivors.[82]

Despite these developments, however, numerous critics of victim participation at the ICC have questioned whether this development within the field of international criminal justice can be deemed worthwhile.[83] They also question whether it still makes sense to include an additional component of meaningful participation for victims in the light of the complexity of the criminal justice process, which now means having to contend with both victim and perpetrator.[84] Thus, navigating the international legal process with an additional actor's interests included is no easy feat in international trials of such a magnitude. This could create tension in terms of balancing the rights of the accused with the meaningful participation of the victims or survivors in question.[85]

Some critics also further contend that the ICC ought to give victims and survivors a stronger platform by paying heed to their individual voices and motivations. Thus far, the court has been criticized for speaking about victims as a single unit or entity especially given that currently the existing narrative on victims has been reduced to single-type category, namely victims of mass atrocities, and a single type of justice, namely justice at the ICC.[86] This result may be offensive to individual victims and survivors who have different desires and needs for recognition of the wrongs committed against them and the type of justice they would like to see meted out.[87]

Furthermore, according to some critics, victim participation through reparations claims should not come to represent symbolic measures of justice such as a public apology, commemoration or memorial only, but instead should always include measures such as monetary compensation and returning property to victims who have been the targets of wrongdoers.[88] Essentially, the objective of ICC reparations is to relieve and alleviate the suffering caused to victims and to promote the deterrence of such crimes while ultimately promoting reconciliation within the wider victim community.[89] In other words these objectives can mostly be carried out through satisfaction in the form of monetary compensation. Thus, the value of reparations in relation to survivors at the ICC will therefore be considered in more detail in Part I of this book.

Part I of this book will in an interrelated way pay heed to the ICC's value as an important transitional justice tool for survivors. It is well known that the main responsibility of the ICC is to investigate and prosecute genocide, war crimes, crimes against humanity and the crime of aggression.[90] However, before the ICC is authorized to intervene in conflict settings states must first be given the primary right to carry out their own investigations and prosecutions.[91] This principle is commonly referred to as the 'principle of complementarity' and it envisions effective investigation and prosecution at both the domestic and international level.[92]

Recently, the ICC's Office of the Prosecutor emphasized that justice for survivors can only be realized through effective investigation and prosecution of mass atrocity crimes at both the domestic and international level but only if there is political will on the part of states that have signed up to the Rome Statute and genuine willingness by states to bring perpetrators of mass atrocity crimes to justice.[93] In other words, in order for justice to be secured for survivors of mass violence there would need to be the optimum functioning of the principle of complementarity as set out under the Rome Statute. The mustering of political will and the willingness of states to initiate an investigation and prosecution underlies the meaning of the principle of complementarity, which by definition delineates that states have the primary right to investigate and prosecute mass atrocity crimes that have occurred on their territories before the ICC may accordingly be authorized to intervene.[94]

Thus, the ICC must be seen as a court of last resort rather than a court of first instance when mass atrocities take place. In this regard, it is necessary for both the ICC and national systems to coordinate with one another in an effort to ensure that lower-ranking perpetrators are prosecuted domestically in addition to the high-level perpetrators that the ICC focuses on at the international level.[95] Furthermore, the Court has reiterated that no person is exempt from criminal responsibility which means that investigations and prosecutions may be instituted against persons in positions of authority, including sitting heads of state, regardless of their official capacity.[96]

There is therefore an assumption, or as others may argue a prerequisite, that states need to be more proactive and ensure that they carry out their investigative and prosecutorial obligations as envisioned under the principle of complementarity. However, given certain fundamental challenges that states often grapple with during transitions such as lack of political will, lack of state resources and lack of capacity, effective justice may be unsuccessful in many instances leaving victims and survivors at the mercy of the transitional state in question.[97] Since the ICC is not in a position to assist with the aforementioned hurdles it has accordingly focused its efforts on urging states to enhance their own judicial capacity through bilateral agreements or rule of law programmes.[98]

Aside from the retributive function of the ICC, namely ensuring that perpetrators are effectively prosecuted for atrocity crimes, the Court also emodies elements of restorative justice, which makes it unique in supporting victims and arguably survivors more readily. Part I of this book will therefore focus extensively on victim participation at the ICC, as well as relatedly on the work for the Trust Fund for Victims. In addition it will flesh out the definition of a victim under the ICC's legal framework as well as focusing more exclusively on the definition and legal category of a survivor and a survivor-centred approach as understood by the ICC.

Part II: Administering Survivor-Centred Justice: Local and Communal Modalities

In continuation of effectively administering justice for survivors of mass atrocity, Part II of this book will address whether customary, informal and/or traditional justice mechanisms can justifiably be seen as a viable avenue to justice for survivors. In the context of Africa, transitional justice has essentially found its roots in the use of traditional justice. Since the 1990s a plethora of judicial and non-judicial mechanisms have been employed by African states, which very often feature restorative tenets of justice such as forgiveness, friendship and compassion between victim and perpetrator, thus mimicking transitional justice objectives as we know them today.[99] These justice mechanisms have been called a variety of names including customary or informal justice mechanisms, traditional justice mechanisms, alternative justice mechanisms and/or local justice mechanisms. The goal of traditional justice mechanisms as understood from an African perspective is usually to secure reconciliation and national unity by drawing on cultural or religious linkages.[100] Some examples of the latter mechanisms include several truth commissions that have been employed over the years in various African countries such as Uganda, Zimbabwe, Nigeria, Ghana, Sierra Leone and South Africa. Other examples include the gacaca courts in Rwanda, the role of the magamba spirits in Mozambique, the mato oput ritual in northern Uganda, the tradition-based practices of the Kpaa Mende in Sierra Leone and the bashingantahe, or wise men, of Burundi.[101]

The use of such mechanisms has essentially been to address large-scale justice needs, keep the cost-effectiveness of the justice system in check and most importantly ensure that political reconciliation is achieved as a final goal.[102] However, this does not necessarily suggest that traditional justice mechanisms provide an adequate measure of justice for victims and survivors undergoing transition, especially if one considers that the gravity of violence committed during conflict situations far exceeds the more ordinary kinds of crime committed on an everyday basis.

Proponents of traditional justice mechanisms nonetheless have stressed the inclusiveness of such systems, which incorporates both victim and perpetrator within the justice process so that these main stakeholders can meaningfully engage with and further empower survivors of mass violence. This in turn is beneficial, in that it enhances the legitimacy of the justice system already in place.[103]

Currently, however, there exists a presumption that justice is by nature retributive, but on closer scrutiny post-conflict societies reveal a much more complex picture whereby victim and perpetrator often switch roles and thus the lines between both actors become blurred.[104] Thus, employing a purely retributive or restorative system of justice may therefore not be the answer or panacea to mass violence.[105] As a result, these more holistic systems of justice are often advocated for in complex post-conflict societies. In this regard, traditional, alternative or local justice mechanisms can be quite valuable in terms of their ability to address large-scale justice needs, their cost-effectiveness, their capacity for truth telling and their ability to promote healing and political reconciliation.[106] Furthermore, proponents of these mechanisms often highlight their inclusive and participatory nature, which in many cases often leads to meaningful engagement between victims and perpetrators.[107]

However, in order for such mechanisms to be of value to survivors and to the societies in which they operate some argue that these mechanisms would need to undergo revision in order to meet the tensions between tradition and modernity since complications arise when these justice mechanisms become subject to scrutiny at the international level, when for instance they are accompanied with blanket amnesties for perpetrators or when they cannot supposedly meet due process standards of the law.[108]

Some findings reveal that purely restorative models of justice will not be able to meet the justice needs of victims and survivors in the context of mass violence simply because perpetrators wield a diminished sense of personal, moral and legal responsibility characterized by the type of crimes they have committed, where in comparison to everyday or ordinary crime, the scale, nature and gravity of the crime and the manner in which it has been committed is exceptional.[109] Furthermore, not all victims find themselves in a position to pardon or forgive their offender, a requirement that is often implicit in a restorative system of justice that functions without any retributive strands.[110] Additionally, states have a further obligation under international law to prosecute perpetrators of mass atrocity in order to prevent similar crimes from occurring on their territories in the future.[111] States cannot violate their legal and human rights obligations and thus it is difficult to forego prosecution in the light of these international obligations.[112] Some convincing arguments therefore suggest that for these mechanisms to be effective a prosecutorial option must be included within their broader framework if they are to meet such international standards and scrutiny, particularly at the ICC.[113]

Furthermore, despite the holistic propensity that many of these mechanisms exude it is noteworthy that when traditional and local justice mechanisms contribute to peacebuilding they also have the potential in some instances to undermine the legality of the justice process.[114] This happens when, for instance, they negatively marginalize or impact vulnerable groups such as women or children and in some cases those in a given community, who feel dissatisfied with the type of justice being dispensed.[115] Needless to say, these shortcomings require careful thought and recalibration for future avoidance. The status quo that is currently deemed as effective justice follows the line of reasoning that prosecution and hence retributive justice is the only adequate source and avenue necessary to exact accountability and appease survivors' rights after prolonged civil wars and mass conflict.[116]

In the light of the aforementioned discussion Part II will consider whether traditional/alternative or local justice mechanisms are capable of and sufficiently effective in addressing the justice needs of survivors. An examination will therefore be made to consider the use of such mechanisms in post-conflict societies, particularly in Africa, with a consideration of their effectiveness and legitimacy as an avenue to justice for post-conflict societies. An additional purpose of this section is to understand how formal justice systems can engage in a complementary manner with such mechanisms.

Part III: Administering Survivor-Centred Justice: Advocacy-Based Approaches

Part III of this volume will focus on the advocacy efforts of NGOs and civil society organizations including other international and regional institutions such as the UN and the AU to understand how these actors advocate justice for survivors of mass atrocities. The objective of this is to draw attention to those efforts that often go unnoticed and to gain a deeper understanding of the pivotal role that such civil society actors and international and regional organizations play on behalf of survivors and additionally to consider the deep impact that they can have in influencing change for survivors.

NGOs have played a fundamental role in ensuring justice for survivors of mass atrocities. Despite these efforts within the field of transitional justice field there is lack of 'comprehensive conceptualization of the role that civil society plays in transitional justice processes'.[117] As a result, the discourse of transitional justice is further narrowed and boasts less scholarship on the role and contribution that civil society currently provides to victims and survivors undergoing transition or emerging from conflict.[118] Furthermore, in recent years there has been an emergence of a 'new' civil society whereby new modes of organization are linked to social movement modalities and other forms of collective action.[119]

Civil society actors, as a result, have changed the way in which justice in transition is dispensed to victims and survivors mainly through the addition and efforts of social movements, the latter of which drives change more democratically and effectively.[120] Social movements have thus been instrumental in forging a new identity with traditional civil society and are thus integral to the creation of the contemporary discourse of transitional justice, 'most notably through victims' movements such as the Madres de Plaza de Mayo in Argentina and the Khulumani Support Group in South Africa'.[121] As social movements are a source of identity for victims, for example, they are able to create and mobilize constituencies more easily as well as to transform the identities of their constituents, and thus a new civil society has emerged.

This new civil society separates itself from traditional civil society, which mainly was concerned with mediating between the individual and the state but instead it integrates and modifies traditional civil society's organizational modes with those of the new social movements, including broader discussions on justice in transition by placing transitional justice closer to contemporary activism and processes.[122] Part of this section will thus delve into a broader understanding of the efforts undertaken by this new civil society to understand how NGOs, through the efforts of social movements, obtain justice for survivors of mass atrocities and influence justice in transition for such survivors.

Along with NGOs international and regional organizations such as the UN and the AU also attempt to give survivors and victims a central place in the advocacy processes that they initiate and implement during transitional justice processes. For instance, in April 2019 the UN passed Resolution 2467 which reinforces and bolsters a survivor-centred approach to preventing and addressing all acts and forms of sexual violence in conflict and post-conflict situations. This also entails encouraging member states to adopt a 'survivor-centred approach ensuring that survivors receive the care required by their specific needs without discrimination'.[123] The UN Security Council has 'urged states to recognize the equal rights of all affected individuals in national legislation and also urged states to apply targeted sanctions against those who perpetrate direct sexual violence during conflict'.[124] By recognizing a survivor-centred approach to sexual violence during conflict the aim of Resolution 2467 is to provide timely assistance to survivors of sexual violence, part of which includes comprehensive health care catering to the specific needs of survivors.[125]

Additionally encapsulated within these efforts is the need to investigate and accordingly prosecute such crimes.[126] Another important aspect of this resolution has also been the emphasis and support it places on 'civil society organizations in supporting survivors of sexual violence through prevention and response efforts including capacity building of survivor led organizations'.[127] Ultimately, the objectives and future impact of this resolution has been considered by many to be ambitious but its benefit lies in its ability to secure peace and security in the long term which is the basis of justice for survivors of mass atrocities.[128]

Like the UN, regional organizations such as the AU have also taken numerous steps in vanquishing violence and vulnerability in humanitarian settings in support of survivors. For instance, in 2014 the UN and the AU entered into a landmark agreement of cooperation on the prevention of and response to conflict-related sexual violence in Africa.[129] The agreement essentially serves as an overarching framework for cooperation between the two aforementioned organizations in various key areas such as combating impunity for perpetrators, capacity building and training to enhance the capacity of peacekeepers and security actors, as well as strengthening national policies, legislation and institutions working on conflict-related sexual violence.[130] The agreement also emphasizes the importance of services for survivors, empowering women and girls, and countering the stigma endured by survivors.[131]

Relatedly and adjacent to this effort the Guidelines on Combating Sexual Violence and its Consequences in Africa (also known as the Niamey Guidelines) were adopted by the African Commission Human and Peoples Rights in May 2017.[132] 'The goal of the aforementioned set of guidelines has been to guide and support member states of the AU in effectively implementing their commitment and obligations to combat sexual violence and its consequences.'[133] The intention of the Niamey Guidelines is to support survivors through essentially assisting states to respond to survivors' concerns and to meet their needs. Since this primary responsibility rests on states the African Commission has garnered and combined strength and support from its member states to meet the needs of survivors of sexual violence by helping to prevent sexual violence and its consequences through a variety of strategies, including protecting and supporting the victims of sexual violence in various ways.[134] The Niamey Guidelines also calls for investigating sexual violence and prosecuting those responsible. This also includes investigating and prosecuting crimes of sexual violence in situations of conflict such as international crime. Finally, states are obliged to guarantee survivors access to 'appropriate, efficient, accessible, timeous and long-lasting reparation for injury and loss suffered by victims of sexual violence, as well as access to appropriate information regarding reparation mechanisms'.[135]

Both the UN and the AU have intensified their efforts to deepen collaboration on the peace and security issues plaguing the African continent. In April 2017 the Joint United Nations-African Union Framework for an Enhanced Partnership in Peace and Security was adopted.[136] This framework has led to a more strategic partnership that seeks to achieve peace and security on the African continent through an underlying emphasis on the importance of humanitarian and human rights law.[137] The framework thus calls for an increased common understanding between the two institutions about the causes of conflict in Africa, to find ways to help to prevent conflict through early warning systems and to identify any potential hotspots as well as using preventive diplomacy as a cooperative mechanism to evade potential conflict situations.[138] There has been a commitment to redouble efforts between both organizations, including coordinating and synergizing efforts across a sequence of responses such as mediation and conflict management.[139] Other areas of joint collaboration emphasized in the framework include efforts to support sustainable peace, regular meetings to review the collaborative partnership and to support the progress of the partnership, and finally to discover ways for both the UN and the AU to identify and mobilize the resources necessary to secure peace and security.[140]

This brief summary of some of the efforts undertaken by civil society organizations attest to the importance of a survivor-centred approach advocated by civil society and major institutions such as the UN and the AU which have the capacity to influence awareness and change for survivors of mass atrocity. Given the vast efforts that the UN and the AU employ in promoting justice for survivors in conflict and post-conflict situations Part

III of this volume will devote itself to an understanding of some of these efforts as well other advocacy-based efforts in order better to grasp how justice for survivors may be advanced within this sphere.

Part IV: Future Prospects for Survivor-Centred Justice

Part IV of this volume examines the prospects for survivors, which may only be made possible through the attainment of peace and security. In this regard the link and/or nexus between peacebuilding and atrocity prevention will come under scrutiny. Given the fact that both aforementioned areas have complementary but distinct goals it is necessary to understand the relationship between peacebuilding and atrocity prevention especially if mass violence is to be prevented or avoided and a peaceful future secured for survivors.[141]

Currently, atrocity prevention can be interpreted as

> a broad range of tools and strategies which aim to prevent the occurrence of mass killings and other large-scale human rights abuses committed against civilians, while peacebuilding as currently defined involves a range of measures targeted to reduce the risk of lapsing or relapsing into conflict by strengthening national capacities at all levels for conflict management, and to lay the foundations for sustainable peace and development.[142]

While historically these separate fields are considered distinctive in that atrocity prevention is steeped in accountability frameworks such as human rights and international criminal justice, and peacebuilding in conflict resolution, their similarity lies in their common goal to prevent mass violence and mass atrocity which creates a nexus between both areas.[143] According to experts and practitioners in both fields, both disciplines need to be integrated in order to secure the most effective solutions in combating cycles of violence and conflict.[144] This would result in a more inclusive approach, which takes into account 'community dialogue, peace education, reconciliation, local mediation and the engagement of different actors at local, national and international level'.[145]

Part IV of this volume will focus on this important nexus and will consider factors such as the obstacles that currently undermine efforts in preventing mass atrocity. Some of these obstacles include but are not limited to

> insufficient or weak institutional governance, the prevalence of non-state armed groups motivated by local disputes, the deep social divisions suffered by many communities with respect to their ethnic and religious identities, the negligent attention and action by regional actors towards the civilian population, hate speech in the media heightening tensions and anger, and the numerous constraints on civil society imposed by some governments including harassment, intimidation and attacks.[146]

Part IV concludes the volume. It will provide practical solutions for use by the international community, such as restoring survivors' human dignity through the use of modern technology in post-conflict societies, as well as taking into consideraion perpetrator, beneficiary and bystander engagement and gender stereotypes in the pursuit of redress and accountability and ultimately in the prevention of future mass atrocities.

Conclusion

The Conclusion will draw on the key insights developed in the chapters in this volume and will provide an assessment of the challenges facing survivor-based justice as well as making recommendations for the optimal ways forward. It should be emphasized that the value of this book lies in bringing together a dense and often inaccessible, albeit highly relevant, discussion on survivors and their experiences. In addition it shines a spotlight on the administration of justice for survivors, thereby allowing for the merging of the juridical, legal, advocacy-based and political aspects of justice, which will provide deeper insight into the availability of policy-orientated solutions that are open to survivors, who might otherwise be unaware of such avenues to justice. Another valuable aspect of this book is that it takes into account the views of experts and practitioners hailing from a variety of different disciplines, institutions and sectors in order to participate and engage on this topic meaningfully, which would not ordinarily occur given the lack of publicity and roundtable discussions on the topic. This book therefore seeks to pay critical attention to voices from the international community in order to overcome the binaries that exist in transitional justice conversations and policy circles. In uniquely being able to take the lessons from across multiple contexts, this book accommodates an equality of voices. It is anticipated that it will help readers to address the most complex set of concerns that plague survivors, namely the most important steps that need to be taken to ensure a holistic range of responses for justice for survivors of mass atrocities. It is pertinent and timely in that it focuses on NGOs, activists and other related allies who can equip survivors with the knowledge and networks they need in order to be proactive leaders in their quest for peace and justice. It is innovative in the sense that thus far there has not been any related literature on the efforts of civil society, and furthermore one that merges these so-called efforts from various sectors into a holistic understanding of justice. In essence, the main goal of this volume is to cater to survivors' justice needs by providing them with a holistic range of sustainable support in the form of theoretical and practical solutions to some of the conundrums entwined with their experiences as survivors and as guidance in their quest for justice.

Notes

1 K. Petty, 'Humanity and National Security: The Law of Mass Atrocity Response Operations', *Michigan Journal of International Law*, 34(4), 2013, pp. 749–750.
2 Ibid.; see also R.J. Rummel, *Death by Government* (New York: Routledge, 1994), pp. 31, 47, 48, 59.
3 B. Fonseka and J. Naples-Mitchell, 'Victim Centered Transitional Justice in Sri Lanka: What Does it Really Mean? Discussion Paper', Center for Policy Initiatives, 2017, available at http://www.cpalanka.org/wp-content/uploads/2017/02/Victim-centred-TJ-1.pdf (accessed 11 June 2019).
4 J. Streitfeld-Hall, 'Responsibility to Protect: Can We Prevent Mass Atrocities Without Making the Same Mistakes', Global Centre for the Responsibility to Protect, 2015, available at https://civicus.org/images/Responsibility%20to%20Protect.pdf (accessed 3 September 2018).
5 M. Mamdani, 'How Shall We Think of Mass Violence: Criminal or Political? Reflections on Nuremberg and CODESA', Paper presented at the Makerere Institute of Social Research, at the Workshop, Public Violence, Justice and the Rule of Law, Kampala, Uganda, 8–9 March 2011; see also T. Mbeki and M. Mamdani, 'Courts Can't End Civil Wars', *The New York Times*, 5 February 2014.
6 Ibid.
7 H. Zehr, *Changing Lenses: A New Focus for Crime and Justice* (Windsor, ON: Herald Press, 2005).
8 D. Orentlicher, 'Settling Accounts: The Duty to Prosecute Human Rights Violations of a Prior Regime', *The Yale Law Journal*, 100(8), 1991, pp. 2537–2615.
9 I. Roestenburg-Morgan, *The Road to Reconciliation: Optimizing the Legitimacy and Efficacy of the ICC Within the African Union and Africa* (Cambridge: Intersentia, 2023).
10 Petty, 'Humanity and National Security'.
11 The Rome Statute of the International Criminal Court, available at https://www.icc-cpi.int/resource-library/documents/rs-eng.pdf (accessed 14 June 2019).
12 A. Bellamy, 'Mass Atrocities and Armed Conflict: Links, Distinctions and Implications for the Responsibility to Protect', The Stanley Foundation, Policy Analysis Brief, 2011, pp. 2–3.
13 Ibid.
14 Petty, 'Humanity and National Security'; see also Rummel, *Death by Government.*
15 Ibid.
16 Ibid.
17 Ibid.
18 Ibid.
19 Ibid.
20 C.S. Villalba, 'Transitional Justice: Key Concepts, Processes and Challenges', Briefing Paper, Institute for Democracy and Conflict Resolution, University of Essex Knowledge Gateway, 2011; see also Roestenburg-Morgan, *The Road to Reconciliation*, p. 141.
21 Ibid.
22 Ibid.
23 Streitfeld-Hall, 'Responsibility to Protect'.
24 Ibid.
25 Ibid.
26 Ibid.
27 Roestenburg-Morgan, *The Road to Reconciliation.*

28 Ibid.; see also K. Annan, 'The Rule of Law in Conflict and Post-Conflict Societies', Report of the UN Secretary-General, 23 August 2004, p. 4.
29 Roestenburg-Morgan, *The Road to Reconciliation*.
30 Ibid.
31 Ibid., p. 142; see also Villalba, 'Transitional Justice'.
32 Ibid., p. 153.
33 Ibid.
34 Ibid.
35 Fonseka and Naples-Mitchell, 'Victim-Centered Transitional Justice in Sri Lanka'.
36 R. Krystall, 'The Subjects of Mass Atrocities: Victims or Survivors?' (blog), *Reinventing Peace* (Somerville, MA: World Peace Foundation, 2014).
37 Ibid.
38 Ibid.
39 Ibid.;, see also R. Gupta, '"Victim" vs. "Survivor": Feminism and Language', *50.50 Gender, Sexuality and Social Justice*, 16 June 2014, available at https://www.opendemocracy.net/5050/rahila-gupta/victim-vs-survivor-feminism-and-language (accessed 28 May 2019).
40 Krystall, 'The Subjects of Mass Atrocities'.
41 Gupta, '"Victim" vs. "Survivor"'.
42 Ibid.
43 Ibid.
44 Krystall, 'The Subjects of Mass Atrocities'; see too Gupta, '"Victim" vs. "Survivor"'.
45 Ibid.
46 Institute for Justice and Reconciliation, Strategic Plan 2017–2020, 10 November 2016.
47 Ibid.
48 Roestenburg-Morgan, *The Road to Reconciliation*, p. 146.
49 Ibid., p. 135.
50 J. Rawls, *A Theory of Justice* (Cambridge: Howard Press, 1981).
51 American Bar Association, 'Human Rights and Access to Justice', available at https://www.americanbar.org/advocacy/rule_of_law/what-we-do/human-rights-access-to-justice.html (accessed 28 May 2018).
52 M. Moscati, 'The Role of Transitional Justice and Access to Justice in Conflict Resolution and Democratic Advancement', Democratic Progress Institute, 2015.
53 Ibid.
54 Roestenburg-Morgan, *The Road to Reconciliation*, p. 184.
55 Ibid.
56 Ibid.
57 M. Soueid *et al.*, 'The Survivor-Centered Approach to Transitional Justice: Why a Trauma-Informed Handling of Witness Testimony is a Necessary Component', *George Washington International Law Review*, 50, 2017–2018, pp. 141–142.
58 See Article 75 of the Rome Statute of the International Criminal Court as well as the ICC Rules of Procedure and Evidence under Rule 85.
59 D. Luban, 'Fairness to Rightness: Jurisdiction, Legality, and the Legitimacy of International Law', in T. Besson, *The Philosophy of International Law* (Oxford: Oxford University Press, 2010).
60 Villalba, 'Transitional Justice', pp. 146–147, and Roestenburg-Morgan, *Road to Reconciliation*, pp. 177–200.
61 Roestenburg-Morgan, *Road to Reconciliation*, p. 200.
62 Ibid., p. 210.
63 Ibid.
64 Ibid.

65 Ibid.
66 Ibid., p. 147.
67 United Nations Human Rights Commission, Human Rights Resolution 9/11, 'Right to the truth', 24 September 2008, A/HRC/RES/9/11. In this connection, an important legal proceeding is the search for the missing and the disappeared, including exhumations.
68 E. Gonzalez and H. Varney, 'Truth Seeking: Elements of Creating an Effective Truth Commission', International Center for Transitional Justice, 2013, available at https://www.ictj.org/publication/truth-seeking-elements-creating-effective-truth-commission (accessed 28 May 2019).
69 Villalba, 'Transitional Justice', p. 49.
70 Soueid *et al.*, 'Survivor-Centered Approach to Transitional Justice', p. 141.
71 Roestenburg-Morgan, *Road to Reconciliation*, pp. 185–190.
72 R. Carranza, 'The Right to Reparations in Situations of Poverty', ICTJ Briefing, Fighting Impunity in Peacebuilding Contexts, The Hague, 2009.
73 Roestenburg-Morgan, *Road to Reconciliation*.
74 See Article 75 of the Rome Statute.
75 Ibid.
76 See 'Trust Fund for Victims', available at https://www.icc-cpi.int/tfv (accessed 28 May 2019).
77 International Center for Transitional Justice, 'Reparative Justice in Theory and Practice', available at https://www.ictj.org/sites/default/files/ICTJ-Global-Reparations-Practice-2007-English.pdf (accessed 28 May 2019).
78 Ibid.
79 Ibid.
80 World Movement for Human Rights, 'Victims at the Center of Justice from 1998 to 2018: Reflections on the Promises and the Reality of Victim Participation at the ICC', December 2018, p. 4.
81 Ibid.
82 C. Garbett, 'The International Criminal Court and Restorative Justice: Victims, Participation and the Processes of Justice', *Restorative Justice: An International Journal*, 5(2), 2017, available at https://www.tandfonline.com/doi/full/10.1080/20504721.2017.1339953 (accessed 12 June 2019).
83 S. SáCouto and K. Cleary, *Victim Participation Before the International Criminal Court* (Washington, DC: War Crimes Research Office, International Criminal Court, 2008).
84 Ibid.
85 See Decision on Victims' Participation in Situation in the Democratic Republic of the Congo in the Case of the Prosecutor v. Thomas Lubanga Dyilo, Case No: ICC-01/04–01/06, Paragraph 78, 18 January 2008.
86 Presentation by M. Kersten at Side Event, 'The Case for Survivor-Centered Justice: Policy Issues and Challenges', hosted by the Institute for Justice and Reconciliation at the 18th Annual Assembly of States Parties, 10 December 2019.
87 Ibid.
88 REDRESS, 'Justice for Victims: The ICC's Reparations Mandate', 20 May 2011, available at http://www.iccnow.org/documents/REDRESS_ICC_Reparations_May2011.pdf (accessed 13 June 2019).
89 Ibid., p. 13.
90 See Article 17 of the Rome Statute of the International Criminal Court, available at https://www.icc-cpi.int/nr/rdonlyres/ea9aeff7-5752-4f84-be94-0a655eb30e16/0/rome_statute_english.pdf (accessed 13 June 2019).
91 Ibid.

92 C. Stahn, 'Fair and Effective Investigation and Prosecution of International Crimes, Inventory and State-of-the-Art: Context, Cluster 1 and Cluster 2', International Nuremburg Principles Academy, p. 5, available at https://www.nurembergacademy.org/fileadmin/user_upload/Fair_and_Effective_Investigation_and_Prosecution_of_International_Crimes.pdf (accessed 12 June 2019).
93 Presentation by P. Mochochoko, Head of the Complementarity Division, Office of the Prosecutor, ICC, presentation given at Side Event, 'The Case for Survivor-Centered Justice: Policy Issues and Challenges', hosted by the Institute for Justice and Reconciliation IJR at the 18th Annual Assembly of States Parties, 10 December 2019.
94 Ibid.
95 Ibid.
96 See Article 15 of the Rome Statute of the International Criminal Court, available at https://www.icc-cpi.int/nr/rdonlyres/ea9aeff7-5752-4f84-be94-0a655eb30e16/0/rome_statute_english.pdf (accessed 13 June 2019).
97 Ibid.
98 Ibid.
99 Report of the AU Panel of the Wise, 'Peace, Justice and Reconciliation in Africa: Opportunities and Challenges in the Fight Against Impunity', International Peace Institute, p, 27, February 2013.
100 L. Huyse, 'Traditional Justice and Reconciliation after Violent Conflict: Learning from Experiences', Institute for Democracy and Electoral Assistance, 2008.
101 Ibid.
102 Roestenburg-Morgan, *Road to Reconciliation*, p. 183.
103 Ibid.
104 Ibid; see also Mbeki and Mamdani, 'Courts Can't End Civil Wars'.
105 Roestenburg-Morgan, *Road to Reconciliation*, p. 152.
106 Ibid., pp. 177–178.
107 Ibid.; see also M. Mutua, 'A Critique in Transitional Justice: The African Experience', in *Rethinking Transitions, Equality and Social Justice in Societies Emerging from Conflict*, Buffalo Legal Studies Research, Paper Series, Paper No. 2012–032 (Intersentia, 2011), pp. 31–45. See also A. An-Na'im, 'From the Neocolonial Transitional to Indigenous Formations of Justice', Editorial Note, *International Journal of Transitional Justice*, 7, 2013, pp. 197–204; see also C. Villa-Vicencio, 'Transitional Justice and Human Rights in Africa', available at http://citeseerx.ist.psu.edu/viewdoc/download?doi=10.1.1.573.424&rep=rep1&type=pdf (accessed 13 June 2019).
108 Roestenburg-Morgan, *Road to Reconciliation*, p. 210.
109 Ibid., p. 152.
110 Ibid., p. 154; see also Zehr, *Changing Lenses.*
111 Orentlicher, 'Settling Accounts'.
112 Ibid.
113 Roestenburg-Morgan, *Road to Reconciliation*, p. 210.
114 Ibid., p. 189.
115 Ibid.
116 Orentlicher, 'Settling Accounts'.
117 P. Gready and S. Robins, 'Rethinking Civil Society and Transitional Justice: Lessons from Social Movements and New Civil Society', *The International Journal of Human Rights*, 2017, p. 1, available at http://eprints.whiterose.ac.uk/116557/3/Rethinking_civil_society_and_transitional_justice_lessons_from_social_movements_and_new_civil_society.pdf (accessed 13 June 2019).
118 Ibid.
119 Ibid., p. 3.
120 Ibid.

121 Ibid.

122 Ibid., pp. 3–10.

123 See Resolution 2467 adopted by the Security Council at its 8,514th meeting on 23 April 2019; see also Security Council, 8514th Meeting (am), 'Security Council Adopts Resolution Calling upon Belligerents Worldwide to Adopt Concrete Commitments on Ending Sexual Violence in Conflict', 23 April 2019, available at https://www.un.org/press/en/2019/sc13790.doc.htm (accessed 13 June 2019).

124 Ibid.

125 Ibid.

126 Ibid.

127 Ibid.

128 What's in Blue, 'In Hindsight: Negotiations on Resolution 2467 on Sexual Violence in Conflict', 2 May 2019, available at https://www.whatsinblue.org/2019/05/in-hindsight-negotiations-on-resolution-2467-on-sexual-violence-in-conflict.php (accessed 13 June 2019).

129 'Landmark Agreement between the African Union and the United Nations to Prevent and Respond to Conflict-Related Sexual Violence', Office of the Special Representative of the Secretary General on Sexual Violence in Conflict, 6 February 2014, available at https://www.un.org/sexualviolenceinconflict/press-release/landmark-agreement-between-the-african-union-and-the-united-nations-to-prevent-and-respond-to-conflict-related-sexual-violence/ (accessed 13 June 2019).

130 Ibid.

131 Ibid.

132 'Guidelines on Combating Sexual Violence and its Consequences in Africa', adopted by the African Commission on Human and Peoples' Rights during its 60th Ordinary Session held in Niamey, Niger from 8 to 22 May 2017, available at http://www.achpr.org/files/instruments/combating-sexual-violence/achpr_eng_guidelines_on_combating_sexual_violence_and_its_consequences.pdf (accessed 13 June 2019).

133 Ibid.

134 Ibid.

135 Ibid.

136 See Joint UN-AU Framework for an Enhanced Partnership in Peace and Security, available at https://unoau.unmissions.org/sites/default/files/jount_un-au_framework_for_an_enhanced_partnership_in_peace_and_security.pdf (accessed 13 June 2019).

137 Ibid.

138 Ibid.

139 Ibid.

140 Ibid.

141 Atrocity Prevention and Peacebuilding, 'Key Insights and Lessons from a Global Consultation by Peace Direct', 2017, available online at: https://www.peacedirect.org/wp-content/uploads/2018/04/Atrocity-Prevention-Executive-Summary-Report_PD.pdf (accessed 14 June 2019).

142 Ibid., p. 7.

143 Ibid.

144 Ibid.

145 These factors were highlighted at Peace Direct during a global consultation of practitioners.

146 Ibid.

References

An-Na'im, A. (2013) 'From the Neocolonial Transitional to Indigenous Formations of Justice', Editorial Note, *The International Journal of Transitional Justice*, vol. 7, pp. 197–220.

Carranza, R. (2009) '*The Right to Reparations in Situations of Poverty*', ICTJ Briefing, presented at Fighting Impunity in Peace Building Contexts, The Hague, September.

Fonseka, B. and Naples-Mitchell, J. (2017) 'Victim-Centered Transitional Justice in Sri Lanka: What Does it Really Mean?' Discussion Paper, Colombo: Center for Policy Alternatives.

Garbett, C. (2017) 'The International Criminal Court and Restorative Justice: Victims, Participation and the Processes of Justice', *Restorative Justice: An International Journal*, vol. 5, no. 2.

Gready, P. and Robins, S. (2017) 'Rethinking Civil Society and Transitional Justice: Lessons from Social Movements and New Civil Society', *The International Journal of Human Rights.*

Huyse, L. (2008) *Traditional Justice and Reconciliation after Violent Conflict: Learning from Experiences*, Stockholm: Institute for Democracy and Electoral Assistance.

Krystall, R. (2014) 'The Subjects of Mass Atrocities: Victims or Survivors?' In *Reinventing Peace*. Somerville, MA: World Peace Foundation.

Luban, D. (2010) 'Fairness to Rightness: Jurisdiction, Legality, and the Legitimacy of International Law', in T. Besson, *The Philosophy of International Law*, Oxford: Oxford University Press.

Moscati, M. (2015) 'The Role of Transitional Justice and Access to Justice in Conflict Resolution and Democratic Advancement', London: Democratic Progress Institute.

Mutua, M. (2011) 'A Critique in Transitional Justice: The African Experience', in *Rethinking Transitions, Equality and Social Justice in Societies Emerging from Conflict*, Buffalo Legal Studies Research, Paper Series, Paper No. 2012–2032, Cambridge: Intersentia, pp. 31–45.

Orentlicher, D. (1991) 'Settling Accounts: The Duty to Prosecute Human Rights Violations of a Prior Regime', *The Yale Law Journal*, vol. 100, no. 8, American University Washington College of Law, pp. 2537–2615.

Petty, K. (2013) 'Humanity and National Security: The Law of Mass Atrocity Response Operations', *Michigan Journal of International Law*, vol. 34, no. 4, p. 749–750.

Rawls, J. (1981) *A Theory of Justice*, Cambridge: Howard Press.

Roestenburg-Morgan, I. (2023) *The Road to Reconciliation: Optimizing the Legitimacy and Efficacy of the ICC Within the African Union and Africa*, Cambridge: Intersentia.

Rummel, R.J. (1994) *Death by Government*. Piscataway, NJ and London: Transaction Publishers.

Sacouto, S. and Cleary, K.A. (2008) 'Victims' Participation in the Investigations of the International Criminal Court', *Transnational Law & Contemporary Problems*, 17(1), p. 1359.

Soueid, M., Willhoite, A.M. and Sovcik, A.E. (2017) 'The Survivor-Centered Approach to Transitional Justice: Why a Trauma-Informed Handling of Witness

Testimony is a Necessary Component', *The George Washington International Law Review*, vol. 50, pp. 141–142.

Streitfeld-Hall, J. (2015) 'Responsibility to Protect: Can We Prevent Mass Atrocities Without Making the Same Mistakes', New York: Global Centre for the Responsibility to Protect.

Villalba, C.S. (2011) 'Transitional Justice: Key Concepts, Processes and Challenges', Briefing Paper, Colchester: Institute for Democracy and Conflict Resolution, University of Essex.

Zehr, H. (2005) *Changing Lenses: A New Focus for Crime and Justice*, Windsor, ON: Herald Press.

Other Documents, Reports and Statutes

African Commission on Human and Peoples' Rights (n.d.) *Guidelines on Combating Sexual Violence and its Consequences in Africa, adopted by the African Commission on Human and Peoples' Rights during its 60th Ordinary Session held in Niamey, Niger from 8 to 22 May 2017*. Available at http://www.achpr.org/files/instruments/combating-sexual-violence/achpr_eng_guidelines_on_combating_sexual_violence_and_its_consequences.pdf.

American Bar Association (n.d.)*Human Rights and Access to Justice*. Available at https://www.americanbar.org/advocacy/rule_of_law/what-we-do/human-rights-access-to-justice.html.

AU Panel of the Wise (2013) *Peace, Justice and Reconciliation in Africa: Opportunities and Challenges in the Fight Against Impunity*, International Peace Institute, p, 27, February.

Bellamy, A. (2011) 'Mass Atrocities and Armed Conflict: Links, Distinctions and Implications for the Responsibility to Protect', Policy Analysis Brief, The Stanley Foundation.

Decision on Victims' Participation in Situation in the Democratic Republic of the Congo in the Case of the Prosecutor v. Thomas Lubanga Dyilo, Case No: ICC-01/04–01/06, Paragraph 78, 18 January 2008.

Gonzalez, E. and Varney, H. (2013) *Truth Seeking: Elements of Creating an Effective Truth Commission*, International Center for Transitional Justice. Available at https://www.ictj.org/publication/truth-seeking-elements-creating-effective-truth-commission.

Gupta, R. (2014) '"Victim" vs. "Survivor", Feminism and Language', *50.50 Gender, Sexuality and Social Justice*. Available at https://www.opendemocracy.net/5050/rahila-gupta/victim-vs-survivor-feminism-and-language.

International Center for Transitional Justice (n.d.) *Reparative Justice in Theory and Practice*. Available at https://www.ictj.org/sites/default/files/ICTJ-Global-Reparations-Practice-2007-English.pdf.

Kersten, M. (2019) Presentation at side event '*The Case for Survivor-Centered Justice: Policy Issues and Challenges*', hosted by the Institute for Justice and Reconciliation at the 18th Annual Assembly of States Parties, 10 December.

Mamdani, M. (2011) '*How Shall We Think of Mass Violence: Criminal or Political? Reflections on Nuremberg and CODESA*', paper presented at the Makerere Institute of Social Research, at the Workshop on Public Violence, Justice and the Rule of Law, Kampala, Uganda, 8–9 March.

Mbeki, T. and Mamdani, M. (2014) 'Courts Can't End Civil Wars', *The New York Times*, 15 February.

Mochochoko, P. (2019) Presentation at side event '*The Case for Survivor-Centered Justice: Policy Issues and Challenges*', hosted by the Institute for Justice and Reconciliation at the 18th Annual Assembly of States Parties, 10 December.

Peace Direct (2017) *Atrocity Prevention and Peacebuilding, Key Insights and Lessons from a Global Consultation by Peace Direct*. Available at https://www.peacedirect.org/wp-content/uploads/2018/04/Atrocity-Prevention-Executive-Summary-Report_PD.pdf.

REDRESS (2011) *Justice for Victims: The ICC's Reparations Mandate*, 20 May. Available at http://www.iccnow.org/documents/REDRESS_ICC_Reparations_May2011.pdf.

Stahn, C. (2020) *Fair and Effective Investigation and Prosecution of International Crimes, Inventory and State-of-the-Art: Context, Cluster 1 and Cluster 2*. Nuremberg: International Nuremburg Principles Academy, p. 5. Available at https://www.nurembergacademy.org/fileadmin/user_upload/Fair_and_Effective_Investigation_and_Prosecution_of_International_Crimes.pdf.

The Office of the Special Representative of the Secretary-General on Sexual Violence in Conflict (2014) *Landmark agreement between the African Union and the United Nations to Prevent and Respond to Conflict-Related Sexual Violence, Office of the Special Representative of the Secretary General on Sexual Violence in Conflict*, 6 February. Available at https://www.un.org/sexualviolenceinconflict/press-release/landmark-agreement-between-the-african-union-and-the-united-nations-to-prevent-and-respond-to-conflict-related-sexual-violence/.

The Rome Statute of the International Criminal Court (n.d.) Available at https://www.icc-cpi.int/resource-library/documents/rs-eng.pdf.

United Nations (2019) *Security Council Adopts Resolution Calling upon Belligerents Worldwide to Adopt Concrete Commitments on Ending Sexual Violence in Conflict*, 23 April. Available at https://www.un.org/press/en/2019/sc13790.doc.htm.

United Nations Human Rights Commission (2008) *Human Rights Resolution 9/11, 'Right to the Truth'*, 24 September.

United Nations Office to the African Union (n.d.) *Joint UN-AU Framework for an Enhanced Partnership in Peace and Security*. Available at https://unoau.unmissions.org/sites/default/files/jount_un-au_framework_for_an_enhanced_partnership_in_peace_and_security.pdf.

Villa-Vicencio, C. (2009) *Transitional Justice and Human Rights in Africa*. Available at http://citeseerx.ist.psu.edu/viewdoc/download?doi=10.1.1.573.424&rep=rep1&type=pdf.

What's in Blue (2019) 'In Hindsight: Negotiations on Resolution 2467 on Sexual Violence in Conflict', 2 May. Available at https://www.whatsinblue.org/2019/05/in-hindsight-negotiations-on-resolution-2467-on-sexual-violence-in-conflict.php.

World Movement for Human Rights (2018) *Victims at the Center of Justice from 1998 to 2018: Reflections on the Promises and the Reality of Victim Participation at the ICC*, December, p. 4.

Part I

The International Criminal Court

1 Justice for Survivors at the ICC?

Assessing the Impact of Victim Participation

Mariana Pena[1]

Introduction

Victim-centred transitional justice seeks to put those affected by conflict at the heart of transitional justice processes.[2] This concept dismisses the notion that victims are mere spectators of judicial and quasi-judicial mechanisms. The advantages of involving victims include benefiting from their intimate understanding of the conflict and related context, as well as ensuring that the justice process can address their demands. Attending to survivors' needs in the aftermath of conflict can arguably guarantee a more lasting impact for transitional justice interventions.[3] Allowing survivors to participate in transitional justice processes improves their experience of justice by ensuring a greater sense of ownership over transitional justice measures.[4]

Criminal justice proceedings have traditionally focused more on the perpetrators of crimes than on those affected by them. That has shifted over the past three decades. Factors that contributed to this shift include increased recognition of the rights of victims of abuse of power and acknowledgement of the limitations of tribunals for which victims were only passive observers.[5]

At the international level, the Rome Statute for the International Criminal Court (ICC) was the first instrument to allow for the participation of victims in international criminal proceedings.[6] Its provisions on victim participation have been considered groundbreaking[7] and innovative.[8] The adoption of such provisions was marked by significant hope that the ICC would offer a victim-centred justice model.[9] It sought to 'break a new path' by involving those 'who [had] traditionally remained voiceless outsiders to the legal process'.[10] Many scholars have claimed that the enactment of victims' rights was a turning point from a retributive justice model to a restorative one.[11]

This chapter will explore the extent to which the hope for a diverse justice model, one that recognizes and puts victims at the centre, has materialized in the ICC's practice. Transitioning from passive observer to an active actor in justice processes requires genuine involvement at all relevant stages. The literature on victim participation in criminal trials refers to 'meaningful participation' as the most effective form of intervention from a survivor's perspective. The ICC Chambers have emphasized that 'meaningful

DOI: 10.4324/9781003212409-3

participation' is not 'purely symbolic.'[12] Commentators who have inquired into the meaningful nature of victim participation conclude that survivors' intervention must be holistic and empowering.[13] In order for survivors' participation in criminal proceedings to be truly meaningful, it must be effective at every stage of their interaction with the Court. Concretely, three main aspects become relevant: the entry point or access to the system; the experience throughout criminal proceedings; and the outcome of the process.

1. *Access*: Facilitating access to justice by those affected by the crimes appears essential to ensure that they can play a central role in proceedings.[14]
2. *Experience*: In order for involvement in justice processes to have a truly empowering effect, the way in which victims experience participation will bear significance.[15]
3. *Outcome*: The outcome refers not only to the end result of the justice process, but also the manner in which judicial proceedings address victims' interests and needs.[16]

After laying out the applicable legal framework, the sections below will study each of these areas by analysing the ICC's law and practice. Such an analysis will be based on a study of relevant Court decisions and commentaries.

This chapter will use the terms 'survivors' and 'victims' interchangeably. While the term 'survivor' better reflects the resilience exhibited by those who have undergone and overcome mass criminality, the term 'victim' is more commonly used in legal writing. Not all survivors consider themselves to be victims and vice versa, so using one single term is not easy. This chapter relies extensively on the literature on participation in transitional justice processes including criminal trials, which almost exclusively uses the terminology 'victim participation'.

Legal Framework

A comprehensive analysis of the Rome Statute scheme on victim participation is beyond the scope of this chapter. This section will outline the main legal provisions and case law relevant to the three aspects analysed in this chapter.

The central provision on victim participation is Article 68(3), which provides as follows:

> Where the personal interests of the victims are affected, the Court shall permit their views and concerns to be presented and considered at stages of the proceedings determined to be appropriate by the Court and in a manner which is not prejudicial to or inconsistent with the rights of the accused and a fair and impartial trial. Such views and concerns may be

> presented by the legal representatives of the victims where the Court considers it appropriate, in accordance with the Rules of Procedure and Evidence.[17]

The scheme is carefully delineated so that victims are to participate 'where their personal interests are affected' and during the stages that the Court considers 'appropriate'.[18] Their participation has a specific purpose, namely to express 'their views and concerns'. Victims intervene in proceedings not as individual parties but as 'participants'.[19] Participation is governed by a set of rules laid out in the ICC legal texts[20] and jurisprudence. While the ICC legal texts contain a number of provisions, much was left to the judges' discretion at the time when those texts were adopted.[21]

According to the legal texts, while victims do not need a lawyer to participate in proceedings, they can appoint one if they so wish. In practice, however, victim participation takes place through a lawyer or 'legal representative' given the complex legal nature of the proceedings. Rule 90 of the ICC Rules of Procedure and Evidence governs the victims' choice of counsel. Rule 90(1) provides that '[a] victim shall be free to choose their legal representative'. However, this right is not absolute given the need to organize collective representation in the light of the vast number of participants.[22] When a group of victims intervening in the same case cannot agree on a common legal representative, Rule 90 provides that the ICC Registry can assist them or that the ICC Chambers or Registry may themselves appoint a lawyer for the group.

When it comes to victims' powers during proceedings, ICC decisions have codified a broad range of procedural rights. These include attending and participating in hearings; making opening and closing statements; putting forward oral and written submissions; calling witnesses and questioning the parties' witnesses; submitting and challenging evidence; and accessing public filings as well as confidential filings that concern them.[23] The Court has claimed that these rights enable 'victims to play a meaningful role that allows them to have a substantial impact on proceedings'.[24] Some of these rights can be exercised directly, while others require a specific application by the victims' legal representative and the relevant Chamber's authorization to proceed. This can be cumbersome, but in certain cases judges have waived the requirement for an application.[25]

Finally, the ICC Statute introduces another major innovation with respect to victims' rights: it grants them a right to reparations in the event of a conviction.[26] In order to realize victims' right to reparations, the Statute created a Trust Fund for Victims, which is tasked with implementing reparations orders through the administration of funds received from the convicted person and voluntary contributions.[27] Acknowledging survivors' urgent needs for material, physical and psychological assistance and, moreover, that criminal trials can be lengthy, the Regulations of the Trust Fund have enabled it to put in place 'assistance' projects while criminal proceedings are ongoing.[28]

Access to Justice

The first question before us is are ICC proceedings accessible? This requires an analysis of the legal conditions to access proceedings (substantive requirements) as well as the necessary steps for victims to introduce themselves to the Court (formal requirements).

Substantive Requirements: Legal Standing

The ICC intervenes in situations of mass atrocities, but its cases cover only a sample of the crimes committed in a certain context. This means that only a limited number of victims from the community that was victimized in a given situation will be able to prove that they have suffered harm as a result of a crime before the Court.[29] In practice, this may lead to tension among different groups of victims,[30] as some will be privileged to see justice done for the crimes they have suffered, to have their voices heard and to obtain reparations, while others will be entirely excluded.[31]

As explained above, participation is granted in relation to certain stages of the proceedings. While access to some proceedings during the pre-trial phase of a case and the trial itself is generally accepted, participation in the earlier stages, including during the investigation and pre-investigation phases, remains restrictive.[32] Recent practice has opened up possibilities for victims to participate in the very early stages of selected proceedings affecting their interests.[33] However, those instances should be considered exceptions to the rule that forecloses participation in early stages.

Exclusion from participation during the investigation phase affects victims' capacity to influence prosecutorial decisions on the contours of future cases, including targeted perpetrators and incidents selected for prosecution.[34] ICC Legal Representative Luc Walleyn claims that the value of participation at the earliest stage is underestimated, because 'the decisions most important for victims are made at this stage'.[35] It is during the investigation that the prosecution selects the specific incidents and charges it will prosecute, and it does so without any checks and balances.[36] Those decisions will significantly impact victims' rights: only those whose crimes are selected for prosecution will be able to participate, and only those for whose crimes the accused is convicted will receive reparations. In short, both the selection and the strength of the evidence presented by the prosecution go to the core of victims' interests.[37] Tibori-Szabó and Hirst explain that 'victim participation at the ICC has been most helpful where … it has held the prosecution accountable for victims' interests'.[38]

Many observers have argued against victim intervention during the investigation phase for good reasons, including the need to preserve the confidentiality and integrity of the investigation, and to avoid unfairly raising expectations at such an early stage.[39] The prosecution itself has claimed that the choice of charges falls within its remit and that 'allowing victims to question its choices … would adversely impact on its prerogatives and undermine its independence'.[40] On the contrary, the ability to question prosecutorial choices early in the proceedings could have prevented adverse decisions being made regarding victims' interests in a number of cases. For example, in the *Ongwen* case, participating victims sought, at the trial stage, to expand the evidentiary basis for crimes of sexual violence. They did so in order to cover crimes committed against boys and men since the prosecutor had only selected crimes against female survivors. The Chamber ruled against the motion because the case had already been consolidated according to the prosecutor's choices.[41]

Formal Requirements: The Application Process

Survivors must apply to participate in proceedings.[42] The application process has evolved over the years as different parts of the Court have sought to enhance its effectiveness.[43] Initially, the application forms were lengthy and requests to participate led to significant litigation. The ICC has sought to address these problems by simplifying the application form and establishing a process for the treatment of applications enabling faster and more straightforward decision-making.[44] For victims, this has resulted in considerably less paperwork and a more speedy treatment of their applications.

In order to apply for participation, survivors must first be aware of their rights, including the possibility of participating in proceedings. Outreach sessions and intermediary assistance play a crucial role here,[45] as it is unlikely that many victims will access the necessary information on their own. Kendall and Nouwen note,

[f]or instance, the application forms [are] available for download on the court's website in English and French, the court's two working languages … They are not easily accessible to people without internet access or reading skills, and they require supplemental identifying documents that can be difficult and costly to obtain.[46]

The Court has also sought to facilitate access to participation by training[47] local organizations or individuals that serve as intermediaries.[48] Relying on local intermediaries has certain advantages, such as their existing trust relationship with members of the community, ability to speak local languages, and context awareness. However, there are also prevalent disadvantages, such as the likelihood of mistakes being made when filling out application forms, possible limitations on the part of intermediaries when explaining the consequences of judicial processes and legal concepts,[49] and difficulties in asserting the victims' informed consent.[50] In addition, survivors do not normally have access to legal advice during this stage,[51] even if the statements made in an application form can have an impact on their rights in relation to the proceedings.[52]

Finally, in recent cases, the Court has set a deadline for the submission of applications before the confirmation of charges and trial proceedings.[53] This can be problematic when there is insufficient time to inform victims and collect applications, or when the security situation or other local conditions (for example, the remote location of communities, and the difficulty in identifying and training intermediaries) cause delays. ICC Legal Representatives Joseph Manoba and Francisco Cox claim that, during the pre-trial phase of the *Ongwen* case, the establishment of a deadline coupled with unavailability of the relevant documentation 'hindered many would have been [*sic*] applicants from applying and participating in the proceedings'.[54]

Experience of Justice: Indirect, Collective Participation

Once victims are granted access to the proceedings, they participate through a legal representative.[55] Scholars have expressed diverse views on the impact of indirect representation on survivors. For example, Haslam and Edmunds argue that indirect contact with the Court may alter the nature and content of victims' contributions.[56] However, evidence suggests that indirect participation is not necessarily against victims' wishes. A survey by the University of California, Berkeley, has concluded that few victims want to participate directly.[57]

Given the physical distance between the Court and the victims' communities, an overwhelming majority of victims will never witness or participate directly in Court proceedings. For this reason, survivors' relationships with their lawyers is likely to shape their participation experience.[58] The sub-sections below will look into interactions between survivors and lawyers in the field, as well as victims' involvement in the choice of legal representative.

Collective Representation

The ICC is mandated to try crimes of mass atrocity. While not all victims will be able or willing to participate, experience in ICC cases shows that the participation of several thousand individuals is the norm.[59] Due to the large number of participants and the need to ensure effective proceedings, legal representation takes a collective form. This means that victims are grouped and assigned a Common Legal Representative for each group.[60] Consequently, despite the Rome Statute's emphasis on survivors' *personal* 'views and concerns', participation happens collectively.[61]

Haslam and Edmunds argue that grouping victims for efficiency considerations risks 'gloss[ing] over the range of potential interests participants might have'.[62] Kendall and Nouwen also worry that individual interests may get lost through the legal representative's inevitable selection of a 'generalizable interests'.[63] Other scholars warn against the risks of presenting victims' interests as homogenous.[64] However, Tenove argues that diversity of views can be overcome by putting in place strategies that seek agreement on positions.[65]

Importantly, some commentators argue that not all aspects of collective participation are negative. Survivors who experience the consequences of isolation and disempowerment as a result of the crimes committed against them could find comfort in the sense of community and joint endeavour that collective participation arguably provides.[66]

Engagement through Consultations

Given the lack of physical access to the Court, survivors access proceedings through consultations. There are two types of consultations that have significant consequences for participants, namely consultations with the Court to identify a common legal representative, and consultations with counsel throughout the proceedings.[67]

Killean and Moffet note that 'the selection of representatives constitutes an important element of victims' legal agency'.[68] As explained in the Legal Framework section, the Court can intervene to identify a common legal representative for a group of victims. In doing so, the Court must adequately weigh up victims' choices following consultations with them.[69] Haslam and Edmunds emphasize that '[e]ffective representation is vital to meaningful victim participation. Achieving it depends in no so small measure on involving victims as fully and directly as possible in choosing their representative.' The extent of the Court's interventionism in the selection of common legal representatives has been a matter of contention in a number of ICC cases.[70] For example, in the *Ntaganda* case, the Court's findings on legal representation and related allocation of legal aid were found to be bluntly at odds with the victims' expressed wish for representation.[71]

Regular consultation with survivors throughout proceedings is the legal representative's responsibility. Counsel must inform clients and seek instructions as per their ethical duties.[72] Tenove notes that 'ongoing consultation is the fundamental basis for [common legal representatives'] claims to speak for victims'.[73] In practice, consultations are a fundamental component through which to achieve adequate and effective legal representation.[74] They can make the difference between genuine and active involvement of participants, on the one hand, or passive and symbolic participation[75] on the other hand.[76] As such, the type, frequency and quality of meetings, the availability of the legal representative, and the level of information flow will matter greatly.

Given the number of survivors represented by each legal team, consultation meetings in most cases involve large groups of victims. In this context, legal representatives need to devise strategies to ensure that there are opportunities for each survivor to be genuinely involved. Some legal teams have provided opportunities for victims to hold individual meetings with their lawyers upon request.[77] Others have organized smaller group gatherings to complement the community meetings, so as to allow for exchanges in a format that could make clients more comfortable.[78] Tibori-Szabó *et al.* emphasize that consultations must be two-way, ensuring that survivors receive updates on the case and can ask questions and share their views.[79]

Meetings are important to build and maintain a relationship of trust between survivors and their legal representatives. The more frequent the meetings, the easier it is to build trust.[80]

Organizing consultations with victims has obvious logistical challenges.[81] Not only is there a large number of survivors, they often inhabit insecure territories or they could be spread out over a vast geographical area. This requires regular travel by the legal representative and members of the legal team, making legal representation costly. Sehmi argues that the ICC must provide victims' lawyers with '[s]ufficient logistical and financial support … so that they are able to meet their professional duties'.[82] This is crucial since '[t]he in-person consultation process with victims is arguably the core function of the [victims' lawyer].'[83] Several victims' representatives have had to litigate over the extent of legal aid.[84] Sehmi notes that the financial and logistical pressures carry significant risks: the legal representative 'might be tempted to act in what he or she believes are the best interests of the victims, without significant in-person consultations'.[85]

As expensive and cumbersome as they may be, consultations may be of significant value for survivors, if undertaken well. They essentially provide participants with a sense of being heard. Receiving first-hand information, as opposed to hearing about developments through the media, can boost survivors' sense of engagement and contribute to their rehabilitation.[86] Manoba and Cox, legal representatives of victims in the *Ongwen* case, argue that 'offering victims an ear to listen to victimisation accounts outside the court room has been fulfilling for many a victim and played an important role in dismantling the victims' sense or feeling of conspiracy of silence by the world'.[87]

Outcome: Survivors' Expectations of Justice

For the purpose of this analysis, outcome refers not only to the end result of the criminal trial, i.e. conviction or acquittal. It also encompasses the effectiveness, from a survivor's perspective, of their intervention in the judicial process. Concretely, this section will study how participation in ICC proceedings addresses survivors' expectations of justice within and beyond the criminal trial.

Fair, Timely and Local Justice?

Survivors naturally expect that proceedings will lead to a fair determination on their case. With respect to the criminal trial, they often expect that justice be done through a conviction. The ICC has been criticized for its low conviction rate. At the time of writing the ICC had handed down five convictions[88] (Lubanga, Katanga, Al Mahdi, Ntaganda, Ongwen), while four accused (Ngudjolo, Bemba, Laurent Gbagbo, Blé Goudé) had been acquitted.[89] Charges were not confirmed in four cases (Abu Garda,

Mbarushimana, Kosgey and Ali), dropped in two cases (Muthaura and Kenyatta), and vacated against further three accused (Ruto, Sang and Simone Gbagbo). One case was declared inadmissible (Al-Senussi).

As explained earlier, the lack of convictions frustrates survivors' access to reparations. While it can be expected that a number of trials will lead to acquittals, the ICC Office of the Prosecutor has been blamed for ineffective investigations and prosecutions.[90] In some cases the accused may be innocent, but in other cases acquittal may be the result of technical procedural errors or insufficient evidence to prove the case beyond reasonable doubt.

Survivors also expect to see justice done without undue delay.[91] Proceedings before the ICC are extraordinarily long and often start many years after the atrocities took place. Factors that negatively influence the timeliness of ICC proceedings include the ICC's cumbersome preliminary examination procedure,[92] the complexity of investigations, and/or the lack of timely arrests.[93] For example, the case against Thomas Lubanga concerned crimes committed in 2002–2003. He was arrested in 2006 and convicted in 2012 (the conviction was confirmed in appeals in 2014). The main reparations decision was adopted in 2017 and, as of October 2021. Sadly, many victims have died while waiting for the resolution of an ICC case.[94]

The ICC sits thousands of kilometres away from the communities it serves. In some cases survivors expect to see justice done in their own communities or in another location closer to home. In other cases they may prefer that proceedings be conducted abroad, for example in highly politicized cases, for fear of destabilization or interference with Court proceedings.[95] According to Article 3(3) of the Rome Statute, the Court can decide to hold proceedings in a location other than its headquarters 'whenever it considers it desirable'. The ICC Chambers and presidency have acknowledged that *in situ* hearings help to bring justice closer to the communities affected by the crimes and can contribute to an improved perception of the ICC.[96] Although the possibility of *in situ* proceedings was studied in six ICC cases, it was sadly never authorized for financial, security or other reasons,[97] despite expressed support from participating victims.[98]

Victims' Procedural Rights

Victims have diverse reasons for participating in proceedings. Prominent reasons include their desire to contribute to justice[99] and to the establishment of the truth.[100] Consequently, their ability to undertake certain procedural steps that can help them to attain those goals goes to the core of their interests. In particular, the right to tender evidence and the right to question witnesses are central to victims' participation experience. The exercise of both of these rights has found a number of limitations in ICC practice.[101] In order to submit evidence, victims must demonstrate that presentation of specific evidence affects their personal interests and can assist the Court in its determination of the truth.[102] Some Chambers have also required that evidence tendered by victims refrains from being duplicative of that submitted by the parties.[103] In addition, victims cannot seek to expand the scope of the case by leading evidence[104] or in any other manner. For example, victims' motions for a re-characterization of the charges in a manner that better reflects the victims' experiences have been rejected.[105]

The approach to victims' ability to question witnesses varies from one ICC Chamber to another. In the *Ongwen* case, judges established that victims' legal representatives should refrain from asking questions that go to the guilt or innocence of the accused, and must therefore limit themselves to questions on the harm caused to victims.[106] This contradicts previous jurisprudence recognizing that questions pertaining to the guilt of an accused concern the victims' 'personal interest' and often can not be separated from questions relating to the harm suffered.[107] Manoba and Cox claim that restricting the scope of questioning goes against established human rights jurisprudence on victims' right to truth.[108]

In addition, as participants in the judicial process, survivors have a right to protection.[109] In practice, the large majority of victim participants will only benefit from so-called in-court measures, involving the use of pseudonyms and the sharing of their identities with other actors in the proceedings on a need-to-know basis only.[110] Some victims' legal representatives have identified shortcomings in the Court's application of these principles in a few concrete situations. Manoba and Cox believe that the judges' inability to appreciate local dynamics may explain the dismissal of particular requests for protection.[111]

Finally, as explained earlier, victims have a variety of opportunities to provide their views on the proceedings. On a number of occasions, victims' representatives have highlighted that the time allotted for victims to provide their input is far too short for the former to conduct meaningful consultations with clients.[112] Keeping a strict timetable is important to ensure the efficiency of the proceedings so that the accused is tried without delay. However, the imposition of deadlines in certain cases often appears irrational and disconnected from the reality on the ground. In one extreme example, victims from Afghanistan were given only two months to provide their views on the opening of an investigation. This required intermediaries to reach out to victims in different provinces to explain ICC proceedings for the first time, and to do so during the harsh winter months and in precarious security conditions.[113] Once the Chamber received victims' views, it took 14 months to deliberate and issue a decision.

Survivors' Needs beyond the Criminal Process

Accountability is one of a victim's main priorities.[114] Mass violence creates other pressing physical, psychological, economic and social needs.[115] 'The destruction of livelihoods, families, deaths, carrying heavy loads etc. has had its share of devastating effect on individuals … these individuals want to see justice done but also need material support such as housing and health care.'[116] These needs are of utmost importance to survivors and, in many cases, prevent them from participating or from doing so meaningfully.[117] These pressing needs, however, tend to be overlooked when the focus is placed squarely on survivors as subjects of the right to participate in judicial proceedings. Survivors do not theorize or compartmentalize their different needs, and their notion of justice may be broader than accountability. For some, justice may encompass recognition and a conviction; for others, it may also include political reform and removal of the root causes that led to conflict; for many, it involves reparations for the harm suffered.[118] This is why the process of participation may naturally create expectations in survivors that they will receive support or assistance to address their most immediate material or physical needs.[119]

Acknowledging this reality and the imperative to restore survivor's dignity,[120] some authors turn to the ICC Trust Fund as the entity that could provide survivors, including those who participate in proceedings, with relief.[121] As explained earlier, the Trust Fund is mandated to implement reparation awards and assistance projects benefiting victims of crimes within ICC jurisdiction. While it has significant potential,[122] in practice the Trust Fund has done too little too late.[123] It has also been criticized for an ineffective discharge of its mandate.[124] Certainly the Trust Fund can do better if reformed.[125] But not all responsibility can be placed on the ICC or the Trust Fund.[126] While certain actors within the ICC may help to bring attention to victims' needs,[127] it does not belong to the Court to address this gap[128] or at least to do so alone. Ideally, government-funded programmes or those put in place by international donors should offer additional support.

Since the ICC can go only so far in meeting victims' needs, it is fair to ask if it has been able to bring victims closer to other goals, such as gaining assistance, reconciliation or accountability through other mechanisms. Ideally, participation in proceedings should be part and parcel of a holistic redress scheme, whereby intervention in an ICC case is complemented by other components. In practice, however, there is disconnection between victim participation and other initiatives addressing survivors' needs. Victim participation that is truly empowering may have a positive knock-on effect on other initiatives originating at the grassroots level, including from the community itself.[129] Some civil society organizations have put in place projects combining assistance to participate in ICC proceedings with other types of support.[130] In addition, lawyers who have represented victims are acutely aware of this gap.[131] Some have sought avenues to assist victims through other projects or advocated for support through other entities.[132] Aside from this, however, participation in ICC proceedings may disappoint survivors because a range of significant needs are likely to remain unaddressed.

Conclusion

This chapter has analysed whether the ICC's promise for a more inclusive, survivor-centred justice model, has materialized in practice. Three main aspects appear relevant to assess whether participation is effective throughout the ICC's intervention from a survivor's point of view, namely access to justice, the participation experience and the outcome of the judicial process. A careful assessment of the ICC's practice in relation to those three features reveals that the Court has fallen short of facilitating truly meaningful and engaging victim participation.

While the Court has sought to ease the process for victims to apply to participate in proceedings, including by making it less bureaucratic and training local intermediaries to assist them, victims face concrete obstacles. In particular, only the victims of the very limited set of crimes selected for prosecution can intervene in proceedings and receive reparations. ICC jurisprudence precludes victims from contributing to the scope of the case, including for the purpose of ensuring that cases are more representative of the crimes they experienced.

Despite budgetary and logistical challenges, survivors' legal representatives have introduced creative practices to ensure that they can be meaningful engaged through consultations throughout proceedings. Challenges remain, however, in relation to consultations with victims on the choice of their legal representative, a fundamental decision that tends to shape their participation experience.

When it comes to the end result of cases, only a handful of ICC cases have led to convictions, which have been handed out with significant delay. Despite survivors' preference in several cases to see justice done closer to home, the Court has never authorized *in situ* proceedings. Positively, survivors have gained a wide variety of procedural rights and can intervene through a legal representative in various ways during the proceedings. However, they have faced limitations in exercising two main rights, namely the right to tender evidence and the right to question witnesses, all of which affects their capacity to partake in the adjudication of justice. Finally, many survivors' needs for material, physical, psychological assistance remain unaddressed or have only been addressed partially and with significant delay.

This assessment demonstrates that although the ICC Statute contains valuable provisions to enable survivors' intervention in criminal proceedings, multiple barriers affect meaningful participation. These include, among others, the physical and cultural distance between the Court and the affected communities, the rigorous legal norms applicable to criminal proceedings, the complexities of litigation for mass atrocities, and budgetary and bureaucratic concerns.

Some of the limitations identified are linked to the normative framework of a criminal tribunal and therefore cannot be overcome. Other constraints, however, arise as a result of ICC policy or practice, and could in principle be surmounted. For example, the Court could pay greater attention to the dynamics of victim participation in criminal proceedings relevant to affected communities, by questioning how decisions on the scope of cases affect survivors, ensuring adequate consultations with survivors, improving staff and officials' understanding of the local context, and linking participation to complementary initiatives in order to address survivors' needs in a more holistic manner.

Notes

1 This chapter was researched and written between August 2020 and January 2021, revised in October 2022 and updated in 2024. All views expressed in this chapter are the author's personal opinion and do not represent the views of any of her current or former employers.

2 M. de Waardt and S. Weber, 'Beyond Victims' Mere Presence: An Empirical Analysis of Victim Participation in Transitional Justice in Colombia', *Journal of Human Rights Practice*, 11(1), 2019.

3 E. Evrard, G. Mejía Bonifazi and T. Destroper , 'The Meaning of Participation in Transitional Justice: A Conceptual Proposal for Empirical Analysis', *International Journal for Transitional Justice*, 15(2) 2021, p. 429.

4 De Waardt and Weber, 'Beyond Victims' Mere Presence', p. 212.

5 R. Sprenkels, *Restricted Access: Promises and Pitfalls of Victim Participation in Transitional Justice Mechanisms* (Utrecht: Impunity Watch, 2017), p. 10.

6 Since then, a number of hybrid tribunals and specialized mechanisms have included similar provisions. See M. Pena, 'Victim Participation in International Criminal Proceedings', in *Max Plank Encyclopaedia of International Procedural Law* (Oxford: Oxford University Press, 2019), para. 4.

7 S. Kelly, 'The Role of Victims in the International Criminal Court: Challenges and Opportunities', *New England Journal of International and Comparative Law*, 18(1), 2012, p. 243.

8 W. Schabas, *An Introduction to the International Criminal Court* (Cambridge: Cambridge University Press, 2014), p. 347.

9 C. Bassiouni, 'Victim's Rights: International Recognition', in *The Pursuit of International Criminal Justice: A World Study on Conflicts, Victimization and Post-Conflict Justice*, ed. C. Bassiouni (Antwerp and Oxford: Intersentia, 2010), p. 617.

10 T. Markus Funk, 'Surveying the Rise of Victims' Rights under International Law (and at the International Criminal Court)', *Eyes on the ICC*, 11, 2015, p. 7.

11 See, for example, ibid., p. 3; L. Paisner, 'Behind the Procedural Curtain', *Eyes on the ICC*, 10(1), 2013–2014, pp. 90–91; and M. Pena and G. Carayon, 'Is the ICC Making the Most of Victim Participation?' *International Journal of Transitional Justice*, 7(3), 2013, p. 524.

12 ICC, *The Prosecutor v. Germain Katanga and Mathieu Ngudjolo Chui*, Decision on the Set of Procedural Rights Attached to Procedural Status of Victims at the Pre-Trial Stage of the Case (ICC-01&04–01/07–474), 13 May 2008, para. 51.

13 L. Moffett, 'Elaborating Justice for Victims at the International Criminal Court: Beyond Rhetoric and The Hague', *Journal of International Criminal Justice*, 13 (2), 2015, pp. 281–311; and Pena and Carayon, 'Is the ICC Making the Most of Victim Participation?' pp. 518–535.

14 Markus Funk, 'Surveying the Rise of Victims' Rights under International Law', and Kelly, 'The Role of Victims in the International Criminal Court'.

15 J. Wemmers, 'Where Do We Belong? Giving Victims a Place in the Criminal Justice Process', *Criminal Law Forum*, 20, 2009, p. 401.
16 Moffett, 'Elaborating Justice for Victims at the International Criminal Court'.
17 Rome Statute of the International Criminal Court, adopted 17 July 1998.
18 M. Cohen, 'Victims' Participation Rights Within the International Criminal Court: A Critical Overview', *Denver Journal of International Law and Policy*, 37 (3), 2009, p. 355.
19 K. Tibori-Szabó and M. Hirst, eds, *Victim Participation in International Criminal Justice* (The Hague: Springer, 2017), p. 4.
20 In addition to the Rome Statute, the ICC Rules of Procedure and Evidence, the Regulations of the Court, Regulations of the Registry contain provisions applicable to victim participation.
21 V. Spiga, 'No Redress without Justice: Victims and International Criminal Law', *Journal of International Criminal Justice*, 10(5), 2012, p. 1389.
22 L. Zegveld, 'Victims as a Third Party: Empowerment of Victims?' *International Criminal Law Review*, 19(2), 2019, p. 335.
23 S. Vasiliev, 'Victim Participation Revisited: What the ICC is Learning about Itself', in *The Law and Practice of the International Criminal Court*, ed. C. Stahn (Oxford: Oxford University Press, 2015), p. 1165; and A. Sehmi, '"Now That We Have No Voice, What Will Happen to Us?" Experiences of Victim Participation in the Kenyatta Case', *Journal of International Criminal Justice*, 16(3), 2018, p. 574.
24 ICC, *The Prosecutor v. Al Hassan*, Decision on Principles Applicable to Victims' Applications for Participation, to Legal Representation of Victims, and to the Manner of Victim Participation in the Proceedings (ICC-01/12–01/18–289-Red-tENG-Corr), 20 March 2019, para. 44.
25 M. Vianney-Liaud and C. Pineau, 'Assessing Victim's Contribution to the Determination of the Truth in the Bemba Case', *Eyes on the ICC*, 12, 2016–2017, p. 61.
26 Article 75, Rome Statute.
27 Article 79, Rome Statute.
28 Regulations of the Trust Fund for Victims (ICC-ASP/4/Res.3), adopted 3 December 2005, para. 50.
29 Rule 85(a) of the ICC Rules of Procedure and Evidence defines victims as 'natural persons who have suffered harm as a result of the commission of any crime within the jurisdiction of the Court'. This provision has been interpreted to require that survivors prove the following to exercise their participatory rights: (a) their identity as a natural person; (b) that the applicant has suffered harm; and (c) that there was a casual link between the harm suffered and the crime(s) charged in the case at hand. See H. Dumont, 'Requirement for Victim Participation', in *Victim Participation in International Criminal Justice*, ed. Tibori-Szabó and Hirst (The Hague: Springer, 2017), 50.
30 M. Juliana Machado, S. Karlsson and L. Rudi, 'The Victims Who Are Not Quite Victim Enough: How the International Criminal Court Creates Divides Within Victim Communities', *Die Friedens-Warte*, 88(3/4), 2013, pp. 216–217.
31 S. Kendall and S. Nouwen, 'Representational Practices at the International Criminal Court: The Gap between Juridified and Abstract Victimhood', in *Law and Contemporary Problems*, 76(3–4), 2014, p. 242.
32 ICC, *Situation in the Democratic Republic of the Congo*, Judgment on Victim Participation in the Investigation Stage of the Proceedings in the Appeal of the OPCD Against the Decision of Pre-Trial Chamber I of 7 December 2007 and in the Appeals of the OPCD and the Prosecutor Against the Decision of Pre-Trial Chamber I of 24 December 2007 (ICC-01/04–556), 19 December 2008.
33 For example, in 2018 the Court allowed participation by victims from Myanmar in a request for a preliminary ruling on jurisdiction filed by the prosecution

prior to an application to open an investigation (see ICC, *Request under Regulation 46(3) of the Regulations of the Court*, Decision on the 'Prosecutor Requests for a Preliminary Ruling on Jurisdiction under Article 19(3) of the Statute' (ICC-RoC46(3)-01/18–37), 6 September 2018, para. 21). In addition, in 2019–2020 the Appeals Chamber allowed victim participation in an appeal lodged by the prosecution concerning a dismissal of a request to open an investigation in Afghanistan, but it rejected direct appeals lodged by victims (see ICC, *Situation in the Islamic Republic of Afghanistan*, Reasons for the Appeals Chamber's oral decision dismissing as inadmissible the victims' appeals against the decision rejecting the authorisation of an investigation into the situation in Afghanistan (ICC-02/17–137), 4 March 2020, para. 23).

34 G. Bitti, 'A Court for Victims?,' in *Victims at the Center of Justice: From 1998 to 2018: Reflections on the Promises and the Reality of Victim Participation at the ICC*, ed. International Federation for Human Rights (FIDH), 2018, p. 11, available at https://www.fidh.org/IMG/pdf/droitsdesvictimes730a_final-2.pdf.

35 L. Walleyn, 'Victims' Participation in ICC Proceedings: Challenges Ahead', *International Criminal Law Review*, 16(6), 2016, p. 999.

36 Moffett, 'Elaborating Justice for Victims', p. 293.

37 M. Pena, 'Victim Participation at the International Criminal Court: Achievements and Challenges Lying Ahead,' *ILSA Journal of International and Comparative Law*, 16(2), 2010, p. 511.

38 Tibori-Szabó and Hirst, *Victim Participation in International Criminal Justice*, p. 4.

39 See, for example, Christine Chung, 'Victims' Participation at the International Criminal Court: Are Concessions of the Court Clouding the Promise?' *Northwestern Journal of International Human Rights*, 6(3), 2008, pp. 519 and 528; and S. SáCouto and K. Cleary, 'Victims' Participation in the Investigations of the International Criminal Court', *Transnational Law & Contemporary Problems*, 17 (1), 2008, p. 105.

40 Pena and G. Carayon, 'Is the ICC Making the Most of Victim Participation?' p. 530.

41 ICC, *The Prosecutor v. Ongwen*, Decision on the Legal Representatives for Victims Requests to Present Evidence and Views and Concerns and related requests (ICC-02/04–01/15–1199-Red), 6 March 2018, para. 57.

42 ICC Rules of Procedure and Evidence, Rule 89. In certain limited cases, victims can participate without lodging an application, specifically with regard to proceedings related to the authorization to open an investigation, and jurisdiction of the Court or admissibility of a case. See Pena, 'Victim Participation in International Criminal Proceedings', para. 21.

43 Moffett, 'Elaborating Justice for Victims', p. 291.

44 ICC, *Chambers' Practice Manual*, 2016, pp. 20–23, available at https://www.icc-cpi.int/iccdocs/other/chambers_practice_manual–february_2016.pdf.

45 K. Tibori-Szabó *et al.*, 'Communication between Victims' Lawyers and Their Counsel', in *Victim Participation in International Criminal Justice*, ed. Tibori-Szabó and Hirst, p. 437.

46 Kendall and Nouwen, 'Representational Practices at the International Criminal Court', pp. 245–246.

47 ICC, *The Prosecutor v. Ongwen*, Decision Establishing Principles on the Application Process (ICC-02/04–01/15–205), 4 March 2015, para. 24.

48 As I have argued elsewhere, experience shows that victims needs support from external parties to access and exercise their rights before international courts. See M. Pena, 'The Role of Intermediaries and Third Parties in Victim Participation', in *Victim Participation in International Criminal Justice*, ed. Tibori-Szabó and Hirst, p. 83.

49 Tibori-Szabó *et al.*, 'Communication between Victims' Lawyers and Their Counsel', p. 437.

50 Avocats sans frontières (ASF), *Modalities of Participation and Legal Representation*, 2013, pp. 10–13, available at https://www.asf.be/wp-content/uploads/2013/11/ASF_IJ_Modes-of-participation-and-legal-representation.pdf.

51 The ICC only provides legal aid after the victim application has been accepted.

52 ASF, *Modalities of Participation and Legal Representation*, p. 31.

53 See, for example, ICC, *Prosecutor v. Al Hassan*, Decision on the procedure for the admission of victims to participate in proceedings for the purposes of trial (ICC-01/12–01/18–661) 12 March 2020, pp. 25–29.

54 J.A. Manoba and F. Cox, 'Victims' Participation in the Ongwen Case: Strengths, Weaknesses and Lessons Learned', in *Victims at the Center of Justice: From 1998 to 2018: Reflections on the Promises and the Reality of Victim Participation at the ICC*, ed. FIDH, p. 50.

55 Spiga, 'No Redress without Justice', p. 1391.

56 E. Haslam and R. Edmunds, 'Common Legal Representation at the International Criminal Court: More Symbolic than Real?' *International Criminal Law Review*, 12(5), 2012, p. 878.

57 Human Rights Center, *The Victims' Court? A Study of 622 Victim Participants at the International Criminal Court* (Berkeley: University of California, School of Law, 2015), p. 72, available at https://humanrights.berkeley.edu/sites/default/files/publications/vp_report_2015_full_rev_b-4.pdf. See also R. Killian and L. Moffett, 'Victim Legal Representation before the ICC and the ECCC', *Journal of International Criminal Justice*, 15(4), 2017, p. 716.

58 A study with focus groups in Kenya and Uganda revealed that survivors consider 'ongoing consultation by the lawyer … as the most important quality of good representation'. See C. Tenove, *Justice and Inclusion in Global Politics: Victim Representation and the International Criminal Court* (Vancouver: University of British Columbia, 2015, p. 255.

59 For example, 5,229 victims participated in the *Bemba* case, 2,129 in *Ntaganda* and 4,107 in *Ongwen*.

60 Where possible, the Court seeks to group all participating victims under one common legal representative. Whenever there is a conflict of interest, the Court must appoint different legal representatives for groups with distinct interests. For example, the Court has appointed different legal representatives for child soldiers on the one hand, and for victims of other crimes including those committed by child soldiers on the other hand. See ICC, *The Prosecutor v. Yekatom and Ngaïssona*, Decision on the Legal Representation of Victims (ICC-01/14–01/18–205), 23 May 2019. The Court has also grouped victims according to geographical criteria when the number of participating victims was particularly high, assigning different legal representatives to victims residing in different areas. See Haslam and Edmunds, 'Common Legal Representation at the International Criminal Court', pp. 885–886.

61 Haslam and Edmunds, 'Common Legal Representation at the International Criminal Court', p. 903.

62 Ibid., p. 889. See also E. Haslam and R. Edmunds, 'Whose Number is it Anyway? Common Legal Representation, Consultations and the "Statistical Victim"', *Journal of International Criminal Justice*, 15(5), 2017, p. 934.

63 Kendall and Nouwen, 'Representational Practices at the International Criminal Court', p.250.

64 Haslam and Edmunds, 'Whose Number is it Anyway?' p. 935.

65 Tenove, *Justice and Inclusion in Global Politics*, pp. 261–262.

66 Sehmi, '"Now That We Have No Voice, What Will Happen to Us?"', p. 583; and 'Victims' Participation in ICC Proceedings, p. 1003.

67 Pena and Carayon, 'Is the ICC Making the Most of Victim Participation?' p. 533.
68 Killian and Moffett, 'Victim Legal Representation before the ICC and the ECCC', p. 722.
69 Haslam and Edmunds, 'Whose Number is it Anyway?' p. 932.
70 Haslam and Edmunds, 'Common Legal Representation at the International Criminal Court', pp. 803, 806–809. See also 'Victims' Participation in ICC Proceedings, pp. 1007–1013 for an account and commentary on the conflicts created by appointment of the ICC's internal Office for Public Counsel for Victims to represent victims.
71 Killian and Moffett, 'Victim Legal Representation before the ICC and the ECCC', pp. 728–729.
72 Article 15 of the ICC Code of Professional Conduct states that 'Counsel shall provide the client with all the explanations reasonable needed to make informed decisions regarding his or her representation'.
73 Tenove, *Justice and Inclusion in Global Politics*', p. 241. See also Simon Robins, 'Towards Victim-Centred Transitional Justice: Understanding the Needs of Families of the Disappeared in Postconflict Nepal', *International Journal of Transitional Justice*, 5(1), 2011, p. 97.
74 Tibori-Szabó *et al.*, 'Communication between Victims' Lawyers and Their Counsel', p. 434.
75 Sehmi, '"Now That We Have No Voice"', p. 580.
76 Tibori-Szabó *et al.* note that 'communication is one of the fundamental rights that participation entails for victims'; see Tibori-Szabó *et al.*, 'Communication between Victims' Lawyers and Their Counsel', p. 442.
77 Individual meetings may be particularly important for survivors of sexual violence.
78 Manoba and Cox, 'Victims' Participation in the Ongwen Case', pp. 50–51.
79 Tibori-Szabó *et al.*, Communication between Victims' Lawyers and Their Counsel', p. 444.
80 Ibid., 437.
81 Ibid., 580.
82 Ibid., 590.
83 Ibid., 584.
84 See, for example, ICC, *The Prosecutor v. Ruto and Sang*, Urgent Request by the Victims' Representative for an order from the Chamber requiring the Registrar to provide appropriate resources for the current mission in Kenya (ICC-01/09–01/11–392-Red), 29 February 2012; and ICC, *Prosecutor v. Ongwen*, Corrected Version of Request for a determination concerning legal aid (ICC-02/04–01/15–434-Corr), 23 May 2016.
85 Sehmi, '"Now That We Have No Voice"', p. 581.
86 Ibid., 583.
87 Manoba and Cox, 'Victims' Participation in the Ongwen Case', p. 53.
88 These statistics only consider cases for 'core crimes' (i.e. genocide, war crimes and crimes against humanity). They, therefore, exclude cases on offences against the administration of justice.
89 The judgment in the Ongwen case has been appealed and is, therefore, not final. At the time of writing, three accused were undergoing trial (*Al Hassan, Yekatom* and *Ngaïssona*), one case was undergoing trial preparations (*Abd-Al-Rahman*), and one case was at the pre-trial stage (*Said*).
90 D. Groome, 'No Witness, No Case: An Assessment of the Conduct and Quality of ICC Investigations', *Penn State Journal of Law and International Affairs*, 3 (1), 2014, pp. 1–29; and P. Labuda, 'The ICC's Evidence Problem: The Future of International Criminal Investigations after the Gbagbo Acquittal',

Völkerrechtsblog, 2019, available at https://voelkerrechtsblog.org/the-iccs-evidence-problem/.

91 FIDH, 2013, p. 11, *Enhancing Victims Rights before the ICC*, available at https://www.fidh.org/IMG/pdf/fidh_victimsrights_621a_nov2013_ld.pdf.

92 A. Pues, 'Towards the "Golden Hour"? A Critical Exploration of the Length of Preliminary Examinations', *Journal of International Criminal Justice*, 15(3), 2017, pp. 438–429 and 448–449.

93 At the time of writing, there were ten pending public arrest warrants (*Kony, Otti, Mudacumura, Harun, Al-Bashir, Banda, Hussein, Saif Gaddafi, Khaled* and *Al-Werfalli*). In addition, four fugitives have died (*Lukwiya, Odhiambo, Muammar Gaddafi* and *Jerbo*).

94 The ICC has developed jurisprudence on the possibility for a deceased victim's relative to take over participation in the even of their demise. See Hirst, Termination of Participation, in *Victim Participation in International Criminal Justice,* ed. Tibori-Szabó and Hirst, pp. 420–424.

95 See, for example, ICC, *Prosecutor v. Ruto and Sang*, Common Legal Representative for Victims' Observations in Relation to the 'Joint Defence Application for Change of Place Where the Court Shall Sit for Trial' (ICC-01/09–01/11–620) 22 February 2013, paras 6–10; and ICC, *Prosecutor v. Kenyatta*, Victims' Observations in relation to the 'Defence Application for change of place where the Court shall sit for Trial' (ICC-01/09–02/11–629), 7 February 2013, para. 8.

96 ICC, *Situation in the People's Republic of Bangladesh/Republic of the Union of Myanmar*, Victims' joint request concerning hearings outside the host State (ICC-01/19–34), 4 August 2020, para. 44.

97 Ibid.

98 See, for example, ICC, *Prosecutor v. Ongwen*, Corrected Version of Submissions on Items Defined for the Status Conference on 23 May 2016 (ICC-02/04–01/15–433-Corr), 13 May 2016, para. 23.

99 Pena, 'Victim Participation at the International Criminal Court', p. 500.

100 Pena and Carayon, 'Is the ICC Making the Most of Victim Participation?' p. 523.

101 Pena, 'Victim Participation at the International Criminal Court', paras 40–42.

102 P. Haynes, 'Victims' Lawyers in the Courtroom: Opening and Closing Statements, Questioning Witnesses, Challenging and Presenting Evidence', in *Victim Participation in International Criminal Justice*, ed. Tibori-Szabó and Hirst, pp. 262–269.

103 Ibid., 269.

104 As explained above, a motion to expand the evidentiary basis in *Ongwen* so as to include sexual violence against male victims was rejected because the case, as conceived by the prosecution, only covered sexual and gender-based crimes committed against female victims.

105 S. SáCouto, 'Victim Participation at the International Criminal Court and the Extraordinary Chambers in the Courts of Cambodia: A Feminist Project', *Michigan Journal of Gender and Law*, 18(2), 2012, pp. 337–339.

106 ICC, *Prosecutor v. Ongwen*, Oral Ruling, Hearing Transcript ICC-02/04–01/15-T-65-Red-ENG, 51–56, 4 April 2017, pp. 51–56.

107 Vianney-Liaud and Pineau, 'Assessing Victim's Contribution to the Determination of the Truth in the Bemba Case', p. 57. See also ICC, *Prosecutor v. Bemba*, Decision (i) Ruling on Legal Representatives' Applications to Question Witness 33 and (ii) Setting a Schedule for the Filing of Submissions in Relation to Future Applications to Question Witnesses (ICC-01/05–01/08–1729), 9 September 2011, para. 15: 'victims have a general interest in the proceedings and in their outcome. As such, they have an interest in making sure that all pertinent questions are put to witnesses'.

108 Manoba and Cox, 'Victims' Participation in the Ongwen Case', p. 52.

109 Pena, 'Victim Participation in International Criminal Proceedings', para. 44.
110 Ibid., para. 45.
111 Manoba and Cox, 'Victims' Participation in the Ongwen Case', p. 54.
112 For example, ICC, *Situation on the Registered Vessels of the Union of Comoros, the Hellenic Republic and the Kingdom of Cambodia*, Request for extension of time to submit Victims' Observations in relation to the article 53 proceedings (ICC-01/13–22), 18 May 2015, para. 10.
113 ICC, *Situation in the Islamic Republic of Afghanistan*, Amicus Curiae Submissions on Behalf of Human Rights Organizations in Afghanistan (ICC-02/17–57), 11 July 2019, para. 22.
114 L. Fletcher, 'Refracted Justice: The Imagined Victim and the International Criminal Court', in *Contested Justice*, ed. C. De Vos S. Kendall and C. Stahn (Cambridge: Cambridge University Press, 2015), pp. 321–322.
115 C. Tenove, *International Justice for Victims? Assessing the International Criminal Court from the Perspective of Victims in Kenya and Uganda*, Africa Portal, Research Paper no. 1, 2013, p. 21, available at https://www.researchgate.net/publication/320386086_International_Justice_for_Victims_Assessing_the_International_Criminal_Court_from_Victims'_Perspectives_in_Kenya_and_Uganda.
116 Manoba and Cox, 'Victims' Participation in the Ongwen Case', p. 53.
117 A. Sehmi, 'A Luxury Victims Cannot Afford: Meaningful Participation at the International Criminal Court', *Kenyans for Peace Truth and Justice Truth & Justice Digest*, 7(9), 2013, p. 4, available at http://africog.org/new/wp-content/uploads/A%20Luxury%20Victims%20Cannot%20Afford%20-%20KPTJ%20JULY%202013.pdf. Sehmi notes that some of the problems that survivors face include poverty, unemployment, lack of medical assistance, the need to obtain food and/or shelter, the need to take care of sick family members, childcare needs, and a lack of transport to attend relevant meetings.
118 J. Wemmers, *Reparation and the International Criminal Court: Meeting the Needs of Victims* (Montreal: International Centre for Comparative Criminology, University of Montreal, 2006), p. 6, available at https://papers.ssrn.com/sol3/papers.cfm?abstract_id=3636291.
119 Moffett, 'Elaborating Justice for Victims', p. 295. See also Human Rights Center, *The Victims' Court?* p. 71.
120 Sehmi, '"Now That We Have No Voice"', p. 585.
121 Ibid., pp. 585–587; and S. Kendall, 'Beyond the Restorative Turn: The Limits of Legal Humanitarianism', in *Contested Justice*, ed. De Vos *et al.*, pp. 369–370.
122 A. Douton and F. Ní Aoláin, 'Between Reparations and Repair: Assessing the Work of the ICC Trust Fund for Victims Under Its Assistance Mandate', *Chicago Journal of International Law*, 19(2), 2019, pp. 546–547.
123 Sehmi, '"Now That We Have No Voice"', p. 587; and REDRESS, *No Time to Wait: Realising Reparations for Victims at the International Criminal Court*, p. 31, available at https://redress.org/wp-content/uploads/2019/02/20190221-Reparations-Report-English.pdf.
124 J. Anderson and S. Van den Berg, 'ICC Trust Fund: The Headless Chicken', *Justice Info*, 8 December 2020, available at https://www.justiceinfo.net/en/46193-icc-trust-fund-headless-chicken.html.
125 Independent Expert Review of the International Criminal Court and the Rome Statute System, Final Report, September 2020, pp. 305–311, available at https://asp.icc-cpi.int/iccdocs/asp_docs/ASP19/IER-Final-Report-ENG.pdf.
126 Fletcher, 'Refracted Justice', p. 324; and Moffett, 'Elaborating Justice for Victims', pp. 295–296.
127 Tenove, *International Justice for Victims?* pp. 25–26.
128 Fletcher, 'Refracted Justice', p. 324.
129 Sehmi, '"Now That We Have No Voice"', p. 589.

130 For example, for several years ASF (Belgium) combined legal assistance to victims participating in ICC proceedings and representation of civil parties intervening in domestic trials in the Democratic Republic of Congo (ASF, Case Study: The Application of the Rome Statute of the International Criminal Court by the Courts of the Democratic Republic of Congo, 2009, p. 2, available at https://asf.be/wp-content/publications/ASF_CaseStudy_RomeStatute_Light_PagePerPage.pdf). Following the 2007–2008 post-election violence in Kenya, Kituo Cha Seria, a local legal advice centre, engaged in advocacy and community awareness to support internally displaced persons, training on the ICC and domestic tribunals, and enabling victims to participate in ICC proceedings (Kituo Cha Sheria, Rationale for a Peace, Justice and Reconciliation Project, available at http://kituochasheria.or.ke/our-programs/peace-justice-reconciliation-programme/.

131 Manoba and Cox, 'Victims' Participation in the Ongwen Case', p. 53.

132 ASF, *Modalities of Participation and Legal Representation*, p. 36.

References

Bassiouni, C. (2010) 'Victim's Rights: International Recognition,', in C. Bassiouni (ed.), *The Pursuit of International Criminal Justice: A World Study on Conflicts, Victimization and Post-Conflict Justice.* Antwerp and Oxford: Intersentia.

Chung, C. (2008) 'Victims' Participation at the International Criminal Court: Are Concessions of the Court Clouding the Promise?' *Northwestern Journal of International Human Rights*, vol. 6, no. 3, pp. 459–545.

Cohen, M. (2009) 'Victims' Participation Rights within the International Criminal Court: A Critical Overview,', *Denver Journal of International Law and Policy*, vol. 37, no. 3, pp. 351–377.

De Waardt, M. and Weber, S. (2019) 'Beyond Victims' Mere Presence: An Empirical Analysis of Victim Participation in Transitional Justice in Colombia,', *Journal of Human Rights Practice*, vol. 11, pp. 209–228.

Douton, A. and Aolaín, F. (2019) 'Between Reparations and Repair: Assessing the Work of the ICC Trust Fund for Victims Under Its Assistance Mandate', *Chicago Journal of International Law*, vol. 19, no. 2, pp. 490–547.

Evrard, E., Mejía Bonifazi, G. and Destrooper, T. (2021) 'The Meaning of Participation in Transitional Justice: A Conceptual Proposal for Empirical Analysis,' *International Journal for Transitional Justice*, vol. 15, no. 2, pp. 428–447.

Fletcher, L. (2015) 'Refracted Justice: The Imagined Victim and the International Criminal Court,' in C. De Vos, S. Kendall and C. Stahn (eds), *Contested Justice.* Cambridge: Cambridge University Press, pp. 302–325.

Funk, T.M. (2015) 'Surveying the Rise of Victims' Rights under International Law (and at the International Criminal Court)', *Eyes on the ICC*, vol. 11, pp. 3–28.

Groome, D. (2014) 'No Witness, No Case: An Assessment of the Conduct and Quality of ICC Investigations', *Penn State Journal of Law and International Affairs*, vol. 3, no. 1, pp 1–29.

Haslam, E. and Edmunds, R. (2012) 'Common Legal Representation at the International Criminal Court: More Symbolic than Real?' *International Criminal Law Review*, vol. 12, no. 5, pp. 871–903.

Haslam, E. and Edmunds, R. (2017) 'Whose Number is it Anyway? Common Legal Representation, Consultations and the "Statistical Victim"', *Journal of International Criminal Justice*, vol. 15, no. 5, pp. 931–952.

Kelly, S. (2012) 'The Role of Victims in the International Criminal Court: Challenges Opportunities', *New England Journal of International and Comparative Law*, vol. 18, no. 1, pp. 243–264.

Kendall, S. (2015) 'Beyond the Restorative Turn: The Limits of Legal Humanitarianism', in C. De Vos, S. Kendall and C. Stahn (eds), *Contested Justice*. Cambridge: Cambridge University Press, pp. 352–376.

Kendall S. and Nouwen, S. (2014) 'Representational Practices at the International Criminal Court: The Gap between Juridified and Abstract Victimhood', in *Law and Contemporary Problems*, vol. 76, nos 3–4, pp. 235–262.

Killian, R. and Moffett, L. (2017) 'Victim Legal Representation before the ICC and the ECCC', *Journal of International Criminal Justic*, 15, no. 4, pp. 713–740.

Machado, M., Karlsson, S. and Rudi, L. (2013) 'The Victims Who Are Not Quite Victim Enough: How the International Criminal Court Creates Divides within Victim Communities', *Die Friedens-Warte*, vol. 88, nos 3/4, pp. 207–231.

Moffett, L. (2015) 'Elaborating Justice for Victims at the International Criminal Court: Beyond Rhetoric and The Hague', *Journal of International Criminal Justic*, vol. 13, no. 2, pp. 281–311.

Pena, M. (2010) 'Victim Participation at the International Criminal Court: Achievements and Challenges Lying Ahead', *ILSA Journal of International and Comparative La*, vol. 16, no. 2, pp. 497–516.

Pena, M. (2019) 'Victim Participation in International Criminal Proceedings', in *Max Plank ·Encyclopaedia of International Procedural Law*. Oxford: Oxford University Press.

Pena, M. and Carayon, G. (2013) 'Is the ICC Making the Most of Victim Participation?', *International Journal of Transitional Justice*, vol. 7, no. 3, pp. 518–535.

Paisner, L. (2013–2014) 'Behind the Procedural Curtain', *Eyes on the ICC*, vol. 10, no. 1, pp. 85–122.

Pues, A. (2017) 'Towards the "Golden Hour"? A Critical Exploration of the Length of Preliminary Examinations', *Journal of International Criminal Justice*, vol. 15, no. 3, pp. 435–453.

Robins, S. (2011) 'Towards Victim-Centred Transitional Justice: Understanding the Needs of Families of the Disappeared in Postconflict Nepal', *International Journal of Transitional Justice*, vol. 5, no. 1, pp. 75–98.

SáCouto, S. (2012) 'Victim Participation at the International Criminal Court and the Extraordinary Chambers in the Courts of Cambodia: A Feminist Project', *Michigan Journal of Gender and Law*, vol. 18, no. 2, pp. 297–360.

SáCouto, S. and Cleary, K. (2008) 'Victims' Participation in the Investigations of the International Criminal Court', *Transnational Law & Contemporary Problems*, vol. 17, no. 1, pp. 73–105.

Schabas, W. (2014) *An Introduction to the International Criminal Court*. Cambridge: Cambridge University Press.

Sehmi, A. (2018) '"Now That We Have No Voice, What Will Happen to Us?" Experiences of Victim Participation in the Kenyatta Case', *Journal of International Criminal Justice*, vol. 16, no. 3, pp. 571–591.

Spiga, V. (2012) 'No Redress without Justice: Victims and International Criminal Law', *Journal of International Criminal Justice*, vol. 10, no. 5, pp. 1377–1394.

Sprenkels, R. (2017) *Restricted Access: Promises and Pitfalls of Victim Participation in Transitional Justice Mechanisms*, Utrecht: Impunity Watch.

Tenove, C. (2015) *Justice and Inclusion in Global Politics: Victim Representation and the International Criminal Court*, Vancouver: University of British Columbia.

Tibori-Szabó, K. and Hirst, M. (eds) (2017) *Victim Participation in International Criminal Justice*. The Hague: Springer.

Vasiliev, S. (2015) 'Victim Participation Revisited: What the ICC is Learning About Itself', in C. Stahn (ed.), *The Law and Practice of the International Criminal Court*, Oxford: Oxford University Press, pp. 1133–1201.

Vianney-Liaud, M. and Pineau, C. (2016–2017) 'Assessing Victim's Contribution to the Determination of the Truth in the Bemba Case', *Eyes on the ICC*, vol. 12, pp. 51–72.

Walleyn, L. (2016) 'Victims' Participation in ICC Proceedings: Challenges Ahead', *International Criminal Law Review*, vol. 16, no. 6, pp. 995–1007.

Wemmers, J. (2009) 'Where Do We Belong? Giving Victims a Place in the Criminal Justice Process', *Criminal Law Forum*, vol. 20, pp. 395–416.

Zegveld, L. (2019) 'Victims as a Third Party: Empowerment of Victims?' *International Criminal Law Review*, vol. 19, no. 2, pp. 321–345.

Legal Filings and Decisions

ICC (13 May 2008) *Prosecutor v. Katanga and Nugdjolo. Decision on the Set of Procedural Rights Attached to Procedural Status of Victims at the Pre-Trial Stage of the Case (ICC-01&04–01/07–474).*

ICC (19 December 2008) *Situation in the Democratic Republic of the Congo. Judgment on Victim Participation in the Investigation Stage of the Proceedings in the Appeal of the OPCD Against the Decision of Pre-Trial Chamber I of 7 December 2007 and in the Appeals of the OPCD and the Prosecutor Against the Decision of Pre-Trial Chamber I of 24 December 2007 (ICC-01/04–556).*

ICC (9 September 2011) *Prosecutor v. Bemba. Decision (i) Ruling on Legal Representatives' Applications to Question Witness 33 and (ii) Setting a Schedule for the Filing of Submissions in Relation to Future Applications to Question Witnesses (ICC-01/05–01/08–1729).*

ICC (29 February 2012) *Prosecutor v. Ruto and Sang. Urgent Request by the Victims' Representative for an order from the Chamber requiring the Registrar to provide appropriate resources for the current mission in Kenya (ICC-01/09–01/11–392-Red).*

ICC (7 February 2013) *Prosecutor v. Kenyatta. Victims' Observations in relation to the 'Defence Application for change of place where the Court shall sit for Trial' (ICC-01/09–02/11–629).*

ICC (22 February 2013) *Prosecutor v. Ruto and Sang. Common Legal Representative for Victims' Observations in Relation to the 'Joint Defence Application for Change of Place Where the Court Shall Sit for Trial' (ICC-01/09–01/11–620).*

ICC (4 March 2015) *Prosecutor v. Ongwen. Decision Establishing Principles on the Application Process (ICC-02/04–01/15–205).*

ICC (18 May 2015) *Situation on the Registered Vessels of the Union of Comoros, the Hellenic Republic and the Kingdom of Cambodia. Request for extension of time to submit Victims' Observations in relation to the Article 53 proceedings (ICC-01/13–22).*

ICC (13 May 2016) *Prosecutor v. Ongwen. Corrected Version of Submissions on Items Defined for the Status Conference on 23 May 2016 (ICC-02/04–01/15–433-Corr).*

ICC (23 May 2016) *Prosecutor v. Ongwen. Corrected Version of Request for a determination concerning legal aid (ICC-02/04–01/15–434-Corr).*

ICC (4 April 2017) *Prosecutor v. Ongwen. Oral Ruling. Hearing Transcript ICC-02/04–01/15-T-65-Red-ENG.*

ICC (6 March 2018) *Prosecutor v. Ongwen. Decision on the Legal Representatives for Victims Requests to Present Evidence and Views and Concerns and related requests (ICC-02/04–01/15–1199-Red).*

ICC (6 September 2018) *Request under Regulation 46(3) of the Regulations of the Court. Decision on the 'Prosecutor Requests for a Preliminary Ruling on Jurisdiction under Article 19(3) of the Statute' (ICC-RoC46(3)-01/18–37).*

ICC (20 March 2019) *Prosecutor v. Al Hassan. Decision on Principles Applicable to Victims' Applications for Participation, to Legal Representation of Victims, and to the Manner of Victim Participation in the Proceedings (ICC-01/12–01/18–289-Red-tENG-Corr).*

ICC (23 May 2019) *Prosecutor v. Yekatom and Ngaïssona. Decision on the Legal Representation of Victims (ICC-01/14–01/18–205).*

ICC (11 July 2019) *Situation in the Islamic Republic of Afghanistan. Amicus Curiae Submissions on Behalf of Human Rights Organizations in Afghanistan (ICC-02/17–57).*

ICC (4 March 2020) *Situation in the Islamic Republic of Afghanistan. Reasons for the Appeals Chamber's oral decision dismissing as inadmissible the victims' appeals against the decision rejecting the authorisation of an investigation into the situation in Afghanistan (ICC-02/17–137).*

ICC (12 March 2020) *Prosecutor v. Al Hassan. Decision on the procedure for the admission of victims to participate in proceedings for the purposes of trial (ICC-01/12–01/18–661).*

ICC (4 August 2020) *Situation in the People's Republic of Bangladesh/Republic of the Union of Myanmar. Victims' joint request concerning hearings outside the host State (ICC-01/19–34).*

Web-based Documents

Anderson, J. and Van den Berg, S. (2020) 'ICC Trust Fund: The Headless Chicken', *Justice Info*. Available at https://www.justiceinfo.net/en/46193-icc-trust-fund-headless-chicken.html.

Avocats Sans Frontières (2009) *Case Study: The Application of the Rome Statute of the International Criminal Court by the Courts of the Democratic Republic of Congo*. Available at https://asf.be/wp-content/publications/ASF_CaseStudy_RomeStatute_Light_PagePerPage.pdf.

Avocats Sans Frontières (2010) *Modalities of Participation and Legal Representation (2013)*. Available at https://www.asf.be/wp-content/uploads/2013/11/ASF_IJ_Modes-of-participation-and-legal-representation.pdf.

International Criminal Court (2016) *Chambers' Practice Manual*. Available at https://www.icc-cpi.int/iccdocs/other/chambers_practice_manual–february_2016.pdf.

International Federation for Human Rights (2013) *Enhancing Victims Rights before the ICC*. Available at https://www.fidh.org/IMG/pdf/fidh_victimsrights_621a_nov2013_ld.pdf.

International Federation for Human Rights (ed.) (2018) *Victims at the Center of Justice: From 1998 to 2018: Reflections on the Promises and the Reality of Victim*

Participation at the ICC. Available at https://www.fidh.org/IMG/pdf/droitsdesvictimes730a_final-2.pdf.

Independent Expert Review of the International Criminal Court and the Rome Statute System (2020) *Final Report.* Available at https://asp.icc-cpi.int/iccdocs/asp_docs/ASP19/IER-Final-Report-ENG.pdf.

Kituo Cha Sheria (n.d.) *Rationale for a Peace, Justice and Reconciliation Project.* Available at http://kituochasheria.or.ke/our-programs/peace-justice-reconciliation-programme/.

Labuda, P. (2019) 'The ICC's Evidence Problem: The Future of International Criminal Investigations after the Gbagbo Acquittal', *Völkerrechtsblog.* Available at https://voelkerrechtsblog.org/the-iccs-evidence-problem/.

REDRESS (2019) *No Time to Wait: Realising Reparations for Victims at the International Criminal Court.* Available at https://redress.org/wp-content/uploads/2019/02/20190221-Reparations-Report-English.pdf.

Sehmi, A. (2013) 'A Luxury Victims Cannot Afford: Meaningful Participation at the International Criminal Court', *Kenyans for Peace Truth and Justice Truth & Justice Digest*, nos 07/09. Available at http://africog.org/new/wp-content/uploads/A%20Luxury%20Victims%20Cannot%20Afford%20-%20KPTJ%20JULY%202013.pdf.

Tenove, C. (2013) 'International Justice for Victims? Assessing the International Criminal Court from the Perspective of Victims in Kenya and Uganda', Africa Portal, Research Paper no. 1. Available at https://www.researchgate.net/publication/320386086_International_Justice_for_Victims_Assessing_the_International_Criminal_Court_from_Victims'_Perspectives_in_Kenya_and_Uganda.

University of California, Berkeley (2015) *The Victims' Court? A Study of 622 Victim Participants at the International Criminal Court.* Available at https://humanrights.berkeley.edu/sites/default/files/publications/vp_report_2015_full_rev_b-4.pdf.

Wemmers, J. (2006) *Reparation and the International Criminal Court: Meeting the Needs of Victims*, International Centre for Comparative Criminology, University of Montreal. Available at https://papers.ssrn.com/sol3/papers.cfm?abstract_id=3636291.

2 The International Criminal Court's Reparations Framework

An Access Point to Justice for Survivors of Mass Atrocities?

Monica Ingber[1]

Introduction

The incorporation of a case-based reparations framework into the Rome Statute of the International Criminal Court (ICC) presents a major advancement within the field of international criminal law. By incorporating a reparations framework into the Rome Statute, the drafters provided the ICC with a dual mandate: first, to investigate and prosecute those who have committed what the global community considers to be the most egregious crimes,[3] and second to place victims at the centre of its proceedings.[4] The inclusion of a number of rights for victims, such as the right to present their views and concerns, the right to protection, as well as the right to claim and receive reparations, serve as the main drivers of the ICC's victim-oriented mandate.[5] Underlying the Court's dual mandate is the notion of restorative justice, which itself is victim-centric and broadly seeks to restore harmony between individuals within the community by instilling a feeling that justice has been done.[6] This can be seen in the case of *The Prosecutor v. Thomas Lubanga Dilyo*, when Pre-Trial Chamber I stated that '[the] reparation scheme provided for in the [Rome Statute] is not only one of the Statute's unique features. It is also a key feature. In the Chamber's opinion, the success of the Court is, to some extent, linked to the success of its reparation system'.[7] In effect, the Court has noted that reparations fulfil the purpose of obliging those responsible for serious crimes to repair the harm done to the victims, and it also enables the Chamber to ensure that offenders account for their actions. Through this, the reparations scheme works to rebalance power between the victims and the perpetrator.

What does this mean for survivors of mass atrocities? In the *Factory of Chorzów* case, the Permanent Court of International Justice found that

> [the] essential principle contained in the actual notion of an illegal act – a principle which seems to be established by international practice and in particular by the decisions of arbitral tribunals – is that reparations must, as far as possible, wipe out all the consequences of the illegal act and re-establish the situation which would, in all probability have existed if the act had not been committed.[8]

DOI: 10.4324/9781003212409-4

When restorative justice is approached along these lines, it is immediately apparent that it is backward looking. This is perhaps why restitution and compensation are the principle modes of reparation since the former aims, as far as it is practicably possible, to return the victim to the situation they were in before the crime was committed, while the latter provides for a monetary award based on calculated damage suffered by the victim. There is an apparent tension, however, between the backward-looking nature of restorative justice and reparations for mass atrocities in post-conflict societies. This tension is located in the legalization of victimhood, which produces a certain knowledge about the constitution of harm and in doing so denies not only the harm suffered by survivors, but also renders them invisible under the law. This is significant if one considers the relationship between justice and reparations to be construed as 'settling the present'.

Conceptualizing Justice

There is little to be gained if justice, in the context of the aftermath of mass atrocities, is understood in relation to its opposite – injustice. This is because thinking of justice/injustice, as a binary opposition, does not explain what justice itself actually means. Instead, when approaching justice in this context, it is more useful to conceptualize it in terms of 'settling the present'. What does a 'settling the present' entail and how should it be theorized?

'Settling the present' does not simply mean the temporal present, but refers more to ἐόν, or 'presencing in unconcealment'.[9] This is significant if we consider that '[at] the beginning of justice, there was *logos*, speech, or language',[10] which locates justice in ἐόν since to speak presences in unconcealment. In other words, 'presencing in unconcealment' is about rendering those who are made invisible present by enabling them to enter into discourse as a subject. As we will see in this chapter, in order to settle the present, one needs to be able to enter into the conversation about justice in the first place. If we consider this in terms of international criminal law, the ability to speak and to be heard arises from a shared epistemology. For example, when looking at modernity, Walter Mignolo noted that modern Western rationality forms the epistemological basis of a 'totality' or a system of knowledge, which is predicated today on neoliberalism, and 'negates, exclude[s], occlude[s] the difference and the possibilities of other totalities'.[11] In other words, the Western cosmology cannot be reconciled with other totalities for the very reason that epistemologies cannot speak to each other. Instead, where separate totalities are formed, they interact either by competing with one another or by collaborating to disqualify knowledge that exists beyond them. International criminal law forms its own totality as a result of the deliberations, discussions, negotiations and disputes that are rooted in the power interests that drive it. In this respect, Burchard argues that what is at stake in international criminal justice is 'normative power', which he frames in terms of social and institutional discursive power.[12] This totality speaks a particular language, one that the particular epistemic (legal) community can hear and which is formed on the basis of a drive towards securing a normative form of justice. This tells us that the way justice is conceptualized is shaped through the particular epistemic community. The result is that knowledge of the 'other' is situated as an 'exteriority-to-totality', which ultimately means that the epistemology of the 'other' cannot be heard. As we will see, the survivor stands in opposition to or outside of the totality[13] due to the way in which the Rome Statute operates.

This speaks to the epistemic privilege of the legal community in deciding on what counts as 'justice' for mass atrocities, on account of the epistemology of the survivor being excluded from the discourse of restorative justice by virtue of remaining an absent present. This can be contrasted to the positionality of the legal victim, who occupies a position of exteriority-in-totality since there is a presumption that ἐόν enables the subsumption of one totality into another as an exteriority-in-totality. The legal victim of mass atrocities is consequently imbued by the legal community with the right of speech, which consequently places them in a position to participate in the restorative justice process.

Methodology

This chapter draws upon the above conceptualization of justice in order to problematize the Rome Statute's reparations framework. In doing so, the author uses discourse analysis to critically evaluate the Court's approach to restorative justice. Discourse analysis centres on the use of language and, as a result, it takes into account the context in which discourse takes place and recognizes that language functions in particular ways.[14] Law can be considered as a system of communication that functions as a social practice. In this respect, Peter Goodrich argues that

> [law] as a linguistic register or as a literary genre, can be described linguistically, or more importantly, discursively, in terms of its systematic appropriation and privileging of legally recognized meanings, accents, and connotations (modes of inclusion), and its simultaneous rejection of alternative and competing meanings, forms of utterance and discourse generally, as extrinsic, unauthorized, or threatening (modes of exclusion).[15]

Goodrich's understanding of the function of legal discourse is important when we consider the epistemological basis of legal texts such as the Rome Statute since it opens an avenue through which it becomes possible to discern how it is that other epistemological standpoints concerning justice become negated.

Epistemologies cannot speak across one another. When considering the incommensurability of epistemologies, it is therefore important to note that knowledge is produced from socially mediated interactions that shape human beings and consequently their knowledge and understanding of the world in which they live.[16] In order to enter into a discussion about justice, one must adopt the discourse of the dominant totality. This negates other totalities since communication can only take place once the individual is subsumed within and begins to speak the language of the dominant totality. By engaging in discourse analysis, it becomes possible to open up and begin to understand the way in which the language of the dominant totality drives the understanding of concepts such as justice. Discourse analysis permits us to begin recognizing the subsumption of one totality into another as an exteriority-in-totality. This consequently provides a means through which a greater understanding of how the 'other', such as the legal victim of mass atrocities, comes to be positioned as an exteriority-in-totality, while survivors largely remain positioned as exteriority-to-totality.

Access to Justice

Access to justice is based upon the ability to enter into, as well as produce, the discourse that serves to settle the present in post-conflict situations. The main problem that this chapter seeks to address is the positionality of survivors as exteriority-to-totality. This positionality makes it impossible to settle the present because survivors cannot contribute to the discourse on justice. It will be argued in this chapter that although it represents a step forward in terms of achieving restorative justice for victims of mass atrocities, the ICC's reparations framework works to create an inside/outside boundary that reinforces the positionality of survivors as exteriority-to-totality. It will be seen that this serves to prevent survivors of mass atrocities from accessing justice, and restorative justice in particular, for the grave human rights breaches they have experienced. In order to show this, the first part of this chapter aims to set out what the ICC's reparations framework entails. Here it will be seen that while the reparations scheme fits with the restorative justice model, its structure creates the space for individuals to be excluded from accessing restorative justice. This is compounded by the exclusions that the reparations scheme itself is subject to, namely those created through both the indictment and the legal designation of individuals as victims. In the second part of this chapter it will be argued that these two means of excluding individuals from legal victimhood relegates them to a non-victim/survivor status. This serves as a barrier to accessing justice for survivors since it positions survivors as exteriority-to-totality. While this presents one of the key findings of this chapter, the main objective thereof is to show that the ICC's reparation framework does, however, leave some room for survivors to access justice through the Trust Fund for Victims' assistance mandate. As such, the third part of this chapter will look at how the mandate of the Trust Fund for Victims attempts to create a space for survivors to access the means of restorative justice through the creation of the 'victim-survivor'. By ushering in the figure of the 'victim-survivor', the Trust Fund is able to work within its legal parameters, while at the same time giving voice to survivors of mass atrocities by enabling them to participate in the construction of restorative justice. The chapter concludes by noting that there is scope for both legal victims and survivors to be given voice as exteriority-in-totality, which ultimately provides an avenue – albeit an imperfect one – for settling the present in post-conflict societies.

The ICC's Reparations Framework

The Legal Framework

The ICC's reparations scheme consists of a case-based framework that is set out in Article 75 of the Rome Statute. A case-based framework means that it is the particular crime that the accused was convicted of which serves to determine the harm for which reparations are actioned. This enables the reparations order to be made directly against the convicted individual on the basis of their personal accountability for the harm they committed. More specifically, Article 75(2) states that 'the Court may make an order directly against a convicted person specifying appropriate reparations to, or in respect of, victims, including restitution, compensation and rehabilitation'.[17] This situates the reparations scheme squarely within the remit of restorative justice since it provides for a direct link to be made between the victim, the perpetrator and the types of reparations normally associated with restorative justice. Article 75(2) also provides the Court with the choice of awarding reparations through the Trust Fund for Victims where the Court deems this to be appropriate.[18] This stipulation in Article 75(2) is particularly important where the convicted person is indigent since the Court is able to make an order directly through the Trust Fund, which is partly funded through donations from states and other parties.[19] As will be seen in the final section of this chapter, the Trust Fund is perhaps the one avenue within the ICC's reparations framework through which survivors of mass atrocities can access justice.

Where the principles of reparations are concerned, the Court is given a measure of discretion to determine those principles that it will act upon when determining the reparations order. Although not explicitly stated in Article 75(1), the principle of *restitutio in integrum*, which is central to reparations within both international law and human rights law, serves as the main guiding principle along with those of proportionality and causality.[20] Article 75(1) specifically imbues the Court with both the power to decide on the principles of reparation and with an obligation to do so by stating that '[the] Court shall establish principles relating to reparations'.[21] We can see here that the impetus towards restorative justice is embedded within the reparations framework since the incorporation of the verb 'shall' into Article 75(1) obliges the Court to act on determining a basis for reparations[22] that is in keeping with the types of reparations called for in the article and which are discussed below.

When determining the principles of reparations, the ICC will look not only at the Rome Statute and the Rules of Procedure and Evidence, but also at applicable treaties, the principles and rules of international law, the national laws of legal systems of the world and case law.[23] Additionally, the Court will apply and interpret the law in a way that is consistent with human rights norms.[24] For instance, in *Lubanga*, the principles that the Court laid out as governing the objectives of reparations included the following: 'relieving suffering, affording justice, deterring future violations, and contributing to rehabilitation and reconciliation'.[25] As Dinah Shelton explains, the Court was able to give effect to these goals by applying reparations in a broad and flexible manner, and by approving the widest possible remedies.[26] Where reparations are concerned, it was set out very clearly in *Factory of Chorzów* that '[it] is a principle of international law that the breach of an engagement involves an obligation to make a reparation in an adequate form'.[27] This provides further evidence of the obligation placed on the Court to determine the principles of reparations since the individual convicted of a crime within the Rome Statute will have been found to have committed a gross human rights breach.

Article 75(1) lists three main types of reparations that the Court can issue: restitution, compensation and rehabilitation.[28] These types of reparations are seen as modalities of restorative justice because together with the choice of individual or collective awards, or both, they have the effect of balancing the needs of the victims, the community and the offender.[29] For instance, restitution has the most direct link to restorative justice since it seeks to return the victim to the position they were in prior to the gross violation of international human rights law and the serious violations of international humanitarian law committed by the perpetrator (examples of restitution might include the restoration of liberty, identity, family life and citizenship), while compensation seeks to provide remedies for economically ascertainable damage such as lost opportunities, lost earnings and damaged property. Likewise, rehabilitation provides for medical and psychological care, as well as legal and social services, which are fundamental to the healing processes for both the individual and the community.[30] What is important with respect to restorative justice is that the inclusion of rehabilitation has moved the reparations scheme away from a transactional model of reparations to a more transformative model.[31] This shift not only allows the Court to play a more active role in any decision-making concerning reparations, but it also enables the capacity of the victim to be taken into account.[32]

In this vein, the inclusion of rehabilitation adds to the restorative justice process since it gives rise to an awareness of the victim's past, current context and potential future.[33] In this respect, Rule 94(f) of the Rules of Procedure and Evidence states that '[claims] for rehabilitation and other forms of remedy'[34] should be included in the victim's requests for reparations. This broadens the scope of the possible forms of redress so that there is the potential to include measures of satisfaction and guarantees of non-repetition, which are missing from Article 75(1). Measures of satisfaction, for instance, include verification of the facts that are usually accompanied by their full disclosure to the community, a declaration or judicial decision that serves to restore the victim's dignity, public apologies and the institution of commemorative monuments within the affected communities. All of these measures focus on the harm sustained and, in doing so, acknowledge the positionality of the victim within the social fabric of the community. Likewise, guarantees of non-repetition are actioned through state policy and tend to include the promotion of law and order, particularly providing for the effective civilian control of military and security forces, ensuring the independence of the judiciary, and promoting respect for human rights within the community, to name but a few examples.[35] Policy changes geared towards the non-repetition of the harm sustained may be broad enough to account for a number of harms, but are at the very least aimed at the particular harm for which they are ordered against. Both measures of satisfaction and guarantees of non-repetition are important to bringing the harm into our purview since they both serve as a means through which to recognize the greater scope of the harms committed. What should be evident so far is that justice within the reparations framework is guided by the way in which the harm is conceptualized and articulated. This is why it is so important for those who have sustained harm as a result of the conflict situation to be able to enter into the conversation about justice.

When considering this, one of the key features of the reparations framework that allows for victims to enter into the conversation about restorative justice is that before making an order, the Court 'may invite and shall take account of representations from or on behalf of the convicted person, victims, other interested persons or interested States'.[36] The use of the word 'may' expresses the possibility of representations being made. This falls short of placing an obligation on the Court to invite representations; however, when the Court does invite the relevant parties to make representations, an obligation is placed on the Court to take account of them. This does not necessarily mean that the victim will receive the type of reparations they see as just; however, what the reparations framework does provide for is an avenue for victims to present what justice might look like in terms of repairing the harm. One point to note is that Article 75(3) allows the Court to invite the convicted person and other interested parties to present their views on reparations. Survivors, however, are seen as falling beyond the scope of 'interested parties'. Instead, the term 'interested parties' can refer to members of global civil society, such as non-governmental organizations (NGOs), as well as intergovernmental agencies who can make representations as *amicus curiae*. This was reinforced in the reparations proceedings in *Lubanga*, where although the Trial Chamber did take note that the views of 'the current victims participating in the proceedings, along with the broader group of victims who may ultimately benefit from a reparations plan'[37] would be heard, the 'broader group of victims' were still considered to be those individuals who could fall within the legal definition of 'victim' rather than those who experienced harm resulting from Lubanga's actions, but who were not included in the indictment.

What becomes evident when we look at the ICC's reparations framework so far, is that although the text of the Statute does not explicitly state the principles on which the Court is to draw upon when making the reparations order, the framework itself is victim-centric and recognizes the central place of victims within the justice process. This is seen in the invitation for victims to make representations and to have a voice in the reparations proceedings.[38] Victim recognition is consequently an important principle driving restorative justice. In addition to this, victim recognition forms an integral part of international human rights law on the basis that harm is not only seen as material in nature, but also contains a moral dimension.[39] With this in mind, the ICC's reparations framework also opens up an avenue for a second constitutive type of reparations to be made through the Trust Fund for Victims. This second constitutive type of reparations is known as assistance measures, which are broader in scope since the assistance mandate focuses on the situation rather than the case. This focus allows the Trust Fund to initiate reparations programmes that are based on a determination of need rather than on culpability.[40] The Rome Statute itself does not refer to assistance measures; however, in providing the Court with the ability to award reparations through the Trust Fund, the reparations scheme itself opens up an avenue for assistance measures to become part of the fabric of the framework itself.[41] The assistance mandate that the Trust Fund is imbued with can be found in Rule 98(5) of the Rules of Procedure and Evidence, which states that '[other] resources of the Trust Fund may be used for the benefit of victims subject to the provisions of Article 79'.[42] The assistance mandate is consequently read into the reference to 'other resources' that are employed for the benefit of victims.

Since assistance measures centre on the needs of victims, they can include development projects, humanitarian relief, aid measures and state subsidies, which are not contingent upon a determination of guilt. More specifically, assistance measures are divided into three categories: physical rehabilitation, psychological rehabilitation and material assistance. These categories are not mutually exclusive, but can work hand-in-hand to provide the community with a means through which they can move forward. For instance, physical rehabilitation enables individuals to re-engage with community life by providing medical care in a variety of forms such as fitting amputees with prosthetic limbs, carrying out necessary surgeries, screening for HIV and providing treatment.[43] Psychological assistance, which is often offered alongside physical rehabilitation, aims to improve the mental wellbeing of individuals who have suffered harm by helping them learn to cope with post-traumatic stress, anxiety, depression and other psychological issues stemming not only from surviving mass atrocities, but also from the need to navigate post-conflict life.[44] Finally, material assistance serves to 'relieve the material and socio-economic harm experienced by victims in situations before the ICC through a variety of livelihood initiatives to improve economic opportunities for victims'.[45] This type of assistance is provided through initiatives such as income generating activities, Village and Saving Loans Associations, improved agricultural techniques, vocational training, and small business development initiatives.[46] The purpose behind these initiatives is to empower not only the victims, but also the wider family and household by focusing on food security and increased agricultural productivity. In doing so, these initiatives are geared towards augmenting social participation within the community and reintegrating more vulnerable members of the community such as women, girls and individuals with disabilities.[47]

As noted above, the assistance mandate is not contingent on the case being tried before the ICC, and this opens up an avenue for survivors of mass atrocities to benefit from reparations programmes so long as they have suffered harm that falls within the jurisdiction of the Court. This is problematic since use of the word 'victim' excludes individuals who have experienced mass atrocities, but whose harms are considered incidental to the crimes committed within the jurisdiction of the Court. With this said, Rule 85(a) of the Rules of Procedure and Evidence allows the ICC to adopt a wide definition of victim as long as a link can be made between the harm suffered and any of the crimes that fall under its jurisdiction.[48] Survivors of mass atrocities could be subsumed under this and so while the reparations framework is victim-centric, the Trust Fund's assistance mandate does provide a way in which survivors can access the means of reparative justice.

So far we have looked at what the ICC's reparations framework has entailed. Accessing restorative justice through this framework, however, is dependent upon factors that enable recognition of the harm to be made. The next section will look at two factors that can prevent this: the indictment and victim status. Both of these are significant to the reparations scheme since eligibility for reparations is not only contingent upon them, but it also provides the impetus for recognizing the individual who has been harmed.

Factors Determining the Recognition of Harm under the Rome Statute

By settling the present, restorative justice allows for society to transition more effectively into post-conflict life. If certain victims are excluded from being acknowledged as victims, it can be more difficult for these individuals to transition and reintegrate effectively into society. Entering into the conversation about justice consequently becomes important since exclusion from the conversation means that from a legal standpoint, survivors cannot be part of determining what is needed for a successful transition into post-conflict society. The ICC's reparations framework is structured in such a way that individuals are subjectified as legal victims only if the harm they suffered falls within the indictment, and if so if they can then demonstrate that they qualify for victim status under the rules set out in Rule 85 of the Court's Rules of Procedure and Evidence. It is to these exclusions that we will now turn in order to demonstrate how an individual is either categorized as a legal victim or as a survivor who stands outside of the reparations framework.

Exclusion 1: The Indictment

The indictment holds great significance with respect to the reparations framework since it determines which crimes the accused is charged with. Article 54 of the Rome Statute provides that the prosecutor must 'take appropriate measures to ensure the effective investigation and prosecution of crimes within the jurisdiction of the Court'[49] and has discretion as to the scope and direction of the investigation.[50] This is important because the focus of the investigation later determines what charges, if any, will be contained in the indictment. If an arrest warrant is issued, it must specifically refer to the crimes within the ICC's jurisdiction that the alleged perpetrator is being accused of committing, as well as a summary of the evidence upon which the allegations are being made.[51] Where the indictment is concerned, the prosecutor is given a measure of discretion on what to include, taking into account the interests of justice.[52] By way of example, in *Lubanga*, there was evidence at the time that the Forces Patriotiques pour la libération du Congo (FPLC – Patriotic Front for the Liberation of the Congo) had committed crimes such as mass murder, rape, mutilation and torture in Ituri Province; however, these crimes did not feature in the charges.[53] Instead, Luis Moreno-Ocampo, who was the ICC Prosecutor at the time, used his prosecutorial discretion and only included one charge in the indictment, which was for the crime of recruiting child soldiers under Rome Statute Article 8(2)(e)(vii). This approach served to exclude anyone who was either a child soldier recruited into Lubanga's forces or his or her immediate parent or relative from being considered a victim. The choice to exclude other crimes for which there is ostensibly sufficient evidence to charge Lubanga served to remove the victims of these crimes from our purview. The result is that when the Court does define who constitutes a victim for the purposes of reparations, anyone whose harm is not resulting from a crime contained in the indictment cannot be considered a victim of the harms committed by the perpetrator. Instead, these individuals become survivors and are precluded from being represented and heard.

The ICC does incorporate a means through which this type of exclusion can be mitigated. Under Rule 103 of the Rules of Procedure and Evidence, the Trial Chamber can consider other information that may be pertinent to the case against the accused.[54] According to Rule 103,

> [at] any stage of the proceedings, a Chamber may, if it considers it desirable for the proper determination of the case, invite or grant leave to

a State, organization or person to submit, in writing or orally, any observation on any issue that the Chamber deems appropriate.[55]

The interpretation of this rule is particularly important because the effect of its interpretation can determine whether or not the charges can be amended. In *Lubanga*, the Trial Chamber provided a narrow interpretation of the word 'case', which meant that observations could only be made in relation to the charges already contained in the indictment. The result that is specific to this case was that observations from NGOs and other international organizations, which pertained to the commission of sexual violence that had taken place under Lubanga's authority, were not allowed to be considered by the Trial Chamber.[56] A broader interpretation of 'case' in this instance would have enabled the Court to amend the charges against Lubanga under Rome Statute Article 61(7)(c)[57] since the information provided by these organizations could have potentially allowed the Court to amend the indictment.

The ability to amend the indictment has the potential of creating an avenue for survivors to become legal victims. Regulation 55 of the Regulations of the Court allows for the modification of the legal facts and, as such, it serves as a means to provide for amendments to be made.[58] The Legal Representatives of Victims attempted to take this route in *Lubanga* by submitting an application in accordance with Regulation 55 to re-characterize the facts so that charges could be brought against Lubanga for war crimes and crimes against humanity, particularly relating to sexual slavery and other forms of sexual violence. Regulation 55, however, is constricted by Rome Statute Article 74(2), which confines it to the facts and circumstances described in the Document Containing the Charges. In *Lubanga*, this meant that the charges could not be amended if the facts did not already include sexual violence and other crimes against humanity.[59] What this demonstrates is that in the first instance there are procedural constraints and interpretations of the Court's rules that prevent survivors of mass atrocities from obtaining the legal status of a victim. In other words, victim classes are missed since the link between the harm and the crime cannot be made given that the crime itself is not included in the indictment. An example of a victim class, which tends to be missed, is children who are born out of rape or other circumstances linked to armed conflict. Consequently, by virtue of falling outside of the scope of the charges, survivors are deemed to be unconnected to the case and therefore cannot participate in the trial or in the reparations proceedings if the accused is convicted.[60] It is contended that although there are utilitarian reasons for limiting the number of victims, predominately relating to both fair trial processes and budgetary constraints, this serves as a means to create a demarcation line between survivors and victims. This has the effect of preventing survivors from speaking and consequently situates survivor speech in opposition to the dominant discourse of the Court, thus excluding survivors from having an impact on the development of the discursive site for which knowledge of the atrocities is produced. This is also seen in the way in which survivors are excluded from obtaining victim status through the Court's interpretation of the definition of 'victim', which can be found in Rule 85 of the ICC's Rules of Procedure and Evidence.[61]

Exclusion 2: The Legal Definition of 'Victim'

The definition of 'victim' in international criminal law is very specific. It derives from the United Nations (UN) Basic Principles and Guidelines on the Right to Remedy and Reparation for Victims of Gross Violations of International Human Rights Law and Serious Violations of International Humanitarian Law. The Basic Principles defines victims as

> persons who individually or collectively suffered harm, including physical or mental injury, emotional suffering, economic loss or substantial impairment of their fundamental rights, through acts or omissions that constitute gross violations of international human rights law, or serious violations of international humanitarian law.[62]

In *Lubanga*, Pre-Trial Chamber I drew both on this definition and on the definition of victims set out in Rule 85 of the Rules on Procedures and Evidence in order to define victims as 'natural persons who have suffered harm as a result of the commission of any crime within the jurisdiction of the court'.[63] A point to note is that Rule 85 includes both natural persons and legal persons such as organizations or institutions that have sustained direct harm to any of their property dedicated to religion, education, art, sciences or charitable purposes, as well as historic monuments, hospitals and other places and objects designated for humanitarian purposes.[64] This provides for a wider scope for who the potential victims might be. This is important, considering that the definition is linked to a number of purposes and procedures within the Rome Statute, including victim participation in proceedings, protection for victims, as well as reparations and assistance.[65]

There are effectively three categories of victims: victims of situations, victims in a case and victims of a convicted person.[66] Those who fall within the first category are given victim status if they meet the criteria set out in Rule 85 in the situation under investigation. A situation is defined as a region or state where the ICC is investigating crimes that fall under its jurisdiction following the Court's decision on admissibility.[67] In effect, victims could be anyone who has suffered harm as a result of the commission of any crime that the Office of the Prosecutor is investigating in that region. The second category of victims in a case are those whose victim status has been determined to be met by the Court based on the eligibility criteria set out in the indictment.[68] Here we see a narrowing of the definition of precisely who might constitute a victim since it is the charges contained in the indictment that will determine whether or not a link can be made between the individual, the harm they have sustained and the crime that the perpetrator has allegedly committed. The final category comprises victims of the convicted person. This further limits the victim pool to those who have been directly or indirectly harmed by the crime that the perpetrator has been found guilty of committing and it is the category most directly tied to the case-based reparations since the reparations order is explicitly made against the convicted person. This excludes anyone who is associated with any of the other crimes under the Court's jurisdiction.[69]

In *Lubanga*, Pre-Trial Chamber I was given the first opportunity to set out the criteria that needed to be met in order to qualify as a victim for purposes of the indictment.[70] In doing so, Pre-Trial Chamber I set out four criteria which have served to guide the Court in subsequent cases. The first victim criterion stipulated in *Lubanga* is that the individual must be a natural person. This is an identity requirement proved through the provision of documentation, such as a birth certificate. Such documentation is often lost, destroyed or no longer obtainable on account of the conflict situation. Two witness statements verifying the individual's identity is therefore considered sufficient for satisfying this criteria in this particular instance.[71]

The second criterion is that the individual must have suffered some harm.[72] In this respect, Article 75 refers to damage, loss or injury as constitutive types of harm that may be claimed; however, there is no set definition of 'harm' either in the Rome Statute or in the Rules of Procedure and Evidence. In *Lubanga*, the Appeals Chamber accepted that harm can either be direct, as in physical, psychological or material harm suffered by the direct victims themselves, or that it may be indirect and therefore include harm suffered by a third person who may have a close relationship with the victim. For instance, loss of a family member, injury or damage stemming from attempts to intervene, as well as material harms resulting from the reintegration of former child soldiers, were all considered to fall within the remit of indirect harm stemming from Lubanga's crimes.[73] A similar approach was adopted in *Katanga*. Here harm was considered in terms of material harm (e.g. the destruction of houses and outbuildings and pillaging), physical harm and psychological harm (such as that resulting from the death of a relative, as well as the psychological harm connected to experiencing the attack on Bogoro).[74] In contrast, the identification of the harm in *Al-Mahdi* was slightly different since the case concerned the destruction of cultural property in Timbuktu. In this case, the Court identified the harm as follows:

1 Property damaged in the attack on protected buildings which reflected Timbuktu's history;
2 Economic loss, particularly that deriving from the loss of tourism and livelihoods, which resulted from the attacks on protected buildings, and;
3 Moral harm stemming from mental pain and anguish which included the loss of childhood opportunities and relationships with those who had fled Timbuktu owing to the attacks on protected buildings, as well as the disruption of culture.[75]

The identification of harm is particularly important for the reparations scheme since it is used as a means to identify the beneficiaries, as well as to gauge the scope and nature of the reparations ordered by the Court. One can see already, however, that the harm itself subjectifies the individual as a legal victim. In doing so, it is tied directly to the third criterion set out in *Lubanga*, which is that the crime itself must fall within the jurisdiction of the Court. As already noted, the inclusion of this criterion means that it is the charges proved at trial that will determine victim eligibility for the purpose of reparations.[76]

The fourth and final criterion is the causal link between the crime and the harm suffered and where survivors of mass atrocities are concerned. This is perhaps the one criterion that serves as the primary mechanism of exclusion.[77] This criterion calls for a nexus between the crime as it is set out in the Rome Statute and the harm committed against the individual to be made. In *Al-Mahdi*, Trial Chamber VIII could not find a link between either the damage sustained to property other than the protected buildings or the infliction of bodily harm to individuals in the course of the destruction of the protected buildings.[78] This meant that even though it was evident that a harm had been committed as a result the presence of Al-Mahdi's armed group in the area, the Court could not recognize those harmed as victims of the crime Al-Mahdi had committed. In effect, the link between the crime and the harm cannot be made without considering whether or not the interpretation of the crime itself includes the individual who has suffered harm. This assertion may seem obvious, but if we go back to *Lubanga* and deconstruct the crime of child soldiering, it will be seen that this is not necessarily straightforward in the context of determining whether or not someone is a legal victim.

Article 8(2)(e)(vii) states that '[conscripting] or enlisting children under the age of fifteen years into armed forces or groups or using them to participate actively in hostilities'[79] is a war crime in the context of a non-international armed conflict. The first two components of this crime, namely conscription and enlistment, are both forms of recruitment and Trial Chamber I in *Lubanga* interpreted these components in terms of their ordinary meaning.[80] For example, enlistment was defined as enrolling on the list of a military body and conscription was considered as compulsory enlistment.[81] The method of recruitment provides the focal point for how and why a child was recruited into an armed group, and although it was considered difficult in *Lubanga* to determine whether a child was conscripted or whether they enlisted, there were a multitude of rationales provided, which included, for example, abduction, poverty and escaping from abusive homes, all of which served to rationalize the recruitment of child soldiers into Lubanga's forces.[82] The important point where the nexus between the harm and the crime committed can be found, however, is in the way the child is *integrated* into the armed group or, in other words, the way they become part of the group. Recruitment and integration are closely aligned since integration has to do with the socialization process that is inherent in incorporating an individual into the group.

Looking at recruitment as a form of integration tells us that the individual recruited into the armed group becomes part of the body of that group. Specifically where child soldiering is concerned, this entails severing the link between the child, their families and their community in order to alienate the child from their previous life and remake them into the image of the armed group.[83] The initiation process is particularly important, so by excluding the commission of sexual violence from the indictment, the Court in *Lubanga* was unable to make the link between sexual violence and the recruitment of girls into Lubanga's forces. Rape and sexual violence have often been thought of as a tool of war rather than as a form of recruitment; however, this type of violence dehumanizes in a way that is similar to acts such as mutilating or murdering family members, since it serves to sever the ties to the family and community.[84] In post-conflict societies, girls are often unable, or find it difficult, to reintegrate into society if they have experienced sexual violence since their families may see them as dishonourable and consequently disown or shun them. For instance, in Congolese society, a strict social hierarchy, which is based upon patriarchal norms, provides for a disempowered status of women. This is evidenced in the Congolese Family Code which places men at the head of the household and gives priority to them in most matters pertaining to family life. As Moley explains, there is an expectation that Congolese women will uphold a high degree of purity. It is on these grounds that '[unlike] men, women are punished for adultery, stigmatized when raped, or forced into marriage when abducted and/or raped'.[85] The result is that women who are victims of sexual violence will find themselves at greater risk of being shunned by their families and the community, particularly if they are unmarried and associated with military men.[86] In the case of women and girls, sexual violence forms part of the inner logic of recruitment and this is something that is difficult to conceptualize within the Rome Statute under Article 8(2)(e)(vii) because the underlying rationale for the commission of sexual violence against women and girls is not considered in terms of a tool of recruitment or incorporation.[87] Likewise, girls are considered to be associated with rather than recruited into the armed group since they fulfil roles such as cooking, cleaning, acting as messengers, porters, spies, as well as providing sexual labour.[88] These roles are often interpreted as affiliated rather than integrative, which places the female child outside of the scope of recruitment since their role, although vital to the overall functioning of the armed group, nevertheless remains outside of it.

In *Lubanga*, Trial Chamber I noted that although the word 'association' is found in the Paris Principles and Guidelines on Children Associated with Armed Forces or Armed Groups and serves to broaden the protection of children, '[this] expression does not form part of the wording of any of the charges the accused faces'.[89] This has repercussions for the third way in which the crime of child soldering can be committed, which is using children to participate in active hostilities. This is because support roles are difficult to incorporate into the language of 'active participation' even when considered in terms of 'indirect participation' which Trial Chamber I sought to do in *Lubanga*. Here indirect participation was contingent upon the provision of an essential support function, and in addition to this the likelihood of either the child's exposure to harm or their exposure to real danger as a potential target of attack.[90] The legal interpretation of 'essential support function' only covers 'acts which by their nature and purpose are intended to cause actual harm to the personnel and equipment of the armed force'[91] which means that the individual carrying out these types of functions are doing so for the purpose of achieving the direct military aims of the armed group. Activities such as diamond mining and providing medical services for wounded combatants fall outside of the scope of essential support function and the consequence of this is that children performing these roles are not considered to be indirect participants in active hostilities, which means that their roles are only associated ones.[92] Characterizations of girls as 'abductees', 'unaccompanied children', 'bush wives' and 'camp followers' also has the effect of placing them outside of the crime of child soldiering since it 'removes the possibility of a girl from being able to occupy an essential support function'.[93] This is because subjectifying females in this way positions them outside of the military function of the armed group. For instance, we seldom think of 'bush wives' as occupying any other role than one of domestic and sexual labour, yet bush wives do play an active role within armed groups since, for example, they are likely to be placed in charge of the compound when the military leader is away and they act as a communication link between the commander and the compound during military operations.[94] Coulter has argued that bush wives have been called upon to advise on military matters including troop movements and war strategies, which certainly makes the case for why bush wives do, at the very least, play an essential support role. The label 'bush wife', however, domesticizes the role that women and girls play within the armed group, which serves to reinforce the idea that they are only associated with armed groups rather than playing an active and military-oriented role within them that has the potential of exposing them to danger from opposing forces.[95] This removes girls from consideration as child soldiers since associated roles fall outside the remit of Article 8(2)(e)(vii).

In order to be designated a victim, the individual must satisfy all four criteria; however, the interpretation of the crime serves as a means to create an inside/outside border that determines the parameters of victimization. When this happens, as has been shown in the example of female child soldiers above, individuals cannot be subjectified as victims in the legal sense. This categorizes them instead as survivors of mass atrocities and consequently places them outside of the 'totality' of international criminal law. This was seen in *Lubanga*, for example, in the trial judges' determination that those individuals harmed by the child soldiers in the FPLC were not considered as either direct or indirect victims of Lubanga's crimes.[96] If the individual is not subjectified as a legal victim they will be excluded from the reparations scheme. The only avenue open to survivors of mass atrocities, as will be discussed below, is through the assistance mandate of the Trust Fund for Victims which, despite its retention of the victim discourse, nevertheless gives survivors some access to the means of restorative justice.

Restorative Justice and the Trust Fund for Victims' Assistance Mandate

For individuals and communities emerging from armed conflict situations, reparations initiate the process of healing primarily because they acknowledge that a harm has been committed. Van Boven has argued that '[i]n devising strategies of justice it must be borne in mind that *lack of reparation* for victims and *impunity* of perpetrators are two sides of the same coin'.[97] This highlights the problematic nature of a case-based reparations system since the interests of justice coming out of a legal framework can be at odds with the concept of justice deriving from the standpoint of survivors. Criminal responsibility is linked to reparations made through the ICC's reparations framework; however, restorative justice need not be linked in the same way. The Trust Fund's dual mandate to action both the ICC's reparations orders and to provide assistance to victims of the situations under investigation provides a starting point for creating opportunities for survivors to enter into the discussion about justice in some capacity.

By virtue of its orientation on situations rather than cases, the Trust Fund's assistance mandate opens it up to creating what the Trust Fund refers to as 'victim-survivors'. The creation of the victim-survivor subjectivity allows survivors to have a voice, albeit a limited one, in the justice process. One example where this can be seen is in Northern Uganda where the Trust Fund's implementing partners engage in community mobilization. As part of this, staff work with local leaders to encourage members of the community to attend information sessions, which are referred to as 'community sensitizations'. These 'community sensitizations' aim to introduce the community to the assistance mandate and the eligibility requirements that must be satisfied in order to benefit from the programmes. This serves to initiate a dialogue with individuals in the community since it includes 'preliminary psychoeducation about trauma and begins a community dialogue about stigma and conflict experiences'.[98] Opening up dialogue helps presence survivors (i.e. presencing in unconcealment) and offers a way for them to begin entering into the conversation about justice. Speech is effectively an act whereby 'relations get constituted and experiences and subjectivities are mediated'.[99] This involves a discourse between speakers and hearers, which affects the subjectivity and experience of survivors.[100] Entering into the participatory process creates a sense of local ownership since victim-survivors are more involved in the design and implementation of the reparations projects by virtue of being able to engage with the Trust Fund's implementing partners and with others in the community.[101] This also produces a healing effect, which is essential to the justice process since it serves to restore the individual's dignity. As Tschudi explains, losing one's dignity is akin to being excluded from humankind. Reparations measures aimed at dealing with the loss of dignity focus on empowerment as a means through which the individual can become rehumanized. This is achieved by creating a space to tell one's story about one's victimization; it serves not only to help to develop a deeper sense of self, but it also deepens the sense of connectedness to the other.[102]

The preceding arguments have shown that survivors stand outside the purview of restorative justice, as it is framed within the Rome Statute, by virtue of the legal processes determining who counts as a victim of the harm committed. The adoption of the language 'victim-survivor' by the Trust Fund provides for a linguistic turn to be made that recognizes survivors and situates them within the discourse of justice. Although the Trust Fund is limited to recognizing harms that fall within the ICC's jurisdiction, this allows it to usher in the figure of the victim-survivor since the reparations programmes can look beyond the specific harms for which the particular cases are based and implement programmes that will lead to a sense that justice is being actioned. This has the effect of bringing survivor discourse into the totality as exteriority-in-totality because it adopts not only the legal language of victim which the legal community understands, but by pairing victims and survivors it also opens up a space for the survivor to be presented. In effect, the linguistic shift does this by changing the discourse to offer a measure of inclusion to 'legal-survivors' by subsuming survivors into the assistance mandate. This has the potential of giving survivors a means through which they can enter into the conversation about justice since it recognizes the subject as a subject who can speak within the reparations process, and it serves to enable the survivor to recognize themselves as having survived a mass atrocity. This dual form of recognition produces a power relationship that, while it remains within a socio-legal model of restorative justice, allows for a negotiation on what justice will look like. This is one of the reasons why the communication strategy and outreach activities of the Trust Fund and its implementing partners is so important. These strategies and activities facilitate the production of the consciousness of violence and suffering experienced and work to develop an understanding of both what reparations mean not only in terms of repairing the harm, but also for 'the new opportunities to engage in a just and peaceful organization of human affairs'.[103] Incorporating survivors as subjects within the dominant totality transforms 'their' knowledge into something that can be understood as encompassing a reality, even if it makes a competing claim to the legal understanding of restorative justice. For instance, the Sierra Leone Truth and Reconciliation Committee has noted that gender inequality prior to the conflict in Sierra Leone contributed to the way in which women and girls were targeted and exploited by armed groups. In effect, women were seen as property to be inherited under customary law and when they returned to the post-conflict community many were viewed as damaged goods. This type of stigmatization limits a woman's chance either to marry or in some cases even to return to their families, which, as Muddel notes, led to severe economic insecurity. Reparations consequently need to challenge the conditions that vulnerable victim-survivors face rather than return them to the situation they were in before the armed conflict, which restorative justice, as outlined in Article 75 of the Rome Statute, tends to focus on.[104] The Nairobi Declaration on Women's and Girl's Right to a Remedy and Reparation acknowledges this particularity by expressing that '[r]eparations must go above and beyond the immediate reasons and consequences of the crimes and violations; they must aim to address the political and structural inequalities that negatively shape women's and girl's lives';[105] however, in order to begin taking this into account, an avenue for creating the necessary dialogue which includes both cultural and gender-sensitive strategies for obtaining information needs to be opened. Engagement by the Trust Fund in community sensitization offers a way of starting the conversation, as well as an avenue for victim-survivors to establish a voice in the conversation about justice.

Although the Trust Fund is established by the Rome Statute, its dual mandate enables the Trust Fund to incorporate victim-survivors into its assistance mandate. While this is limited by the parameters within which it works and with the funding available to it, the nature of the assistance mandate has enabled the Trust Fund to shift some of the language of legal victimhood through the discursive construction of the victim-survivor to allow the survivor to appear in situation-based reparative processes.

Conclusion

The Basic Principles and Guidelines on the Right to a Remedy and Reparation for Victims of Violations of International Human Rights and Humanitarian Law stipulate that reparations shall be 'effective and adequate'.[106] To do so, reparations need not only to meet the needs of victims, they also need to meet the needs of survivors. If justice means 'settling the present', then dialogue needs to be created between those actioning reparations and the individuals and communities who have survived grave breaches of human rights. It has been argued throughout this chapter that this is contingent upon dialogue taking place between epistemologies. For example, the Court in *Lubanga* attempted to find out what type of reparations the victims of Lubanga's crimes, as well as the affected communities, felt would help them to achieve restorative justice by '[endorsing] the Registry proposal for a multidisciplinary team of experts to engage in a preliminary consultative phase involving victims and affected communities'.[107] Through this consultation process, many of Lubanga's victims were able to express their desire to receive individual reparations. For instance, in Bogoro, which was used by

Lubanga between 2002 and 2003 as a battlefield and training camp for child soldiers, as many as 80% of victims expressed the desire for individual reparations.[108] In addition to engaging with affected communities in Ituri Province, the Court also heard testimony from victims during the reparations proceedings as to what they felt would be an appropriate award. Similarly to the community consultations, the victims represented in Court almost unanimously felt that individual reparation awards would be appropriate; however, Trial Chamber I nevertheless placed a greater emphasis on collective reparations and rehabilitation for child soldiers in its judgment on reparations.[109] What this shows is an incompatibility between what justice means to victims and what it means to the Court. The victim, as exteriority-in-totality, has their consciousness represented through the voice of their legal representative who is placed in a position to express the desires of the victim. The legal representative is, however, also a product of the same epistemological standpoint of the legal community. This means that a potential discontinuity of knowledge and understanding is created when it comes to expressing the victim's consciousness since the dominant understanding of justice is always that stemming from the Court rather than being organically constituted. To this effect, Mignolo has argued that '[t]ranslation in the rhetoric of modernity … was always unidirectional and served the need of imperial designs … [a] modern/colonial translation that captures and transforms people, cultures, and meanings into what is legible and controllable for those in power'.[110] Although Mignolo is speaking about the relationship between modernity and coloniality, one can see here how the process of becoming an exteriority-in-totality takes place. This demonstrates that victims of mass atrocities and the legal community can only really enter into a dialogue about restorative justice if the victim reconceptualizes justice so that knowledge and understanding of justice is approached from the same direction. This is not the case with survivors since they remain, as we have seen, outside of the totality.

As argued above, the potential shift for survivors from occupying a position of exteriority-to-totality and to the position of exteriority-in-totality takes place through the Trust Fund's assistance mandate, which places them in a parallel position to legal victims in terms of being able to enter into the conversation about justice. The ICC has started to acknowledge this, which is a step in the right direction where restorative justice is concerned. This can be seen, for example, when the Appeal Court in *Lubanga* issued a revised reparations order that considered the possibility of including assistance measures for those who were subjected to sexual and gender-based violence, but who did not qualify for victim status based on the charges.[111] It was decided that these individuals would be covered under Regulation 50(a) of the Trust Fund's Regulations, which enables the Trust Fund to implement assistance activities.[112] This, the Court indicated, could come through the referral to competent NGOs operating in the area, who offer services to those who have been, for instance, victims of sexual and gender-based violence.[113] This provides an avenue for survivors to have a voice in the construction of reparations programmes geared towards their needs, thus allowing for a measure of access to justice for the harms committed against them.

With this in mind, it should not be forgotten that the ICC's reparative framework is subject to a particular legal discourse that can only be heard within the parameters set out in the Rome Statute. As we have seen, exclusions from the reparations framework which occur at both the charging stage and with respect to determining legal victimhood, have the effect of creating a barrier to justice for those who find themselves outside of the framework. For instance, case-based reparations exclude certain individuals as victims as a result of focusing on the causal link between the harm sustained and the acts the accused has been convicted of committing. This makes sense where international criminal justice and reparations are concerned because the ICC is required to protect the rights of the convicted person and must ensure that they are not ordering reparations for harms that did not result from the crimes that the accused had been convicted of. This was seen in *Lubanga* where the harm focused exclusively on child soldiers as the direct victims of Lubanga's crimes and on their relatives as indirect victims, yet excluded those who were harmed by the child soldiers themselves. While more work needs to be done in order to enable survivors of mass atrocities to enter into discussions about restorative justice, recognizing the barriers for survivors to access justice is at least a step in the right direction. We can see this with the Trust Fund's assistance mandate, which opens up a space for survivors to enter into the conversation about justice by virtue of shifting the language from 'victim' to 'victim-survivor'. As argued in the chapter, this allows the Trust Fund to operate within the parameters set out in the Rome Statute and the Rules of Procedure and Evidence, while also providing reparative assistance to victims of conflict situations. An example of this can be found through the continuation of the assistance programmes in the Central Republic of Africa following the ICC's Appeal Chamber's overturning of Jean-Pierre Bemba Gombo's conviction for war crimes committed in the republic.[114] The assistance mandate and the Court's recognition of the pertinence of this mandate to victim-survivors therefore suggests that although exclusions arising from the ICC's reparations framework serve to create a barrier to accessing justice for survivors of mass atrocities, the potentiality of such access for survivors can be achieved through the actions of the Trust Fund. This ultimately provides an avenue through which to settle the present by providing survivors with a means to enter into the conversation about justice.

Notes

1 The author wishes to thank Jayan Nayar for introducing her to the theory underpinning this chapter. The author would also like to thank Daniel Lowe and Lorenzo Pasculli for their thoughtful insights which helped to shape and solidify this chapter. The views put forward are solely those of the author and

do not represent the views of the International Criminal Court or the Trust Fund for Victims.

2 Rome Statute of the International Criminal Court, Article 75.

3 These are considered to be the four core crimes in international criminal law: war crimes, crimes against humanity, genocide and aggression. Rome Statute, Article 5.

4 E. Dwertmann, 'Historical and Legal Context of Reparations for Victims of Crimes under International Law (Overview)', in *The Reparations System of the International Criminal Court: Its Implementation, Possibilities, and Limitations*, ed. Eva Dwertmann (Leiden: Brill Nijhoff, 2010), p. 26.

5 A. Balta, M. Bax and R. Letschert, 'Trial and (Potential) Error: Conflicting Visions on Reparations Within the ICC System', *International Criminal Justice Review*, 29(3), 2019, p. 222.

6 J. Brathwaite, 'Building Legitimacy through Restorative Justice', in *Legitimacy and Criminal Justice: International Perspectives*, ed. Tom Tyler (New York, Russell Sage, 2007), p. 148.

7 *The Prosecutor v. Thomas Lubanga Dyilo*, 'Decision on the Prosecutor's Application for a Warrant of Arrest, Article 58,' ICC-01/01–04/06, 10 February 2006, p. 60.

8 *Germany v. Poland* (Factory at Chorzów) (Merits) Judgment of the Permanent Court of International Justice, 13 September 1928, p. 47.

9 Heidegger argues that truth belongs to the substance of Being. Drawing on Parmenides, he uses the Greek word 'ἐόν' (Being, or the act of Being) to express the way that truth is revealed. Heidegger's use of ἐόν has subsequently been translated into English as 'presencing in unconcealment'. Martin Heidegger, *Off the Beaten Track*, trans. Y. Young and K. Hayes (Cambridge: Cambridge University Press, 2002), p. 261.

10 J. Derrida, 'Force of Law: The Mystical Foundation of Authority', in *Deconstruction and the Possibility of Justice*, ed. Drucilla Cornell, Michael Rosenfeld and David Gray Carlson (New York: Routledge, 1992), p. 10.

11 W. Mignolo, 'Delinking: The Rhetoric of Modernity, the Logic of Coloniality and the Grammar of Decoloniality', *Cultural Studies*, 21(2), 2007, p. 451.

12 C. Burchard, 'From Open Normativity to Normative Openness: Addressing the Elephant in the Room, That Is, the Fact of Justificatory Pluralism in International Criminal Justice', in *Philosophical Foundations of International Criminal Law: Foundational Concepts*, ed. M. Bergsmo and E.J. Buis (Brussels: Torkel Opsahl Academic EPublisher, 2019), pp. 4–7.

13 J. Nayar, 'The Politics of Hope and the Other-in-the World: Thinking Exteriority', *Law Critique*, 24, 2013, p. 67.

14 See, for example, G. Brown and G. Yule, *Discourse Analysis* (Cambridge: Cambridge University Press, 1983).

15 P. Goodrich, *Legal Discourse: Studies in Linguistics, Rhetoric, and Legal Analysis* (London: Palgrave Macmillan, 1990), p. 3.

16 See, for example, N. Hartsock, 'The Feminist Standpoint: Developing the Ground for a Specific Feminist Historical Materialism', in *Discovering Reality*, ed. Sandra Harding and Merrill B. Hintikka (Dordrecht: D. Reidel Publishing Company, 1983), p. 106.

17 Rome Statute, Article 75(2).

18 The Trust Fund for Victims was established by Rome Statute Article 79.

19 International Criminal Court, *Rules of Procedure and Evidence*, CC-PIDS-LT-02–002/13_Eng, Rule 98; and *Establishment of a fund for the benefit of victims of crimes within the jurisdiction of the Court, and of the families of such victims*, The Assembly of States Parties, Resolution ICC-ASP/1/Res.6, 9 September 2002.

20 O. Amezcua-Noriega, 'Reparation Principles under International Law and their Possible Application by the International Criminal Court: Some Reflections', *Essex Transitional Justice Network*, 1, 2011, pp. 2–4.
21 Rome Statute, Article 75(1).
22 *Report of the Preparatory Committee on the Establishment of an International Criminal Court*, United Nations Diplomatic Conference of Plenipotentiaries on the Establishment of an International Criminal Court (A/2/Conf. 183/2/Add.1), 14 April 1998.
23 Examples include the Universal Declaration of Human Rights, the United Nations Convention against Torture, the International Covenant on Civil and Political Rights, and the United Nations Basic Principles on the Right to a Remedy and Reparation.
24 Rome Statute, Article 21.
25 D. Shelton, 'Introductory Note to the International Criminal Court: Situation in the Democratic Republic of the Congo, Prosecutor v. Thomas Lubanga Dyilo, Decision Establishing the Principles and Procedures to be Applied to Reparations', *Introductory Legal Materials*, 51(5), 2017, p. 971.
26 Ibid.
27 *Germany v. Poland* (Factory at Chorzów) Judgment of the Permanent Court of International Justice (Claim for Indemnity), 26 July 1927, p. 21.
28 Rome Statute, Article 75(1), and Rome Statute Article 75(2).
29 C. Holger, R.J. Arsovska and I. Aertsen, 'Challenging Restorative Justice: State-based Conflict, Mass Victimisation and the Changing Nature of Warfare', in *Restoring Justice after Large-scale Violent Conflicts: Kosovo, DR Congo, and the Israeli-Palestinian Case*, ed. Ivo Aertsen, Jana Arsovska, Holger C. Rohne, Marta Valiñas and Kris Vanspauwen (Uffculme: Willan Publishing, 2008), p. 14.
30 Office of the United Nations High Commissioner for Human Rights, *Rule-of-Law Tools for Post-Conflict States Reparations Programmes* (New York: United Nations, 2008), p. 7.
31 A. Di Giovanni, 'The Prospect of ICC Reparations in the Case Concerning Northern Uganda: On a Collision Course with Incoherence?' *Journal of International Law and International Relations*, 25(2), 2006, p. 26.
32 C. Sperfeldt, 'Rome's Legacy: Negotiating the Reparations Mandate of the International Criminal Court', *International Law Review*, 17, 2016, pp. 368–369.
33 A. Goggans, 'The Case for Interpersonal Reparations', Fellowship of Reconciliation, available at https://wagingnonviolence.org/forusa/2019/02/case-for-interpersonal-reparations/.
34 International Criminal Court, *Rules of Procedure and Evidence*, Rule 94(f).
35 'Basic Principles and Guidelines on the Right to a Remedy and Reparation for Victims of Gross Violations of International Human Rights Law and Serious Violations of International Humanitarian Law', United Nations General Assembly (A/RES/60/147), 21 March 2006.
36 Rome Statute, Article 75(3).
37 *The Prosecutor v Thomas Lubanga Dyilo*, 'Decision Establishing the Principles and Procedures to be Applied to Reparations,' ICC-01/04–01/06, 7 August 2012, P. 87.
38 Rome Statute, Article 75(3).
39 Amezcua-Noriega, 'Reparation Principles under International Law and their Possible Application by the International Criminal Court,' p. 5.
40 F. Val-Garijo, 'Redressing Victims of International Crimes: The International Criminal Court and the Trust Fund for Victims', *Comunitania: International Journal of Social Work and Social Sciences*, 2011, p. 85.
41 Article 79(3) sets out that the Trust Fund for Victims shall be managed in accordance with the criteria determined by the Assembly of States Parties. Rome Statute, Article 79(3).

42 International Criminal Court, *Rules of Procedure and Evidence*, Rule 98.
43 The Trust Fund for Victims, *Physical Rehabilitation*, available at https://trustfundforvictims.org/en/what-we-do/assistance-programmes/physical-rehabilitation.
44 The Trust Fund for Victims, *Psychological Rehabilitation*, available at https://trustfundforvictims.org/en/what-we-do/assistance-programmes/psychological-rehabilitation.
45 The Trust Fund for Victims, *Material Support*, available at https://trustfundforvictims.org/en/what-we-do/assistance-programmes/material-support.
46 Ibid.
47 Ibid.
48 International Criminal Court, *Rules of Procedure and Evidence*, Rule 85(a).
49 Rome Statute, Article 54.
50 Ibid.
51 Ibid., Article 58.
52 K. Smith, 'Prosecutor v. Lubanga: How the International Criminal Court Failed the Women and Girls of the Congo', *Howard Law Journal*, 2011, pp. 54–480.
53 A. Wiersing, '*Lubanga* and its Implications for Victims Seeking Reparations at the International Criminal Court', *Amsterdam Law Forum* 4, no.3 2012, p. 27.
54 International Criminal Court, *Rules of Procedure and Evidence*, Rule 103.
55 Ibid.
56 Smith, 'Prosecutor v. Lubanga', p. 482.
57 Rome Statute, Article 61(7)(c).
58 International Criminal Court, *Regulations of the Court* (ICC-BD/01–05–16), Regulation 55.
59 J. Tan, 'Sexual Violence against Children on the Battlefield as a Crime of Using Child Soldiers: Square Pegs in Round Holes and Missed Opportunities in *Lubanga*', in *Yearbook of International Humanitarian Law*, ed. Terry D. Gill, Robin Geiß, Robert Heinsch, Tim McCormack, Christophe Paulussen and Jessica Dorsey (The Hague: T.M.C. Asser Press, 2012), p. 146.
60 Rome Statute, Article 68.
61 International Criminal Court, *Rules of Procedure and Evidence*, Rule 85.
62 'Basic Principles and Guidelines on the Right to a Remedy and Reparation for Victims of Gross Violations of International Human Rights Law and Serious Violations of International Humanitarian Law', United Nations General Assembly Resolution 60/147, 16 December 2005.
63 *The Prosecutor v. Thomas Lubanga Dyilo*, 'Judgment pursuant to Article 74 of the Statute', ICC-01/04–01/06–2842, 14 March 2012, pp. 16–19.
64 International Criminal Court, *Rules of Procedure and Evidence*, Rule 85.
65 Rome Statute, Article 68, and Rome Statute Article 75.
66 S. Kabalira, *The Right to Reparations under the Rome Statute of the International Criminal Court (ICC): The Content of the Right and its Implementation in the Light of the Early Case Law of the Court* (Oisterwijk: Wolf Legal Publishers, 2016), p. 180.
67 Ibid., p. 181.
68 Ibid.
69 Ibid., p. 182.
70 The Pre-Trial Chamber effectively 'pre-judges' the case before a ruling is made on the guilt of the accused. This is pursuant to Rule 85(a); however, the purpose of this is to make and formally acknowledge a connection between the victim and the accused. The standard of proof for victim qualification here is lower than that required for conviction. International Criminal Court, *Rules of Procedure and Evidence*, Rule 85(a). See also T. Markus Funk, *Victim's Rights and*

Advocacy at the International Criminal Court (Oxford: Oxford University Press, 2010), p. 102.

71 *The Prosecutor v. Thomas Lubanga Dyilo*, 'Judgment pursuant to Article 74 of the Statute,' pp. 16–19.

72 Ibid.

73 *The Prosecutor v. Thomas Lubanga Dyilo*, 'Judgment on the appeals against the 'Decision establishing the principles and procedures to be applied to reparations' of 7 August 2012,' ICC-01/04–01/06A A 2 A 3, March 3 2015.

74 *The Prosecutor v. Germain Katanga*, 'Order for Reparations pursuant to Article 75 of the Statute', ICC-01/04–01/07, 24 March 2017.

75 *The Prosecutor v. Ahmad Al Faqi Al Mahdi*, 'Reparations Order', ICC-01–12–01/15–236, 17 August 2017.

76 International Criminal Court, *Rules of Procedure and Evidence*, Rule 85(a); C. McCarthy, *Reparations and Victim Support in the International Criminal Court* (Cambridge: Cambridge University Press, 2012), p. 150.

77 McCarthy, *Reparations and Victim Support in the International Criminal Court*, p. 150; *The Prosecutor v. Thomas Lubanga Dyilo*, 'Situation in the Democratic Republic of the Congo in the Case of *the Prosecutor v. Thomas Lubanga Dyilo*: Summary of the 'Judgment pursuant to Article 74 of the Statute'. ICC-01–01/01–06, 14 March 2012.

78 *The Prosecutor v. Ahmad Al Faqi Al Mahdi*, 'Reparations Order'.

79 Rome Statute, Article 8(2)(e)(vii).

80 *The Prosecutor v. Thomas Lubanga Dyilo*, 'Judgment pursuant to Article 74 of the Statute.'

81 Ibid.

82 M. Wessels, *Child Soldiers: From Violence to Protection* (Cambridge, MA: Harvard University Press, 2006), p. 71.

83 F. McDonnell and G. Akallo, *Girl Soldier: A Story of Hope for Uganda's Children* (Grand Rapids, MI: Chosen Books, 2007), p. 118.

84 M. Ingber, 'Gender Imaginaries, Child Soldiering, and International Criminal Law', in *The Asian Yearbook of Human Rights and Humanitarian Law*, ed. Javaid Rehman, Ayesha Shahid and Steve Foster (Leiden: Brill Nijhoff, 2019), p. 181; C. Coulter, *Bush Wives and Girl Soldiers: Women's Lives through War and Peace in Sierra Leone* (New York: Cornell University Press, 2009), p. 142.

85 N. Moley, 'Methods of Reparations in the International Criminal Court: The Impossibility of Individual Awards in the Democratic Republic of Congo', *UCLA Journal of International Foreign Affairs*, 17, 2013, p. 272.

86 Ibid., pp. 271–273. See also D. Nduwimana, 'Reintegration of Child Soldiers in Eastern Congo: Challenges and Prospects', the International Peace Support Training Centre Nairobi, Kenya, Occasional Paper Series 4(2), 2013, pp. 8–9.

87 Ingber, 'Gender Imaginaries, Child Soldiering, and International Criminal Law', p. 181.

88 Wessels, *Child Soldiers*, p. 71.

89 United Nations Children's Fund (UNICEF), *The Paris Principles: Principles and Guidelines on Children Associated with Armed Forces or Armed Groups*, February 2007.

90 *The Prosecutor v. Thomas Lubanga Dyilo*, 'Judgment pursuant to Article 74 of the Statute', pp. 285–286.

91 Noelle Quenivet, quoted in International Justice Monitor, 'UN Envoy to Testify on Interpretation of Charges, available at www.ijmonitor.org/2010/01/un-envoy-to-testify-on-interpretation-of-charges; Ingber, 'Gender Imaginaries', p. 186; *The Prosecutor v. Thomas Lubanga Dyilo*, 'Judgment pursuant to Article 74 of the Statute', p. 285.

92 Ingber, 'Gender Imaginaries', p. 187.

93 Ibid.
94 Coulter, *Bush Wives and Girl Soldiers*, p. 130.
95 Ibid.
96 M. Drumbl, *Reimagining Child Soldiers in International Law and Policy* (Oxford: Oxford University Press, 2012), p. 18.
97 T. van Boven, 'The Perspective of the Victim', in *The Universal Declaration of Human Rights: Fifty Years On*, ed. Yael Danieli, Elsa Stamatopoulou and Clarence Dias (Boca Raton, FL: CRC Press, 1999), p. 16; emphasis added.
98 A. Dutton and F.N. Aoláin, 'Between Reparations and Repair: Assessing the Work of the ICC Trust Fund for Victims under its Assistance Mandate', *Chicago Journal of International Law*, 19(2), 2019, p. 503.
99 L. Alcoff and L. Gray, 'Survivor Discourse: Transgression or Recuperation?' *Signs*, 18(2), 1993, p. 264.
100 Ibid.
101 M. Suchkova, 'The Importance of a Participatory Reparations Process and its Relationship to the Principles of Reparation', *Essex Transitional Justice Network Briefing Paper*, 5, 2011, p. 2.
102 F. Tschudi, 'Dealing with Violent Conflicts and Mass Victimization: A Human Dignity Approach', in *Restoring Justice after Large-scale Violent Conflicts: Kosovo, DR Congo, and the Israeli-Palestinian Case*, eds. Ivo Aertsen, Jana Arsovska, Holger C. Rohne, Marta Valiñas and Kris Vanspauwen (Uffculme: Willan Publishing, 2008), p. 48.
103 J. Torpey, '"Making Whole What Has Been Smashed": Reflections on Reparations', *The Journal of Modern History*, 73(2), 2001, p. 343.
104 K. Muddel, 'Limitations and Opportunities of Reparations for Women's Empowerment', available at https://www.ictj.org/sites/default/files/ICTJ-Global-Limitations-Reparations-2009-English.pdf; Suchkova, 'The Importance of a Participatory Reparations Process and its Relationship to the Principles of Reparation', p. 9.
105 *Nairobi Declaration on Women's and Girl's Right to a Remedy and Reparation*, International Meeting on Women's and Girl's Right to a Remedy and Reparation, Nairobi, March 2007, available at https://reparations.qub.ac.uk/assets/uploads/NAIROBI_DECLARATIONeng.pdf.
106 'Basic Principles and Guidelines on the Right to a Remedy and Reparation for Victims of Gross Violations of International Human Rights Law and Serious Violations of International Humanitarian Law', United Nations General Assembly (A/RES/60/147), 21 March 2006.
107 Shelton, 'Introductory Note to the International Criminal Court', p. 972.
108 Moley, 'Methods of Reparations in the International Criminal Court', pp. 253–254.
109 *The Prosecutor v. Thomas Lubanga Dyilo*, 'Situation in the Democratic Republic of the Congo in the Case of the *Prosecutor v. Thomas Lubanga Dyilo*: Decision Establishing the Principles and Procedures to be Applied to Reparations,' ICC-01/04–01/06–2904, 7 August 2012, p. 16.
110 W.D. Mignolo, *The Idea of Latin America* (Oxford: Blackwell Publishing, 2005), p. 144. Quoted in R. Vázquez, 'Translation as Erasure: Thoughts on Modernity's Epistemic Violence', *Journal of Historical Sociology*, 24(1), 2011, p. 30.
111 *The Prosecutor v Thomas Lubanga Dyilo* 'Judgment on the Appeals against the 'Decision establishing the principles and procedures to be applied to reparations' of 7 August 2012,' ICC-01/04–01/06A A 2 A 3, March 3 2015, pp. 77–78.
112 The Assembly of States Parties, *Regulations of the Trust Fund for Victims*, ICC-ASP/4/Res.3, available at www.trustfundforvictims.org/sites/default/files/imce/Latest updated Regulations of the Trust Fund for Victims.pdf.

113 *The Prosecutor v Thomas Lubanga Dyilo*, 'Judgment on the Appeals against the 'Decision establishing the principles and procedures to be applied to reparations' of 7 August 2012', pp. 77–78.

114 International Criminal Court, 'Following Mr Bemba's acquittal, Trust Fund for Victims at the ICC decides to accelerate launch of assistance programme in Central African Republic,' 13 June 2018, available at www.icc-cpi.int/Pages/item.aspx?name=180613-TFVPR.

References

Aertsen, I., Arsovska, J., Rohne, H., Valiñas, M. and Vanspauwen, K. (eds) (2008) *Restoring Justice after Large-scale Violent Conflicts: Kosovo, DR Congo, and Israeli-Palestinian Case.* Uffculme: Willan Publishing.

Alcoff, L. and Gray, L. (1993) 'Survivor Discourse: Transgression or Recuperation?' *Signs*, vol. 18, no. 2, pp. 260–290.

Amezcua-Noriega, O. (2011) 'Reparation Principles under International Law and their Possible Application by the International Criminal Court: Some Reflections', Briefing Paper no. 1, *Essex Transitional Justice Network*, pp. 2–12.

Balta, A., Manon, B. and Letschert, R. (2019) 'Trial and (Potential) Error: Conflicting Visions on Reparations Within the ICC System', *International Criminal Justice Review*, vol. 29, no. 3, pp. 221–248.

Bergsmo, M. and Buis, J. (eds) (2019) *Philosophical Foundations of International Criminal Law: Foundational Concepts.* Brussels: Torkel Opsahl Academic EPublisher.

Brathwaite, J. (2007) 'Building Legitimacy through Restorative Justice', in T. Tyler (ed.), *Legitimacy and Criminal Justice: International Perspectives.* New York: Russell Sage, pp. 146–162.

Brown, G. and Yule, G. (1983) *Discourse Analysis.* Cambridge: Cambridge University Press.

Burchard, C. (2019) 'From Open Normativity to Normative Openness: Addressing the Elephant in the Room, That Is, the Fact of Justificatory Pluralism in International Criminal Justice', in M. Bergsmo and E. Buis (eds), *Philosophical Foundations of International Criminal Law: Foundational Concepts.* Brussels: Torkel Opsahl Academic EPublisher, pp. 1–21.

Cornell, D., Rosenfeld, M. and Carlson, D. (eds) (1992) *Deconstruction and the Possibility of Justice.* New York: Routledge.

Coulter, C. (2009) *Bush Wives and Girl Soldiers: Women's Lives through War and Peace in Sierra Leone.* New York: Cornell University Press.

Danieli, Y., Stamatopoulou, E. and Dias, C. (eds) (1999) *The Universal Declaration of Human Rights: Fifty Years On.* Boca Raton, FL: CRC Press.

Derrida, J. (1992) 'Force of Law: The Mystical Foundation of Authority', In D. Cornell, M. Rosenfeld and D. Carlson (eds), *Deconstruction and the Possibility of Justice.* New York: Routledge, pp. 3–67.

Di Giovanni, A. (2006) 'The Prospect of ICC Reparations in the Case Concerning Northern Uganda: On a Collision Course with Incoherence?' *Journal of International Law and International Relations*, vol. 25, no. 2, pp. 25–64.

Drumbl, M. (2012) *Reimagining Child Soldiers in International Law and Policy.* Oxford: Oxford University Press.

Dutton, A. and Ní Aoláin, F. (2019) 'Between Reparations and Repair: Assessing the Work of the ICC Trust Fund for Victims under its Assistance Mandate', *Chicago Journal of International Law*, vol. 19, no. 2, pp. 490–547.

Dwertmann, E. (2010) 'Historical and Legal Context of Reparations for Victims of Crimes under International Law (Overview)', in E. Dwertmann (ed.), *The Reparations System of the International Criminal Court: It's Implementation, Possibilities, and Limitations.* Leiden: Brill Nijhoff, pp. 13–27.

Dwertmann, E. (ed.) (2010) *The Reparations System of the International Criminal Court: It's Implementation, Possibilities, and Limitations.* Leiden: Brill Nijhoff.

Funk, T.M. (2010) *Victim's Rights and Advocacy at the International Criminal Court.* Oxford: Oxford University Press.

Gill, T., Geiß, R., Heinsch, R., McCormack, T., Paulussen, C. and Dorsey, J. (eds) (2012) *Yearbook of International Humanitarian Law.* The Hague: T.M.C. Asser Press.

Goggans, A. (2019) 'The Case for Interpersonal Reparations', *Fellowship of Reconciliation.* Available at https://wagingnonviolence.org/forusa/2019/02/case-for-interpersonal-reparations/.

Goodrich, P. (1990) *Legal Discourse: Studies in Linguistics, Rhetoric, and Legal Analysis.* New York: Palgrave Macmillan.

Harding, S. and Hintikka, M. (eds) (1983) *Discovering Reality.* Dordrecht: D. Reidel Publishing Company.

Hartsock, N. (1983) 'The Feminist Standpoint: Developing the Ground for a Specific Feminist Historical Materialism', in S. Harding and M. Hintikka (eds), *Discovering Reality.* Dordrecht: D. Reidel Publishing Company, pp. 283–310.

Heidegger, M. (2002) *Off the Beaten Track*, trans. J. Young and K. Hayes. Cambridge: Cambridge University Press.

Ingber, M. (2019) 'Gender Imaginaries, Child Soldiering, and International Criminal Law', in J. Rehman, A. Shahid and S. Foster (eds), *The Asian Yearbook of Human Rights and Humanitarian Law.* Leiden: Brill Nijhoff, pp. 169–191.

International Justice Monitor (2010) 'UN Envoy to Testify on Interpretation of Charges'. Available at: www.ijmonitor.org/2010/01/un-envoy-to-testify-on-interpretation-of-charges.

Kabalira, S. (2016) *The Right to Reparations under the Rome Statute of the International Criminal Court (ICC): The Content of the Right and its Implementation in the Light of the Early Case Law of the Court.* Oisterwijk: Wolf Legal Publishers.

McCarthy, C. (2012) *Reparations and Victim Support in the International Criminal Court.* Cambridge: Cambridge University Press.

McDonnell, F. and Akallo, G. (2007) *Girl Soldier: A Story of Hope for Uganda's Children.* Grand Rapids, MI: Chosen Books.

Mignolo, W. (2007) 'Delinking: The Rhetoric of Modernity, the Logic of Coloniality and the Grammar of Decoloniality', *Cultural Studies*, vol. 21, no. 2, pp. 449–514.

Mignolo, W. (2005) *The Idea of Latin America.* Oxford: Blackwell Publishing.

Moley, N. (2013) 'Methods of Reparations in the International Criminal Court: The Impossibility of Individual Awards in the Democratic Republic of Congo'. *UCLA Journal of International Foreign Affairs*, vol. 17, pp. 251–282.

Muddel, K. (2009) 'Limitations and Opportunities of Reparations for Women's Empowerment', International Centre for Transitional Justice. Available at www.ictj.org/sites/default/files/ICTJ-Global-Limitations-Reparations-2009-English.pdf.

Nayar, J. (2013) 'The Politics of Hope and the Other-in-the World: Thinking Exteriority', *Law Critique*, vol. 24, pp. 63–85.

Nduwimana, D. (2013) 'Reintegration of Child Soldiers in Eastern Congo: Challenges and Prospects', *The International Peace Support Training Centre Nairobi, Kenya*, Occasional Paper Series, vol. 4, no. 2, pp. 1–40.

Rehman, J., Shahid, A. and Foster, S. (eds) (2019) *The Asian Yearbook of Human Rights and Humanitarian Law*. Leiden: Brill Nijhoff.

Rohne, H., Arsovska, J. and Aertsen, I. (2008) 'Challenging Restorative Justice: State-based Conflict, Mass Victimisation and the Changing Nature of Warfare', in I. Aertsen, J. Arsovska, H. Rohne, M. Valiñas and K. Vanspauwen (eds), *Restoring Justice after Large-scale Violent Conflicts: Kosovo, DR Congo, and Israeli-Palestinian Case*. Uffculme: Willan Publishing, pp. 3–45.

Shelton, D. (2017) 'Introductory Note to the International Criminal Court: Situation in the Democratic Republic of the Congo, Prosecutor v. Thomas Lubanga Dyilo, Decision Establishing the Principles and Procedures to be Applied to Reparations', *Introductory Legal Materials*, vol. 51, no. 5, pp. 971–1017.

Smith, K. (2011) 'Prosecutor v. Lubanga: How the International Criminal Court Failed the Women and Girls of the Congo', *Howard Law Journal*, vol. 54, pp. 467–500.

Sperfeldt, C. (2016) 'Rome's Legacy: Negotiating the Reparations Mandate of the International Criminal Court', *International Law Review* vol. 17, pp. 351–377.

Suchkova, M. (2011) *The Importance of a Participatory Reparations Process and its Relationship to the Principles of Reparation*. Essex Transitional Justice Network. Briefing Paper 5, pp. 2–23.

Tan, J. (2012) 'Sexual Violence against Children on the Battlefield as a Crime of Using Child Soldiers: Square Pegs in Round Holes and Missed Opportunities in Lubanga', in T. Gill, R. Geiß, R. Heinsch, T. McCormack, C. Paulussen and J. Dorsey (eds), *Yearbook of International Humanitarian Law 2012*. The Hague: T.M. C. Asser Press, pp. 117–151.

Torpey, J. (2001) '"Making Whole What Has Been Smashed": Reflections on Reparations', *The Journal of Modern History*, vol. 73, no. 2, pp. 333–358.

Tschudi, F. (2008) 'Dealing with Violent Conflicts and Mass Victimization: A Human Dignity Approach', in I. Aertsen, J. Arsovska, H. Rohne, M. Valiñas and K. Vanspauwen (eds), *Restoring Justice after Large-scale Violent Conflicts: Kosovo, DR Congo, and Israeli-Palestinian Case*. Uffculme: Willan Publishing, pp. 46–69.

Tyler, T. (ed.) (2007) *Legitimacy and Criminal Justice: International Perspectives*. New York: Russell Sage.

Val-Garijo, F. (2011) 'Redressing Victims of International Crimes: The International Criminal Court and the Trust Fund for Victims', *Comunitania: International Journal of Social Work and Social Sciences*, pp. 81–97.

Van Boven, T. (1999) 'The Perspective of the Victim', in Y. Danieli, E. Stamatopoulou and C. Dias (eds), *The Universal Declaration of Human Rights: Fifty Years On*. Boca Raton, FL: CRC Press, pp. 13–26.

Vázquez, R. (2011) 'Translation as Erasure: Thoughts on Modernity's Epistemic Violence', *Journal of Historical Sociology*, vol. 24, no. 1, pp. 27–44.

Wessels, M. (2006) *Child Soldiers: From Violence to Protection*. Cambridge, MA: Harvard University Press.

Wiersing, A. (2012) 'Lubanga and its Implications for Victims Seeking Reparations at the International Criminal Court', *Amsterdam Law Forum*, vol. 4, no. 3, pp. 21–39.

Cases

Germany v. Poland (Factory at Chorzów), 1927. *Judgment of the Permanent Court of International Justice (Claim for Indemnity)*. Series A, no. 9.

Germany v. Poland (Factory at Chorzów), 1929. *Judgment of the Permanent Court of International Justice*. Series A, no. 17.

The Prosecutor v. Ahmad Al Faqi Al Mahdi, 2017. *Reparations Order*. ICC-1–12–01/15–236.

The Prosecutor v. Germain Katanga, 2017. *Order for Reparations pursuant to Article 75 of the Statute*. ICC-01/4–1/07.

The Prosecutor v. Thomas Lubanga Dyilo, 2015. *Judgment on the appeals against the 'Decision establishing the principles and procedures to be applied to reparations'* of 7 August 2012. ICC-01/4–1/06A A 2 A 3.

The Prosecutor v. Thomas Lubanga Dyilo, 2012. *Situation in the Democratic Republic of the Congo in the Case of the Prosecutor v.* Thomas Lubanga Dyilo: Decision Establishing the Principles and Procedures to be Applied to Reparations. ICC-01/4–1/06.

The Prosecutor v. Thomas Lubanga Dyilo, 2006. *Decision on the Prosecutor's Application for a Warrant of Arrest*, Article 58. ICC-01/1–4/06.

The Prosecutor v. Thomas Lubanga Dyilo, 2012. *Decision establishing the principles and procedures to be applied to reparations*. ICC-01/4–1/06.

The Prosecutor v. Thomas Lubanga Dyilo, 2012. *Judgment pursuant to Article 74 of the Statute*. ICC-01/4–1/6–2842.

Publications and Documents Published by International Organizations

International Criminal Court (2018) *Following Mr Bemba's acquittal, Trust Fund for Victims at the ICC decides to accelerate launch of assistance programme in Central African Republic*. Available at www.icc-cpi.int/Pages/item.aspx?name=180613-TFVPR.

International Criminal Court. *Regulations of the Court. ICC-BD/01–05–16.*

International Criminal Court. *Rules of Procedure and Evidence. CC-PIDS-LT-02–002/13_Eng.*

International Criminal Court (2012) *Situation in the Democratic Republic of the Congo in the Case of the Prosecutor v. Thomas Lubanga Dyilo: Summary of the 'Judgment Pursuant to Article 74 of the Statute.' ICC-01–01/01–06.*

International Meeting on Women's and Girl's Right to a Remedy and Reparation (2007) *Nairobi Declaration on Women's and Girl's Right to a Remedy and Reparation*. Available at https://reparations.qub.ac.uk/assets/uploads/NAIROBI_DECLARATIONeng.pdf.

Office of the United Nations High Commissioner for Human Rights (2008) *Rule-of-Law Tools for Post-Conflict States Reparations Programmes.*

United Nations (1998) *Report of the Preparatory Committee on the Establishment of an International Criminal Court*. UN Diplomatic Conference of Plenipotentiaries on the Establishment of an International Criminal Court. A/2/Conf. 183/2/Add.1.

The Assembly of States Parties (2002) *Establishment of a fund for the benefit of victims of crimes within the jurisdiction of the Court, and of the families of such victims.* Resolution ICC-ASP/1/Res.6.

The Assembly of States Parties (n.d.) *Regulations of the Trust Fund for Victims*. ICC-ASP/4/Res.3. Available at www.trustfundforvictims.org/sites/default/files/imce/Latest updated Regulations of the Trust Fund for Victims.pdf.

Trust Fund for Victims (n.d.) *Material Support*. Available at https://trustfundforvictims.org/en/what-we-do/assistance-programmes/material-support.

Trust Fund for Victims (n.d.) *Physical Rehabilitation*. Available at https://trustfndforvictims.org/en/what-we-do/assistance-programmes/physical-rehabilitation.

Trust Fund for Victims (n.d.) *Psychological Rehabilitation*. Available at https://trustfundforvictims.org/en/what-we-do/assistance-programmes/psychological-rehabilitation.

United Nations Children's Fund (UNICEF) (2007) *The Paris Principles: Principles and Guidelines on Children Associated with Armed Forces or Armed Groups.*

United Nations General Assembly (2006) *Basic Principles and Guidelines on the Right to a Remedy and Reparation for Victims of Gross Violations of International Human Rights Law and Serious Violations of International Humanitarian Law.* A/RES/60/147.

United Nations General Assembly (2005) *Basic Principles and Guidelines on the Right to a Remedy and Reparation for Victims of Gross Violations of International Human Rights Law and Serious Violations of International Humanitarian Law.* Resolution 60/147.

United Nations General Assembly (1998) *Rome Statute of the International Criminal Court* (last amended 2010). Available at https://www.refworld.org/docid/3ae6b3a84.html.

3 Concretizing a Legal Definition of a 'Survivor' and Spearheading a Survivor-Centred Approach at the International Criminal Court

Ingrid Roestenburg-Morgan

Introduction

A pertinent feature of post-conflict societies is the need to achieve stability, peace and accountability through a range of processes focused on justice, truth telling, reparations, institutional reform and reconciliation.[1] Better understood as transitional justice such processes include judicial and non-judicial processes that are used to achieve justice for victims and survivors of mass atrocities.[2] Transitional justice solutions have continued to evolve and are becoming more localized in favour of a more progressive and context-specific response to achieving justice. Since its inception transitional justice has elevated victims' rights by advocating for redress and reparations mainly via state responsibility and individual criminal responsibility for these particular actors.[3] The rights and dignity of the victim thus occupy a central space in transitional justice processes. In recent years the rights and dignity of the survivor have also become a prominent topic in the field of transitional justice.

International criminal justice is a vital component of transitional justice processes, and has made significant strides in terms of upholding the rights that should accrue to victims. This has been particularly visible at the International Criminal Court (ICC) where victims are now accorded a space allowing them to participate in criminal trials as well as giving them the opportunity to receive reparations.[4] The provision of support for victims' rights by civil society actors has resulted in stronger rights for both victims and survivors in the human rights and international criminal justice sectors, by holding the latter to account.[5] This includes the ICC where the focus on victims' rights and jurisdiction for victims has become a fundamental area for monitoring the overall success of the Court.

There has been a significant shift within international circles from the commonly held terminology and positionality of a 'victim' to that of a 'survivor' with increasing emphasis being placed on the concept of a 'survivor' as the more encompassing and empowering term of the two. Both terms have been used in different contexts and in various ways, but this has led to unclear and flexible definitions of these terms. This impacts the current

DOI: 10.4324/9781003212409-5

understanding of what constitutes a 'victim' at the ICC because it creates confusion around the meaning of 'victim' especially when the latter identifies as a 'survivor'.

The main objective of this chapter is thus to seek clarification of the definition of 'victim' and 'survivor' and to focus on the relevance of and the differences between a 'victim-centred' approach and the more novel 'survivor-centred' approach.

The chapter will begin by providing a clear definition of a 'victim', before proceeding to analyse the characteristics of a 'victim-centred' approach. The chapter then turns its attention to the ICC to understand its role as a meaningful transitional justice actor, and examines the responsibility that it has and owes towards the victims and survivors of mass atrocities. This will include a brief analysis of the role that the ICC occupies as a transitional justice actor and its accompanying legal obligation to victims and survivors of mass crimes.

A further aim of the chapter will be to trace the origins of the definition of a 'survivor' in order to build a case in support of a legal definition of the term survivor which could be adopted at the level of the ICC. The chapter in essence advocates for a formalized legal definition of the term that could be used by the ICC in order to support survivors as a legal category and to ensure the protection of their rights and dignity. The chapter also seeks to outline the problematic gap that the lack of a legal definition creates for the ICC which is linked a 'survivor-centred' approach..

Defining Victim and Victim-Centred Justice under Transitional Justice

The voices and agency of victims are increasingly being highlighted through transitional justice processes and transitional societies.[6] The reasons for the centrality of victims' rights in transitional contexts is meant to legitimize transitional justice processes such as prosecutions, truth commissions and other processes in both a moral and a legal attempt to give recognition to victims of mass atrocity.[7] While this has resulted in a deeper enquiry into the role of and rights for victims under transitional justice it has also resulted in the politicization of victims' rights. Victims have been depicted by proponents as innocent, vulnerable, blameless and deserving of justice. These persons have a vested interest in the justifiability of harms inflicted and the cause of the conflict but are less concerned about the victim's actual needs and wants.[8] Victimhood has as a result become very politicized within the framework of transitional justice processes in that although the victims themselves have become more prominent, it has simultaneously and ironically limited victims' voices and their agency.[9]

The primary reason for this shortcoming is because a victim who wants to access the rights that they are entitled to as well as strengthening their agency under transitional justice processes requires official acknowledgement from international institutions and judicial actors that they can in fact be classified as a 'victim' by fulfilling certain criteria. Thus, in order to be classified as a victim the individual in question must be accorded the appropriate legal status based on the qualification of the legal definition of the term 'victim'. A general understanding of a 'victim' within the criminal justice system, for example, is someone who has suffered harm as a result of criminal conduct. Punishment is no longer viewed as the only redress owed to victims of crime at the domestic level and many national criminal legal systems have evolved and adapted their penal codes to ensure that the proper recognition is accorded to victims.[10]

The concept of a 'victim' under international law, however, is more nuanced and contains different categories of victims.[11] These are victims of crime, victims of abuse of power, victims of gross violations of international human rights law and of serious violations of international humanitarian law, victims of enforced disappearance, victims of violations of international criminal law and, finally, victims of terrorism.[12] All the aforementioned categories 'have their own definition, as well as a catalogue of listed rights which builds the legal status of each victim'.[13] The most pivotal development in supporting victimhood and victims' rights has been the 1985 United Nations (UN) Declaration of Basic Principles of Justice for Victims of Crime and Abuse of Power, which has spearheaded the centrality of victims' rights under international law and has provided clarity in terms of the definition of who constitutes a victim. According to the aforementioned UN Declaration, a victim can be defined as follows:[14]

> 1. 'Victims' means persons who, individually or collectively, have suffered harm, including physical or mental injury, emotional suffering, economic loss or substantial impairment of their fundamental rights, through acts or omissions that are in violation of criminal laws operative within Member States, including those laws proscribing criminal abuse of power.
> 2. A person may be considered a victim, under this Declaration, regardless of whether the perpetrator is identified, apprehended, prosecuted or convicted and regardless of the familial relationship between the perpetrator and the victim. The term 'victim' also includes, where appropriate, the immediate family or dependants of the direct victim and persons who have suffered harm in intervening to assist victims in distress or to prevent victimization.

This definition must be seen as a forerunner and the basis upon which other listed categories of 'victim' definitions have been built.[15] For example, under the definition of 'victims of violations of international criminal law' the definition and positionality of the victim is determined under the Rome Statute of the ICC. Under Rule 85 of the Rules of Procedure and Evidence of the ICC:

> (a) 'Victims' means natural persons who have suffered harm as a result of the commission of any crime within the jurisdiction of the Court;

(b) Victims may include organizations or institutions that have sustained direct harm to any of their property which is dedicated to religion, education, art or science or charitable purposes, and to their historic monuments, hospitals and other places and objects for humanitarian purposes.

In other words, Rule 85 covers both natural and legal persons who have directly or indirectly suffered harm as a result of the commission of any crime that falls under the jurisdiction of the ICC. Rule 85 constitutes a significant advancement for international criminal law considering that historically international criminal law accorded scant recognition to the legal standing of victims, thus preventing them from becoming parties to the relevant criminal proceedings in question.[16] Within the international criminal justice system, however, the balancing of victims' and perpetrators' rights places further restrictions upon the full realization of victims' rights due to the need to extend equal treatment and rights to both of these parties. As a result, victims' expectations and needs may suffer under international criminal proceedings for a number of reasons.[17] For example, victims may not have a voice during proceedings; may not be able to participate in a case that might concern them, may not be treated with respect and fairness, may not be adequately updated on the progress, developments and outcomes of the case in question and may not be able to obtain economic and emotional redress.[18] To compensate for these shortcomings a 'victim-centred' approach has over time become a more popular approach within the spectrum of international and non-governmental organizations (NGOs) and is increasingly and consciously being subscribed to by international actors such as the UN and other NGOs.

The Victim-Centred Approach

When taking a 'victim-centred' approach, the victim's wishes, safety and wellbeing are prioritized in all matters and in all procedures. The approach is generally defined as the systematic focus on the needs and concerns of a victim to ensure the compassionate and sensitive delivery of services in a non-judgmental manner. The UN High Commissioner for Refugees (UNHCR), for instance, uses the following definition in relation to victims of sexual exploitation and abuse and sexual harassment:

> a victim-centred approach is a way of engaging with victim(s) that prioritizes listening to the victim(s), avoids re-traumatization, and systematically focuses on their safety, rights, well-being, expressed needs and choices, thereby giving back as much control to victim(s) as feasible and ensuring the empathetic and sensitive delivery of services and accompaniment in a non-judgmental manner.[19]

A victim-centred approach thus seeks to minimize the re-traumatization associated with criminal justice processes or related accountability processes by providing the support of victim advocates and service providers, empowering victims as engaged participants in the process, and giving them the opportunity to play a role in seeing the perpetrators of crimes committed against them being brought to justice. A victim-centred approach is usually implemented through policies and accompanying mechanisms that are meant to monitor the extent to which the approach is adopted, integrated and brought to life in practice.[20]

It is clear from the above criteria outlined by UNHCR associated with a victim-centred approach that victims are no longer passive recipients in legal processes but are now empowered to seek justice on their own terms. Similarly, under transitional justice processes victim participation in the design and execution in programmes of truth telling, reparations and accountability have become a well-established norm among states that undertake transitional justice measures and have as a result facilitated and drawn much-needed attention to victim-centred approaches not only domestically but also internationally.[21] Whereas some domestic trials incorporate some level of victim participation others are more conservative and generally speaking on a domestic level, victim-centred justice still remains limited.[22] International criminal justice, on the other hand, has more overtly tailored its approach to victim participation in the prosecution process, namely investigation, prosecution and trial, as well as in witness protection programmes and emergency reparations. This has been demonstrated at the ICC where victims' rights and a victim-centred approach has become more relevant and more prominent, thereby underpinning and steering the existing mandate of the Court.[23]

The ICC as a Pivotal Transitional Justice Tool and its Mandate towards Victims

The ICC's mandate towards victims follows more specifically from the jurisdiction it exercises over the most serious crimes of concern to the international community as a whole, namely the crime of genocide, war crimes, crimes against humanity and the crime of aggression. The ICC's mandate towards victims may be made easier if it is understood as the Court having a responsibility to prosecute offenders on behalf of victims, to include and protect victims during its criminal proceedings and to make reparations to or compensate victims. This mandate towards victims must furthermore be understood in light of the ICC being a transitional justice actor whereby it may be used as one of the many tools in contexts of transition to exact accountability for heinous crimes committed against victims of mass atrocities in an attempt to secure redress for the latter and peace and security in fragile contexts.[24] The ICC can thus be seen as an institution that was set up to secure lasting peace for the benefit of victims and the international community at large. Thus, while it primarily serves as an accountability mechanism, ultimately its chief function is to maintain international peace and security. In other words, the Court is one of the integral components or tools in a transitional justice setting which is needed to address mass atrocities through accountability by securing lasting peace and upholding victims' rights.[25]

The ICC's Responsibility to Prosecute on Behalf of Victims and Survivors

The objectives central to all international criminal tribunals, including the ICC, is to prosecute persons responsible for the most serious violations of international humanitarian law and to fight impunity.[26] This is clearly enunciated not only in the statutes of all ad hoc tribunals but also under the Preamble to the Rome Statute of the ICC which outlines the necessity of prosecutions and places an obligation on the states parties to the statute to prosecute international crimes that fall within their jurisdiction. The necessity of prosecutions for international crimes are that such crimes are deemed so inhumane and shocking to the conscience of humanity that it would be an omission not to exact accountability for them. Besides placing a legal duty on states and the international community at large tribunals have a moral duty to ensure that prosecutions following mass atrocities are followed up on. Victims and survivors of violent crime and human rights abuses seek respect for their rights and accountability from their leaders. The ICC was therefore established with the goal and purpose of directly prosecuting perpetrators of mass atrocities.

Punishment from an international legal perspective is necessary because 'it has a deep impact on victims and survivors and by extension on societies'.[27] Many victims and survivors who have been psychologically scarred and violated as the result of cruelty inflicted during mass killings, rape and other heinous crimes need the assurance that such crimes will not be committed again, as well as the personal security that those responsible will face punishment through incarceration. Thus, prosecutions are an essential tool towards achieving justice for both victims and survivors and society at large.

Victim Participation at the ICC and the ICC's Protection of Victims

Victim participation at the ICC may also be seen as one of the ways in which the Court has contributed towards a victim-centred approach. Victim participation is a new phenomenon that was devised as a means to give victims a voice during criminal proceedings at the ICC. Victims may therefore make representations before the judges of the Court to present their views and concerns.[28] Victim participation also involves victims and their legal representatives, receiving access to confidential material which can affect their personal interests.[29] Victims also have the right to question witnesses once their identities have been disclosed, as well as the right to tender and challenge the admissibility and the relevance of evidence presented by both the prosecution and the defence, which with the exception of the ICC does not usually exist in any domestic or other criminal justice systems.[30]

Although victim participation has been a giant leap in facilitating a victim-centred approach at the ICC it has also been subject to criticism and resistance. Those who oppose victim participation argue that the participation of victims could destabilize proceedings especially if the victim group is too large.[31] Arguments made by both the prosecution and the defence have shown that victim participation could compromise the integrity and independence of investigations and furthermore undermine the presumption of innocence of the defendant in question.[32] Victims who wish to qualify as 'victims' within the ICC framework must do so as victims *prima facie* which often results in the need for the provision of a more stringent proof of identity by the judges of the Court and is hence more time-consuming during the process of victim qualification.[33] Furthermore, a large majority of victims are indigent which places a huge financial strain on the Court because it is obliged to pay for legal assistance for such victims. Consequently, this leads to the legal aid scheme being depleted with limited funds becoming available to legal representatives of victims and therefore less interaction between victims and their legal counsel.[34] (See Chapter 1 in this volume which highlights the problems that can be encountered by victims and their legal representatives.) Despite these criticisms and shortcomings, victim participation at the ICC has been viewed as a major achievement in the international criminal justice system and has contributed substantially to the strengthening of the rights of victims through the ICC's victim participation programme.

Aside from victim participation, the protection of victims also qualifies as an important aspect of the Court's further commitment to victims' rights. Given the scale and nature of the crimes committed, the seniority and power of those under investigation and prosecution, victim protection is imperative at the level of the ICC.[35] The Victims and Witnesses Unit has been established in the Registry to address the issue of victims' protection. Once the nature of the threat to victims has been ascertained then protective measures are implemented accordingly. Relatedly, a victim support programme remains in place to offer psychological, social, economic and legal support to victims.

Reparations for Victims

Part of the justice process at the ICC is to provide support to victims who have suffered as a result of the conflict they have endured. Victims are also entitled to redress or reparations based on the individual criminal responsibility of perpetrators. Perpetrators are expected to be held criminally responsible by the domestic state in question where the crime has been committed and/or where legally and jurisdictionally appropriate by the ICC for the crime of genocide, war crimes, crimes against humanity and the crime of aggression, as stipulated under the Rome Statute.[36] Reparations are thus directly provided to victims or indirectly to their family members who have suffered as a result of the victim's loss as stipulated and pursuant to Article 75 of the Rome Statute. The Rome Statute and the ICC's Rules of Procedure and Evidence lays out the rights available for victims, who must first qualify as an ICC 'victim' before reparations may be granted.[37] The Court may also 'order individuals to pay reparations to other individuals and it has the option of granting individual and collective reparations which may take the form of 'restitution, indemnification and rehabilitation'. Reparations may also more broadly impact victims' families and the wider community by contributing 'to the rebuilding of war-torn societies, by advancing truth and by acknowledging the gravity of the crimes committed'.[38]

Chapter 2 in this volume notes that the basic purpose of reparations is essentially to elevate victims' rights to a higher status than is generally accorded in the international justice process and to make it a legitimate concern for the public to take into account. Victims should avoid being viewed as persons only waiting to accept financial handouts but as persons deserving of acknowledgement and respect. Initially, victims were given no significant place or public acknowledgement in the international criminal justice process and their needs were often marginalized with many other priorities given priority in the criminal justice rankings.[39]

Article 75 of the Rome Statute provides for the establishment of a Trust Fund for Victims, which outlines the ICC's reparations mandate and gives victims a voice in order to exercise their rights within the international criminal justice system.[40] The Trust Fund is an important mechanism that facilitates the effective implementation of reparations ordered by the Court and is central to the success of ICC reparations being provided to victims. Thus far the Trust Fund for Victims has proven to be a critical source of assistance to victims and has ensured that meaningful reparations can be provided to victims and their families as initially envisioned by the Rome Statute.[41]

In order to complement the Trust Fund for Victims and the ICC it is imperative that reparations are streamlined with national reparations programmes and international organizations such as the International Organization for Migration and the Office of the High Commissioner for Human Rights to repair the harm suffered by victims to enable a more holistic and victim-centred response to be made to victims within a transitional justice setting.[42]

Reflections on Whether the ICC Does Follow a Victim-Centred Approach to Justice

It is clear that the ICC grants victims a central role in its justice process by enabling them to be more meaningfully engaged as witnesses. The Rome Statute has made victims' rights a reality through its victim participation programme 'by shifting the perception of victims from that of passive recipients of justice to one of active rights holders'.[43] This can contribute to the process of healing and the recognition of victims in the international and transitional justice landscapes making victims more visible and more vocal, thereby ultimately contributing to their agency.[44]

This interaction of victims featuring more overtly within the criminal justice system has also endowed the ICC with a restorative function and purview making the ICC a valuable transitional justice tool. 'The inclusiveness of a victim's constituency at the ICC seems to a large extent to be consistent with the restorative model of justice, since it seeks to connect international criminal justice to the process of social reconciliation typical of the restorative justice paradigm.'[45] Reconciliation and social healing of both the individual and the society forms part of such a paradigm and thus the right of victims to participate in criminal proceedings for the wrongs committed against them contributes to the recovery of individual victims and aids in the restoration of society as a whole.[46]

However, despite this innovative development of victim participation at the ICC, which many believe qualifies the ICC as a victim-centred institution, on closer scrutiny some shortcomings undermine a fully victim-centred approach at the ICC. Some of these hurdles include:

- the adversarial nature of the trial proceedings giving rise to less dialogue between victim and perpetrator;
- the presumption of innocence and rights of the alleged perpetrator that undermine the responsibility and remorse of the perpetrator towards the victim;
- the ICC's primary mandate which urges the Court to prosecute and punish those most responsible inevitably taking precedence over any opportunity for participatory conflict resolution;
- the real extent to which the ICC could contribute to genuine reconciliation and eradicate or undo victimization which in ICC jurisdictional contexts takes place in an overtly violent and large-scale manner;
- and finally the extent to which the ICC can actually succeed in restoring victims' rights and their dignity including that of the wider community through symbolic reparations which still remain inadequate in meeting victims' basic needs.

These identifiable shortcomings undermine the ICC's restorative justice purview in support of victims and compromise its strict adherence to a victim-centred approach. Other shortcomings that may be seen as inconsistent with the 2005 UN Basic Principles which limit the rights of victims to participate fully in ICC proceedings include (i) the narrowing of charges at a later stage of the trial proceedings which may exclude the participation of victims who have initially qualified as victims; (ii) the judicial discretion by the judges of the ICC may further limit the participation of victims at various stages of the proceedings such as during the appeal stage; and (iii) victims' presentation of evidence which may be at odds with the prosecution's case also remains questionable.[47]

The ICC appears to have been able to meet the key principles supporting a victim-centred approach as evidenced through its statutes and policy documentation.[48] However, the questionable key principle is the issue of re-traumatization of victims during trial proceedings. Re-traumatization refers to secondary or additional victimization during victims and survivors interactions with service providers and institutions.[49] Given that the trial process is one that is adversarial in nature there is always the risk that victims and survivors will be exposed to an intimidating and difficult process which will often include direct confrontation with the perpetrator and other court officials which may intentionally and/or unintentionally re-traumatize victims and survivors through the use of 'negative statements, behaviors, and attitudes'.[50]

> Re-traumatization encompasses victim-blaming and explicitly or implicitly accusing someone of failing to prevent what happened to them. It also includes other negative attitudes and behaviors, such as dismissive or unresponsive actions, as well as statements that minimize what the victim or survivor has experienced.[51]

The issue of re-traumatization can easily be subsumed under the purview of restorative justice and remains a hurdle that the ICC must overcome in order fully to meet the principles of a victim-centred approach. Despite this, the recognition of victims' rights at the ICC has contributed to the rule of law, bolstering the ICC's credibility and legitimacy as a transitional justice actor. Transitional justice actors such as the ICC should therefore do their best to focus on victims' needs. A victim-centred approach places victims more centrally at the core of any institutional strategy.

From the prevailing discussion it has become clear that the ICC has made strategic steps in following a victim-centred approach within the limitations of the criminal justice system which it operates in. Given the adversarial nature of the criminal justice process there will always be a balancing of victims' rights against those of the defendants in order to afford both an equal measure of justice. However, it is imperative that the ICC should not lose sight of the needs and perceptions of victims, victim communities and vulnerable groups if it is to play an active role as a transitional justice actor. Furthermore, the fact that the Court occupies a role as accountability mechanism and peace builder for victims who occupy this legal status under the Court's statutes and therefore are a legal category further begs the question whether individuals who identify as survivors also have the right to reparations and representation at the ICC? This conundrum exists because currently a 'survivor' does not fall into a legal category generally defined by the law, nor is this word universally used in all contexts. For the purposes of this discussion it is therefore imperative to provide more clarity about the terminology of a 'survivor' as a category under transitional justice within the international community and under international law.

Current Understandings of the Term 'Survivor'

Increasingly, the international community and the transitional justice sector has seen the emergence of the term 'survivor' as an alternative or interchangeable word to the term 'victim'. This gradual shift in terminology stems from the fact that throughout history victims have often been depicted as 'passive, weak, traumatised, stigmatised, powerless, and in extreme cases, even as mentally ill'.[52] This led to the popularization of the term 'survivor' by activists, particularly feminists, development practitioners and international organizations, who began to recognize the power that words convey in promoting or undermining the agency and autonomy of individuals.[53] By tracing the historical roots of the word 'survivor' it becomes apparent that the word's connotations are steeped in its relationship to sexual and gender-based violence. The term 'survivor' became more commonly used when individuals who were sexually assaulted in the aftermath became more empowered after the relevant violation in question. These persons deliberately chose to heal and share their experiences of sexual assault in a more autonomous way instead of only focusing on the experience of the violation itself.[54] The shift in terminology from 'victim' to 'survivor' thus emphasized the heroism, mostly of women, in overcoming the scourge of rape or sexual violence which was often accompanied by powerlessness and shamefulness.[55] The definition of a survivor is deemed to represent triumph over despair, strength over weakness and heroism over the trauma of sexual assault.[56]

The term itself was popularized by activists and feminists during the 1970s and 1980s when feminists strategically used it 'to win over public sympathy and government funding' to support women suffering from domestic abuse and violence in the United Kingdom.[57] A distinction then emerged between victims and survivors whereby women who were deemed to be victims were portrayed as being 'trapped' in their domestic situations and provided a convincing explanation as to why they returned to their domestic abusers. 'Activists cited psychological motives such as being trapped by fear, love, guilt or societal expectations of a woman's role, that is, they constructed a narrative in which the victim could not be held responsible for her misfortunes.'[58] This narrative of abused women as victims who were 'passive and helpless' and who could not be held responsible for their fates eventually began gnawing at feminists who began to view this narrative as less than convincing to support a feminist understanding of the term 'victim'. This was mainly due to the diminished agency that the concept was beginning to convey or accord to women in abusive relationships.[59] As a result, the adoption of the term 'survivor' reasserted victims' and women's rights within the political and development arenas in that it now portrayed women as 'free agents' with the ability to make their own personal choices regardless of the dire circumstances they faced or found themselves in because of the resilience they demonstrated by staying with their abusers. This transition in terminology from 'victim' to 'survivor' also meant that certain states or donors who preferred the term survivor rather than victim were willing to support and spearhead this transition since they appreciated the connotation of agency and power now accorded by the term.[60]

From a more generalized perspective there are a number of different connotations of the term survivor; some describe a survivor as someone who has overcome traumatic experiences such as road accidents, illness or disease, injustices such as discrimination or racism, and natural disasters.[61] A legal understanding of the term gives rise to a legal vacuum (lacuna) because the term survivor has not been defined under international law and the Rome Statute. However, in practice it has become commonplace and is increasingly referred to by legal professionals and policymakers in various policy documents, speeches and communications. It may thus be argued that the term is becoming universally accepted which means that from an international legal perspective it is imperative that a legal definition be coined.

Under transitional justice the term survivor also requires further reflection. Mahmood Mamdani, for instance, draws attention to the realities inherent in societies transitioning from mass conflict to peace where is no clear perpetrator. This is because both victim and perpetrator trade places during mass conflict and each side has their own narrative of victimhood.[62] Transitional societies therefore bring into question the victim-perpetrator dichotomy, which may be limiting in depicting the realities of post-conflict societies. Given the rigidity of roles accorded to victims and perpetrators an oversimplification of these roles has arisen, creating a good and evil narrative whereby victimhood is politically constructed.[63] Such a narrative is rarely quite straightforward because it excludes a majority of experiences taking place during conflict and only reflects the dominant narrative such as was the case in Rwanda where the transitional government was absolved from all its crimes and where the Hutu were collectively held accountable.[64] According to Mamdani, there is no template with which to define mass violence in instances where violence is politically motivated and where victims and perpetrators trade places, each having their own narrative of victimhood.[65] An assumption thus exists that the perpetrator is always the perpetrator and never the victim or vice versa. This then leads to diminished agency on the part of the victim and the demonization of the perpetrator, which in Mamdani's view creates or feeds the cycle of violence even further.[66] To break this cycle Mamdani suggests that the victim narrative should be displaced with that of a survivor narrative whereby victims' perpetrators, beneficiaries and bystanders may all be seen as part of a new community of survivors following mass violence or conflict.[67]

An example of the complexity of adhering to the victim-perpetrator dichotomy in transitional societies may be the situation in relation to child soldiers where the latter in essence can occupy the role of both victim and perpetrator. In situations such as these, a blurring of the lines between the categories of victim and perpetrator takes place, creating confusion especially when actors such as these can legitimately switch roles between victim and perpetrator.[68] Thus, in instances such as these where perpetrators identify as victims they could also be in a position to further identify as survivors because survivors often shift in and out of victimization.

Developing and Concretizing a Legal Definition of the Term 'Survivor'

The consequences of a fluid victim-perpetrator status ought to have implications in the way which transitional societies and institutions such as the ICC will respond to and address such a status. The impact of a fluid status, which swings between victim, perpetrator and survivor, will also have an impact on the adjudication of international crimes, victim participation and reparations should such a fluid status be formally recognized and accepted by the ICC. The *Ongwen* case serves as a good example of this and is the only case at the ICC where the duality of the status of the accused was contested.[69] As part of his defence, Dominic Ongwen's defence team held that he was a victim, and not a perpetrator based on the fact that the Lord's Resistance Army abducted him as a young child, brutalized him for almost three decades and forced him to commit the most heinous crimes, which he was being charged with at the ICC.[70] His defence team held that his role as child soldier could not be ignored and that the Trial Chamber should therefore not overlook his status as a victim.[71] Despite this plea, Ongwen's defence team's arguments were rejected on the basis that his role as a child soldier did not directly diminish his criminal responsibility for the crimes that he committed.[72] Unfortunately, this was a missed opportunity for the Trial Chamber in question to engage on and recognize this unique status which would have provided more clarity and subsequently a unique precedent on some of the more complex issues that continue to challenge international criminal law and transitional justice, namely victimhood, the dual and legal status of both victim and perpetrator, and the recognition of the complexities surrounding such individuals' culpability given their ambiguous status.

The issue of legal status situates the position of a person as determined by the law. A person's legal status accords clarity to the privileges, obligations, powers or restrictions as declared by the relevant legislation in question.[73] Under international law all human rights bodies and judicial institutions create rights for victims. The ICC does the same under the Rome Statute where victims' rights includes the right of participation, the right to present evidence, the right to protection and the right to reparations.[74] The term victim thus denotes a person's legal status as it outlines the extent to which an individual can exercise certain participatory rights and protections, which are not readily available to every person involved in international criminal proceedings.[75] With the term survivor being used more readily in the international legal arena it is incumbent upon international institutions such as the ICC to consider legitimizing this term by endowing such individuals with an independent status within the legal framework of the Court. Like victims, those who identify as survivors have the right to be treated with dignity, respect and fairness within the international criminal justice system through the recognition of their distinct status as survivors. Negating the status of the term survivor and making use of the term victim trivializes a survivor's identity without any real or true recognition of such a unique and distinct identity and role within the international criminal justice system and diminishes a survivor's dignity.

Based on the ICC's mandate towards victims and survivors of mass atrocities and its role as a leading judicial transitional justice actor, the ICC should consider developing a legal definition of the term survivor to uphold the dignity and rights of a category of individuals who lack a legal identity. The definition for instance could read as follows:

> A survivor means any person who individually and collectively suffered from harm, mainly of a sexual nature which results in physical or mental injury, emotional suffering, economic loss or substantial impairment of their fundamental rights, through acts or omissions that are in violation of criminal laws operative within domestic jurisdictions and within the jurisdiction of the International Criminal Court. Survivors during their process of recovery are fragile and may be re-traumatized or reinjured emotionally. They may shift in and out of victimization and victim-survivor status. Survivors may also further identify as both victim and perpetrator in ambiguous contexts of mass conflict if there is a blurring or duality in their status. They may periodically return to their mental and emotional suffering, or they may continue to strive to maintain emotional, mental, spiritual, and physical health. Survivors feel empowered to make healthy decisions about their lives and they actively pursue informal and formal support systems geared towards their full recovery.[76]

Based on this skeleton definition of the term survivor the ICC's Working Group on Amendments should consider developing a formal legal definition that takes into account the etymology of the term together with its nascent connotations. This is important in order to bring clarity and consistency to the term survivor, which forms the foundational underpinnings of a survivor-centred approach that was recently adopted by the Office of the Prosecutor.[77] Moreover, it is particularly important because it fills the legal gap that would cover the categories of individuals who identify solely as survivors and not as victims, and those who occupy a dual or tripartite identity or status such as perpetrators who identify as both victim and/or survivor.

A Survivor-Centred Approach

A survivor-centred approach has its early roots in conflict-related sexual violence with the promulgation of UN Resolution 1325 in October 2000 when women, peace and security became a priority issue for the UN Security

Council during that particular period. The most recent addition to this work has been the further promulgation of UN Resolution 2467 which makes a distinct reference to adopting a survivor-centred approach to conflict-related sexual violence.[78] An understanding of a survivor-centred approach generally follows that the survivor's dignity, rights, agency and empowerment are upheld and protected at all costs usually in relation to any conflict-related sexual violence.[79] In other words, all the relevant actors who investigate, collect, research, monitor and use any data gathered are encouraged to follow such an approach thereby ensuring that survivors are protected from further harm, stigma and/or discrimination.[80] Definitions of such an approach while containing many of the aforementioned elements are often tailored by organizations such as the UN and various NGOs in alignment with each of the latter's culture, mission and values. Interestingly, the term survivor in these contexts also follows more loosely defined or subjective definitions following the lack of a formalized definition unlike in the case of a victim.

By placing the survivor at the heart of a survivor-centred approach a survivor's agency and self-determination is reinforced which allows the survivor to gain more control over their life.[81] Such agency may be defined as the ability of an individual to make strategic choices and to act on those choices, and this is an important part of empowerment because it implies exercising one's choices in a way which challenges power relations that are central to a survivor's wellbeing.[82] Some direct indicators of agency include freedom of movement, freedom from violence, decision-making on a range of topics and an inherent belief in one's self-worth and ability. The promotion of agency is therefore fundamental to the adoption of a survivor-centred approach.[83]

Some general or guiding principles in implementing a survivor-centred approach include confidentiality, safety, respect and non-discrimination.[84] Confidentiality entails not sharing information to any party without the informed consent of the survivor in question and in some instances within limit.[85] Safety of the survivor is also an important tenet of the approach and includes the protection of the survivor's physical, emotional and psychological safety. Respect covers the right of the survivor to be treated with respect and dignity the latter of which is a fundamental and inalienable human right.[86] According to the Universal Declaration of Human Rights, the right to be treated with dignity means that all human beings are born free and equal in dignity and rights and should therefore be treated in a spirit of brotherhood.[87] Similarly, the right to be free from discrimination under a survivor-centred approach means that survivors should be afforded equal rights without any unfair discrimination on the basis of gender, disability, race, ethnicity or tribe, colour, language, religious or political beliefs and/or class.[88]

A forerunner of the survivor-centred approach has been the recently released Murad Code which has complemented and strengthened the understanding and guidance on the implementation of a survivor-centred approach.[89] Named after Nobel Laureate Nadia Murad, the Murad Code has been described as a global code of conduct for gathering and using information relating to systematic and conflict-related sexual violence. It distils existing minimum standards for the safe, effective and ethical use of information obtained from victims and survivors.[90] It seeks to ensure that people who interact with survivors of systematic and conflict-related sexual violence do so in a way which is conscientious, ethical and respectful.[91] While the Murad Code is voluntary and rooted in international law it is not binding on relevant professional actors who interact with survivors, but since its inception it has garnered tremendous support from governments, national authorities, international organizations, civil society and other relevant stakeholders.[92] It is hoped that the Code could win global support and adherence from professional bodies and institutions who regularly interact with survivors. The Murad Code is inventive because the agency of survivors is placed centre stage along with various principles and commitments which are interconnected and mutually reinforcing.[93]

Closely associated or encompassed within the context of a survivor-centred approach is a trauma-informed approach.[94] Often a survivor-centred approach is accompanied with the use of a trauma-informed approach which is increasingly becoming cited and used in policy and practice.[95] A trauma-informed approach may be defined as an approach which considers the needs of the survivor or victim throughout the intended process. In the context of a criminal justice process a trauma-informed approach allows the victim or survivor to work through the trauma while participating in the criminal justice process.[96] The aim of this approach is to prevent re-traumatization through sensitive care of the victim or survivor which depends on the practitioner in question understanding and realizing what trauma is and then recognizing the signs, symptoms and widespread impact of trauma on the particular individual and/or community.[97] The key principles of this approach include ensuring the psychological and emotional safety of the survivor, building trust between staff and survivor, restoring the survivor's choice and control, facilitating collaboration and connection between survivors, ensuring survivors' empowerment by giving them a strong voice and decision-making ability and finally ensuring that practitioners are culturally and gender sensitive.[98]

In this regard, demonstrating cultural sensitivity requires that practitioners be aware of the relationship that culture has on survivors of sexual and gender-based violence. 'Culture should extend broadly not only to race and ethnicity but should also include sensitivity to gender, age, disability, language, literacy, sexual orientation and any set of beliefs that guide an individual.'[99] Gender sensitivity falls under the aforementioned umbrella of culture and aims to understand and take account of the societal and cultural factors involved in gender-based exclusion and discrimination in the most diverse spheres of public and private life.[100]

Practitioners engaging with survivors must therefore receive ongoing education and training on cultural and gender competency and the latter should form part of the policies and practices of organizations working with survivors.[101] As part of cultural sensitivity there is also the need to use the language and vernacular of the individual in question.[102] Furthermore, there must be 'zero tolerance policies against any form of harassment discrimination, racist language or homophobia.'[103] Therefore, law enforcement practitioners, prosecutors and medical examiners must be sufficiently trained to deal with cultural and gender proclivities in order to establish trust and safety with survivors.[104]

Understanding the individual context in which the crimes involving the survivor took place and identifying the relevant cultural traditions and social norms are important to minimize any negative repercussions against the survivor in question.[105] It is clear that a survivor-centred approach seeks to empower survivors by focusing on their needs as well as allowing their voices to be heard. Furthermore, a survivor-centred approach almost always encompasses a reliance on ancillary approaches such as a trauma-informed approach or gender-sensitive approach which remains attentive to the needs of survivors. There must be cultural and gender sensitivity to afford survivors equal treatment in order to avoid any form of discrimination and powerlessness. In other words, a survivor-centred approach must be empowering to the extent that survivors are able to meaningfully participate in the decisions that directly affect them so that they retain intimate control over those decisions that impact them and those that they decide upon.

Final Reflections and Most Recent Developments at the ICC with Regard to Survivors and a Survivor-Centred Approach

It is highly likely that a transitional justice institution and actor such as the ICC will benefit from a survivor-centred approach given its close relationship to individuals who experience mass violence and conflict-related sexual violence. The Court's association with victims and victims' rights and its usage of the terminology of a 'victim' in all of its policies and communications has been commonplace until very recently. At the time of writing in December 2023 the Office of the Prosecutor published an updated policy on gender-based crimes in which references to and acknowledgement of survivors and a survivor-centred approach feature prominently.[106]

This new policy on gender-based crimes that was spearheaded by the ICC's new prosecutor Karim Khan supersedes the original policy which was first published by his predecessor Fatou Bensouda in 2014, and makes clear that the Office of the Prosecutor is committed to an intersectional and survivor-centred approach in its work on gender-based crimes.[107] The policy also states that the Office of the Prosecutor will 'integrate a survivor-centred and trauma-informed approach in its work with victims and witnesses exposed to GBC [gender-based crimes] and other atrocity crimes'.[108] On reading the policy it also becomes clear that the Office of the Prosecutor has largely borrowed its understanding of implementing a survivor-centred approach from the Murad Code which has contributed to this development. Additionally, the Office of the Prosecutor's recent policy highlights that in tandem to a survivor-centred approach it will employ, *inter alia*, a trauma-informed approach, gender competence, due diligence and a culturally sensitive approach when dealing with gender-based crimes.[109] The adoption of such a comprehensive methodology in dealing with victims and survivors of gender-based crimes is indicative of a holistic approach that is indeed consistent with what a survivor-centred approach should in fact entail.

The Office of the Prosecutor furthermore gives recognition to survivors as a distinct category by taking the position that 'it is for an individual to decide if they prefer to be identified as a 'victim', 'survivor', or both.[110] The policy uses both terms with some flexibility often utilizing 'victim' (at times with a 'witness') when referring to the Rome Statute or ICC jurisprudence or procedures, and 'survivor' when focusing more closely on the experiences or needs of the individual.'[111] In other words, through its policy the Office of the Prosecutor views victims and survivors at times as distinct and at other times as fluid categories, whereby victims may identify as survivors and vice versa. The policy asserts that 'many of the victims and witnesses the Office engages are survivors of atrocity crimes, including possible GBC'.'[112] Thus, the Office of the Prosecutor's understanding of survivors is to a large degree consistent with the skeleton legal definition of the term survivor developed and provided for earlier in this chapter. Currently, the legal determination of who can be classified as a victim based on the criteria at the ICC is complex and will become more difficult in certain instances such as when an individual identifies solely as a survivor and not a victim, or has a tripartite identity such as a 'victim-perpetrator-survivor'. While in the former instance a survivor may be classified as a victim because they meet the criteria of a victim as stipulated by the ICC they may not want to be labelled as such and therefore may forfeit any redress or justice due to them by not being able or empowered to pursue their own interests under the ICC's legal framework. In the second instance the individual concerned may be classified as a victim but could identify as a survivor or indeed as both, yet at the same time they might be a perpetrator. This then may limit the rights of individuals who as a result of their complex identities are prevented from claiming the justice that is due to them because they do not identify with or fit into the legal category of victim that the ICC has accorded to them.

Conclusion

Based on the discussion developed in this chapter it becomes clear that survivors should be recognized as a legal category that is separate from that of victims at the ICC based on their distinct and particular identities. As the chapter has demonstrated survivors may see themselves as victims, perpetrators or solely as survivors or even a combination of the latter categories. During or in the aftermath of conflict, transitional or post-conflict societies give rise to convoluted identities where victimhood becomes controversial. This is because the roles accorded to victim and perpetrator in such contexts is sometimes blurred resulting in a diminished or one-sided understanding of victimhood. The ICC as a pivotal transitional justice actor should therefore be cognizant of this dilemma and seek to provide more clarity into the identities and legal categories of individuals who identify as survivors or who identify with multiple or a combination of identities following conflict. This is because the ICC as a judicial institution and a transitional justice actor has an obligation towards victims and survivors of mass atrocities, so promoting or enabling the latter's interests remains a large part of the mandate of the Court. Furthermore, the chapter shows that a legal gap currently exists as a result of the lack of a legal definition of the term survivor which as a result may limit or diminish the rights of individuals who identify as such.

In addition, if a judicial institution such as the ICC is to rely on a survivor-centred approach a legal definition of a survivor, which forms the foundation or crux of the approach, ought to accompany the approach. This is because currently the definition of the term survivor still remains a subjective, vague and loosely defined term under transitional justice and international criminal law. It will be valuable for the ICC to concretize a legal definition of the term survivor in order to support and spearhead the effective adherence and implementation of a survivor-centred approach, which could in the future provide more uniformity in terms of the definition of the term and the approach amongst international institutions, NGOs and other like-minded international organizations that support and advocate for survivors of conflict-related violence.

Finally, a legal definition will assist in providing survivors with the necessary legal standing or *locus standi*, which would enable them to participate in ICC proceedings if they are able to prove that there is a connection between the offence committed against them and the harm or damage they suffered as a result. Like with victims at the ICC a survivor's legal standing may be denied if they cannot prove a direct and specific interest as specified *mutatis mutandis* for victims under Rule 85 of the Rome Statute. The importance and additional benefit of equipping them with a legal identity and status contributes not only to upholding survivors' rights and dignity but goes directly to their agency, which is a crucial element of a survivor-centred approach to justice. In supporting both victims and survivors, transitional justice actors such as the ICC must cater to the needs and uphold the identities and dignities of those recovering from mass atrocity crimes for whom the Court has been set up in the first place for. The voices of survivors can only be heard if influential institutions such as the ICC recognize their unique identity, uphold their dignity and provide a platform for their effective participation. It is thus incumbent upon transitional justice institutions such as the ICC to pave the way for meaningful justice for survivors who depend on the Court for the protection of their dignity and rights.

Notes

1 C.S. Villalba, 'Transitional Justice: Key Concepts, Processes and Challenges', Briefing Paper, Institute for Democracy and Conflict Resolution, University of Essex Knowledge Gateway, 2011.
2 Ibid.
3 D. Orentlicher D. 'Settling Accounts: The Duty to Prosecute Human Rights Violations of a Prior Regime', *The Yale Law Journal*, 100(8), 1991, pp. 2537–2615. See also the UN Basic Guidelines on the Right to Remedy and Reparation for Victims of Gross Violations of International Human Rights Law and Serious Violations of International Humanitarian Law, adopted and proclaimed by General Assembly Resolution 60/147 of 16 December 2005. See too the ICC website, 'Victims Participation and Reparations', and Article 75 of the Rome Statute, available at http://www.icc-cpi.int/en_menus/icc/structure%20of%20the%20court/victims/reparation/Pages/reparation%20for%20victims.aspx (accessed 24 January 2023).
4 Ibid.
5 Ibid.
6 C. Lawther, '"Let Me Tell You": Transitional Justice, Victimhood and Dealing with a Contested Past', *Social & Legal Studies*, 30(6), 2021, pp. 890–912.
7 L. Fletcher and H. Weinstein, 'Transitional Justice and the Plight of Victimhood', in *Research Handbook on Transitional Justice*, ed. C. Lawther, L. Moffett and D. Jacobs (Cheltenham: Edward Elgar, 2017), pp. 244–266.
8 Lawther, 'Let Me Tell You'.
9 Ibid.
10 M. Rauschenbach and D. Scalia, 'Victims and International Criminal Justice: A Vexed Question?' *International Review of the Red Cross*, 90(870), 2008, pp. 441–449.
11 C. Fernández de Casadevante Romani, 'International Law of Victims', in *Max Planck Yearbook of United Nations Law*, ed. A. von Bogdandy and R. Wolfrum, vol. 14 (Leiden: Brill, 2010), p. 219–272.
12 Ibid.
13 Ibid.
14 UN Declaration of Basic Principles of Justice for Victims of Crime and Abuse of Power. Adopted 29 November 1985 by General Assembly Resolution 40/34.
15 Fernández de Casadevante Romani, 'International Law of Victims'.
16 Ibid.
17 Rauschenbach and Scalia, 'Victims and International Criminal Justice'.
18 H. Strang, *Repair or Revenge: Victims and Restorative Justice* (Oxford: Oxford University Press, 2002).
19 UNHCR, *Policy on a Victim-Centred Approach in UNHCR's Response to Sexual Misconduct: Sexual Exploitation and Abuse and Sexual Harassment*, 1 December 2020, available at https://www.unhcr.org/uk/media/policy-victim-centred-approach-unhcrs-response-sexual-misconduct.
20 Ibid.
21 J. Mendez, 'Victims as Protagonists in Transitional Justice', *International Journal of Transitional Justice*, 10(1), March 2016, pp. 1–5.
22 Ibid.
23 Ibid.
24 I. Morgan, *The Road to Reconciliation? Optimising the Legitimacy and Efficacy of the International Criminal Court within the African Union and Africa*, Human Rights Research Series, vol. 102 (Cambridge: Intersentia, 2023).
25 Ibid.
26 See IMT Charter Article 6, ICTY Statute, Art, 1, ICTR, Art. 1, SCSL Statute, Art. 1, ECCC Statute, Art. 1

27 K.C. Moghalu, 'Prosecute or Pardon? Between Truth Commissions and War Crimes Trials', in *Peace versus Justice: The Dilemma of Transitional Justice in Africa*, ed. C.L. Sriram S. and Pillay (Oxford: James Currey and Durban: University of KwaZulu Natal Press, 2009 and 2010), p. 87
28 See Article 75 of the Rome Statute.
29 E. Baumgartner, 'Aspects of Victim Participation in the Proceedings of the International Criminal Court', *International Review of the Red Cross*, 90(870), 2008, pp. 409–440.
30 P. Katonene, 'An Analysis of the Difficulties related to Victim Participation before the ICC and Extraordinary Chambers in the Courts of Cambodia', thesis, University of the Western Cape, Cape Town, 2012, pp. 1–87.
31 Ibid.
32 Ibid.
33 Ibid.
34 Ibid.
35 S. Uma, 'Victims at the Heart of International Criminal Justice', *The Wire*, 2021, available at https://thewire.in/rights/victims-at-the-heart-of-international-criminal-justice (accessed 24 April 2023).
36 Villalba, 'Transitional Justice', p. 5.
37 Victims should meet the definition as spelled out in the ICC's Rules of Procedure and Evidence. Rule 85 of the ICC Rules of Procedure and Evidence define 'victims' as 'natural persons who have suffered harm as a result of the commission of any crime within the jurisdiction of the ICC'.
38 The Redress Trust and Forensic Risk Alliance, 'The International Criminal Court's Trust Fund for Victims: Analysis and Options for the Development of Further Criteria for the Operation of the Trust Fund for Victims', Discussion Document, 2003.
39 L. Margarrel, 'Reparations in Theory and Practice', Reparative Justice Series (New York: International Center for Transitional Justice, 2007), p. 2.
40 See Article 75 of the Rome Statute.
41 REDRESS, *No Time to Wait: Realising Reparations for Victims at the International Criminal Court* (London: REDRESS, 2019), pp 1–68.
42 Ibid.
43 Fédération Internationale pour les droits humains (FIDH), 'Whose Court Is It?' *Judicial Handbook on Victims Rights at the International Criminal Court* (FIDH, in collaboration with the Ministry of Foreign Affairs of the Netherlands, 2021).
44 A. Cuppini, 'A Restorative Response to Victims in Proceedings before the International Criminal Court: Reality or Chimaera?' *International Criminal Law Review*, 2021.
45 Ibid.
46 Ibid.
47 C.M. Bassiouni (2012) 'Victim Rights and Participation in ICC Proceedings and in Emerging Customary International Law', ICC Forum, 2012, available at https://iccforum.com/reparations (accessed 17 October 2023).
48 See the Rome Statute and the ICC's Rules of Procedure and Evidence Concerning Victims' Rights. See also Office of the Prosecutor Policy Paper on Victims' Participation, April 2010, available at https://www.icc-cpi.int/sites/default/files/iccdocs/otp/Policy_Paper_on_Victims_Participation_April_2010.pdf.
49 N. Katirai, 'Retraumatized in Court', *Arizona Law Review*, 62, Arizona Legal Studies Discussion Paper, no. 19–10, 2020, pp. 81–123.
50 Ibid.
51 Ibid.
52 L.J. Hepworth, 'Victim? Survivor? The Importance of the Language We Use to Talk about People Who Have Experienced Sexual Violence', Guest Blog,

RSACC: Rape and Sexual Abuse Counseling Centre, available at https://www.rsacc-thecentre.org.uk/guest-blogs/victim-survivor-the-importance-of-the-language-we-use-to-talk-about-people-who-have-experienced-sexual-violence/ (accessed 10 May 2023).

53 Ibid.

54 C. Glover, 'Community Voices: What Does the Term "Survivor" Mean Exactly?' GOMAG, 2018, available at https://gomag.com/article/this-is-what-survivor-centered-healing-looks-like/ (accessed 21 September 2023).

55 R. Gupta, '"Victim" vs "Survivor": Feminism and Language', Open Democracy, 2014, available at https://www.opendemocracy.net/en/5050/victim-vs-survivor-feminism-and-language/ (accessed 21 September 2023).

56 Ibid.

57 Ibid.

58 Ibid.

59 Ibid.

60 Ibid.

61 Hepworth, 'Victim? Survivor?'

62 M. Mamdani, 'Beyond Nuremberg: The Historical Significance of the Post-Apartheid Transition in South Africa', Makerere Institute of Social Research Working Paper No. 23, 2015, available at https://misr.mak.ac.ug/sites/default/files/publications/2018/02/MISR%20WP%2023%20Mamdani.pdf.

63 M. Hourmat, 'Victim-Perpetrator Dichotomy in Transitional Justice: The Case of Post-Genocide Rwanda', *Narrative and Conflict: Explorations in Theory and Practice*, 4(1), 2016, pp. 43–67.

64 Ibid.

65 Mamdani, 'Beyond Nuremberg'.

66 Ibid.

67 Ibid.

68 K. Fox, *The Complex Combatant: Constructions of Victimhood and Perpetratorhood in Gulu District, Northern Uganda*, Independent Study Project Collection 2458, 2016, https://digitalcollections.sit.edu/isp_collection/2458 (accessed 12 October 2023).

69 See 'Situation in Uganda: *The Prosecutor v. Dominic Ongwen* ICC-02/04–01/15, Case Information Sheet, available at https://www.icc-cpi.int/sites/default/files/CaseInformationSheets/OngwenEng.pdf (accessed 2 November 2023).

70 'Situation in Uganda in the case of *The Prosecutor v. Dominic Ongwen*', Public Redacted Version of 'Corrected Version of "Defence Closing Brief", filed on 24 February 2020', 13 March 2020, available at https://www.icc-cpi.int/sites/default/files/CourtRecords/CR2020_00998.PDF (accessed 20 October 2024).

71 Ibid.

72 Ibid.

73 A. Peters, *Beyond Human Rights: The Legal Status of the Individual in International Law* (Cambridge: Cambridge University Press, 2016).

74 Ibid.

75 Ibid.

76 The author's definition includes merging of certain aspects of the definition of a 'victim' as included under the ICC's Rules of Procedure and Evidence (Rule 85) and as well as from the definition of 'survivor' as developed by Celia Williamson in conjunction with the Lucas County Human Trafficking Coalition in 2017.

77 OTP Policy on Gender Based Crimes, Crimes Involving Sexual, Reproductive and Other Gender Based Violence, December 2023, available at https://www.icc-cpi.int/sites/default/files/2023-12/2023-policy-gender-en-web.pdf (accessed 12 February 2024).

78 See UN Resolution 1325, adopted by the UN Security Council at its 4,213th meeting held on 31 October 2000, available at https://peacemaker.un.org/sites/peacemaker.un.org/files/SC_ResolutionWomenPeaceSecurity_SRES1325%282000%29%28english_0.pdf (accessed 12 February 2024). See also UN Resolution 2467, adopted by the Security Council at its 8,514th meeting held on 23 April 2019, available at https://documents.un.org/doc/undoc/gen/n19/118/28/pdf/n1911828.pdf?token=uvZ6gaJh1z5IbhaH8I&fe=true (accessed 12 February 2024).

79 See 'The Survivor-Centred Approach and Referral Pathways', in *Handbook for UN Field Missions on Preventing and Responding to Conflict-Related Sexual Violence* (New York: United Nations, 2020), pp. 35–37, available at https://www.un.org/sexualviolenceinconflict/wp-content/uploads/2020/06/2020.08-UN-CRSV-Handbook.pdf (accessed 12 February 2024).

80 Ibid.

81 Ibid.

82 W. Chang *et al.*, 'What Works to Enhance Women's Agency: Cross-cutting Lessons from Experimental and Quasi-experimental Studies', J-PAL Working Paper, 2020, p. 4.

83 Ibid., pp. 6–8.

84 USAID'S Collective Action to Reduce Gender-Based Violence (CARE-GBV) (2021), 'How to Implement a Survivor-Centered Approach in GBV Programming', December 2021, pp. 3–5, available at https://makingcents.com/wp-content/uploads/2021/01/CARE-GBV-03-Survivor-centered-v9-508c.pdf (accessed 20 October 2024).

85 Ibid.

86 Ibid.

87 Article 1, Universal Declaration of Human Rights, Proclaimed by the United Nations General Assembly in Paris on 10 December 1948, available at https://www.un.org/en/about-us/universal-declaration-of-human-rights (accessed 13 February 2024).

88 USAID, 'How to Implement a Survivor-Centered Approach in GBV Programming'.

89 See Murad Global Code of Conduct for Gathering and Using Information about Systematic and Conflict-Related Sexual Violence, 13 April (2022), available at https://www.muradcode.com/murad-code (accessed 13 February 2024).

90 Ibid.

91 Ibid.

92 Ibid.

93 Ibid.

94 M. Milam, N. Borello and J. Pooler, 'The Survivor-Centered, Trauma-Informed Approach', United States Attorney's Bulletin, 2017, pp. 39–43.

95 Ibid. See also Murad Global Code of Conduct for Gathering and Using Information about Systematic and Conflict-Related Sexual Violence, available at https://www.muradcode.com/murad-code (accessed 20 October 2024).

96 Milam *et al.,* 'The Survivor-Centered, Trauma-Informed Approach'.

97 Ibid.

98 S.N. Jumarali, N. Nnawulezi, S. Royson, C. Lippy, A.N. Rivera and T. Toopet, 'Participatory Research Engagement of Vulnerable Populations: Employing Survivor-Centered, Trauma-Informed Approaches', *Journal of Participatory Research Methods*, 2(2), 2021.

99 See *Wisconsin Adult Sexual Assault Response Team Protocol*, Wisconsin Coalition Against Sexual Assault, 2011, pp. 43–46.

100 Ibid.

101 Ibid.

102 Ibid.

103 Ibid.

104 Ibid.
105 Ibid.
106 OTP Policy on Gender Based Crimes, Crimes Involving Sexual, Reproductive and Other Gender Based Violence.
107 Ibid.
108 Ibid.
109 Ibid.
110 Ibid.
111 Ibid.
112 Ibid.

References

Baumgartner, E. (2008) 'Aspects of Victim Participation in the Proceedings of the International Criminal Court', *International Review of the Red Cross*, vol. 90, no. 870, pp. 409–440.

Cuppini, A. (2021) 'A Restorative Response to Victims in Proceedings before the International Criminal Court: Reality or Chimaera?' *International Criminal Law Review.*

Fernández de Casadevante Romani, C. (2010) 'International Law of Victims', in A. von Bogdandy and R. Wolfrum (eds), *Max Planck Yearbook of United Nations Law*, vol. 14. Leiden: Brill, pp. 219–272.

Fletcher, L. and Weinstein, H. (2017) 'Transitional Justice and the Plight of Victimhood', in C. Lawther, L. Moffett and D. Jacobs (eds), *Research Handbook on Transitional Justice.* Cheltenham: Edward Elgar, pp. 244–266.

Fox, K. (2016) 'The Complex Combatant: Constructions of Victimhood and Perpetratorhood in Gulu District, Northern Uganda', *Independent Study Project Collection*, p. 2458.

Garcia-Godos, J. and Sriram, C.L. (2013) *Transitional Justice and Peacebuilding on the Ground, Victims and Ex-combatants.* Abingdon: Routledge, p. 5.

Hourmat, M. (2016) 'Victim-Perpetrator Dichotomy in Transitional Justice: The Case of Post-Genocide Rwanda', *Narrative and Conflict: Explorations in Theory and Practice*, vol. 4, no. 1, p. 43.

Jumarali, S.N., Nnawulezi, N., Royson, S., Lippy, C., Rivera, A.N. and Toopet, T. (2021) 'Participatory Research Engagement of Vulnerable Populations: Employing Survivor-Centered, Trauma-Informed Approaches', *Journal of Participatory Research Methods*, vol. 2, no. 2.

Katirai, N. (2020) 'Retraumatized in Court', *Arizona Law Review*, vol. 62, Arizona Legal Studies Discussion Paper, no. 19–10, pp. 81–123.

Katonene, P.M. (2012) 'An Analysis of the Difficulties Related to Victim Participation before the ICC and Extraordinary Chambers in the Courts of Cambodia'. Thesis, University of the Western Cape, pp. 1–87.

Lawther, C. (2021) '"Let Me Tell You": Transitional Justice, Victimhood and Dealing with a Contested Past', *Social & Legal Studies*, vol. 30, no. 6, pp. 890–912.

Mamdani, M. (2015) 'Beyond Nuremberg: The Historical Significance of the Post-Apartheid Transition in South Africa', Makerere Institute of Social Research-Working Paper no. 23.

Mendez, J. (2016) 'Victims as Protagonists in Transitional Justice', *International Journal of Transitional Justice*, vol. 10, no. 1, March, pp. 1–5.

Moghalu, K.C. (2010) 'Prosecute or Pardon? Between Truth Commissions and War Crimes Trials', in C.L. Sriram and S. Pillay (eds), *Peace versus Justice: The*

Dilemma of Transitional Justice in Africa. Woodbridge: James Currey and Pietermaritzburg:University of KwaZulu Natal Press, p. 87.

Morgan, I. (2023) *The Road to Reconciliation? Optimising the Legitimacy and Efficacy of the International Criminal Court within the African Union and Africa*. Human Rights Research Series, vol. 102. Cambridge: Intersentia.

Orentlicher, D. (1991) 'Settling Accounts: The Duty to Prosecute Human Rights Violations of a Prior Regime', *The Yale Law Journal*, vol. 100, no. 8, pp. 2537–2615.

Rauschenbach, M. and Scalia, D. (2008) 'Victims and International Criminal Justice: A Vexed Question?' *International Review of the Red Cross*, vol. 90, no. 870, pp. 441–449.

Strang, H. (2002) *Repair and Revenge: Victims and Restorative Justice*. Oxford: Oxford University Press.

Villalba, C.S. (2011) '*Transitional Justice: Key Concepts, Processes and Challenges*', Briefing Paper, Institute for Democracy and Conflict Resolution, University of Essex Knowledge Gateway, p. 5.

Blogs Reports, Policies, Handbooks and other Web-based Documents

Chang, W.et al. (2020) 'What Works to Enhance Women's Agency: Cross-cutting Lessons from Experimental and Quasi-experimental Studies, *J-PAL Working Paper*, p. 4.

Fédération Internationale pour les droits humains (FIDH) (2021) *'Whose Court Is It?' Judicial Handbook on Victims Rights at the International Criminal Court*. Paris: FIDH in collaboration with the Ministry of Foreign Affairs of the Netherlands.

Glover, C. (2018) 'Community Voices: What Does the Term "Survivor" Mean Exactly?' *GOMAG*. Available at https://gomag.com/article/this-is-what-survivor-centered-healing-looks-like/ (accessed 21 September 2023).

Gupta, R. (2014) '"Victim" vs "Survivor": Feminism and Language', Open Democracy. Available at https://www.opendemocracy.net/en/5050/victim-vs-survivor-feminism-and-language/ (accessed 21 September 2023).

Hepworth, L.J. (n.d.) 'Victim? Survivor? The Importance of the Language We Use to Talk about People Who Have Experienced Sexual Violence', Guest Blog, Rape and Sexual Abuse Counseling Centre. Available at https://www.rsacc-thecentre.org.uk/guest-blogs/victim-survivor-the-importance-of-the-language-we-use-to-talk-about-people-who-have-experienced-sexual-violence/ (accessed 10 May 2023).

Margarrell, L. (2007) *Reparations in Theory and Practice*, Reparative Justice Series. New York: International Center for Transitional Justice, p. 2.

Milam, M., Borello, N. and Pooler, J. (2017) 'The Survivor-Centered, Trauma-Informed Approach', *United States Attorney's Bulletin*, pp. 39–43.

Murad Global Code of Conduct for Gathering and Using Information about Systematic and Conflict-Related Sexual Violence, 13 April2022. Available at https://www.muradcode.com/murad-code.

OTP Policy on Gender Based Crimes, Crimes Involving Sexual, Reproductive and Other Gender Based Violence, December2023. Available at https://www.icc-cpi.int/sites/default/files/2023-12/2023-policy-gender-en-web.pdf.

REDRESS (2019) *No Time to Wait: Realising Reparations for Victims at the International Criminal Court*. London: REDRESS, pp. 1–68.

The Redress Trust and Forensic Risk Alliance (2003) *The International Criminal Court's Trust Fund for Victims: Analysis and Options for the Development of Further Criteria for the Operation of the Trust Fund for Victims*, Discussion Document.

Uma, S. (2021) 'Victims at the Heart of International Criminal Justice', *The Wire*. Available at https://thewire.in/rights/victims-at-the-heart-of-international-criminal-justice (accessed 24 April 2023).

United Nations (2020) 'The Survivor-Centred Approach and Referral Pathways', in *Handbook for UN Field Missions on Preventing and Responding to Conflict-Related Sexual Violence*, pp. 35–37. Available at https://www.un.org/sexualviolenceinconflict/wp-content/uploads/2020/06/2020.08-UN-CRSV-Handbook.pdf (accessed 12 February 2024).

USAID (2021) 'How to Implement a Survivor-Centered Approach in GBV Programming', *in Collective Action to Reduce Gender-Based Violence*, December (Washington, DC: Development Professionals), pp. 3–5.

Wisconsin Coalition Against Sexual Assault (2011) *Wisconsin Adult Sexual Assault Response Team Protocol*, pp. 43–46.

United Nations Documentation, Resolutions and Case Law

Situation in Uganda: The Prosecutor v. Dominic Ongwen ICC-02/4–1/15.

UN Basic Guidelines on the Right to Remedy and Reparation for Victims of Gross Violations of International Human Rights Law and Serious Violations of International Humanitarian Law, adopted and proclaimed by General Assembly Resolution 60/147 of 16 December 2005.

UN Resolution 1325, adopted by the UN Security Council at its 4,213th meeting on 31 October 2000. Available at https://peacemaker.un.org/sites/peacemaker.un.org/files/SC_ResolutionWomenPeaceSecurity_SRES1325%282000%29%28english_0.pdf (accessed 12 February 2024).

UN Resolution 2467, adopted by the Security Council at its 8,514th meeting on 23 April 2019. Available at https://documents.un.org/doc/undoc/gen/n19/118/28/pdf/n1911828.pdf?token=uvZ6gaJh1z5IbhaH8I&fe=true (accessed12 February 2024).

UNHCR (2020) *Policy on a Victim-Centered Approach in UNHCR's response to Sexual Misconduct: Sexual Exploitation and Abuse and Sexual Harassment*. Available at https://www.unhcr.org/uk/media/policy-victim-centred-approach-unhcrs-response-sexual-misconduct.

United Nations Declaration of Basic Principles of Justice for Victims of Crime and Abuse of Power. Adopted 29 November 1985 by General Assembly Resolution 40/34.

Statutes

IMT Charter – Charter of the Military Tribunal

UN-ICTY Statute – Statute of the United Nations International Criminal Tribunal for the Former Yugoslavia

UN-ICTR Statute – Statute of the International Criminal Tribunal for Rwanda

SCSL Statute – Statute for the Special Court of Sierra Leone

ECCC Statute – Law on the Establishment of the Extraordinary Chambers

RS – Rome Statute of the International Criminal Court

ICC RPE – International Criminal Court Rules of Procedure and Evidence

UDHR – Universal Declaration of Human Rights

Part II

Informal and Traditional/ Customary Justice Mechanisms

4 An Assessment of the Viability of Incorporating Healing Ceremonies into Local Transitional Justice Initiatives for Addressing Violence Associated with Mass Atrocities in Africa

Michael Raila Odhiambo

Introduction

The effects of mass atrocities and similar events of extreme violence on survivors may continue long after the laying down of arms or the cessation or de-escalation of hostilities. Coming out of such events alive is often just the beginning of a long and fragile transition into peace, social stability and development. Yet, in the aftermath of such traumatic events, those left behind will often have to piece together a viable social community, not just co-existing together but truly getting along peacefully and sustainably in the new post-violence order regardless of their designation as survivors, victims or perpetrators.

If communities recovering from mass atrocities are to come together into a coherent, peaceful and prosperous whole, then they must confront the stark realities presented by the newly pacified environment. They will need to deal with physical and mental disorders wrought by the trauma of violence; rebuild broken economic infrastructures, mend shattered social institutions, including families and relationships; create new friendships, alliances and networks; decide on whether and how to integrate members of the community from all sides of the conflict; find a way to share resources and political power, and generally engage in the business of 'getting on' with their lives.

Whether and how such communities move on from the trauma and destruction of mass violence and evolve into peaceful and prosperous societies will ultimately depend on the cultural and material resources available to them to achieve such an objective. This refers to the local practice and the legitimacy and efficacy of accepted or internalized notions of justice in resolving the root causes of the conflict, and their ultimate translation into sustainable peace and development. The author recognizes that in addition there is an economic and social aspect on which sustainable peace and development are contingent, but considers it to be beyond the scope of this chapter.

Many societies in Africa have over the centuries developed their own indigenous ways of coping in the aftermath of wars and violent conflict,

DOI: 10.4324/9781003212409-7

which are built upon their own worldviews and understandings of justice as well as their historical experiences. The African Union Transitional Justice Policy (AUTJP) highlights the Mato Oput (Uganda), Gacaca (Rwanda), Magamba spirit mediums (Mozambique), Fambul Tok or 'family talk' (Sierra Leone) and the Bashingantahe (Counsel of Wise Men) in Burundi as examples of innovative local transitional justice processes in Africa.[1] It is notable that all of these traditional processes involve an element of healing rituals. For the purposes of this chapter, however, it will be sufficient to consider in some detail the Magamba spirit mediums of Mozambique,[2] as these have been widely researched and documented.

Based on documentary desktop research, this chapter therefore draws on some of these documented indigenous systems to build a case for the recognition of healing ceremonies as a viable option to be taken seriously in the practice of transitional justice. The scope of this chapter is therefore limited to the practical experience and application of these notions and is focused on defining the possible role of traditional healing ceremonies as an element of transitional justice within the framework of the newly adopted AUTJP.

This chapter is divided into five sections that are designed to develop the argument that even though traditional healing ceremonies have not been systematically used as part of transitional justice processes, they are deeply rooted in the cultural practices of many African societies and can be oriented to fit into the AUTJP framework.

The chapter starts with a brief elaboration on the concept of survivors. The second section then sets the context for healing ceremonies in Africa, locating them within the worldview of the concerned communities and reviewing data from selected examples to demonstrate their efficacy. The third section considers a specific application of healing ceremonies in the context of restorative justice and deals with some perceived shortcomings of traditional justice systems. Having established the efficacy of healing ceremonies, the fourth section sets the stage for the application of healing ceremonies in Africa by setting out a normative and legal framework based on the African Charter on Human and Peoples Rights. Finally, the chapter concludes with some observations on the way forward.

Contextualizing Survivors/Victims

This chapter recognizes the contested nature of concepts and terms related to justice in general but at the same time appreciates the depth of research undertaken by the African Union (AU) on transitional justice in particular, and takes as a point of departure the African Charter-based formulation of justice and related concepts. It therefore adopts the AU conception and definition of notions such as 'justice', 'traditional justice', 'transitional justice', 'transition', 'victims' and 'rule of law'.[3] For instance, 'victims' are herein defined as 'persons who, individually or collectively, have suffered harm, including physical or mental injury, emotional suffering, economic loss or substantial impairment of their fundamental rights, through acts or omissions that constitute gross violations of international human rights law, or serious violations of international humanitarian law'. As a legal status, this definition of 'victim' is consistent with other internationally recognized definitions.[4] In so far as far as criminal judicial processes are concerned the recognition of victimhood clearly has important implications for the individuals or groups concerned as it may generate specific rights as well as impose certain obligations on judicial institutions.[5]

The term 'victim' is also quite often used interchangeably with the term 'survivor', in such a way that whether one is referred to as a victim or a survivor is a matter of preference for the individual concerned. It is recognized that individuals may not wish to be referred to as victims so as not to be burdened by the stigma and memory of their experience, and that they may find the term survivor more empowering.[6] For example, McIntosh applies the same meaning to victims and survivors as 'people who have been harmed physically, mentally, socially, or economically in the context of mass atrocities'.[7]

In this chapter we argue that these understandings and definitions of survivors/victims are more appropriate in the context of retributive criminal procedures. When it comes to healing ceremonies and other culturally based transitional justice measures that are far removed from criminal legal institutions an expanded and more nuanced understanding of 'survivors' is called for.

This is not to diminish the importance of survivors/victims in the post-conflict situation, but simply to recognize that the legal categorizations and associated implications assume a less prominent role in communally based conceptions of mass violent behaviour compared to their more individually oriented conceptions in criminal legal processes.

In the examples from Mozambique described below, mass violence is associated with the agency of 'bad' spirits associated with angry ancestors. Fault is therefore not ascribed to individuals or groups but to the contamination of the society by evil spirits.[8] It is this contamination or spiritual impurity that leads to suffering through, for example, poor harvests, illness, bad lack, infertility and even violence. In this sense, healing ceremonies cleanse or wash away the evil spirits via whose agency mass violence is faulted. It is clear, therefore, that for the purposes of such healing, especially when it is aimed at reconciliation, the categorization of individuals as victims/survivors or perpetrators serves no discernible purpose.

It is preferable, then, to use the expression 'survivor communities' to relay an understanding of the notion of 'survivors', who may well include individuals who were agents of criminal activity during the conflict phase but who are presently part of a community. When violence is protracted we may also find individuals playing different roles at different times. For example, acts of revenge and counter-attacks may lead individuals to assume the role of victim in one moment and that of perpetrator the next, and vice versa.

Thus, according to Huyse and Salter, many 'informal systems tend to draw more on ritual elements and to emphasize the community dimension of criminal behavior over individual accountability'.[9] They see a clear benefit to such processes especially in complicated legal situations where things are not clearly defined in black and white.

> [T]the 'guilty', 'not guilty', 'victim', 'perpetrator' dichotomies can be misleading and even harmful. Violent conflicts characterised by moral 'grey zones', in which different forms of guilt and innocence are mixed, are complicated territory for criminal law and render the delivery of clear verdicts a difficult exercise.[10], [11]

The fluid nature of these identities and the complexity of cases presented by situations of mass violence render their adjudication by criminal judicial institutions difficult, to say the least. Giving the very appropriate example of Sierra Leonian and Ugandan child soldiers who have been forcibly recruited and forced to commit criminal acts, Baines describes such situations as ones of 'shifting 'perpetrator-victim' identities'.[12] Thus, for traditional methods of transitional justice with a focus on the communal as opposed to the individual dimension of criminal behaviour it would be a difficult and unnecessary effort to attempt to pin down these identities. Therefore, there is a preference to label these specific legal categories of individuals or groups 'survivor communities' rather than as survivors/victims.

The African Experience of Healing Ceremonies in Post-Conflict Peace

The context of healing ceremonies described here involves a belief in the agency of spirits in the causal chain of events in the physical realm so that violence and the ensuing trauma can be explained and resolved through ritual, thereby allowing individuals and societies to confront their particular histories of violence. These rituals then become the means to engage with and intervene in the actions of the spirits in order to restore normalcy. They also provide space to expunge the traumatic events and find a resolution to lingering problems. The ceremonies include purification, cleansing, homecoming, welcoming, reconciliation and other similarly named rituals.

Healing ceremonies, as a cultural practice applied to the resolution of conflict, will necessarily be based upon particular understandings of justice expressed in the values, beliefs and customary practices of societies emerging from mass violence. Anyone who has experienced mass violence will agree that violence, or even the spectre of it, is deeply traumatizing. It is suggested, therefore, that in the wake of such violence, affected societies and individuals need to confront the trauma in order to heal and move on. The argument that is made is that cultural understandings and conceptualizations of trauma and its causes can inform highly effective treatments which can, with the requisite knowledge and skill, be applied to heal societies and possibly open their path to justice, accountability and reconciliation.[13]

It is suggested that because every society's experience of violence and mass atrocity is unique to their individual circumstances, there cannot be a single prescription on how they react to the aftermath of such events. Healing ceremonies are therefore necessarily local and specific to the community within whose cultural orbit they are relevant and applicable, and there can be no generalization as to their practice and efficacy. What is fairly common throughout Africa, though, is the worldview that life transcends the physical reality as we know it, and that spirits are both real and active in our lives. Bojuwoye captures this aptly:

> The traditional African worldview is premised on the interrelationship between the living and the non-living, natural and supernatural elements and the material and the immaterial. The emphasis on spiritual phenomena is also another important aspect of this worldview, particularly the belief that deceased individuals transform into invisible ancestral spirits and involve themselves in all aspects of life, including assisting individuals in obtaining good fortune, assisting with interpersonal relationships, and promoting good health and preventing illness.[14]

According to Green and Honwana, anthropological research in Mozambique and Angola has shown that certain communities in these countries have a worldview and understanding of life that includes an active belief in the potent agency of the spirits of the dead.[15] They directly relate psychological trauma resulting from war to the action of the spirits of the dead angry at the injustice and mistreatment experienced at the hands of their living killers and next-of-kin. Such spirits are able to come back to haunt the living, seeking justice. Spirits not given a proper send-off into the world of the ancestors are considered to be so angry that they could harm their killers or even passers-by in the areas haunted by them.[16]

Green and Honwana use the concept of 'social pollution'[17] to describe the contamination of a social system through acts or omissions inconsistent with accepted cultural and behavioural norms. For example, acceptable norms regulating death protocols within communities may demand that the dead are accorded a certain level of decency performed through established rituals in the way that corpses are handled and disposed of in the period following death. Such rituals would ensure that the spirits of the dead are properly positioned in the world of the ancestors. A breach or non-observance of these protocols may thus attract the wrath of the departed. Locals therefore fear that such spirits of the dead pose a danger not only to their killers but also to people in the vicinity of the scenes of death. Consequently, social pollution may arise from the proximity with death and bloodshed brought about by war. In this situation, killers or witnesses to killings as well as next-of-kin who abandon corpses could pollute or contaminate the social body and therefore cleansing and purification rituals will be necessary to allow them to be reintegrated in the community.

Healing ceremonies are thus performed with the aim of providing physical and psychosocial healing to affected individuals and societies on the path towards rehabilitation and reintegration, reconciliation, forgiveness and eventually peace and development. For normalcy to be restored and for the affected communities to have a chance of lasting peace and prosperity both the society and the individuals in it must undergo a process of healing to deal with the trauma and the physical, psychological and moral dislocation caused by mass violence and conflict. Without healing such societies remain troubled by unresolved issues and will struggle to make the transition to peace and stability, and therefore there is an imperative element to these healing ceremonies that would make them a particularly useful component of an indigenous approach to transitional justice.

To recognize the importance of healing ceremonies, therefore, is to recognize the plurality of ways to conceive, internalize and experience justice. It is to accept and respect the fact that while there may be human agents responsible for violence, there are people who believe that the agency of spiritual forces is also implicated, and their vision of justice would not be complete without addressing the spiritual dimension. In the quest for peace and stability after mass atrocities, therefore, where such ceremonies are functional and able to achieve a peaceful transition, they should be considered not merely as an afterthought, but as a key component to which other transitional and secular justice processes may be added. The use of healing ceremonies in the context of transitional justice, however, can only be justified if their efficacy in establishing post-conflict rehabilitation can be demonstrated. In the sections that follow we examine several documented applications of healing ceremonies in the context of the reconciliation of perpetrators with victims, as well as the rehabilitation and reintegration of survivors into the community.

Efficacy of Healing Ceremonies among Survivors: Some Examples

Several studies on healing ceremonies in Africa point to their efficacy in ensuring post-conflict harmony. For example, Babatunde has examined the efficacy of traditional practices in the rehabilitation of victims of torture in the oil-rich Niger Delta region of Nigeria.[18] He describes and analyses the conflict over oil resources that saw militant youth and government security agents commit heinous acts of extreme violence, including murder, rape and the maiming and kidnapping of the civilian population. Healing ceremonies and reconciliatory processes carried out by local communities themselves were successfully applied to reconcile the victims and perpetrators. According to Babatunde,

> [t]raditional methods of purification and healing carried out by customary healers, priests and other spiritual authorities are of utmost importance for the mental and spiritual rehabilitation of victims and

> perpetrators. The mental healing of victims, who were deeply traumatized by the experiences of torture during violent conflict, is an aspect of peace-building that is at least as important as material reconstruction … healing and reconciliation rituals have been an essential component of rehabilitation processes in many local communities in the Niger Delta region. It calls for national governments, and regional and international institutions to recognize the cultural importance of such rituals and their potential relevance and significance for victims of torture.[19]

While the rituals were performed at the behest of the local communities and not as part of an officially sanctioned judicial process, many elements of transitional justice can already be discerned that could be imported into a national transitional justice policy. For example, the rituals had as a main objective the reconciliation of the victims and perpetrators and their reintegration into society; prior mutual consent by both the victims and perpetrators to submit to the reconciliation process and healing rituals was always obtained; narration of the atrocities through story telling by the victims facilitated the admission of guilt and the seeking of forgiveness by the perpetrators; compensation was paid to the victims and ritual cleansing to protect the community was performed; and ties to a common ancestry and strong values of kinship and community were instrumental to the acceptance and legitimacy of the whole process.

In another study carried out in the context of disarmament, demobilization and reintegration programmes, Babatunde examines the crucial role and effectiveness of traditional cultural practices within the reintegration of child soldiers in post-conflict Liberia and Burundi.[20] He argues that traditional cultural practices are integral to the success of reintegration of child soldiers in post-conflict African states. Babatunde's study prescribes the prioritization of the psychosocial aspects of traditional reconciliation rituals and cleansing ceremonies given that not only are they rooted in traditional cultural practices, but they fulfil the need for rehabilitation programmes that target severely psychologically traumatized child solders to be therapeutic. Such rituals and ceremonies are therefore well placed to complement interventions by secular state institutions and international organizations whose goal is the reintegration of child soldiers. They can also be useful for retributive justice and truth telling in the aftermath of civil war and genocide.[21]

The use of child soldiers in violent conflicts and wars is a common feature in Africa, and child soldiers have been used to commit atrocious and horrifying acts of war in Liberia, Sierra Leone, Burundi, Uganda, the Central African Republic and elsewhere. Children can be coerced into being enlisted as soldiers in wars. Not only are such child soldiers deprived of the protections of human rights such as health, education and normal development opportunities, but they suffer terrible injustices including physical and emotional violence such as rape, sexual slavery, prostitution and forced labour.[22]

The reintegration of child soldiers, who, due to the conditions of war or mass violence, are likely to be detached, desensitized, undisciplined, disposed to violence, lacking in social skills and possibly suffering from depression, anxiety and other mental and psychological disorders, would be virtually impossible without healing. It is therefore clear that child soldiers, whose status as criminal perpetrators is legally problematic[23] but whose victimhood is arguably demonstrable,[24] need personal healing to deal with the physical and mental disorders arising from violent situations, as well as psychosocial healing as part of a society that on the one hand violated their innocence and right to a peaceful existence while on the other endured the violent disorder meted out by the child soldiers as part of warring factions. Such healing, if it is to be effective and legitimate, must be performed within the cultural milieux of the child soldiers by recognized institutions of the societies to which they belong.

Such rituals are necessary because they can help to generate acceptance of the child soldiers by their receiving communities, whose acceptance is crucial for resolving mental health issues such as post-traumatic stress disorder (PTSD), anxiety and depression. Community-based approaches in this context have been found to lessen distrust, increase tolerance and facilitate reconciliation.[25] On the other hand, the re-establishment of trust and acceptance in the community can be achieved with community mediation and forgiveness or cleansing rituals. Such a participatory approach allows the community to confront impunity and feel included in decisions about accepting returning child soldiers.[26]

The importance of traditional rituals or healing ceremonies is not only due to their positive individual and societal therapeutic value, but also to the inadequacy of Western therapy in dealing with psychological trauma in traditional African settings. Green and Honwana have questioned the appropriateness and effectiveness of Western psychotherapeutic techniques for PTSD, originally developed to treat American veterans of the Vietnam War, in treating child soldiers in Africa.[27]

They raise issue with therapeutic techniques revolving around the individual patient. These ignore relevant conceptions of disease, trauma and healing in Mozambique where locals believe that 'ancestral and malevolent spiritual forces have a role to play in causing and healing of affliction'. These Western techniques that focus on the individual not only ignore the worldview and cultural orientation of the patient but also exclude the active participation of family and community in the healing process.

Green and Honwana also point to evidence from across Africa showing the efficacy of indigenous therapy in treating mental or psychiatric disorders, highlighting comparative studies that have shown that 'virtually all psychotherapies do the patient some good and all are potentially effective when embedded within social and cultural specificities'.[28] They find that psychotherapy performed by indigenous African healers on patients sharing a common African culture may be as effective as that performed by Western specialists.

Similarly, Stark has studied the effects of traditional cleansing ceremonies (purification rituals) on girl soldiers who survived rape in Sierra Leone and found that cleansing ceremonies contributed to their improved psychosocial health and facilitated reintegration.[29] Stark attributes this positive outcome to the fact that the ceremonies are a symbolic gesture of reconciliation with designated roles for both the community and the girls, to which all the parties concerned expressed mutual consent. Furthermore, the rituals facilitated a 'spiritual transformation' of the girls, allowing them to leave behind negative perceptions associated with the contamination of war and forge a new path as fully rehabilitated and accepted members of society.[30]

Healing Ceremonies and Restorative Justice

The abovementioned examples show to that to a large extent traditional healing ceremonies have been used to positive effect in the reintegration and reconciliation of victims/survivors and perpetrators. They can therefore be put to good and effective use, especially as part of a holistic strategy to deal with post-conflict trauma. However, their potential as elements of a deliberately crafted transitional justice policy, while clearly evident-based on the data, is still rather hypothetical. To really bring home the efficacy of healing rituals within the proper context of transitional justice, a brief consideration of the Magamba spirits phenomenon in Mozambique is useful.

Igreja and Dias-Lambranca describe the role of Magamba spirits in the context of restorative justice in the post-war Gorongosa region of central Mozambique .[31] The Mozambican war was one of the bloodiest and longest in the recent history of conflict in Africa. The signing of a peace agreement between the government and rebel forces in 1992 marked the end of the civil war, and the beginning of a journey towards a hopefully peaceful, prosperous and stable Mozambique. Tasked with managing the transition from war to peace, however, the powers that be tried to implement their own vision of justice which attempted a blanket erasure of the past based on the perhaps mistaken belief that past traumas and injustices were best forgotten in order to facilitate national reconciliation. They chose to focus instead on other socioeconomic and political aspects aimed at establishing a post-conflict democratic and market-based economy.

With no particular strategy for restorative justice post-civil war adopted by the authorities, the war survivors in Gorongosa are credited with proactively resorting to indigenous cultural resources to repair their broken individual and collective lives. The institution of the Magamba spirits provided a credible path to healing and rehabilitating a community torn apart by decades of bloody war and also facilitated peace and reconciliation.

Magamba refer to the spirits of dead soldiers who return to the land of the living to exact justice for perceived wrongs suffered at the hands of the living during their transition from life to death and in the afterlife. Magamba spirits operate by possessing their targets and causing great affliction and suffering, and it is the process of healing from these afflictions performed by recognized Magamba healers that provides the space to engage with the violent legacy of the past, acknowledge wrongdoing, seek forgiveness and attain both individual and collective freedom from trauma.

Gorongosa happened to be the epicentre of the civil war and to ignore its violent past in a policy of 'forget and move on' would be to turn a collective blind eye to the numerous deaths that occurred in this place. It would trivialize the suffering and humiliation experienced by civilian victims who died under fire from the air force of the Frente de Libertação de Moçambique, (FRELIMO – Mozambique Liberation Front); it would erase from collective memory the suffering of the women and children subjected to forced labour and sexual slavery, as well as the humiliation, torture, murder and forced separation meted out to families by the cruel Gandira system of the Resistência Nacional Moçambicana (RENAMO – Mozambican National Resistance). It would also be to ignore the complete devastation occasioned by the extreme acts of violence that destroyed the social fabric that had held the community together. The agency of the Magamba spirits ensured that the community would never forget its violent past but would instead confront it and heal itself through rehabilitation. As the community, through the institution of the Magamba spirits was able to remember, the emergence of feelings of revenge and reignition of violent episodes to settle wartime scores among community and family members was reported to be largely absent in the post-civil war Gorongosa.

Igreja and Dias-Lambranca also analyse the ethnographic significance of the Magamba spirits and their utility as a vehicle for restorative justice: they enable the community (comprising of both the living and the dead) to be accountable for the shameful acts committed during the war; they provide a possibility to channel in a positive way the negative feelings and bad memories carried over from the war; they provide a safe space for the community to confront its past and transform its legacy of the war; they provide a space for the spirits to safely vent their anger about acts committed during the war; they provide restorative justice by resolving lingering issues and allowing the survivors to reconcile and continue their life with dignity and social stability.[32]

The institution of the Magamba spirits demonstrates the potential of healing ceremonies as a vehicle for transitional justice. One can only imagine how much more effective the efforts of the Mozambican authorities would have been in establishing post-civil war peace and stability had they worked with the community by recognizing and incorporating their efforts in a coordinated transitional justice policy.

Perceived Shortcomings of Healing Ceremonies

No system of justice is perfect but what is of crucial importance is whether any perceived shortcomings could be cured or repaired without harming the core value of the system. Several perceived shortcomings have been raised with regard to traditional justice systems in general. These include the possibility of perpetuation of oppressive and unequal power relations inherent in patriarchal systems and gender inequality.

Stark, for instance, questions whether strengthening traditional systems such as cleansing ceremonies might have the unintended consequence of also strengthening harmful traditional practices such as female circumcision.[33] This is ostensibly because the recognition of healing ceremonies empowers the healers who perform them and because such healers also perform female initiation rites such as circumcision then their raised profile in the community can encourage the practice of harmful traditional practices.

Similarly, Igreja and Dias-Lambranca also caution that the institution of the Magamba spirits, despite its positive values, also has a gender bias.[34] Seemingly, unlike male soldiers killed in the war who are able to return as spirits to claim justice, female soldiers who suffered the same fate are unable to do the same.[35] Consequently, the institution of the Magamba spirits is entrenched in a structurally gender-biased system that helps to reinforce patriarchal power, and this is problematic because it goes against the country's commitment to create an equal society.

Now, the abovementioned shortcomings are important but must be taken in their proper context, not forgetting that fundamentally transitional justice does not mean justice as usual. It often involves political compromise and a recalibration of priorities, and sometimes it is important to first secure the right to life itself, such that the rehabilitation of a stable and viable community should be given priority.

Gender relations in any particular community represent a manifestation of the power relations within that community. An unequal power structure that favours men at the expense of women and other vulnerable categories of society is clearly undesirable. In order not to reproduce such unequal power dynamics, there is a need to understand how power is constructed, distributed and contested within a particular society. The ultimate aim should be to create viable communities that are able to resolve inequalities within their systems through internal contestations of power, and here Williams' model of dialogic democracy is instructive.[36]

According to Williams, effective change can be driven by promoting or empowering the internal voices that challenge the dominant representations of unequal power relations within a given society. Therefore, interventions should focus on empowering challenge within the internal dialogue of cultural communities so that they can trigger change within their own local and national systems. This can be done, for example, through awareness raising and civic education to build the capacity of women in shaping the gender relations to which they are subject. Supporting and empowering the agency of women to assert their own equality through employing effective tools to create change will result in outcomes that enjoy legitimacy and ownership within the target communities.[37]

In the context of healing ceremonies and the risk of perpetuating unequal power relations, priority should first be given to creating a viable society (through healing), and then on empowering women to drive change internally towards equality. In this way patriarchy can be addressed without the imposition of paternalistic interventions – good intentions notwithstanding.

With regard to the Magamba spirits, an overly legalistic view of gender equality should not blind us to the overall utility of the institution. Gender equality is important but to attempt to view elements of the spiritual domain in the legal terms that regulate physical life would be futile for the simple reason that the supernatural spiritual domain is by definition not subservient to the physical and operates beyond the secular laws of physical human beings. Furthermore, the collective logic of the Magamba institution does not easily lend itself to analysis on the basis of gender. Having said that, and as Igreja and Dias-Lambranca themselves recommend, addressing the gender bias in the Magamba institution will require an expert and holistic intervention that is aimed at giving voice to the excluded women, while also addressing other aspects of their social economic status so that they are better able to respond to their current predicament.

It will be apparent from the framework of the new AUPTJ that these shortcomings are not fatal to an orderly implementation of a well-thought-out transitional justice policy that includes traditional healing practices. With appropriate modifications, checks and balances can be included to make such ceremonies feasible.

The AUTJP recommends certain measures which could act as benchmarks and standards for successful African traditional justice mechanisms, including

> the use of functioning local reconciliation mechanisms among the various sectors of the community; institutional and legal reforms that recognize alternative and traditional dispute resolution mechanisms in matters of accountability and reconciliation; and provision of technical and political support to local communities and traditional leaders for adapting and using their traditional justice mechanisms for addressing their transitional justice needs.[38]

The Normative and Legal Basis for Healing Ceremonies in Africa

In the sections above we have established the efficacy and potential of healing ceremonies for individual and collective trauma as well as in a transitional justice setting. We have also addressed some potential shortcomings of healing ceremonies. We now proceed to consider the normative and legal basis that would set the stage for their application as part of a coordinated transitional justice policy.

The history of mass violence in Africa shows that a justice process with a relentless and narrow focus on tackling impunity through judicial retribution and punishment of offenders and perpetrators of mass violence events does not necessarily equate to post-conflict peace and justice, and many states emerging from such events are increasingly recognizing and applying transitional justice principles in seeking to resolve the underlying root causes of such conflicts and to create lasting peace and justice.

The AU defines transitional justice as

> the judicial and non-judicial measures that transitional societies adopt for advancing rehabilitation and reparations of victims, holding perpetrators of violence accountable, restoring social harmony and national cohesion, and transforming institutions, policies and processes aimed at achieving a just political and socioeconomic system, having particular regard to the gendered and generational burden of violence. Such a transformative conception of transitional justice allows and calls for combining contextually relevant criminal justice processes and restorative and redistributive as well as structural justice approaches.[39]

This formulation of transitional justice by the AU, considered in the light of the African Charter, is indicative of the norms underpinning traditional justice mechanisms in Africa generally. Compared to other regional international human rights instruments, the African Charter is unique in its orientation towards family, community and group rights, reflecting the value placed by Africans on culture and tradition (Articles 27, 29). The drafters of the African Charter clearly saw rights and duties, on the one hand, and individuals and people on the other, as not only complementing each other in the realization of human rights for all, but also consistent with their adherence to the declarations, conventions and other instruments adopted by other treaty bodies (Article 18). They saw virtue in their historical tradition and the values of African civilization which in their view should inspire and characterize their reflection on the concept of human and peoples' rights (preamble).

This community-centric construction of the African Charter makes it particularly amenable to the incorporation of African traditional justice methods in transitional justice processes. As opposed to retributive forms of justice based on the individual, an African Charter based the formulation of transitional justice gravitates towards reconciliation, participation, dialogue and restitution. While individual rights and the violation of such rights are still considered important, so too are group dynamics evident in the mobilization of violence on the basis of ethno-cultural, religious or regional collective identities, for example.[40]

From a legal point of view, the African Charter and several other legal instruments in Africa support the application of transitional justice processes. These include the Maputo Protocol, the African Children's Charter, the African Charter on Democracy, Elections and Governance and the AU Convention for the Protection and Assistance of Internally Displaced

Persons in Africa. These instruments, taken together, provide a legal basis as well as a comprehensive scope sufficient to address conceivable violations as well as multiple issues and interests of concern to the formulation and implementation of a functional transitional justice policy by any state party.

Each of these instruments articulates specific rights and obligations related to transitional justice, and looking at the African Charter, for instance, one finds the legal basis for the application of healing ceremonies within transitional justice processes in the right to cultural life (Article 17 (2)), the right to development (Article 22), and on the duty to preserve African cultural values (Article 29 (7).

Within the African normative and legal framework, therefore, transitional justice processes in general and traditional healing ceremonies in particular have an prominent place. The AUTJP recognizes this important role and recommends that they be adapted and used alongside other formal mechanisms to address justice, peace, accountability, social cohesion, reconciliation and healing.[41]

States parties are therefore called upon to

1 support and respect community-based accountability mechanisms that seek to foster integration and reconciliation;
2 promote communal dispute settlement institutions at appropriate levels for relevant cases, provided that a person shall not be compelled to undergo any harmful traditional ritual;
3 explore alternative and non-formal dispute resolution mechanisms where necessary;
4 integrate generic African practices into international norms and standards that would enhance international commitment to end impunity and promote peace, justice and reconciliation; and
5 recognize the contribution of positive traditional practices and customary norms in Africa that have proven to be useful complements to criminal prosecutions for certain categories of crimes.[42]

Conclusion

Within the African Union's formulation of transitional justice articulated in its Transitional Justice Policy, is the idea of incorporating healing ceremonies into local transitional justice initiatives for addressing violence associated with mass atrocities in Africa viable?

It is the author's hope that the argument developed in this chapter point to an answer in the affirmative. Given the African experience of mass violence, the trauma associated with it and the innovative solutions described above, traditional healing ceremonies certainly have a place in modern transitional justice practice in Africa. This chapter has shown that for those communities that believe in the agency of ancestral spirits, healing ceremonies that incorporate this worldview are effective in healing both individual and communal trauma. They have been used effectively to reintegrate former child soldiers into their communities, and they have successfully reconciled former perpetrators with their victims. It was shown that there exists both a moral and legal basis as well as a well-thought-out toolkit based on the AUTJP to aid counties in transition implement a transitional justice policy involving healing ceremonies. It was also demonstrated that their perceived shortcomings are not fatal to such a project and can be addressed using inclusive and participative methodologies.

Despite their proven usefulness and application in several societies in Africa, traditional justice mechanisms in general and healing ceremonies in particular do not enjoy universal acceptance internationally. This is understandable, as belief in the agency of spiritual forces in the commission of crime is not universal, and the communal ascription of fault that accompanies such a belief goes against the logical grain of the legal and normative principles underpinning contemporary legal thought and practice.[43] It is therefore anticipated that there will not be a sudden uptake of healing ceremonies as part of transitional justice practices in Africa.

The acceptance and recognition of traditional healing ceremonies as a legitimate and authoritative part of a transitional justice will only happen if African states assert their cultural knowledge and wisdom by applying their own time-tested methods to contemporary exigencies of transitional justice. As we have seen in the foregoing sections, traditional communities have a moral and legal right which their states have an obligation to uphold on the basis of autonomy and equality in dignity and rights as laid down in the Universal Declaration of Human Rights and every major international human rights instrument since.

There must be a willingness on the part of the mainstream legal and international community to accept and respect traditional communities as they are, within their proper cultural constructs, practising their cultural and traditional beliefs while retaining their identity as legitimate members of the global human community. Eventually this boils down to respecting the worldviews of others, even when they do not fit into our own cosmological construction of the world we live in and share. We must come to terms with the fact that there is no monopoly of thought and belief, and when society is broken by violence and mass atrocities we must heal it the best way we know how.

Notes

1 African Union, *Transitional Justice Policy* (Addis Ababa: African Union, 2019), available at https://au.int/sites/default/files/documents/36541-doc-au_tj_policy_eng_web.pdf (accessed 25 October 2024).

2 The focus on Mozambique is not to suggest that the rituals do not exist elsewhere. We simply intend to demonstrate, by taking advantage of existing documentation, the efficacy of healing ceremonies within the context of a community

that has experienced long periods of mass violence and one that has a particular cosmology and outlook of life that views suffering in general and trauma in particular through a communal lens.

3 African Union, *Transitional Justice Policy*, ss 16–22, pp. 3–4.

4 A similar wording is found for example in the United Nations Basic Principles on the Right to a Remedy and Reparation for Victims of Gross Violations of Human Rights and Serious Violations of International Humanitarian Law (Basic Principles).

5 For instance, reparations for victims will only be available to those designated as such. The International Criminal Court defines in its statute certain rights for victims, such as the right to protection from threat, intimidation, coercion and duress; the right to participation in proceedings; and the right to reparations.

6 So-called survivor-centred approaches find it empowering to respect the choice of individuals or groups in defining both their status and their condition as they are best informed about what happened to them. See, for example, OECD, *Eliminating Gender-based Violence: Governance and Survivor/Victim-centred Approaches* (Paris: OECD Publishing, 2021), available at https://doi.org/10.1787/42121347-en.

7 S. McIntosh, *Pursuing Justice for Mass Atrocities: A Handbook for Victim Groups* (Washington, DC: United States Holocaust Memorial Museum, 2021), p. xii.

8 P. Gastrow, *Bargaining for Peace: South Africa and the National Peace Accord* (Cambridge: Cambridge University Press, 1995).

9 L. Huyse and M. Salter, 'Introduction: Tradition-Based Approaches in Peacemaking, Transitional Justice and Reconciliation Policies', in L. Huyse and M. Salter (eds), *Traditional Justice and Reconciliation after Violent Conflict: Learning from African Experiences, International Institute for Democracy and Electoral Assistance* (Stockholm: International IDEA, 2008).

10 R. Shaw, L. Waldorf with P. Hazan, *Localizing Transitional Justice: Interventions and Priorities after Mass Violence* (Stanford, CA: Stanford University Press, 2010).

11 A. Hinton (ed.) *Transitional Justice: Global Mechanisms and Local Realities After Genocide and Mass Violence* (New Jersey: Rutgers University Press, 2011).

12 E. Baines, 'Complex Political Perpetrators: Reflections on Dominic Ongwen', *Journal of Modern African Studies*, 47, 2009, pp. 163–191.

13 In the AU's conceptualization, in situations of mass atrocity, justice, accountability, reconciliation and healing are interlinked and interdependent and must be looked at broadly. See, for example, African Union, *Report of the African Union High-Level Panel on Darfur (AUPD)* (Abuja: African Union, 2009), ss 199, p. 47.

14 O. Bojuwoye, 'Traditional Healing Practices in Southern Africa: Ancestral Spirits, Ritual Ceremonies, and Holistic Healing', in R. Moodley and W. West (eds), *Integrating Traditional Healing Practices into Counselling & Psychotherapy* (Thousand Oaks, CA: Sage Publications, 2005), p. 55.

15 E.C. Green and A. Honwana, 'Indigenous Healing of War-Affected Children in Africa', *High Plains Applied Anthropologist*, 21(1), spring 2001, p. 94.

16 Ibid.; see also V. Igreja and B. Dias-Lambranca, 'Restorative Justice and the Role of Magamba Spirits in Post-civil War Gorongosa, Central Mozambique', in L. Huyse and M. Salter (eds), *Traditional Justice and Reconciliation after Violent Conflict: Learning from African Experiences* (Stockholm: International Institute for Democracy and Electoral Assistance, 2008).

17 Green and Honwana, 'Indigenous Healing of War-Affected Children in Africa', p. 95.

18 A.O. Babatunde, The Efficacy of Traditional Cultural Practices in the Rehabilitation of Victims of Torture in Nigeria's Niger Delta', *Torture*, 28(3), 2018, available at https://doi.org/10.7146/torture.v28i3.111184.

19 Ibid., p. 59.

20 A.O. Babatunde, 'Harnessing Traditional Practices for Use in the Reintegration of Child Soldiers in Africa: Examples from Liberia and Burundi', *Intervention*, 12(3), 2014, pp. 379–392.

21 Ibid., p. 388.

22 G. Machel, 'International Conference on War Affected Children: The Impact of Armed Conflict on Children. A Critical Review of Progress Made and Obstacles Encountered in Increasing Protection for War-Affected Children', Winnipeg, Canada, 2000; S. Stavrou and R. Stewart, *The Reintegration of Child Soldiers and Abducted Children: A Case Study of Palaro and Pabbo Gulu District, Northern Uganda* (Pretoria: Institute for Security Studies, 2000).

23 For example, is a child below the age of criminal liability who shoots and kills guilty? Does the fact that a child soldier is forcibly recruited make them a victim when they commit atrocities to which they have become hardened? These are complicated legal questions.

24 It is arguable that a child enlisted to fight and thereby forced to endure violent and terrible encounters, even when they pull the trigger, is a victim of society's failure to accord them the conditions for a normal childhood with its attendant rights.

25 C. Bragg, 'Challenges to Policy and Practice in the Disarmament, Demobilisation, Reintegration and Rehabilitation of Youth Combatants in Liberia', Sussex Migration Working Paper no. 29 (Brighton: University of Sussex Centre for Migration Research, 2006), T.S. Betancourt, I.I. Borisova, T.P. Williams, R.T. Brennan, T.H. Whitfeld, M. de la Soudiere, J. Williamson and S.E. Gilman, 'Sierra Leone's Former Child Soldiers: A Follow-up Study of Psychosocial Adjustment and Community Reintegration', *Child Development*, 81(4), 2010, pp. 1077–1095.

26 G. Maina, 'An Analytical Evaluation of the Reintegration Process of Formerly Abducted Children in Northern Uganda and the Role of the Various Actors', *Journal of Peace, Conflict and Development*, 14, 2009.

27 Green and Honwana, 'Indigenous Healing of War-Affected Children in Africa'.

28 Ibid.

29 L. Stark, 'Cleansing the Wounds of War: An Examination of Traditional Healing, Psychosocial Health and Reintegration in Sierra Leone', *Intervention*, 4(3), 2006, pp. 206–218.

30 Ibid.

31 Igreja and Dias-Lambranca, 'Restorative Justice and the Role of Magamba Spirits in Post-civil War Gorongosa, Central Mozambique'.

32 Ibid., p. 80.

33 Stark, 'Cleansing the Wounds of War', pp. 206–218.

34 Igreja and Dias-Lambranca, 'Restorative Justice and the Role of Magamba Spirits'.

35 We do not understand why this is so, but the inherent logic in this practice cannot be sufficiently analysed outside the confines of the spiritual worldview of the society concerned. For example, Tim Allen and Anna Macdonald's expression on the same point that '[i]n Mozambique only the spirits of men killed during the civil war are allowed to return to the realm of the living to claim justice' seemingly misallocates the agency of the spirits to the living: the Magamba spirits do not wait for permission in order to act. See Allen and Macdonald, 'Post-Conflict Traditional Justice', p. 13.

36 S.H. Williams, 'Democracy, Gender Equality, and Customary Law: Constitutionalizing Internal Cultural Disruption', *Indiana Journal of Global Legal Studies*, 18(1), 2011, pp. 65–85.

37 Ibid., p. 65.

38 African Union, *Transitional Justice Policy*, ss 58, p. 12.

39 AUTJP, cited in African Commission on Human and Peoples' Rights (ACPHR), *Study on Transitional Justice and Human and Peoples' Rights in Africa* (Banjul: ACPHR, 2019), ss 63, p. 18, available at https://achpr.au.int/sites/default/files/files/2020-11/achprtransitionaljusticeeng.pdf.
40 Ibid., ss 201, p. 57.
41 Ibid., ss 56, p. 16.
42 Ibid., ss 57, p. 16.
43 For instance, communal conceptions of responsibility for crime are completely alien to the better-known legal construction of criminal conduct that requires *mens* and *actus rea* in the legal formulation of crime.

References

African Union (2009) *Report of the African Union High Level Panel on Darfur (AUPD)*. Abuja: African Union.

African Union (2019) *Transitional Justice Policy.* Addis Ababa: African Union. Available at https://au.int/sites/default/files/documents/36541-doc-au_tj_policy_eng_web.pdf.

Babatunde, A.O. (2014) 'Harnessing Traditional Practices for Use in the Reintegration of Child Soldiers in Africa: Examples from Liberia and Burundi', *Intervention*, vol. 12, no. 3, pp. 379–392.

Babatunde, A.O. (2018) 'The Efficacy of Traditional Cultural Practices in the Rehabilitation of Victims of Torture in Nigeria's Niger Delta', *Torture*, vol. 28, no 3. Available at https://doi.org/10.7146/torture.v28i3.111184.

African Commission on Human and Peoples' Rights (ACPHR) (2019) *Study on Transitional Justice and Human and Peoples' Rights in Africa.* Banjul: ACPHR. Available at http://www.un.org/en/peacebuilding/pdf/doc_wgll/justice_times_transition/26_02_2008_concept_note.pdf.

Allen, T. and Macdonald, A. (2013) 'Post-Conflict Traditional Justice: A Critical Overview', Justice and Security Research Programme, Paper 3.

Baines, E. (2009) 'Complex Political Perpetrators: Reflections on Dominic Ongwen', *Journal of Modern African Studies*, vol. 47.

Betancourt, T.S., Borisova, I.I., Williams, T.P., Brennan, R.T., Whitfeld, T.H., de la Soudiere, M., Williamson, J. and Gilman, S.E. (2010) 'Sierra Leone's Former Child Soldiers: A Follow-up Study of Psychosocial Adjustment and Community Reintegration', *Child Development*, vol. 81, no. 4, pp. 1077–1095.

Bojuwoye, O. (2005) 'Traditional Healing Practices in Southern Africa: Ancestral Spirits, Ritual Ceremonies, and Holistic Healing', in R. Moodley and W. West (eds), *Integrating Traditional Healing Practices into Counselling & Psychotherapy.* Thousand Oaks, CA: SAGE, pp. 61–72.

Bragg, C. (2006) 'Challenges to Policy and Practice in the Disarmament, Demobilisation, Reintegration and Rehabilitation of Youth Combatants in Liberia', Sussex Migration Working Paper no. 29. Brighton: University of Sussex Centre for Migration Research.

Gastrow, P. (1995) *Bargaining for Peace: South Africa and the National Peace Accord.* Cambridge: Cambridge University Press.

Green, E.C. and Honwana, A. (2001) 'Indigenous Healing of War-Affected Children in Africa', *High Plains Applied Anthropologist*, vol. 21, no. 1, spring.

Hinton, A. (ed.) (2011) *Transitional Justice: Global Mechanisms and Local Realities After Genocide and Mass Violence.* New Jersey: Rutgers University Press.

Huyse, L. and Salter, M. (2008) 'Introduction: Tradition-Based Approaches in Peace-making, Transitional Justice and Reconciliation Policies', in L. Huyse and M. Salter (eds), *Traditional Justice and Reconciliation after Violent Conflict: Learning from African Experiences, International Institute for Democracy and Electoral Assistance.* Stockholm: International IDEA.

Igreja, V. and Dias-Lambranca, B. (2008) 'Restorative Justice and the Role of Magamba Spirits in Post-civil War Gorongosa, Central Mozambique', in L. Huyse and M. Salter (eds), *Traditional Justice and Reconciliation after Violent Conflict: Learning from African Experiences.* Stockholm: International Institute for Democracy and Electoral Assistance.

Machel, G. (2000) '*International Conference on War Affected Children: The Impact of Armed Conflict on Children. A Critical Review of Progress Made and Obstacles Encountered in Increasing Protection for War-Affected Children*'. Winnipeg, Canada.

Maina, G. (2009) 'An Analytical Evaluation of the Reintegration Process of Formerly Abducted Children in Northern Uganda and the Role of the Various Actors', *Journal of Peace, Conflict and Development*, no. 14.

McIntosh, S. (2021) *Pursuing Justice for Mass Atrocities: A Handbook for Victim Groups.* Washington, DC: United States Holocaust Memorial Museum.

OECD (2021) *Eliminating Gender-based Violence: Governance and Survivor/Victim-centred Approaches.* Paris: OECD Publishing.

Shaw, R., Waldorf, L. with Hazan, P. (2010) *Localizing Transitional Justice: Interventions and Priorities after Mass Violence.* Stanford, CA: Stanford University Press.

Stark, L. (2006) 'Cleansing the Wounds of War: An Examination of Traditional Healing', Psychosocial Health and Reintegration in Sierra Leone', *Intervention*, vol. 4, no. 3, pp. 206–218.

Stavrou, S. and Stewart, R. (2000) *The Reintegration of Child Soldiers and Abducted Children: A Case Study of Palaro and Pabbo Gulu District, Northern Uganda.* Pretoria: Institute for Security Studies.

Williams, S.H. (2011) 'Democracy, Gender Equality, and Customary Law: Constitutionalizing Internal Cultural Disruption', *Indiana Journal of Global Legal Studies*, vol. 18, no. 1, pp. 65–85.

5 Local Justice in Darfur

A Necessary and Effective Component of Survivor-Centred Justice?

Mohammed Elgizoly Adam[1]

Introduction

This chapter asks whether local justice mechanisms can assist victims and survivors of atrocities in Darfur. In many African states, including the Republic of Sudan, people resort to local justice mechanisms when war erupts and the national legal system falls short of assisting those in need. Very little attention has been paid to the significance of local justice mechanisms in Darfur, which can play an important role in pursuing justice for the victims of mass atrocities. The national legal system currently lacks well-trained lawyers, judges and investigative institutions to ensure speedy and fair trials for victims, survivors and alleged perpetrators. The massive scale of the atrocities committed in Darfur over past few decades has led both victims and survivors to seek justice mainly under the auspices of the International Criminal Court (ICC) based in The Hague, Netherlands, but also through the local Sudanese justice mechanisms. Although many political actors in Darfur, including victims and survivors, have essentially pursued prosecutions at the international level, local justice mechanisms have in the past been used to broker peace agreements, such as those signed in Abuja in 2006, Doha in 2011 and Juba in 2020.[2] This analysis is therefore based on a review of the relevant literature on the Sudanese legal system, the background and root causes of the conflict in Darfur, and local justice mechanisms rooted in traditional practices. It is supplemented by research based on interviews with individuals who are familiar with local justice mechanisms in Darfur.[3]

This chapter will trace the relevant history of Sudan, Darfur and its civil institutions. The conflict in Darfur is one of the most complex on the continent. This chapter will therefore delve into the root causes of the conflict, including the issues of ethnicity, ecology and the prolonged neglect of the country at the hands of the central government in the capital, Khartoum, which have contributed to the perpetration of mass atrocities in both Darfur and the rest of the country since 2003.

The chapter will also provide an overview of the current Sudanese legal mechanisms and assess their potential to address the large-scale human

DOI: 10.4324/9781003212409-8

rights violations that continue to take place in Darfur and in the peripheral regions of the country. The question of transitional justice is critical for the future of Sudan and for achieving peace and stability. The December Revolution of 2018 ended the rule of the infamous former President Omer Hassan Ahmed al-Bashir and raised the hopes of the victims and survivors of mass atrocities of attaining justice.[4] The failure to address victims' and survivors' demands for justice may potentially undermine political negotiations since disputing parties fear accountability if accused of human rights violations.[5] Therefore, political will is key to transitional justice in post-conflict situations.[6] Whether local justice mechanisms such as those described in this chapter can play a decisive role has yet to be seen. This chapter will explore the intricacies of meeting the justice needs of victims and survivors in the current Sudanese transitional justice setting through an evaluation of the Sudanese legal system and its politics.

Historical Background

Sudan is a diverse, multi-ethnic and multi-religious country. Before the secession of South Sudan, it was the tenth largest state in the world. The former country of Sudan comprised 597 tribes and over 133 languages and racially Sudanese people identified themselves as Arab or African.[7] Since independence in 1956, Sudan has acknowledged the Arab culture and race as the primary national identity of the country.[8] The country's assimilation of this national identity is one of the main reasons for the long Sudanese civil war that eventually led to the secession of the south.[9] The central government imposed Islamic and Arabic culture (Islamization and Arabization) on all the Sudanese people despite the cultural and ethnic diversity of the country,[10] and as a result the issue of national identity has played a crucial role in the wars in the Blue Nile state, the Nuba Mountains and Darfur.[11]

It is also widely recognized in Africa that politicians use ethnicity or religion as a tool to attain their political objectives, irrespective of the consequences of their actions. One scholar has observed that 'ethnicity is a means through which conflicts in many African countries are conducted and remains a powerful tool for political mass mobilization'.[12] Conflicts can easily take on tribal or ethnic dimensions and can shape the nature of crimes and the concept of justice. For instance, if a rebel group or a pro-government militia recruits from a certain tribe, the other members of that tribe are perceived as supporters or affiliates of such armed groups, regardless of their role in the conflict. This ethnic polarization can often result in fighters targeting civilians and carrying out widespread abuses against civilians. This is what transpired in Darfur on a large scale.

From the Middle Ages up until the 20th century, Darfur was an independent entity.[13] During this period Darfur was in an continual process of state formation until the Turkish-Egyptian forces and their allies invaded the region, along with their allies, the Khartoum slave traders, in the 1870s. A

British military expedition killed Ali Dinar, the Sultan of Darfur, in 1916 and then incorporated the region into the rest of Sudan.[14] A civil service was established that was responsible for the administration of the country.[15] To maintain security, the British officially implemented a 'native administration' in the country in 1932 as a method of indirect rule.[16] During this period of colonization the central government paid little attention to the Darfur region, and its people were denied the right to education, health care and political participation.[17] The governor of Darfur from 1934 to 1941 noted his administration's success in restricting 'access to education to the sons of tribal leaders, and created a ruling class for many years to come'.[18] This historical marginalization continues today and is one of the contributory factors to the current crisis in Darfur.

In 1955, on its departure, the colonial administration relinquished power to the elites in Khartoum who were unfamiliar with remote regions such as Darfur and who knew little about Darfur's social and cultural background.[19] As a result, little has changed in this regard since Sudan's independence[20] because although the British established medical, judicial and educational institutions as well as other civil service institutions, these institutions diminished over time, and eventually became dysfunctional. The tribal administration continued to function despite the state's continual interference[21] and in the 1970s during the Nimeiry regime and the 1990s during the Al Bashir administration the government tried its best to adjust the native administration to serve its policies and political agenda in the region.[22] The central government exploited the tribes politically by favouring one tribe over the next. While it has not been established if this administration in its current form can act as a mechanism on its own to settle the ongoing conflict in Darfur, given the long history of this mechanism, it could be an option for an effective mechanism for conflict resolution if adjusted or modified.[23]

Brief History of the Darfur Conflict

Currently, the majority of Darfurians are Sunni Muslims, and religion has never been a significant source of conflict in the region. Ethnicity, however, has historically been a major issue as different groups have competed for resources.[24] The ethnic dimensions of the Darfur conflict should not be overstated, however.[25] The existing situation has been described as a simple conflict between Arabs and Africans, in which Arabs have carried out atrocities with the support of the central government. Hence there is an assumption that Arabs are criminals and cannot be described as victims who, according to the United Nations (UN) Declaration of Basic Principles of Justice for Victims of Crime and Abuse of Power, are 'persons who, individually or collectively, have suffered harm, including physical or mental injury, emotional suffering, economic loss or substantial impairment of their fundamental rights'.[26] This assumption contradicts the reality on the ground, as

Arab communities have long borne the brunt of horrific abuses, and Darfurian rebel forces have been accused of grave human rights violations. The infamous Janjaweed militia[27] has represented the Arab tribes of Darfur, while the rebels are seen to represent the African tribes. This has resulted in millions of Darfurian civilians from various tribes suffering greatly on account of the violence perpetrated against them, while large numbers have been displaced and forced into refugee camps.

One of the worst humanitarian crises of the 21st century took place in 2002 and 2003 in Darfur[28] when three ethnically African tribes – the Zaghawa, Masalit and Fur peoples – formed an alliance in rebellion against the central government.[29] During this period the rebels formed two armed movements: the Sudan Liberation Army and the Justice and Equality Movement.[30] Both armed movements claimed that the central government intentionally neglected the region and that it was unwilling to address the historical imbalances and economic disparities inherent there, thus forcing them to take action.

In response, the central government waged a counter-insurgency by encouraging the Arab militia groups to fight alongside its army against the rebels.[31] Between 2003 and 2005 the violence intensified significantly with the government leading large-scale attacks on civilians, whom they accused of supporting or harbouring rebels. It has been alleged that these government forces committed war crimes, crimes against humanity and possibly genocide.[32] Human rights organizations and the UN have alleged that thousands of civilians have lost their lives, while millions have been forced to flee their homes as a result of the large-scale destruction. Furthermore, a significant number of civilians have been reported missing.[33] In addition to the violations allegedly committed by the al-Bashir government and its ally, the Janjaweed militia, the International Commission of Inquiry on Darfur found credible evidence that serious human rights violations have taken place in the region.[34]

To avoid a similar situation to that which took place in Rwanda in 1999, the UN Security Council, acting under Chapter VII of the UN Charter, therefore adopted Resolution 1593 on 31 March 2005, and referred the situation in Darfur to the prosecutor of the ICC based on Article 13(b) of the Rome Statute.[35] Since these developments, the international legal avenue used has not as yet resulted in the desired accountability for the crimes committed and the grave human rights violations committed by all the implicated parties, which continues to impede the quest for justice in Darfur.

The Potential of Local Justice Mechanisms

The demand for justice in Darfur is led by the central government and serves as a political solution to the current hostilities. This section will provide an overview of the Sudanese legal system and will describe how customary courts function and play an important role in local dispute mechanisms. It then discusses the interaction of local justice mechanisms with state institutions.

Sudan's Legal System from Past to Present

The Sudanese legal system draws on various, sources namely national legislation, customary law and legal traditions. In Darfur, both the statutory and customary courts are commonly used to resolve disputes. Although one may assume that domestic law prevails local justice processes are viewed with more confidence by the community. Legitimacy in essence reflects the society's consent to comply with rules established by a fair and impartial authority,[36] which has the authority to issue binding judgments.[37] In parts of Sudan, including Darfur, local justice mechanisms may benefit from greater trust and acceptance. As a local judge has noted, '[i]n Darfur, most people prefer local courts more than formal [statutory] courts. Hence it is safe to aver that these mechanisms enjoy more legitimacy than statutory courts in Darfur.'[38]

To better understand the role that local justice mechanisms might play in addressing Darfur's justice deficit, it is useful to explain the origins and functions of these mechanisms.

The 'Native Administration' or Customary Court System

The 'native administration' or customary courts system developed through a series of Acts and ordinances in 1922, 1925, 1927 and 1928, respectively, and was eventually codified in 1932.[39] These ordinances regulated the administrative and judicial power of the tribal leaders and established a hierarchical court system in Sudan.[40] These customary courts are presided over by native administrative or tribal leaders.[41] The hierarchy of tribal leaders follows a strict order: the king, or sultan, rules over non-Arabs, equivalent to the ruling Arab nazir.[42] The Omda (mayor) presides over hundreds of sheikhs and reports to the kings or nazirs.[43] The government provides the latter with a monthly salary to run and keep records of their courts.[44]

In Darfur, there are currently over 200 functioning customary courts[45] whose legal foundations were established by the Towns and Rural Regulations of 2004.[46] Informed and experienced judges who are often tribal leaders oversee these courts.[47] Other judges are native administration leaders who are appointed by the government. In essence, however, all customary judges are appointed by the chief justice after consultation with the native administration in the area concerned.[48]

The local statutory courts are subject to the customary courts, and statutory judges thus endorse the decisions of the customary courts. Customary court records and documentation are retained for future examination should any discrepancies arise.[49] In other words the formal legal system is authorized to verify and affirm decisions and proceedings undertaken at the customary courts. Parties who appear before the customary courts therefore have a right to appeal in the formal courts.[50]

Customary law is unwritten law based on historical practices, traditions and societal customs, and the customary courts' business is underpinned by these customs and traditions, but only if these customs do not contradict either religious Sharia law or statutory law. These courts use both statutory and Islamic Sharia law as the main influence overseeing customs and traditions. Sharia law plays an important role in certain matters such as inheritance, family issues, divorce, alimony and child custody. Since the majority of Darfurians are Sufi Muslims, they often resort to Sharia law to resolve family issues. The judges of the native administration courts are therefore expected to be knowledgeable about the customs and traditions of people residing in the areas concerned.[51] Since Sharia law has a great influence on the customs and traditions in Darfur it is imperative that judges are aware of its foundations.

Customary courts mostly adjudicate cases related to land disputes, minor injuries and sometimes issues related to violence. They also have the power to issue summons and arrest warrants and can impose punishment on convicted parties, including fines, imprisonment and corporal punishment. They also have the discretion to refer serious cases to statutory courts when unable to effectively deal with particular cases. In the past, customary courts were mandated to impose sentences and adjudicate on serious crimes, including murder and rape; however, currently these courts only deal with minor criminal infractions.[52]

The Statutory Legal System

Postcolonial Sudan inherited a common law system from the British and some aspects of Sharia law from Egypt. The legal system is functional in certain legal areas such as property, tort and contract law, but it is less effective in criminal law, human rights and international crimes at a substantive and procedural level. As the legal system was largely imported from colonial powers, it is unsurprising that people often resort to the customary courts rather than relying on the formal legal system in most parts of the country.

Sudan's judiciary consists of the Constitutional Court, the National Supreme Court, the National Court of Appeals and other national courts. The National Judiciary Service Commission undertakes the overall management of the national judiciary.[53] The judiciary comprises courts to deal with both civil and criminal cases. The lowest courts are the rural and town courts with jurisdiction over land and family issues as well as minor criminal offences. District courts[54] have a broader jurisdiction in civil and criminal matters,[55] and provincial courts have jurisdiction over commercial and personal status cases for non-Muslims and can hear appeals on decisions of the district courts.[56] Each provincial or state capital has a Court of Appeal and a

Supreme Court that functions as a final court of appeal. The Constitutional Court is separate from the judiciary structure and was established in 1998.[57]

The primary role of the Constitutional Court is to judge the constitutionality of the laws, hear cases about the fundamental rights that are constitutionally guaranteed, and arbitrate between the lower courts, where there are jurisdictional conflicts. For decades, the government exerted considerable influence over the judiciary system in Sudan.[58] Although the interim Constitution of 2005 and the Constitution of 2019 provided that the judiciary system must be independent, the judiciary frequently appears to serve the interests of the government.[59] Since 1989 the independence of judges has been seriously undermined in Sudan.

When al-Bashir seized power in a military coup, he ensured that he controlled the judiciary branch.[60] The regime immediately started to remove its opponents from the judiciary and replaced them with new government affiliates and cadres from the ruling Islamic Brotherhood Organization.[61] Despite the change and the successful removal of the al-Bashir regime, the Sudanese judiciary system still remains under the influence of the Islamic Brotherhood Organization and its cadres. Hence in order to have an independent judiciary system there must be serious political will to make legal reform feasible.

The Sudanese courts, including the Constitutional Court, are not well suited to protect fundamental human rights. They do not interpret the law to give effect to the constitutional rights of the executive branch of the government.[62] Many legal scholars argue that the law is quite ambivalent and vague in Sudan,[63] since many of the statutory laws are the outcome of a series of political changes, namely colonization, Egypt's influence and Islamization, which together have created a hybrid legal system. Moreover, Sudan's judges lack the necessary expertise, training and knowledge when dealing with sensitive human rights cases[64] and reference to international human rights law is only visible in the interim Constitution of 2005 and the Sudan's Constitution of 2019.[65]

The Interaction of Local or Traditional Justice Mechanisms with State Institutions

Judiyya Proceedings

Local justice in Darfur involves the traditional justice system, known as the *judiyya* process, and the town and rural courts or customary courts. Judiyya consists of two forms of dispute resolution: mediation and arbitration. Judiyya is purely traditional and is not governed by formal law; however, it often interacts with the formal Sudanese legal system. Native administration leaders – nazirs, omdas, sheikhs, kings or sultans – usually conduct judiyya proceedings, playing a significant role as judiyya mediators or *ajaweed*. Some of these leaders are appointed as heads of customary courts, but judiyya processes take place separately and independently from state institutions and customary courts. However, judges may rely on judiyya proceedings in their rulings.

Ajaweed or judiyya mediators exercise certain powers; for instance, they can issue arrest warrants and transfers of the accused and they may formally request that a prosecutor or statutory judge refer a certain case to them. A judge or prosecutor has the discretion to decide to transfer the case if the parties to the dispute formally agree. The ajaweed may also refer a case to the national judiciary if the parties fail to reach an agreement and the mediators are unable to assist in the resolution of the case.

Judiyya in essence is an arbitration and mediation process and not a formal judicial proceeding.[66] The ajaweed are respected members of the community and they must have a good reputation, remain neutral and be competent in Sudanese traditions and customs.[67] Judiyya can assist with matters pertaining to domestic violence, land disputes, incidents involving injury or death, as well as tribal feuds.[68] Its objectives are to achieve a compromise between parties rather than impose punishment.[69] In other words, it has a restorative purview. Each of the disputed parties has the right to reject the advice handed down by judiyya mediators but if the parties accept the judgment, the ruling of the judiyya is then binding.[70] The primary principle is that both opposing parties ought to abide by the recommendations of the ajaweed; however, if one of the parties is dissatisfied with the decision, the mediators might adjudicate once more to reconsider the case in question.[71]

In order to gain an understanding of the benefits of judiyya as a local justice mechanism a number of interviews were conducted with members of various courts to elicit their views on judiyya. Some of their views are summarized and represented in this section to highlight the benefits and shortcomings of judiyya as understood from local perspectives and in order to demonstrate the legitimacy and popularity of this mechanism in administering justice in Sudan.

Interviews show that the judiyya settlement is faster, lenient and inclusive for all the parties involved. The parties may file a complaint at the police station and then only later can ajaweed mediators become involved in the dispute once both parties have agreed on their involvement.[72] Judiyya records can also be tendered and used as evidence in both formal and informal court processes which is beneficial in the administration of justice and less time-consuming. As one interviewee also mentioned, a number of reconciliatory or restorative elements are associated with judiyya and there is no winner or loser in the outcomes of the process. The issues are deliberated deeply upon until both parties are happy with the outcomes, according to the interviewees. It was mentioned that the parties often leave the settlement being reconciled to one another with no hard feelings between them. Furthermore, records from judiyya proceedings can be submitted and tendered as evidence, and ajaweed mediators may also appear as witnesses in formal courts of law.

As Professor Abdullahi El-Tom has highlighted, some of the shortcomings of the judiyya process include a lower standard of evidence, lack of fair trial, and an undermining of the presumption of innocence principle.[73] El-Tom further argues that even with the requisite adjustment, juddiyya may still not be able to handle cases of mass atrocity in Darfur.[74] Additionally, enhancing or modifying the judiyya process to meet some level of international fair trial standards will diminish some of its functionality.[75]

From the discussions with interviewees it has become clear that judiyya needs further research in order to highlight the areas where it falls short and the areas where modifications may be needed. Local justice mechanisms must be viewed as a complementary means to the domestic legal system.[76] It is imperative that grave or mass crimes due to the noted shortcomings of informal justice such as judiyya are adjudicated in the formal court system, while the local justice or traditional systems should deal with crimes of a lesser severity and more with reconciliation.

Town and Rural Courts

Town and rural courts are considered to occupy the lowest tier of the formal Sudanese court system.[77] These courts are sometimes referred to as traditional, native and king courts; however, this chapter will refer to them as town and rural courts. Administrative leaders often chair these courts or a recommended person appointed by the chief justice. The latter also determines the jurisdictions or powers of the town and rural courts. These courts apply traditional and formal law so long as the former does not contradict Sharia or formal law. The legal foundation for the establishment of these courts is the Towns and Rural Courts Regulation of 2004.[78] However, the actual power of these courts depends on their order establishment. These courts have both criminal and civil jurisdiction, and they have the power to issue arrest warrants and the discretion to determine different forms of punishment. Furthermore, people coming before these courts have the right of appeal to formal courts. Judges allocated to the district courts have supervisory power over these courts, while judges of the general court are responsible for the functioning of these courts. These courts are more accessible than the formal courts. Currently, out of 80 town and rural courts 47 remain in use, while the remainder have been closed down owing to the ongoing conflict in the country.

Town and rural courts are also regarded as being more legitimate than formal courts in Darfur because they are longstanding, familiar and therefore well-established courts. In an interview,[79] it was purported that because judges of the town and rural courts hail from the communities concerned and because they understand the complexities and intricacies of the people and their culture these courts enjoy a large measure of legitimacy from the local population. People prefer them because these courts are procedurally swifter in deciding cases and judgments and are often consensus based. For serious *hudud* crimes, regarded as capital offences in Islamic jurisprudence, the formal courts are in a better position to adjudicate on crimes of a severe nature. Most cases concern coming before town and rural courts concern land issues, matrimonial law and minor criminal offences.[80]

Justice for Victims and Survivors of Mass Atrocities in Darfur

This chapter has sought to outline the role of the formal courts compared to that of the customary or informal courts in Sudan in an attempt to show how informal justice systems may complement formal justice systems providing a measure of legitimacy and ownership for victims and survivors. Although victims and survivors of mass atrocities in Sudan have the right to determine the form of justice they seek, criticisms against international prosecutions suggest that the latter could have disappointing outcomes in the context of Darfur. This is primarily because international prosecutions in post-conflict states tend to have protracted judicial processes and funding issues. Furthermore, it may be practically difficult for international justice to take into consideration the full extent of the views of victims and survivors. Justice cannot be meaningfully administered without the full involvement and perceptions of the majority of victims and survivors in the context of transition. A possible way forward for war-affected communities is a conversation about what may happen through reconciliatory processes. In times of post-conflict situations, each group forms their own narrative of what occurred, in part because of a lack of communication and long-term bitterness.[81] Thus, giving each group the opportunity to listen to the other's story might create a sense of empathy and understanding, which could lead to reconciliation. It is therefore imperative to put in place a transitional mechanism to ensure a space for victims and survivors. This section will examine the proposal for a Special Court for Darfur and will go on to explore the limitations of an international transitional justice mechanism such as the ICC and the potential for local justice mechanisms to address justice needs within the Darfurian community.

A Special Court for Darfur Based on Lessons Learned

The idea of a Special Court for Darfur is not a novel one. In 2005 the Sudanese government established the Special Criminal Court for the Events in Darfur (SCCED) one day after the ICC's chief prosecutor had announced the opening of an investigation into the conflict in Darfur.[82] The Sudanese government in response wanted to try the alleged crimes domestically,[83] and therefore sought to challenge the jurisdiction of the ICC. The Sudanese Ministry of Justice referred to Article 17 of the Rome Statute[84] which stipulates that a case may be deemed inadmissible if the state in question is investigating or prosecuting the same crimes in question and unless the state concerned is unwilling or unable to do so.[85] According to Human Rights Watch, one year after the establishment of the SCCED, evidence showed that the Sudanese authorities appeared to be reluctant to prosecute alleged grave human rights violations in Darfur.[86] No government official was ever charged before the SCCED, although several perpetrators and various crimes were named.[87]

Separately, the Doha and Juba peace agreements also gave rise to the suggestion to establish a special court with a mandate to prosecute gross human rights violations in Darfur.[88] Similar to the implementation process of the Doha peace agreement, this envisioned court did not prosecute a single case.[89] The Sudanese peace agreement which was signed in Juba in October 2020 also stipulated the advisability of the establishment of a special court with jurisdiction to prosecute any grave human rights violations falling outside the jurisdiction of the ICC in Darfur.[90] However, the authorities did not set up such a court, nor did they follow through on their commitments to cooperate with the ICC. It is notable that the agreement in question paid little attention to the available local justice mechanisms.[91]

Calls for international prosecutions have been repeatedly politicized for over the last two decades. In lengthy interviews held with camp leaders for internally displaced persons regarding their preference for and perceptions of justice, they held that their top priority was to hand over the accused persons to the ICC.[92] This was because they had lost confidence in the domestic system and therefore had turned to international justice in the hope of seeing al-Bashir and others standing trial at the ICC.

However, given the limitations of international prosecutions and the large-scale human rights violations which have occurred on the territory the call for a Special Court for Darfur, as envisioned in various peace agreements including the Juba Peace Agreement, may be more effective and legitimate and function in a way that is complementary to the Sudanese legal and customary system as well as to the ICC.[93] Some have argued that a Special Court could also overcome the obstacle of temporal jurisdiction concerning crimes committed in Darfur between 2003 to 2004.[94] This principle clearly holds that no person can be prosecuted for a crime that does not exist in the Sudanese Criminal Code at the time in question. The latter Code has, however, been amended since 2009 to include international crimes.[95] A Special Court could potentially overcome this legal conundrum and prosecute war crimes, crimes against humanity and genocide committed during the missed period in question.[96]

Based on lessons learned from previous conflicts in African countries Darfur can also learn a lot.[97] A similar situation can be gleaned from the Special Court for Sierra Leone where the latter was granted jurisdiction over war crimes, crimes against humanity and genocide including having temporal jurisdiction over international crimes committed in the past.[98]

In the case of Sierra Leone, a Truth and Reconciliation Commission (TRC) was established under the auspices of the UN, which functioned together with the Special Court for Sierra Leone (SCSL).[99] The assumption was that the TRC would deal with reconciliation and the bulk of the lesser crimes, while the SCSL dealt with grave crimes that were committed during the war.[100] The TRC focused more on public hearings, where perpetrators and victims have the opportunity to present their stories.[101] Some argue that the TRC did not incorporate local justice mechanisms and focused merely on Western models of truth telling and reconciliation and that as a result there were no significant constructive outcomes.[102] The lesson to be learned from the Sierra Leonean model of transitional justice is how the inclusion of culture, local justice mechanisms, traditions or customs was incorporated into legal processes.[103]

Lessons from South Sudan that have many similarities to the case of Darfur are also valuable because of the regions' shared history and culture. In 2018 the opposing South Sudanese leaders reached an agreement to end the civil war in the Republic of South Sudan.[104] The peace agreement proposed a hybrid court or commission that would comprise transitional justice, truth telling, reconciliation and healing to address the mass human rights violations that were committed against civilians in 2013.[105] To remain objective and impartial and avoid political influence, the agreement provided that the hybrid court must be independent and have primacy over the national courts and that the majority of judges must be appointed from other African countries.[106] The material jurisdiction of this court would include war crimes, crimes against humanity and genocide committed in South Sudan[107] in 2013 until the end of the transitional period.[108]

The lessons learned from the case of Rwanda are also valuable to Dafur. Darfur can learn from the use of local justice mechanisms such as the Gacaca courts because of their similarities with the judiyya and RTCs. The Rwandese example shows how laws were adopted to give rise to a local justice mechanism which would be well equipped to deal with the atrocities which took place during the Rwandan genocide.[109] The most heinous crimes remained within the ambit of the statutory courts, and the less serious ones, such as looting, burning, or property damage were referred to the Gacaca courts.[110] These courts have since decided over a million cases and held thousands of individuals who were responsible for grave human rights violations accountable.[111] Despite its evident successes, some have argued that there were many shortcomings, such as widening racial division between Rwandans, political abuse by the government for necessary support from various constituencies'[112] the impression of victor's justice, fair trial shortcomings and compromised witness protection were highlighted.[113]

The similarities of Gacaca with the judiyya and town and rural courts mainly revolve around the use of traditions and culture, the public nature of their meeting, the close relationship with the domestic legal systems in place and the less retributive nature of these local justice mechanisms. However, there will still be difficulties in Darfur if a local justice mechanism such as Gacaca is utilized. For instance, given that the court system in Darfur is primarily ethnic-based it will be difficult for such a mechanism to play a role in administering justice in the post-conflict phase because ethnicity and tribalism still play a significant role in Darfur.[114] Furthermore, these customary courts and processes have been chaired by the chief leaders of dominant tribes or ethnicities in the area who might have been involved in the conflict.[115] Despite the limited inclusion of ethnic minorities, it will still be difficult to maintain impartiality throughout the process. Furthermore, as reiterated earlier on in this chapter, the shortcomings of the proceedings of the judiyya or the town and rural courts include the issue of concerns about fair trials, gender bias and political influence.[116] Furthermore, male tribal leaders dominate these processes despite the fact that women are the most marginalized and affected segment of society and remain absent from any leadership role in such proceedings.[117] Moreover, there are legitimacy concerns as well where for decades, the central government has influenced tribal leaders, and therefore the credibility of tribal leaders has become questionable.[118] It may however, be possible to make some amendments to judiyya regarding women's participation, fair trial and impartiality; however, this will be challenging in the light of intersecting discriminations and entrenched patriarchy. If a Special Court is to exist there must be an honest debate about the need to include women and other marginalized groups in the process as well as the importance of training local judges in the knowledge of the law. Addressing such shortcomings could help to bridge the gap between the local justice mechanisms utilized and international human rights standards.

Conclusion

In 2008 the AU formed a panel which focused on the conflict in Darfur and carried out a comprehensive study analysing the root causes, and providing possible solutions. The panel's report concluded that the issues of justice and reconciliation are intertwined in Darfur and that therefore they cannot be addressed separately. They must be addressed procedurally and conceptually to achieve peace and security in the country as whole. The justice issue has become more polarized following the arrest warrant issued against al-Bashir in 2009 by the ICC. Currently, most of the perpetrators responsible for the mass atrocities remain at large. Even when operating at full capacity, the ICC can only handle a few cases at a time, and the remainder will require prosecution domestically. Therefore, it is of paramount importance to reform the national legal system of Sudan in order to achieve adequate justice. As this chapter has demonstrated Sudan can benefit from its existing, well-established and diverse legal heritage, which includes customary law, common law and Islamic Sharia law.[119] As the AU Panel's report concludes justice and reconciliation are intertwined issues and must therefore be approached in an integrated manner. Moreover, it is necessary to strengthen the current legal system in order to establish a special court to deal with crimes that were committed in Darfur. Establishing a hybrid court to address grave crimes committed in Darfur without modifying the current legal system will not ensure a viable transitional justice mechanism that is able to deal with the serious atrocities committed against victims and survivors in Darfur.[120] The

AU panel resolved that the solution must be found within the country, thus supporting the view that local justice mechanisms could be indispensable in pursuit of justice, peace and security in Darfur.

The chapter has shown that judiyya could be a useful local justice mechanism especially given the role it has played in adjudication and dispute resolution in Darfur. It would be shortsighted to label it as currently ineffective or weak, without considering how it could be modified to function effectively in a post-conflict situation. Undoubtedly, dealing with grave crimes such as war crimes, crimes against humanity and genocide is challenging with even the most sophisticated legal system in place. However, the fundamental issue is to develop an efficient, effective and feasible legal means or mechanism to deal with the scale and nature of the crimes committed and which take into account international fair trial standards and human rights. Essentially, such a mechanism must aim to deliver justice to the countless number of victims and survivors who have borne the brunt of endless suffering and who crave justice, peace and security. It is therefore imperative to strengthen the available local justice mechanisms sufficiently in order for them to be viewed as viable transitional justice mechanisms.

Notes

1 The author is a Sudanese survivor living in the Netherlands. He would like to acknowledge the editing efforts of Adrienne Fricke in this chapter.

2 Darfur Peace Agreement, 5 May 2006, available at https://www.refworld.org/docid/4c0375d62.html; see also Doha Document for Peace in Darfur, 14 July 2012, available at https://www.refworld.org/docid/5a8430814.html, Juba Agreement for Peace in Sudan (accessed 3 October 2020).

3 Due to the security situation and limited access to remote areas in Darfur, these interviews were conducted by telephone. Throughout these interviews the author followed the No Harm Principles and took into account the privacy of the interviewees.

4 *Draft Constitutional Charter for the 2019 Transitional Period*, Sudan (4 August 2019), available at https://www.refworld.org/docid/5ec7fc374.html.

5 Although a full discussion of contemporary Sudanese political negotiations lies outside the scope of this chapter, the history of the December 2018 revolution, the establishment of a civilian-led transitional government in 2019, the military coup in October 2021, and the subsequent struggles within the al-Burhan government all highlight the ongoing need for transitional justice mechanisms that can satisfy civilian demands for justice on a large scale. For the former civilian Minister of Justice's perspective see, for example, N. Abdulbari, 'A Transitional Period Constitutional Question in Sudan', *Just Security* (blog), 16 February 2022, available at https://www.justsecurity.org/80164/a-transitional-period-constitutional-question-in-sudan/. For a discussion of the civilian-led government period, and the draft constitutional commitments to justice, see D. Johnson, 'Revolution, Peace, and Justice in Sudan', *University of Pennsylvania Journal of International Law*, 43(1), 2021, pp. 187–192.

6 E. Skaar, 'On Sudan Transitional Justice: 'No Victorious Army Has Ever Been Prosecuted', Radio Dabanga, 19 January 2020, available at https://bit.ly/3vgpCyL.

7 Johnson, 'Revolution, Peace, and Justice in Sudan', pp. 187–192.

8 J. Hāshim, To Be or Not To Be: Sudan at Crossroads (Dar es Salaam: Mkuki na Nyota, 2019), pp. 1–32.

9 Ibid.

10 Ibid.

11 Ibid.

12 P. Pamela, 'Ethnicity and Tribalism: Are These the Root Causes of the Sudanese Civil Conflicts?' *Africa Economic Analysis*, 2007, pp. 1–2.

13 A. De Waal, 'Who are the Darfurians? Arab and African Identities, Violence and External Engagement', *African Affairs*, 104(415), 2005, pp. 181–205.

14 Ibid.

15 Ibid.

16 The three main pillars of the native administration were the interests of the state and its constituencies in an apportioned part of the country, land management, and administering justice in that apportioned territory. See also J. Tubiana V. Tanner, M.A. Abdul-Jali, 'Traditional Authorities' Peacemaking Role in Darfur', United Institute of Peace, 2012, pp. 1–5, available at https://files.ethz.ch/isn/155469/PW83.pdf.

17 B.A. Kritz and J. Wilson, 'No Transitional Justice without Transition: Darfur Case Study', *Mich. St. U. Coll. LJ Int'l L.*19, 2010, pp. 475–478

18 Ibid.

19 M. Mukhtar, 'Marginalization and Ethnicization in Sudan: How the Elite Failed to Stabilize a Diverse Country', Contemporary Arab Affairs, 3(4), 2010, pp. 551–558.

20 De Waal, 'Who Are the Darfurians?'

21 J. Morton, 'Conflict in Darfur: A Different Perspective', HTSPE Resource Paper, Hemel Hempstead, 2004, pp.1–23.

22 M. Adam, 'Future Prospects for Native Administration and Local Governance in Darfur: War in Darfur and the Search for Peace', 2007, pp. 1–11.

23 De Waal, 'Who Are the Darfurians?'

24 Morton, 'Conflict in Darfur'.

25 De Waal, 'Who Are the Darfurians?' In Sudan, rebel leaders in Darfur have often said that they are fighting for all Sudan and that their organization represents all tribes in Darfur. See, for example, 'SLM statement on the secular state', *Sudan Tribune*, 3 January 2007, available at https://sudantribune.com/article19977/.

26 UN General Assembly, Declaration of Basic Principles of Justice for Victims of Crime and Abuse of Power: resolution adopted by the General Assembly, 29 November 1985, A/RES/40/34, available at https://www.refworld.org/docid/3b00f2275b.html (accessed 12 March 2022). There is a robust debate in the literature on the usefulness of the term victim. See, for example, K. Dillenburger, M. Fargas and R. Akhonzada, 'Victims or Survivors?' *International Journal of the Humanities*, 3(5), 2006, pp. 1–1. For clarity, this chapter uses the terms survivor and victim interchangeably. Lawyers, prosecutors and judges may prefer the term victim, while NGOs or other community-based advocates are likely to use the term survivor. See, e.g., Sexual Assault Kit Initiative, 'Victim or Survivor: Terminology from investigation through prosecution', US Department of Justice, Bureau of Justice Assistance, available at https://dojmt.gov/wp-content/uploads/Victim-or-Survivor-Terminology-from-Investigation-Through-Prosecution.pdf.

27 The Janjaweed militia was created and supported during al-Bashir's regime; it mainly comprised members of nomadic Arab tribes who had been in competition with Darfur's settled African farmers over land and other issues for some time.

28 *Washington Post*, 'Why Africa's Migrant Crisis Makes No Sense to Outsiders', 27 April 2016, available at https://wapo.st/3pdsUiJ.

29 Pamela, 'Ethnicity and Tribalism'.
30 Ibid.
31 International Crisis Group, 'Sudan's Spreading Conflict (III): The Limits of Darfur's Peace Process', *Africa Report*, no. 211, 27 January 2014, pp. 1–2, available at https://www.refworld.org/docid/52e7c8954.html.
32 Amnesty International 'Sudan: Omar al-Bashir Must Face Justice for Recent and Past Crimes', 14 May 2019, available at https://www.amnesty.org/en/latest/news/2019/05/sudan-omar-al-bashir-must-face-justice-for-recent-and-past-crimes/.
33 International Crisis Group, 'Sudan's Spreading Conflict (III)', pp. 1–2
34 United Nations, International Commission of Inquiry on Darfur Report to the Secretary-General, 25 January 2005, pp. 1–3
35 Security Council, Security Council Resolution, S/RES/1593 (2005), 31 March 2005.
36 For a discussion of the history of the terms and their uses, see T. Justice and A. Liebling, 'Legitimacy and Criminal Justice: An Introduction', in *Legitimacy and Criminal Justice: An International Exploration* (Oxford: Oxford University Press, 2013), pp. 1–376. See also M. Franck, 'The Power of Legitimacy and the Legitimacy of Power: International Law in an Age of Power Disequilibrium', *Am. J. Int'l L*, 100, pp. 88–93, and H.G. Cohen *et al., Legitimacy and International Courts: A Framework* (New York: Cambridge University Press, 2018).
37 United Nations, International Commission of Inquiry on Darfur Report to the Secretary-General.
38 Omda Ismail Goma, 'An Interview Regarding the Legitimacy of RTC in Darfur', 2 February 2022, on file with the author.
39 Adam, 'Future Prospects for Native Administration and Local Governance in Darfur'.
40 Ibid.
41 Tubiana *et al.*, 'Traditional Authorities' Peacemaking Role in Darfur'.
42 Ibid.
43 A. El-Tom, 'From War to Peace and Reconciliation in Darfur, Sudan: Prospects for the Judiyya', *African Dialogue Monography Series*, 2(2) 2012, pp. 99–106.
44 Ibid.
45 Tubiana *et al.*, 'Traditional Authorities' Peacemaking Role in Darfur'.
46 Available at https://redress.org/wp-content/uploads/2021/09/Towns-and-Rural-Areas-Courts-Regulations-2004-English.pdf. See also 'UNAMID Hands Over Nertiti Rural Court to the Sudanese Judiciary', 5 December 2018, available at https://unamid.unmissions.org/unamid-hands-over-nertiti-rural-court-sudanese-judiciary.
47 Tubiana *et al.*, 'Traditional Authorities' Peacemaking Role in Darfur'.
48 Ibid.
49 REDRESS, Sudan Legal resources (Town and Rural Areas Courts Regulations (2004)), available at https://redress.org/sudan-legal-resources/.
50 Tubiana *et al.*, 'Traditional Authorities' Peacemaking Role in Darfur'.
51 Ibid.
52 Y. Mohammed, 'The Role of Legal Traditions in Conflict Resolution and Reconciliation Procedure in Darfur', interview with Radio Dabanga, 2020, available at shorturl.at/dqzIM.
53 United Kingdom Home Office, *Country of Origin Information Report - Sudan*, 11 September 2012, available at https://www.refworld.org/docid/505192fe2.html.
54 Ibid. In Sudan, the judicial system includes four types of courts, namely the regular courts that mainly deal with criminal and civil matters, special mixed security courts, military courts, and tribal courts that usually address disputes over land, water rights or family issues. The regular courts include the Court of Appeal, the public courts, and the district court or Court of the First Instance.
55 Ibid.

56 Ibid.
57 Ibid.
58 Ibid.
59 O. Lutz and A.B. Mohamed, 'The Rule of Law and Human Rights in Sudan: Challenges and Prospects for Reform', *Institutional Reforms Series*, 2, 2014, pp. 1–2.
60 International Commission of Juris, 'Attack on Justice 2000: Sudan', 13 August 2001, available at https://www.icj.org/sudan-attacks-on-justice-2000-sudan/.
61 Ibid.
62 REDRESS, *Criminal Justice and Human Rights: An Agenda for Effective Human Rights Protection in Sudan's New Constitution*, March 2012, available at https://www.refworld.org/docid/5064158b2.html.
63 Lutz and Mohamed, 'The Rule of Law and Human Rights in Sudan'.
64 Ibid.
65 REDRESS, *Criminal Justice and Human Rights.*
66 A.S. Wahab, 'The Sudanese Indigenous Model for Conflict Resolution: A Case Study to Examine the Relevancy and the Applicability of the Judiyya Model in Restoring Peace within the Ethnic Tribal Communities of the Sudan' (Fort Lauderdale, FL: Nova Southeastern University, 2018), pp. 25–26, available at https://nsuworks.nova.edu/shss_dcar_etd/87/ (accessed 24 October 2024).
67 Ibid.
68 Ibid.
69 Ibid.
70 Austrian Centre for Country of Origin and Asylum Research and Documentation (ACCORD), *Darfur: COI Compilation*, July 2014, pp. 1–86, available at https://www.refworld.org/docid/53ce74e64.htm.
71 Ibid.
72 In an interview with Omda Magbual, native administration leader in Darfur East Jebel Marra, 20 January 2021.
73 Professor Abdullahi El-Tom was head of the Anthropology department at Maynooth University. He grew up in Darfur and he has been actively involved in Darfur issues since the war erupted in 2003. He has written numerous articles about the conflict in Darfur.
74 El-Tom, 'From War to Peace and Reconciliation in Darfur, Sudan', pp. 99–108.
75 Ibid.
76 Interview with Prof. Sara Nouwen, 'The possibility of transitional justice in Sudan', 20 June 2020, Radio Dabanga, available at https://bit.ly/3pkR5Mh.
77 Tubiana *et al.*, 'Traditional Authorities' Peacemaking Role in Darfur'.
78 'Towns and Rural Areas Courts Regulations, 2004'; based on Article 10 of this regulation, at their discretion, the Chief Justice might revoke an appointment of the president, deputy president, or member of any town and rural court.
79 M. Abdalrahim Ahmed, 'An Interview Regarding Local Justice Mechanisms Advantages and Disadvantages of RTC', 24 February 2022. He is the head of the Al Dain Town Court, one of the oldest in Darfur.
80 O.I. Goma, 'An Interview Regarding the Legitimacy of RTC in Darfur', 2 February 2022. The latter is the head of Tululo Rural Court in Central Darfur. The interviewee emphasized that people prefer town and rural courts because of the communication, culture and language.
81 Ibid.
82 Human Rights Watch, 'Lack of Conviction: The Special Criminal Court on the Events in Darfur', 8 June 2006, available at https://www.refworld.org/docid/44c765c74.html.
83 Ibid.
84 Ibid.

85 UN General Assembly, Rome Statute of the International Criminal Court (last amended 2010), (17 July1998).
86 Human Rights Watch, 'Lack of Conviction'.
87 Ibid.
88 Doha Document for Peace in Darfur (2011) Article 59.
89 Radio Dabanga, interview conducted on 19 June 2020 by Mohammed Adam with Bashir Niam, senior negotiator during the Doha Peace talks in 2011, available at https://soundcloud.com/radio-dabanga/19-6-2020a?in=radio-dabanga/sets/0mnqouyns2zs.
90 Juba Agreement: Summary and Analysis (International IDEA) Version 5, 23 October 2020, pp. 1–19.
91 Ibid.
92 Radio Dabanga, 'Darfur Displaced Community Leaders: Justice Is Top Priority', 17 March 2020, available at https://www.dabangasudan.org/en/all-news/article/darfur-displaced-community-leaders-justice-is-top-priority.
93 Ibid.
94 Ibid.
95 Lutz and Mohamed, 'The Rule of Law and Human Rights in Sudan'.
96 Kritz and Wilson, 'No Transitional Justice without Transition'.
97 Ibid.
98 Austrian Centre for Country of Origin and Asylum Research and Documentation (ACCORD), *Darfur.*
99 S. Conner, 'Structural and Socioeconomic Approaches to Justice: Transformative Justice in Nicaragua's 'Dual Transition', *Transitional Justice*, 111, 2022, pp. 7–30.
100 Ibid.
101 Ibid.
102 G. Young, 'Transitional Justice in Sierra Leone: A Critical Analysis', *United Nations Peace and Progress*, 1(1), 2013, pp. 3–11.
103 Ibid.
104 Revitalized Agreement on the Resolution of the Conflict in the Republic of South Sudan (R-ARCSS), 12 September 2018.
105 J. Akech, 'Rethinking Transitional Justice in South Sudan: Critical Perspectives on Justice and Reconciliation', *International Journal of Transitional Justice*,14 (3), 2020, pp. 585–588.
106 Ibid.
107 Ibid.
108 Ibid.
109 T. Longman, 'An Assessment of Rwanda's Gacaca Courts', *Peace Review*, 21(3), 2009, pp. 304–306.
110 R. Thakur and W. Schabas (eds), *Atrocities and International Accountability: Beyond Transitional Justice*, Tokyo: United Nations University Press, 2002, pp. 1–164.
111 Timothy, 'An Assessment of Rwanda's Gacaca Courts', pp. 304–309.
112 S. Thomson, 'The Darker Side of Transitional Justice: The Power Dynamics behind Rwanda's Gacaca Courts', *Africa*, 81(3), 2011, pp. 373–378.
113 Longman, 'An Assessment of Rwanda's Gacaca Courts'.
114 El-Tom, 'From War to Peace and Reconciliation in Darfur, Sudan'.
115 Ibid.
116 Kritz and Wilson, 'No Transitional Justice without Transition'.
117 Ibid.
118 Ibid.
119 African Union, *Report of the African Union: High Level Panel on Darfur* (AUPD), PSC/AHG/2(CCVII), 29 October 2009.
120 Ibid.

References

Abdulbari, Nasredeen (2022) 'A Transitional Period Constitutional Question in Sudan', *Just Security*, 16 February.

Abdul-Jalil, Adam, Azzain, Adam and Yousuf, Adam (2007) *Future Prospects for Native Administration and Local Governance in Darfur: War in Darfur and the Search for Peace.* Cambridge, MA: Harvard University Press.

Akech, Joseph Geng (2020) 'Rethinking Transitional Justice in South Sudan: Critical Perspectives on Justice and Reconciliation', *International Journal of Transitional Justice*, vol. 14, no. 3.

Cohen, Harlan Grant*et al.* (2018) *Legitimacy and International Courts: A Framework.* Cambridge: Cambridge University Press.

Conner, Sean (2022) 'Structural and Socioeconomic Approaches to Justice: Transformative Justice in Nicaragua's 'Dual Transition', *Transitional Justice*, vol. 111, January.

De Waal, Alex (2005) 'Who Are the Darfurians? Arab and African Identities, Violence and External Engagement', *African Affairs*, vol. 104, no. 415.

Dillenburger, Karola, Fargas, Montserrat and Akhonzada, Rym (2006) 'Victims or Survivors?' *International Journal of the Humanities*, vol. 3, no. 5.

El-Tom, Abdullahi (2012) 'From War to Peace and Reconciliation in Darfur, Sudan: Prospects for the Judiyya', *African Dialogue Monography Series*, vol. 2, no. 2.

Franck, Thomas M. (2006) 'The Power of Legitimacy and the Legitimacy of Power: International Law in an Age of Power Disequilibrium', *Am. J. Int'l L*, vol. 100.

Hāshim, Jala (2019) *To Be or Not to Be: Sudan at Crossroads: A Pan-African Perspective.* Dar es Salaam: Mkuki na Nyota Publishers.

Johnson, Darin E.W. (2021) 'Revolution, Peace, and Justice in Sudan', *University of Pennsylvania Journal of International Law*, vol. 43, no. 1.

Kritz, Brian A. and Wilson, Jacqueline (2010) 'No Transitional Justice Without Transition: Darfur – A Case Study', *Mich. St. U. Coll. LJ Int'l L.*, vol. 19.

Longman, Timothy (2009) 'An Assessment of Rwanda's Gacaca Courts', *Peace Review*, vol. 21, no. 3.

Mamdani, Mahmood (2009) *Saviors and Survivors: Darfur, Politics, and the War on Terror.* New York:Pantheon Books.

Morton, James (2004) '*Conflict in Darfur: A Different Perspective*'. doi:10.2139/ssrn.4474147.

Morton, James (2011) *How to Govern Darfur? Modern Threats to a Social Contract Developed over Three Centuries*, Sir William Luce Publication Series 12, School of Government and International Affairs, Durham University. doi:10.2139/ssrn.2158374.

Musa, Abdu Mukhtar (2010) 'Marginalization and Ethnicization in the Sudan: How the Elite Failed to Stabilize a Diverse Country', *Contemporary Arab Affairs*, vol. 3, no. 4.

Oette, Lutz, and Abdelsalam Babiker, Mohamed (2014) 'The Rule of Law and Human Rights in Sudan: Challenges and Prospects for Reform', *Institutional Reforms Series*, vol. 2.

Paglia, Pamela (2007) 'Ethnicity and Tribalism: Are These the Root Causes of the Sudanese Civil Conflicts?' *Africa Economic Analysis.*

Sexual Assault Kit Initiative (2015) *Victim or Survivor: Terminology from Investigation through Prosecution.* Available at https://www.sakitta.org/toolkit/docs/Victim-or-Survivor-Terminology-from-Investigation-Through-Prosecution.pdf.

Shelton, Dinah (2013) *The Oxford Handbook of International Human Rights Law.* Oxford: Oxford University Press.

Tankebe, Justice and Liebling, Alison (2013) 'Legitimacy and Criminal Justice: An Introduction', in *Legitimacy and Criminal Justice: An International Exploration.* Oxford: Oxford University Press.

Thakur, Ramesh and Schabas, William (2002) *Atrocities and International Accountability: Beyond Transitional Justice.* Tokyo; New York; Paris: United Nations University Press.

Thomson, Susan (2011) 'The Darker Side Of Transitional Justice: The Power Dynamics behind Rwanda's Gacaca Courts', *Africa*, vol. 81, no. 3.

Tubiana, Jérôme, Tanner, Victor and Abdul-Jalil, MusaAdam (2012) *Traditional Authorities' Peacemaking Role in Darfur.* Washington, DC: US Institute of Peace.

Tyler, Tom R. (2009) 'Legitimacy and Criminal Justice: The Benefits of Self-Regulation', *Ohio St. J. Crim. L*, vol. 7.

Wahab, Abdul S. (2018) *The Sudanese Indigenous Model for Conflict Resolution: A Case Study to Examine the Relevancy and the Applicability of the Judiyya Model in Restoring Peace within the Ethnic Tribal Communities of the Sudan*, Doctoral Dissertation. Fort Lauderdale, FL: Nova Southeastern University. Available at https://nsuworks.nova.edu/shss_dcar_etd/87/.

Young, Graeme (2013) 'Transitional Justice in Sierra Leone: A Critical Analysis', *United Nations Peace and Progress*, vol. 1, no. 1.

Statutes and Legislation

Towns and Rural Areas Courts Regulations (2004).

Darfur Peace Agreement (5 May 2006).

Doha Document for Peace in Darfur (14 July 2012).

Revitalized Agreement on the Resolution of the Conflict in the Republic of South Sudan (R-ARCSS) (12 September 2018).

Draft Constitutional Charter for the 2019 Transitional Period, Sudan (4 August 2019).

Juba Agreement for Peace in Sudan (3 October 2020).

Resolutions, Principles, Decisions and Reports

African Union, *Report of the African Union: High Level Panel on Darfur (AUPD), PSC/AHG/2(CCVII)* (29 October 2009).

Austrian Centre for Country of Origin and Asylum Research and Documentation (ACCORD), *Darfur: COI Compilation.*

Home Office, *Country of Origin Information Report: Sudan* (11 September 2012).

Human Rights Watch, '*Lack of Conviction: The Special Criminal Court on the Events in Darfur*' (8 June 2006).

International Crisis Group, 'Sudan's Spreading Conflict (III): The Limits of Darfur's Peace Process', *Africa Report*, vol. 211 (27 January 2014).

Juba Agreement: Summary and Analysis (International IDEA) Version 5 (23 October 2020).

REDRESS, *Criminal Justice and Human Rights: An Agenda for Effective Human Rights Protection in Sudan's New Constitution* (March 2012).

Revitalised Agreement on the Resolution of the Conflict in the Republic of South Sudan (R-ARCSS) (12 September 2018).

Rome Statute of the International Criminal Court (adopted on 17 July 1998, entered into force on 1 July 2002) vol. 2187, no. 38544, Depositary. Available at https://www.icc-cpi.int/sites/default/files/2024-05/Rome-Statute-eng.pdf.

Security Council, *Security Council Resolution* [*S/RES/1593 (2005)*] (31 March2005).

United Nations, *International Commission of Inquiry on Darfur Report to the Secretary-General* (25 January 2005).

United Nations, '*Legality and Legitimacy in International Order*', Policy Brief, no. 5 (2008).

United Nations General Assembly, *Declaration of Basic Principles of Justice for Victims of Crime and Abuse of Power: Resolution/Adopted by the General Assembly, 29 November 1985, A/RES/40/34.*

Websites and Interviews

Mohammed Abdelsalam, 'Transitional Justice in Darfur', interview with Radio Dabanga (in Arabic), 13 April2020.

Mohammed Abdalrahim Ahmed, 'Local Justice Mechanisms: Advantages and Disadvantages of RTC', 24 February2022.

Amnesty International, 'Sudan: Omar al-Bashir Must Face Justice for Recent and Past Crimes', 14 May2019.

Omda Ismail Goma, 'The Legitimacy of RTC in Darfur', 2 February2022.

International Commission of Juris, 'Attack on Justice 2000: Sudan', 13 August2001.

Omda Magbual, native administration leader in Darfur East Jebel Marra, interview, 20 January2021.

Yasin Mohammed, 'The Role of Legal Traditions in Conflict Resolution and Reconciliation Procedure in Darfur', interview with Radio Dabanga, 2020.

Bashir Niam, senior negotiator in the peace talks held in Doha, interview, 2020.

Sara Nouwen, 'The Possibility of Transitional Justice in Sudan', 20 June2020.

Radio Dabanga, 'Darfur Displaced Community Leaders: Justice Is Top Priority', 17 March2020.

Elin Skaar, 'On Sudan Transitional Justice: 'No Victorious Army Has Ever Been Prosecuted', Radio Dabanga.

Sudan Tribune, 'SLM Statement on the Secular State', 3 January2007.

'UNAMID Hands Over Nertiti Rural Court to the Sudanese Judiciary', 5 December2018. Interviews conducted by Mohammed Adam, Transitional Justice Programme Manager, Radio Dabanga.

Washington Post, 'Why Africa's Migrant Crisis Makes No Sense to Outsiders', 27 April2016.

Part III
Advocacy

6 Survivor Inclusion in Transitional Justice

Towards Meaningful Justice for Survivors

Camila Fernandes Thomaz and Malini Laxminarayan

Introduction

> When victims speak with their own voices, justice, peace and democracy also win.[1]

Conflict-related sexual violence (CRSV) has dramatic consequences on the lives of survivors,[2] affecting their physical, psychological and socio-economic wellbeing. The stigma associated with this type of violence is especially debilitating and can be exacerbated by the criminal justice system, which has been criticized for re-traumatizing survivors[3]. When survivors are afraid or ashamed to speak out, their chances of accessing justice and reclaiming their rights decrease or disappear entirely.[4] In addition, the low conviction rate for reported cases creates a cycle of impunity for perpetrators, which severely impacts peace and the rule of law.[5]

Transitional justice mechanisms play a vital role in dealing with the past and helping communities to come to terms with the atrocities that occurred. More specifically, transitional justice aims to recognize the dignity of individuals by acknowledging and providing redress for human rights violations to prevent the recurrence of abuses. Due to its flexible and dialogue-based approach, survivors often perceive transitional justice as a better model for achieving justice.[6]

The discipline of transitional justice has explored to a large extent the role at grassroots level where ordinary people rather than elites make the decisions and collectively influence transitional justice policy. Victims and survivors themselves are one vital element when referring to the affected population that may serve as a crucial driver within transitional justice. Yet despite the increased attention to victims' rights in policy and academia and the adoption of more survivor-centred approaches to transitional justice, most often the role of survivors is too narrow and superficial to ensure meaningful participation. Whether included as consultees or witnesses, survivors are hardly ever decision-makers, which leads to a sense of lack of ownership and control over the process.[7]

Achieving meaningful justice, therefore, requires a survivor-centred approach in which survivors are active during all stages of the process. By

DOI: 10.4324/9781003212409-10

calling for a survivor-centred approach with meaningful survivor participation, the authors refer to a process in which those affected and their needs take centre stage in the development, decision-making and implementation of transitional justice initiatives.[8] To ensure meaningful participation, survivors must be allowed to fundamentally challenge the assumptions, objectives and processes of transitional justice interventions.[9].

One catalyst for enhancing such meaningful participation is to offer platforms through which survivors can organize themselves, learn from one another and strengthen their solidarity, working towards a larger social movement in search of justice. These platforms may take the form of organized survivor networks, or they may be considered within the context of a given initiative. In this chapter, the authors will explore different spaces that promote the meaningful participation of survivors in demanding and developing strategies to reclaim their rights, including access to justice.

The impact and potential of survivors' meaningful participation in transitional justice is an under-researched area in transitional justice[10]. In this chapter, through an examination of three case studies, the authors aim to demonstrate that transitional justice initiatives can benefit – and are benefiting – from an active role of those with a key stake in the process, namely survivors of human rights abuses.

This chapter will present six characteristics determining whether platforms are *more* or *less* survivor-led. The first characteristic is measuring the extent to which survivors have or need to acquire – through capacity building – the skills and knowledge to be recognized as experts and work independently. The second characteristic centres around the role played by non-governmental organizations (NGOs) and civil society organizations (CSOs) in these initiatives. NGOs and CSOs may play a complementary role, a facilitative role, or they may be mostly absent but offer guidance and support when needed, depending on their focus and expertise. Partnerships constitute the third characteristic identified given the importance of collaborating with key nationally and internationally recognized actors and the wider impact they can have. Another crucial attribute is the role of survivors in these different networks and initiatives, namely as consultees or key stakeholders with real decision-making power. The resources available to develop such platforms define the fifth characteristic. Finally, the sixth characteristic will explore the potential of partnerships in leveraging these platforms' positioning in the CRSV landscape and transitional justice policy setting. It is important to note that neither of these characteristics is static or binary; rather, they evolve over time and exist within a spectrum of possibilities.

To further explore *how* to provide a platform where survivors and victims can play leading roles in demanding their rights and becoming agents of change in the process towards greater justice and the rule of law, the chapter will proceed as follows: the first section will briefly outline transitional justice and the link with survivor-centred justice. The third section will examine the interconnectedness between the rule of law, access to justice and survivor social movements and networks. The fourth section will present three cases of platforms varying in their degree of complexity and survivor-led focus to illustrate how survivors can take a key role in advocacy. The fifth section will concretely link survivor participation to an enhanced rule of law. Finally, the sixth section will offer some conclusions and reflections on how to move forward, focusing on the importance of promoting a shift from survivor-centredness to survivor leadership in achieving meaningful change.

Transitional Justice, Survivor Inclusivity and the Rule of Law

CRSV affects millions of women, girls, men and boys globally, but most victims do not have access to the necessary psychological, medical, socio-economic and legal assistance.[11] The consequences are devastating and they not only impact the wellbeing of victims but society at large, particularly when there are no mechanisms in place to address the damage caused.

There is increasing recognition that the traditional criminal justice system is unable to bring a sense of justice to survivors of sexual violence.[12] Therefore, in recent years, there has been increasing acknowledgement that alternative mechanisms within transitional justice may be more appropriate. Developed with the aim of restoring dignity to victims, transitional justice refers to a range of mechanisms that aim to deal with the harms and trauma of the past.[13] Both judicial and non-judicial mechanisms may be implemented by states to ensure that human rights abuses do not go unpunished, but rather form a (collective) narrative and look towards the future in terms of reconciliation and improvement of the wellbeing of harmed parties.[14] Among these mechanisms are truth commissions, legal and criminal justice avenues, reparations and apologies.[15] The aims of such mechanisms include truth-finding, strengthening the rule of law, victim compensation, reconciliation, public deliberation, accountability and punishment, a public platform for survivors and victims and long-term development.

When theorizing on transitional justice, we may adopt the perspective that prioritizes the notion of justice, or the perspective that focuses on the moment of transition.[16] When exploring the notion of justice, questions about the forms of justice arise and, more importantly, which forms of justice meet the needs of survivors. Corresponding with existing transitional justice mechanisms, these forms may be retributive, restorative, punitive or corrective. Furthermore, questions characterizing the focus on transition may also ask about the type of society, the population or the aims of its government as outcomes of a successful transition. The broader aim is essentially to create an inclusive society to enhance the rule of law.

Participatory Approaches to Transitional Justice

Civic mobilization is a key element to understanding transitional justice theory. It has long been studied in terms of its role within the larger transitional justice landscape and numerous examples can be given where affected communities effectively mobilize to make demands on justice and accountability.[17] Where local communities can define and address local problems and ensure that power is transferred from the dominant elite to those who are subordinate in the process, the participation of civil society leads to empowerment.[18]

In this chapter, the authors understand the concept of civil society as broader than only the role of NGOs; instead, we also consider social movements and collective behaviours contesting the mainstream as an integral part of civil society.[19] This view of civil society encompasses invited spaces (those designed and controlled by governments) but also claimed spaces (those chosen or developed by people themselves).[20] Furthermore, as described by Evrard *et al.*,[21] this spatial lens

> was linked to growing scholarly critiques of state-centric and elite-managed transitional justice, leading authors to highlight the important functions performed by civil society, not limited to the support of certain (human rights) NGOs for formal TJ processes, but also including a wide range of groups, movements and collectives that mobilize at the grassroots level in line with communities' and victims' self-identified needs and interests. The spatial metaphor has great analytical potential, as it redirects attention from a purely institutional perspective to a more actor-oriented approach.

Following this actor-oriented approach claimed spaces where the voices of survivors of CRSV are prevalent enhance our understanding of the notion of (transitional) justice. Without survivors' input, transitional justice mechanisms may fail to meet the needs of survivors and communities. The argument of this chapter – that survivors' meaningful participation leads to better outcomes in transitional justice – rests on the assumption that there is a well-researched and practised link between survivors' voices and transitional justice, securing the relationship between a survivor-centred approach with greater recognition of the survivors and a strengthened rule of law. The notion of enhancing the rule of law through such an inclusive approach is confirmed by numerous scholars and the international community, including the United Nations (UN) Special Rapporteur on the promotion of truth, justice, reparations and guarantees of non-recurrence, emphasizing that the meaningful participation of survivors and victims is not only beneficial but is, moreover, required to achieve the aims of transitional justice.[22]

As expressed by Orentlicher,[23] where victims are included in the design of programmes and policies, they can (re)ignite their full civic membership. In this context, it is crucial to connect participation and citizenship. The participation of individuals, namely those who are particularly aggrieved and disempowered, in transitional justice procedures not only encourages their agency but also paves the way for survivors to exercise their political right to equal participation and influence the social and political structures of society.[24] By including survivors and victims in the development and implementation of transitional justice processes, the mechanisms themselves become more relevant for the affected communities, contribute to local ownership and grassroots impact and, as noted above, directly address the grievances of survivors.[25] For this reason, transitional justice mechanisms provide an opportunity to increase victim participation and improve the legitimacy of governments and institutions.

Survivors of CRSV are driven by a desire for recognition of the wrongs done, guarantees of non-repetition, connectedness and a voice in the justice process.[26] Recognition is closely related to validation while guarantees of non-repetition are linked to the prevention of CRSV. The sense of connectedness comes from the wish to regain their sense of belonging in the community and, finally, having a voice can be understood in terms of being listened to as well as to survivors' active participation in the justice process.[27] These characteristics are at the centre of the conceptualization of justice by survivors. In the next section, the authors will examine how social movements in the context of CRSV have the potential to enhance transitional justice.

Survivor Movements to Enhance Transitional Justice and the Rule of Law

Survivor movements, like other social movements, represent social forms of political struggle in which survivors and victims engage and act together as collectives to challenge the socio-political status quo.[28] These movements operate outside institutionalized lines of action and they promote or resist change across the existing socio-economic, political and cultural systems of authority.[29]

Survivor movements[30] place survivors in leadership roles, provide a sense of power and self-assurance and enhance collective identity.[31] The empowerment of survivors by adopting leadership roles helps them to internalize their identities as enabled and influential, leading to their ability to assert a public voice. The perception of a common identity is also crucial to ensure the successful mobilization of the movement's activities. Melucci provides more insight into this concept,[32] arguing that collective identity is not a given, but rather a process that is strengthened through a common language among members.[33]

An important view of Melucci[34] is the role of the emotional involvement of activists, which has been tested by others. Research indicates that emotional bonds and solidarity between activists can encourage them to continue their work, despite setbacks and other forms of repression.[35] While this concept of collective identity within the theoretical literature encompasses a range of definitions, relationships and interactions, it is important to note that contributions from research indicate that survivors do not only seek justice for themselves but also others, including future generations, their families and fellow survivors. Thus, forming a collective identity for survivors is crucial to ensure a unison voice in their demands for justice.[36]

In addition to a collective identity, an earlier view around social movements, namely the resource mobilization theory, believes that resources are key factors in determining whether social movements are successful. According to this perspective, resources such as money, knowledge, skills and the media contribute to more effective movements. These resources have been broken down into five types by Edwards and McCarthy, who have categorized them as being moral, cultural, social-organizational, material and human.[37] Moral resources refer to solidarity and sympathetic support from those who are not direct beneficiaries. Cultural resources refer to knowledge on how to complete specific tasks related to advocacy activities in a given context. Social-organizational resources are those resources that help to spread the message of a group or network, such as holding community meetings, public demonstrations, and strikes. Material resources refer to the financial and physical assets of the movement while human resources refer to labour, experience and expertise. These movements also benefit from obtaining linkages to other groups and external support.[38]

Furthermore, social movements thrive on the notion of the meaningful participation of those involved, because they are direct beneficiaries and best placed to demand their rights. Participation can extend to various forms, ranging from expression, provision of information and consultation, to decision-making. It is the latter form that is most interesting, particularly concerning survivor movements and promoting survivor-centred initiatives.

Understanding 'Meaningful Participation' in the Context of CRSV

Survivors have a unique insight into the realities of their communities and a normative view of what is owed to them. Therefore, providing survivors with decision-making power and trusting them with responsibilities that accompany such power is key. One remarkable example where survivors are not passive actors, but rather leaders or equal participants with a large portion of control is the case of survivor networks. In recent years, survivor networks have proved successful in taking important steps towards achieving meaningful justice for survivors of CRSV.

Survivor networks are structured as social movement organizations with varying degrees of organization in which survivors who share the same grievances come together around a common cause.[39] In this context, we can consider the spatial lens described above and look at survivor networks as 'claimed spaces'. These networks play a crucial role in coordinating and mobilizing the community, and they also have an important connective role in linking the ideologies of the movement to ground-level mobilization.[40]

Survivor networks from all around the globe organize public events and awareness-raising campaigns to shine a light on the devastating consequences of sexual violence and involve the community in a collective fight against impunity for these crimes. Representing thousands of survivors, these networks' advocacy and activism pressure governments to act and implement policies that adequately protect and uphold the rights of survivors. Furthermore, survivor networks play a key role in eliminating the stigma around sexual violence, providing survivors with the understanding that they are not alone, that others have suffered the same and that this violence is systemic and beyond their control.

Social movements made up of survivors provide a safe platform for them to speak out and demand justice on their terms. Both individual survivor activists and survivor networks, if provided with the resources and the support needed, can thrive through different levels of participation and roles.

The question that remains is *how can we concretely envisage survivor participation in networks and movements, taking what we know from social movement theory?* As identified above, several factors of social movement theory contribute to the success and growth of social movements. These were leadership, knowledge (particularly around advocacy), external support, meaningful participation, material resources, space to build a collective identity and solidarity.

Method to Apply the Framework to Practice

To answer the above question, we aim to conceptualize the efforts of survivor networks and activists by applying the six identified factors to existing networks. It is important to note that these characteristics are not static, but rather evolve over time. These characteristics are not binary either; they exist in a spectrum with a whole range of possibilities and combinations where each can contribute to enhancing meaningful participation of survivors, with the overarching goal of ensuring more impactful justice for survivors.

Table 6.1 Framework for assessing survivor networks

Factors identified in social movement theory	*Elements needed for survivor networks and activists*
Leadership	Capacity-building efforts
Knowledge	Capacity-building efforts; platform for activists to exchange with one another
External support	Active role of CSOs/NGOs; partnerships
Meaningful participation	Consultees versus decision-makers
Material resources	Space/resources to develop own initiatives
Space to build a collective identity	Platform for activists to exchange with one another
Solidarity	Platform for activists to exchange with one another

Conceptualization of the Characteristics

Although unlikely to be ubiquitous, these characteristics are explained as follows:

- *Capacity-building efforts to become independent actors and leaders.* Movements and networks provide an opportunity for individuals to gain the skills and proficiency to become influential actors on the policy stage. Thus, we use this term to refer to the knowledge and cultural resources needed to conduct effective advocacy and awareness-raising. Through training, coaching programmes and study visits, to name just a few, survivors can gain these skills. Importantly, they can form their advocacy messages and goals and learn how best to implement an advocacy strategy. Furthermore, these forms of capacity building strengthen leadership skills.
- *The active role of CSOs and NGOs.* One characteristic that is different for each network is the role played by other CSOs or NGOs. By focusing efforts on collaboration with CSOs and NGOs, networks and activists can build external support, which is key to a successful movement. With their expertise and organizational capacities, CSOs and NGOs can play a complementary or facilitative role or offer guidance and support to survivor networks when needed. This support can sometimes be indispensable, especially during the early stages until the network is fully developed and becomes self-sustainable. CSOs and NGOs have the material, financial and human resources necessary to establish a network and – especially when speaking about local CSOs and NGOs – they also have increased legitimacy and recognition which can help to raise relevant public attention to the continued use of sexual violence as a weapon of war and call for the changes needed to end sexual violence and achieve justice. As these organizations enhance the political participation of survivors, they allow survivors to promote changes to the society from within its current existing sociopolitical setting, and not apart from it.[41]
- *Consultees versus decision-makers.* The role of CSOs and the level of independence (partially brought about by capacity-building activities), in addition to the approach of external actors in interacting with survivor activists and networks, will impact their level of participation in decision-making processes. We distinguish between consultees and decision-makers. In both cases, survivors are recognized as key stakeholders to ensure that their needs are reflected in policies, programmes and other initiatives. For survivors to be more empowered as equal actors, they may adopt roles as decision-makers, where they not only inform about their needs but also shape the programmes and policies that concern them. Such a distinction addresses the factors related to meaningful participation.
- *Space/resources to develop their own initiatives.* The role of NGOs and CSOs could still range from high levels of involvement to a more

supervisory role, to no involvement at all. However, when networks have sufficient support and space to carry out their initiatives, there is more ownership and freedom to pursue more survivor-led goals and to advocate for justice on their own terms.

- *Platform for survivor activists and networks to exchange with one another.* Learning exchanges with other survivor networks and other forms of exchanges further equip survivors with the necessary skills to become leaders and central figures of the movement. Both at the national and global level, this may take the form of online platforms helping survivors and victims to connect to others. In addition to online and offline meetings where they can learn from each other, they are also able to feel supported and empowered. Opportunities to come together, share stories and develop action plans are likely to lead to greater solidarity and understanding of a collective identity, particularly when, as was noted earlier, an emotional exchange takes place.
- *Partnerships.* One key procedural step in obtaining change within the transitional justice context and other settings is to become recognized as a key player within the CRSV landscape. In addition to adopting such a positioning, networks and activists will also largely benefit when they engage in both formal and informal partnerships, therefore gaining external support with NGOs, legal professionals, ministries, churches and traditional leaders, key international actors and others who can complement their work in a valuable way. By achieving this positioning, networks gain legitimacy and can more meaningfully exercise their active participation, ensuring that their voices are not absent from important decision-making processes and events.

Survivor networks' advocacy targets are context-specific and so are the networks' priorities and methods for achieving meaningful justice for survivors. Survivor networks operate differently and they can take many forms, varying in their degree of survivor-centredness and leadership. Although these cases are not stationary, for the purposes of this chapter the authors will present three examples in which survivors' (leading) role in advocacy has led to significant steps towards justice.

Survivor Networks in Practice

Many initiatives where aggrieved parties have played a major role in developing or implementing transitional justice mechanisms achieved meaningful change, namely in many countries in Latin America. There is undeniably no single inclusive approach, but rather different approaches that can place survivors centre stage, ranging from survivor-centred to truly survivor-led initiatives, as noted above. The three examples were chosen for different reasons. The first, SEMA, the Global Network of Victims and Survivors to End Wartime Sexual Violence, has been working under the principle of 'nothing about us without us', with the overarching goal of ensuring that survivors' voices are made central. The 'Network of Women Victims and Professionals' in Colombia has a similar aim to include survivors' voices in peace and transitional justice processes but adds an interesting aspect related to the potential role of professionals in survivor networks. Finally, an initiative rather than a network entitled 'Call It What It Is Campaign' will be explored to demonstrate that it is not only survivor networks that have the potential to bring justice to survivors but that ensuring the meaningful participation of survivors in campaigns can also achieve this goal.

In the section below, the aim of the authors is not to model survivor networks and campaigns, but rather to portray it in the light of the six characteristics identified in the previous section based on social movement theory. Our aim is not to compare them either: when introducing these three cases, we acknowledge their unique benefits and flaws and reflect on their intrinsic and structural differences that make their survivor-centredness and leadership distinctive in nature. By selecting two examples of survivor networks, and one of an international campaign we aim to encourage organizations working with survivors to enhance survivor-centred initiatives and entrust survivors with decision-making power.

Platforms to Enhance Meaningful Participation and Justice to Survivors of CRSV

SEMA, the Global Network of Victims and Survivors to End Wartime Sexual Violence

SEMA, the Global Network of Victims and Survivors to End Wartime Sexual Violence, gathers victims and survivors of CRSV from 21 countries around the world. SEMA members mobilize collectively to speak out about the reality and consequences of CRSV, demand justice and accountability and work together to reclaim their space as agents of change. The global network advocates for survivors' rights to receive holistic care – including medical, legal, psychological and socio-economic assistance – and compensation to rebuild their lives. SEMA is seen as a safe international platform for survivors to come together and strengthen one another. By bringing together survivors from different generations, continents and cultures to learn from each other, SEMA is breaking new ground by adding an international dimension to previous approaches.

Since its creation, survivors have taken the lead and expressed their desire to establish a global survivor-led and survivor-centred movement and, together, decided on concrete next steps. Making sure that SEMA truly reflects their needs, survivors have identified the strategic priorities of the network and the path forward for their joint advocacy. This survivor-centred approach has allowed survivors to build the network on their terms and has transformed them into decision-makers.

The Mukwege Foundation, a survivor-driven international NGO, has played a crucial facilitative role in connecting grassroots survivor networks with SEMA for mutual support, learning and growth. In addition to the global network SEMA, the Mukwege Foundation has set up national survivor networks in several countries, such as the Democratic Republic of the Congo, the Central African Republic and Ukraine. Providing support to these networks through capacity building, setting up communication channels, connecting members to other organizations and stakeholders, and supporting them in their advocacy endeavours, the Mukwege Foundation works with local partners to guide and support the women who take part in these networks.

So far, SEMA members have been receiving capacity-building training to help them to acquire the necessary skills and knowledge to participate in the discussions that concern them and gain recognition as experts capable of finding innovative solutions at the local, national and international level. However, the global network – similar to the national networks – was established with the goal of becoming survivor-led. Therefore, the current role of the Mukwege Foundation is intended to be replaced by an advisory role in the future, once the network becomes self-sustainable and, in all matters, survivor-led.

Furthermore, international NGOs can act as a bridge between international organizations and survivors, promoting partnerships with key national and international actors. Through the Mukwege Foundation, SEMA members are invited to speak at numerous international conferences and meetings where they advocate for their rights and urge policymakers to be included in the discussions that concern them. Recently, SEMA members have spoken at the Human Rights Council, the North Atlantic Treaty Organization (NATO) headquarters in Brussels, Belgium, numerous side events of the UN General Assembly, and dozens of international conferences and debates; they have contributed to academic research and policy reports and they have shaped the draft of a code of conduct for documenters of CRSV.

This partnership between NGOs and survivor networks can enhance survivors' (political) participation and, ultimately, contribute to achieving true justice for survivors. In this case, on the one hand, the Mukwege Foundation has helped to boost the reach of the network with its contacts and made it possible for survivors from different continents to meet, connect and support each other. On the other hand, the Mukwege Foundation –being a survivor-driven human rights organization – has also gained extremely valuable insights from its close relationship with survivors. Over the past few years the Mukwege Foundation has learned about the local context in each country from the survivors themselves and partners on the ground, and it has shaped its programmes to make them more meaningful for survivors. Survivors benefit from the expertise of NGOs but the latter also gain extremely valuable insight from their work with survivors, namely on how to engage and include survivors in policy discussions and how to better to prioritize and reflect survivors' needs in policies, programmes and other initiatives.

SEMA has made the call for reparations one of the network's advocacy priorities. In 2019 SEMA joined forces with Dr Denis Mukwege and Nadia Murad – the 2018 Nobel Peace Prize laureates – which culminated in the establishment of the Global Survivors Fund, a new, innovative and survivor-centred mechanism to provide reparations and other forms of redress to survivors of CRSV globally. Since the outset, SEMA has been consulted by the Fund to understand the potential impact of the programmes at the local level and to explore how reparations can best serve individuals and their communities, depending on the context. The achievements of the innovative approach of the Fund will be further examined in the next chapter.

The Network of Women Victims and Professionals (Red de Mujeres Víctimas y Profesionales)

Red de Mujeres Víctimas y Profesionales (the Network of Women Victims and Professionals) provides psychosocial support and empowers victims[42] so that they understand their rights and seek justice and reparation for the crimes committed against them. The network supports women who speak out about sexual violence and inspires other victims who have not yet broken the silence to do so and continue their path towards healing.

The network has organized more than 19 documentation days in which more than 1,200 victims have denounced the crimes of sexual violence committed against them. At the time of writing the network in Colombia had documented more than 650 cases of sexual violence. Throughout the years, these initiatives have been developed and implemented in partnership with other local and international organizations such as the Investigation and Accusation Unit of Colombia's Special Jurisdiction for Peace. The documentation days offer victims a space where they feel comfortable and safe to denounce the crimes of sexual violence before the Office of the Attorney General and the Ombudsman's Office, something that they would not have done otherwise.

Within the network, the relationship between victims and professionals is one of mutual learning and collaboration. Initiatives such as the documentation days are carried out throughout the country and the survivor coordinators of the network play a crucial role in identifying the victims in each region, coordinating the activities with the other partner organizations and ensuring victims' access to psychological support during the process of documentation. The legal professionals design the programmes and protocols with the victims' insights and provide training on several topics, including the Colombian peace agreement, protection and safety of activists, access to justice and transitional justice mechanisms. Thus, professionals play a crucial role in teaching victims about the laws and policies in the country and helping victims to understand their rights so that they can become fully fledged actors in civil society.

With survivors occupying the main leadership positions of the network, they are not only consulted in the processes, but they shape all the strategic decisions of the network and carry out the programmes all over the country. The Colombian network is an example of how victims and professionals can complement each other and enhance the survivor-led component and meaningfully exercise their active (political) participation.

Women's Initiatives for Gender Justice: The 'Call It What It Is' Campaign

The 'Call It What It Is' campaign aims to promote the work of civil society towards a survivor-centred understanding of what makes violence sexual and it has resulted in the development of the Civil Society Declaration within the Hague Principles on Sexual Violence. This tool ensures that practitioners, whether legal practitioners, NGOs or policymakers, do not trivialize or overlook certain types of violence. The Hague Principles indicate to all relevant stakeholders – including practitioners working to support survivors – that although stakeholders may think they understand sexual violence and claim that definitions of sexual violence are incomplete, they will not have a full understanding until input from survivors is accounted for.

The initiative was developed by the Women's Initiatives for Gender Justice, which has been guiding the process since its inception and ensuring the inclusion of survivor voices. Other organizations[43] are also included in a partnership, working both with survivors and legal practitioners to ensure that all perspectives are included. While the development of the Hague Principles on Sexual Violence[44] included survivors in a predominantly consultative role, it is expected that their role will become essential during the upcoming implementation stage, while the NGO role will become less of an imperative, although still necessary.

After consulting with survivors to understand the most relevant tools to implement the Hague Principles in their advocacy work, a toolkit was developed that encourages survivors and victims to lead their advocacy efforts, moving one step further away from consultation towards advocates and decision-makers in terms of awareness-raising and policy. To carry out the activities outlined in the toolkit and to continue national efforts of the campaign, survivor activists require a capacity-building stage to fully grasp the extent and possibilities provided by the Hague Principles on Sexual Violence. Through such capacity building, they may learn, for example, how best to target their audiences, how to effectively spread the message on sexual violence and how to implement their messaging into their existing efforts to demand their rights as CRSV survivors and victims.

The toolkit,[45] particularly one that involved survivor activists in its development, will also create a space for survivors to develop their initiatives, which was also identified as an important characteristic of any effort geared towards survivor-led work. Going beyond capacity building, such a tool enhances the independence of an individual or a network. The 'Call It What It Is' campaign and subsequent survivor advocacy toolkit illustrates how survivor-led initiatives will make survivors more autonomous. Furthermore, this method can also be applied to other projects that aim to include survivors' voices.

More Survivor-Centred Justice

Despite the tremendous advances in recognizing victims' rights and their crucial role in post-conflict societies, this agenda has yet to be fully realized at both the national and international level. What is notable is that even when the process of achieving justice for survivors is survivor-centred, it often fails to ensure the meaningful participation of survivors. A survivor-centred approach[46] focuses on prioritizing the rights, needs and wishes of survivors and victims, yet it does not necessarily address their role in obtaining their rights. Meaningful participation, however, requires the empowerment of survivors and the space to adopt leadership roles in the process, while considering the local context and recognizing that justice means different things for different people.[47] The cases illustrated in the previous section demonstrate that, although there is no single universal approach, when survivors are empowered and entrusted with decision-making they can contribute to unprecedented achievements in attaining justice.

In the case of SEMA, the network has created a safe space for survivors to come together and support each other on their healing and reconciliation path. The exchanges between survivors bring to light the similarity of their experiences in the wider context of systematic use of sexual violence as a weapon of war. This creates a powerful sense of strength, unity and solidarity among survivors. Furthermore, survivors' leadership in developing their survivor-centred awareness-raising campaigns not only allows them to document their testimonies in creative and bold ways, but also provides them with a sense of ownership in the way they speak out ensuring that their experiences are (correctly) documented.

Another way in which SEMA has contributed to unprecedented success is the launch of the Global Survivors Fund, where the programmes are designed together with survivors so that the schemes commensurate the harm inflicted upon them and reflect the needs of individuals or groups of survivors, from development to implementation. Three SEMA members[48] have seats on the Global Survivors Fund's Board, surpassing the consultee threshold and making sure that they are key players at all levels of decision-making. The board members are treated as equal partners and are considered as primary stakeholders, adding to their empowerment and allowing them to regain their dignity and rebuild their lives. The shared learning between survivors and the collaboration among all stakeholders yield more productive and context-sensitive outcomes and can achieve genuine justice for survivors.

In Colombia, with the support from other partners, the Network of Women Victims and Professionals is fighting against impunity for crimes of sexual violence by launching the first public civil society information system to compile and systematize the complaints from victims. The system – although originally designed by professionals – is currently managed by survivors and it enables the network to follow up on documented cases, all the while ensuring due process and making sexual violence in Colombia visible. The creation of a survivor-centred and survivor-led platform that centralizes information and gives voice to hundreds of victims of sexual violence is a major step towards truth finding and justice to survivors in Colombia.

Based on the information gathered in the collective and individual complaints documented by the network and systematized in the online platform, the network has submitted several reports to Colombia's Special Jurisdiction for Peace and Truth Commission. The network aims to reclaim survivors' rightful participation in the transitional justice process in Colombia and, in the process, become recognized as a major player within the CRSV landscape. The case of the Colombian network demonstrates that it is possible to empower victims so that they work together with professionals as equal partners and complement one another's work based on their available expertise. This process not only empowers victims by allowing them to regain their dignity but also contributes to better outcomes for transitional justice and the rule of law.

The 'Call It What It Is' campaign is an unparalleled initiative providing recognition to survivors of sexual violence as those whose expertise is best placed to inform practitioners about sexual violence. For transitional justice measures, this accuracy is crucial and it ought to be the first step before developing programmes and policies for victims. Without fully understanding how laws can be stipulated and enforced inclusively, how victims can gain access to legal recourse, and which characteristics are accounted for when deciding on eligibility for reparations programmes, a large number of survivors and victims would be excluded from transitional justice efforts. This could potentially constitute an example of best practice to the International Criminal Court and other bodies whose aims are intimately linked to the mandate of ending impunity for grave crimes and delivering justice for survivors.

This campaign launched in 2019 had a first phase in which practitioners agreed on the necessity of taking a step back and understanding what constitutes sexual violence in the eyes of those harmed. This is not only an important milestone in recognizing the harm done but also in acknowledging and affirming survivors' crucial role throughout the reconciliation process. With survivors placed at the centre of this campaign, the aim remains to continue to use the Hague Principles on Sexual Violence and to provide survivors with the necessary skills and knowledge so that they can apply it to their work.

Conclusion

The international victims' rights movement has been gaining momentum in recent years and there has been a push for victims and survivors' rights to be echoed in legislation and other internationally adopted resolutions. There is also plenty of research on transitional justice and the importance of civil society's participation but, despite the shift from NGOs, UN bodies and other organizations in recognizing the need for greater survivor inclusion in the decisions that concern them, the question of 'meaningful participation' remains highly unexplored. There is an increasing amount of attention paid to *why* this is important; however, further research is needed to solidify the concept of meaningful participation. In this chapter, we unpack the concept of meaningful participation of survivors of CRSV and reject preconceived ideas and expectations about transitional justice and its objectives. Looking at survivor movements, it has become clear that survivors can – and are – effectively demanding their rights and achieving significant milestones.

What the current chapter does is to provide a practical lens through which better to understand how to optimize civil society's – and in particular survivors' – participation in transitional justice. Building on the evidence from three case studies, this chapter is a first attempt at better understanding how survivor participation – including in leadership roles – can lead to more meaningful (transitional) justice. SEMA, the global network of survivors, has contributed to creating a global collective narrative around CRSV and it has shed light on the enormous potential and strength of an internationally coordinated network of survivors. This is further confirmed by the important role played by survivors of CRSV in the launch of the Global Survivors Fund, created to provide reparations to victims of CRSV and where survivors are part of decision-making. In the case of the Network of Women Victims and Professionals, we have demonstrated how victims are fighting to end the cycle of impunity and contribute to truth finding in Colombia while taking the most out of their partnership with professionals. Finally, the 'Call It What It Is' campaign laid the foundation for a more meaningful and deep understanding of sexual violence in the eyes of the survivors, not only impacting all forms of transitional justice but also ensuring that the basis for all the policies and programmes implemented truly reflect their experiences. With increasingly more involvement in future phases, the campaign aims to equip survivors to become agents of change while giving them the space to shape and implement the Hague Principles and toolkit created. In summary, these cases illustrated how, when supported effectively, organized survivor efforts can lead to meaningful change within transitional justice.

Social movement theory was reviewed in this chapter, not to test it but to provide a new framework that can be applied to survivor movements in a more structured manner. Before understanding how to promote meaningful justice, it is important to understand the factors that impact survivor networks, namely those identified in terms of social movements, namely leadership, knowledge, external support, meaningful participation, material resources, a space in which to build a collective identity and solidarity. Although it is recognized this is a simplified view of push and pull factors ensuring successful survivor movements, the authors are not aware of studies or literature specifically applying these theories to CRSV, and therefore an explorative approach was adopted. Such an approach allows for the conceptualization of survivor activism and of the relevant characteristics that strengthen the efforts of survivor networks, as borrowed from various theories around social movements. The identified characteristics include capacity building, the potentially beneficial role of NGOs, the space and resources to develop their own initiatives, providing a platform for activists to exchange with one another, partnerships and encouraging survivors' roles as decision-makers. Further work on this topic is needed to explore other elements that were not discussed in this chapter. For example, a more in-depth understanding of how to develop survivor networks may include the factors that ensure high-quality advocacy work, such as the creation of a formalized structure.[49]

In this chapter, the authors explored how existing transitional justice theory around civic mobilization can be applied to network building. This examination was done by (1) briefly presenting a background to transitional justice in terms of participatory approaches; (2) presenting an overview of survivor movements within social movement theory to understand how these notions have been and can be applied to transitional justice; (3) discussing meaningful participation in terms of survivor networks; (4) presenting a practical framework that can help networks to understand how to best to function; and (5) illustrating this framework through three existing networks or initiatives that contain elements of survivor-centred, meaningful participation. As a result, this chapter demonstrated how the meaningful participation of survivors has contributed to reaching important milestones in the context of CRSV.

The rule of law will only function in a society that engages those who are geared towards effecting the desired changes. By promoting survivor advocacy, civil society amplifies other voices and puts pressure on those developing and implementing transitional justice mechanisms. Indeed, survivors and victims are best placed to inform on the necessary steps towards accountability, not only as witnesses in criminal proceedings but also as experts who can demand and exercise their rights.

Finally, the arguments we put forth can extend further in a more encompassing view of victims' and survivors' rights: *how can survivors be best equipped to impact transitional justice in meaningful ways?* With this analysis, we hope that NGOs, UN agencies, organizations working on survivors' rights, scholars, policymakers and other stakeholders will pause to reflect on the benefits of survivor-centred initiatives and develop mechanisms and tools that support meaningful participation of survivors in transitional justice and the rule of law.

Notes

1 Ángela María Escobar, a survivor of CRSV, during the event *Survivors of Sexual Violence Step Up and Speak Out for Transitional Justice* on 12 October 2020, organized by the Mukwege Foundation, UN Women and the UN Office of the

Special Representative of the Secretary-General on Sexual Violence in Conflict, marking the 20th anniversary of UN Security Council Resolution 1325 on Women, Peace, and Security.

2 The terminology used in the literature on sexual violence has gradually shifted from 'victims' to 'survivors', emphasizing the agency, empowerment and resilience of those who have lived through the experience. The chapter follows this terminology but, in some cases, the term 'victims' is used as a legal term of reference.

3 J. Shapland, J. Willmore and P. Duff (1985) *Victims in the Criminal Justice System* (Aldershot: Gower, 1985); J.L. Herman, 'Justice from the Victim's Perspective', *Violence Against Women*, 11(5), 2005, pp. 571–602; and F. Marsh and N.M. Wager, 'Restorative Justice in Cases of Sexual Violence: Exploring the Views of the Public and Survivors', *Probation Journal*, 62(4), 2015, pp. 336–356.

4 J.L. Leatherman, *Sexual Violence and Armed Conflict* (Cambridge: Polity Press, 2011).

5 Marsh and Wager, 'Restorative Justice in Cases of Sexual Violence'.

6 T, Van Camp and J. Wemmers, 'Victim Satisfaction with Restorative Justice: More Than Simply Procedural Justice', *International Review of Victimology*, 19(2), 2013, pp. 117–143; and Marsh and Wager, 'Restorative Justice in Cases of Sexual Violence'.

7 C. Garbett, 'The International Criminal Court and Restorative Justice: Victims, Participation and the Processes of Justice', *Restorative Justice*, 5(2), 2017, pp. 198–220; and M. de Waardt and S. Weber, 'Beyond Victims' Mere Presence: An Empirical Analysis of Victim Participation in Transitional Justice in Colombia', *Journal of Human Rights Practice*, 11(1), 2019, pp. 209–228.

8 P. Lundy and M. McGovern, (2008) 'The Role of Community in Participatory Transitional Justice', in *Transitional Justice from Below: Grassroots Activism and the Struggle for Change*, ed. Kieran McEvoy and Lorna McGregor (Oxford: Hart Publishing, 2008), pp. 99–120.

9 E. Evrard, G.M. Bonifazi and T. Destrooper, 'The Meaning of Participation in Transitional Justice: A Conceptual Proposal for Empirical Analysis', *International Journal of Transitional Justice*, 2021, pp. 1–20.

10 Ibid.

11 N.I. Dossa, M. Zunzunegui, M. Hatem and W.D. Fraser, 'Mental Health Disorders among Women Victims of Conflict-Related Sexual Violence in the Democratic Republic of Congo', *Journal of Interpersonal Violence*, 30(13), 2014, pp. 1–22; E. Sidebotham, J. Moffatt and K. Jones, 'Sexual Violence in Conflict: A Global Epidemic', *The Obstetrician and Gynaecologist*, 18(4), 2016, pp. 247–250; and C. Koos, 'Sexual Violence in Armed Conflicts: Research Progress and Remaining Gaps', *Third World Quarterly*, 38(9), 2017, pp. 1935–1951.

12 H.F. Antonsdottir, 'Decentring Criminal Law: Understandings of Justice by Victim-Survivors of Sexual Violence and their Implications for Different Justice Strategies', Lund University, 2020.

13 T.D. Olsen, L.A. Payne and A. Reiter, *Transitional Justice in Balance: Comparing Processes, Weighing Efficacy* (Washington, DC: United States Institute of Peace Press, 2010).

14 Ibid., and C. Brants and K. Klep, 'Transitional Justice: History-Telling, Collective Memory and the Victim Witness', *International Journal of Conflict and Violence*, 7 (1), 2013, pp. 36–49.

15 D. Crocker, 'Reckoning with Past Wrongs: A Normative Framework,' *Ethics and International Affairs*, 13(1), 1999, pp. 43–64.

16 S. Buckley-Zistel, T. Beck, C. Braun and F. Mieth, 'Transitional Justice Theories: An Introduction,' in *Transitional Justice Theories*, ed. Susanne Buckley-Zistel, Teresa Koloma Beck, Christian Braun and Friederike Mieth (New York: Routledge, 2014), pp. 1–16.

17 P. Gready and S. Robins, 'Rethinking Civil Society and Transitional Justice: Lessons from Social Movements and 'New' Civil Society', *The International Journal of Human Rights*, 21(7), 2017, pp. 956–975; and Evrard *et al.*, 'The Meaning of Participation in Transitional Justice'.
18 R. Sithole, 'Whose Justice? Rethinking Transitional Justice from the Bottom Up', *Journal of Law and Society*, 35(2), 2008, pp. 265–292.
19 Gready and Robins, 'Rethinking Civil Society and Transitional Justice'.
20 A. Cornwall, 'Spaces for Transformation? Reflections on Issues of Power and Difference in Participation in Development', in *Participation: From Tyranny to Transformation? Exploring New Approaches to Participation in Development*, ed. Samuel Hickey and Giles Mohan (London: Zed Books, 2005), pp. 75–91.
21 Evrard *et al.*, 'The Meaning of Participation in Transitional Justice'.
22 *Report of the Special Rapporteur on the promotion of truth, justice, reparation and guarantees of non-recurrence, Pablo de Greiff* (A/HRC/21/46), 9 August 2012.
23 *Independent Study on Best Practices, Including Recommendations, to Assist States in Strengthening Their Domestic Capacity to Combat All Aspects of Impunity, by Professor Diana Orentlicher* (E/CN.4/2004/88), 27 February 2004.
24 A. Cornwall, 'Beneficiary, Consumer, Citizen: Perspectives on Participation for Poverty Reduction', *Sida Studies*, 2, 2000, pp. 1–92; T. Bundschuh, 'Enabling Transitional Justice, Restoring Capabilities: The Imperative of Participation and Normative Integrity', *International Journal of Transitional Justice*, 9(1), 2015, pp. 10–32; and de Waardt and Weber, 'Beyond Victims' Mere Presence', pp. 209–228.
25 D. Taylor, 'Victim Participation in Transitional Justice Mechanisms: Real Power or Empty Ritual?' (Utrecht: Impunity Watch, 2014).
26 Antonsdottir, 'Decentring Criminal Law', and R. Holder and A. Robinson, 'Claiming Justice: Victims of Crime and their Perspectives of Justice', *International Review of Victimology*, 27(2), 2021, pp. 129–137.
27 C. McGlynn and N. Westmarland, (2019): 'Kaleidoscopic Justice: Sexual Violence and Victim-Survivors' Perceptions of Justice,' *Social & Legal Studies*, 28(2), 2019, pp. 179–201; and Antonsdottir, 'Decentring Criminal Law'.
28 M. de Buser and C. Kim, 'Social Movements against Corruption and Sexual Violence in India', *Asian Journal of Social Science*, 44(1–2), 2016, pp. 7–33.
29 S. Cummings, 'Law and Social Movements: An Interdisciplinary Analysis', in *Handbook of Social Movements Across Disciplines*, ed. Conny Roggeband and Bert Klandermans (Cham: Springer, 2017), pp. 233–270.
30 We do not aim to provide a comprehensive overview of social movement theory. We do, however, borrow from different theories in order to illustrate how social movements can benefit victims and survivors of CRSV.
31 K. Klenke, *Women and Leadership: A Contextual Perspective* (New York: Springer, 1996); and Gready and Robins, 'Rethinking Civil Society and Transitional Justice'.
32 A. Melucci A, 'The New Social Movements: A Theoretical Approach', *Social Science Information*, 19(2), 1980, pp. 199–226.
33 C.F. Fominaya, 'Collective Identity in Social Movements: Central Concepts and Debates', *Sociology Compass*, 4(6), 2010, pp. 393–404.
34 A. Melucci, 'The Process of Collective Identity', in *Social Movements and Culture*, ed. H. Johnston and B. Klandermans (Minneapolis: University of Minnesota Press, 1995), pp. 41–63.
35 Ibid.
36 R. Holder and A. Robinson, 'Claiming Justice: Victims of Crime and their Perspectives of Justice', *International Review of Victimology*, 27(2), 2021, pp. 129–137.
37 B. Edwards and J.D. McCarthy, *The Blackwell Companion to Social Movements* (Malden, MA: Blackwell, 2004), pp. 116–152.

38 M. Zald and J. McCarthy, 'Resource Mobilization and Social Movements: A Partial Theory', in *Social Movements in an Organizational Society: Collected Essays*, ed. N. Mayer, M. Zald and J.D. McCarthy (New York: Routledge, 2017), pp. 15–48.

39 For the purposes of this chapter, we assert that while a fully recognized victim/survivor movement has yet to surface, there are networks and individuals active in changing the CRSV landscape and an undeniable momentum is taking place.

40 M. Zald and J. McCarthy, 'Resource Mobilization and Social Movements: A Partial Theory', *American Journal of Sociology*, 82(6), 1977, pp. 15–48.

41 M. de Buser and C. Kim, 'Social Movements against Corruption and Sexual Violence in India: Urban Middle Class Approaches', *Asian Journal of Social Science*, 44(1), 2016, p. 7.

42 Here we use the term victim as the Colombian network has consciously decided on this terminology to ensure that they are recognized as individuals whom the legal framework protects.

43 A full list of organizations that contributed can be found here, under acknowledgement, available at https://thehagueprinciples.org/about-the-hague-principles/.

44 The Hague Principles of Sexual Violence include (1) the Civil Society Declaration on Sexual Violence; (2) International Criminal Law Guidelines on Sexual Violence; and (3) Key Principles for Policy Makers on Sexual Violence. See https://4genderjustice.org/ftp-files/publications/The-Hague-Principles-on-Sexual-Violence.pdf. More information on the methodology and history can be found at https://thehagueprinciples.org/about-the-hague-principles/.

45 For more information or to see the current stage of development, see https://thehagueprinciples.org/tools-for-the-use-of-the-principles/.

46 For more information, see https://www.endvawnow.org/en/articles/1499-survivor-centred-approach.html.

47 For a discussion on the concept of meaningful participation, see D. Taylor, 'Victim Participation in Transitional Justice Mechanisms: Real Power or Empty Ritual?' (Utrecht: Impunity Watch, 2014). For the purposes of this chapter, we particularly emphasize the active role that survivors and victims may take, namely through leadership or participation in decision-making processes or design and implementation of processes.

48 The three members of the global network were chosen based on their interest and qualifications. They attend all meetings and have an equal place at the table where decisions are taken.

49 M. Laxminarayan and B. Duerr, 'Engaging Survivors of Conflict-Related Sexual Violence in Social Movements', in *Peace, Reconciliation and Social Justice Leadership in the 21st Century*, ed. H.E. Schockman, V. Hernandez and A. Boitano (Bingley: Emerald Publishing, 2019), pp. 263–278.

References

Antonsdottir, H.F. (2020) *Decentring Criminal Law: Understandings of Justice by Victim-Survivors of Sexual Violence and their Implications for Different Justice Strategies*, Lund University.

Brants, C. and Klep, K. (2013) 'Transitional Justice: History-Telling, Collective Memory and the Victim Witness,' *International Journal of Conflict and Violence*, vol. 7, no. 1, pp. 36–49.

Buckley-Zistel, S.K. Beck, T. Braun, C. and Mieth, F. (2014) 'Transitional Justice Theories: An Introduction', in Susanne Buckley-Zistel, Teresa Koloma Beck, Christian Braun and Friederike Mieth (eds), *Transitional Justice Theories*. New York: Routledge, pp. 1–16.

Bundschuh, T. (2015) 'Enabling Transitional Justice, Restoring Capabilities: The Imperative of Participation and Normative Integrity', *International Journal of Transitional Justice*, vol. 9, no. 1, pp. 10–32.

Cornwall, A. (2000) 'Beneficiary, Consumer, Citizen: Perspectives on Participation for Poverty Reduction', *Sida Studies*, no. 2, pp. 1–92.

Cornwall, A. (2005) 'Spaces for Transformation? Reflections on Issues of Power and Difference in Participation in Development', in Samuel Hickey and Giles Mohan *(eds), Participation: From Tyranny to Transformation? Exploring New Approaches to Participation in Development*. London: Zed Books, pp. 75–91.

Crocker, D. (1999) 'Reckoning with Past Wrongs: A Normative Framework', *Ethics and International Affairs*, vol. 13, no. 1, pp. 43–64.

Cummings, S.L. (2017) 'Law and Social Movements: An Interdisciplinary Analysis', in Conny Roggeband and Bert Klandermans (eds), *Handbook of Social Movements Across Disciplines*. Cham: Springer, pp. 233–270.

DeBuser, M. and Kim, C. (2016) 'Social Movements against Corruption and Sexual Violence in India', *Asian Journal of Social Science*, vol. 44, no. 1–2, pp. 7–33.

DeWaardt, M. and Weber, S. (2019) 'Beyond Victims' Mere Presence: An Empirical Analysis of Victim Participation in Transitional Justice in Colombia', *Journal of Human Rights Practice*, vol. 11, no. 1, pp. 209–228.

Ines Dossa, N., Zunzunegui, M.V., Hatem, M. and Fraser, W.D. (2014) 'Mental Health Disorders among Women Victims of Conflict-Related Sexual Violence in the Democratic Republic of the Congo', *Journal of Interpersonal Violence*, vol. 30, no. 13, pp. 1–22.

Edwards, B. and McCarthy, J.D. (2004) *The Blackwell Companion to Social Movements*. Malden, MA: Blackwell, pp. 116–152.

Evrard, E., Bonifazi, G.M. and Destrooper, T. (2021) 'The Meaning of Participation in Transitional Justice: A Conceptual Proposal for Empirical Analysis', *International Journal of Transitional Justice*, pp. 1–20.

Fominaya, C.F. (2010) 'Collective Identity in Social Movements: Central Concepts and Debates', *Sociology Compass*, vol. 4, no. 6, pp. 393–404.

Garbett, C. (2017) 'The International Criminal Court and Restorative Justice: Victims, Participation and the Processes of Justice', *Restorative Justice*, vol. 5, no. 2, pp. 198–220.

Gready, P. and Robins, S. (2017) 'Rethinking Civil Society and Transitional Justice: Lessons from Social Movements and "New" Civil Society', *The International Journal of Human Rights*, vol. 21, no. 7, pp. 956–975.

Herman, J.L. (2005) 'Justice from the Victim's Perspective', *Violence Against Women*, vol. 11, no. 5, pp. 571–602.

Holder, R.L. and Robinson, A.L. (2021) 'Claiming Justice: Victims of Crime and their Perspectives of Justice', *International Review of Victimology*, vol. 27, no. 2, pp. 129–137.

Klenke, K. (1996) *Women and Leadership: A Contextual Perspective*. New York: Springer.

Koos, C. (2017) 'Sexual Violence in Armed Conflicts: Research Progress and Remaining Gaps', *Third World Quarterly*, vol. 38, no. 9, pp. 1935–1951.

Laxminarayan, M. and Duerr, B. (2019) 'Engaging Survivors of Conflict-Related Sexual Violence in Social Movements,' in H. Eric Schockman, Vanessa Hernandez and Aldo Boitano (eds), *Peace, Reconciliation and Social Justice Leadership in the 21st Century*. Bingley: Emerald Publishing, pp. 263–278.

Leatherman, J.L. (2011) *Sexual Violence and Armed Conflict*. Cambridge: Polity Press.

Lundy, P. and McGovern, M. (2008) 'The Role of Community in Participatory Transitional Justice', in Kieran McEvoy and Lorna McGregor (eds), *Transitional Justice from Below: Grassroots Activism and the Struggle for Change*. Oxford: Hart Publishing, pp. 99–120.

Marsh, F. and Wager, N.W. (2015) 'Restorative Justice in Cases of Sexual Violence: Exploring the Views of the Public and Survivors', *Probation Journal*, vol. 62, no. 4, pp. 336–356.

McGlynn, C. and Westmarland, N. (2019) 'Kaleidoscopic Justice: Sexual Violence and Victim-Survivors' Perceptions of Justice', *Social & Legal Studies*, vol. 28, no. 2, pp. 179–201.

Melucci, A. (1980) 'The New Social Movements: A Theoretical Approach', *Social Science Information*, vol. 19, no. 2, pp. 199–226.

Melucci, A. (1995) 'The Process of Collective Identity', in H. Johnston and B. Klandermans (eds), *Social Movements and Culture*. Minneapolis: University of Minnesota Press, pp. 41–63.

Olsen, T.D., Payne, L.A. and Reiter, A.G. (2010) *Transitional Justice in Balance: Comparing Processes, Weighing Efficacy*. Washington, DC: United States Institute of Peace Press.

Shapland, S., Willmore, J. and Duff, P. (1985) Victims in the Criminal Justice System. Aldershot: Gower Publishing.

Sidebotham, E., Moffatt, J. and Jones, K. (2016) 'Sexual Violence in Conflict: A Global Epidemic', *The Obstetrician and Gynaecologist*, vol. 18, no. 4, pp. 247–250.

Sithole, R. (2008) 'Whose Justice? Rethinking Transitional Justice from the Bottom Up', *Journal of Law and Society*, vol. 35, no. 2, pp. 265–292.

Taylor, D. (2014) *Victim Participation in Transitional Justice Mechanisms: Real Power or Empty Ritual?* Utrecht: Impunity Watch.

Van Camp, T. and Wemmers, J.-A. (2013) 'Victim Satisfaction with Restorative Justice: More Than Simply Procedural Justice', *International Review of Victimology*, vol. 19, no. 2, pp. 117–143.

Zald, M.N. and McCarthy, J.D. (2017) 'Resource Mobilization and Social Movements: A Partial Theory', in Mayer N. Zald and John D. McCarthy (eds), *Social Movements in an Organizational Society: Collected Essays*. New York: Routledge, pp. 15–48.

7 UN Women

Paving the Way towards a Survivor-Centred Approach to Justice

Emily Kenney and Rozafa Kelmendi[1]

Introduction

In April 2019 the United Nations (UN) Security Council adopted its ninth resolution on women, peace and security, in which it recognized the need for survivor-centred approaches in preventing and responding to sexual violence in conflict and post-conflict situations.[2] Several years later, although the term 'survivor-centred approach' has continued to grow in usage within the UN system, there is no commonly accepted definition of this term within the organization.[3] The objective of this chapter is to examine programming implemented by one UN entity, UN Women, supporting access to justice for survivors of conflict-related sexual violence (CRSV) in order to understand better the key elements of what a survivor-centred approach looks like in practice, and to move towards a working definition of the term.

What is a 'survivor-centred approach' to preventing and responding to CRSV? The chapter uses examples from UN Women's programming on justice for CRSV in Kosovo[4] and Guatemala, which are both contexts where UN Women has consistently engaged in work on justice for CRSV over a period of many years, and has adopted an innovative survivor-centred approach with impressive results.[5] Examining UN Women's work in these two contexts, the chapter highlights three key elements which have helped the organization to place the rights, needs, expertise, capabilities and aspirations of survivors at the centre of its efforts by (1) supporting survivors to participate meaningfully in and lead justice efforts; (2) encouraging states to provide redress for CRSV, while ensuring adequate procedures to protect survivors throughout the justice process and to enable safe spaces conducive to their meaningful participation and leadership; and (3) focusing on how justice for survivors can contribute to social transformation by chipping away at gender inequality, a root cause of conflict and CRSV. Through its examination of UN Women's programming, this chapter seeks to support the field of practitioners, both within and outside the UN, to develop further the concept of a survivor-centred approach and put it into practice – to ensure that survivors of human rights violations are at the heart of all efforts to strengthen access to justice and transformative reparations. As such, the chapter concludes with a brief set of recommendations for the UN,

DOI: 10.4324/9781003212409-11

its member states and civil society to advance further a survivor-centred approach to justice for CRSV.

Background

With gender equality and women's participation and leadership at the centre of its work, UN Women's programming on justice for CRSV makes a good starting point for examining how the UN interprets and puts a survivor-centred approach into practice. UN Women is one of the youngest members of the UN system, created by the General Assembly in 2010.[6] The organization promotes gender equality and the empowerment of women and girls with a unique mandate: supporting the strengthening of *normative* frameworks for gender equality and women's empowerment; working with member states, at their request, in implementing obligations and commitments relating to gender equality through *operational* activities, including programming on access to justice and support for CRSV survivors; and *coordinating*, leading and promoting the accountability of the UN system in its work on gender equality and women's empowerment.[7] UN Women is also unique in that it has a mandate to work on development issues *and* on peace and security issues, which enables the organization to work on transformative justice in development, humanitarian and peacebuilding contexts.[8] UN Women is also the UN system's lead on women, peace and security (WPS)[9] and its support for gender-sensitive transitional justice and rule of law in conflict-affected countries is an integral part of its activities to advance the WPS agenda. UN Women's work on justice for CRSV is most often approached through the framework of transitional justice, which includes a range of judicial and non-judicial mechanisms and processes, such as truth commissions, criminal trials, reparations and guarantees of non-repetition or non-recurrence.[10] Although this chapter focuses on examples of programming from UN Women, other entities in the UN system are also working to advance survivor-centred justice, including through UN-wide coordination mechanisms, such as UN Action Against Sexual Violence in Conflict and the UN Global Focal Point on the Rule of Law.

UN Women is unique in the UN system for its strong relationships with women's civil society organizations. The global women's movement led the initiative to create UN Women and is still a key constituency for the organization today. Civil society partnerships, including with associations and networks of victims and survivors of CRSV, are a cornerstone of the organization's work. UN Women benefits in all respects from the ingenuity and dedication of women's organizations, women peacebuilders and women human rights defenders. Many of the innovative practices and concepts explored in this chapter were developed and advocated for by civil society and survivors of CRSV in Guatemala and Kosovo. UN Women's 'approach' in these contexts was to simply to trust the expertise of these individuals and organizations, and to work in solidarity with them to advance their cause.

Increasingly, reports from UN entities and official UN documents use the term 'survivor' – particularly when discussing CRSV and sexual and gender-based violence, in order to emphasize the empowerment and resilience of those who have experienced violations.[11] At the same time, the term 'victim' is also common in UN documents, particularly when focusing on legal and medical rights and issues. Sometimes both terms are used interchangeably in the same text.[12] Although this chapter most often uses the term 'survivor' in recognition of individual and collective agency, it is important to note that it is always the right of the individual who experienced a violation to determine for themselves how they prefer to be identified. This is, after all, at the heart of a survivor/victim-centred approach.

At the outset, it is also important to make clear that, although this chapter focuses mostly on female survivors of CRSV, who were the focus of UN Women's programming in Guatemala and Kosovo, people of all genders experience sexual violence in conflict. A gender-sensitive approach to preventing and responding to CRSV requires a nuanced understanding of the gender inequality that underpins sexual violence, regardless of the gender of the victim or survivor.[13] Pre-existing vulnerability to oppression and marginalization, on the basis of gender identity or sexual orientation, as well as intersectional discrimination on the basis of religious, political or ethnic identity, disability, age, indigeneity, etc., informs how victims and survivors experience sexual violence and its after-effects.

Putting a Survivor-Centred Approach into Practice

In a thematic report on victim participation, the UN's special rapporteur on truth, justice, reparations and guarantees of non-repetition asserts that robust victim participation is likely to improve the end result of a transitional justice process, and that 'participation in itself provides a measure of recognition to, and empowerment of, victims'.[14] In Kosovo, survivors played a leading role in developing and implementing a reparations programme to redress CRSV, and are now working with investigators and prosecutors to pursue criminal cases against perpetrators. In Guatemala, a group of indigenous survivors of CRSV won a groundbreaking conviction in the *Sepur Zarco* case of two former military officers convicted for rape and sexual slavery, and a wide-ranging reparations judgment. The survivors are now leading the efforts to ensure implementation of the reparations judgment. In Kosovo and Guatemala, UN Women programming has supported survivors in their quest to access justice by centring their rights, needs and aspirations. This includes supporting survivors as rights-holders, decision-makers and agents of change; supporting justice institutions and government as duty-bearers with an obligation to provide redress to survivors in a safe and dignified manner; and addressing the wider social impact of gender inequality, social stigma and the root causes of CRSV. These elements are outlined in the following sections.

Survivors Participate Meaningfully in and Lead Justice Efforts

Victims and survivors of CRSV have a right to a remedy for the harm they suffered from individual perpetrators and from the state.[15] Survivors should also be able to exercise their autonomy to safely participate in, and lead, justice efforts. The right to participate in public affairs is enshrined in a number of human rights texts, including the Universal Declaration on Human Rights and the International Covenant on Civil and Political Rights.[16] The Convention on the Elimination of All Forms of Discrimination against Women (CEDAW) specifically calls for states parties to eliminate discrimination against women in the political and public life of the country, and to accord to women the right, on equal terms with men, to participate in the formulation and implementation of government policy and to hold public office at all levels of government.[17] Furthermore, participation is a core principle of a human rights-based approach to development.[18]

The UN's support to survivors of CRSV seeking access to justice often focuses on their protection and participation as beneficiaries of processes: as victims testifying in court, as witnesses making statements to a truth commission, or as applicants to a reparations programme.[19] This emphasis makes sense, given the myriad barriers that survivors of CRSV often face in achieving basic access to justice.[20] UN policy guidance on transitional justice also stresses the importance of consultation with survivors to understand their priorities and ensure that they inform the design and implementation of transitional justice processes.[21] However, a survivor-centred approach necessitates taking a step further: survivors must not only have *access* to justice processes and be *consulted* on process design and implementation. Survivors, among others, should have a real opportunity to *lead* in transitional justice processes.[22]

Survivors of CRSV face discrimination and stigma, and are often among the most marginalized members of their society.[23] Examples from UN Women's programming in Guatemala and Kosovo highlight the steps taken to support survivors to overcome or remove obstacles and become leaders in defining, demanding and – ultimately – beginning to achieve justice. This section of the chapter explores how, in both contexts, UN Women worked in solidarity with CRSV survivors, civil society organizations and human rights defenders, and in collaboration with government and other international actors and UN agencies to support survivors in claiming their right to redress and making sure that their voices are heard in the process. In both contexts, UN Women's approach began with a process of listening to survivors, seeking to understand their needs and what they saw as the roadblocks to their participation and leadership, and working together to identify and implement creative solutions.

Guatemala

The rights of indigenous peoples in Guatemala were at the heart of the country's internal armed conflict, which began in 1954 with a military coup and the reversal of land reforms that had benefited indigenous farmers. The conflict lasted for 36 years and cost more than 200,000 lives.[24] The majority of those killed – 83 per cent – were indigenous Maya people.[25] In 1982 government armed forces attacked the community of Sepur Zarco in eastern Guatemala, killing or forcibly disappearing Mayan Q'eqchi' leaders who had angered their landlords by seeking to obtain legal titles to their ancestral lands.[26] The armed forces then began systematically to subject women in the community to sexual and domestic slavery at their military outpost outside the community.[27]

In February 2016 11 Maya Q'eqchi' indigenous women from Sepur Zarco became a rare exception to the 'rule' of impunity for CRSV when their abusers, two former senior military officers, were convicted of crimes against humanity, including sexual slavery.[28] The *Sepur Zarco* case resulted in a landmark verdict for Guatemala, and for the world, as it was the first conviction ever by a national court for the international crime of sexual slavery. The court also issued a wide-ranging reparations decision which included compensation for the women who brought the case to court, as well as collective, transformative reparations measures aimed at the state to address the root causes of the violations that the women and their indigenous communities experienced, including improving access to health and education in their community.[29]

The *Sepur Zarco* case is remarkable for its judicial precedent, but even more so for the role of the survivors, now respectfully known as the *abuelas* (grandmothers) of Sepur Zarco, as leaders in steering the course towards justice. The *Sepur Zarco* case involved 15 victims, but only 11 survived to see the trial.[30] Three individuals (a woman and her two daughters) were murdered, and the defendants in the *Sepur Zarco* trial were convicted for these murders, along with the charges of sexual violence and sexual and domestic slavery. One of the victims died between giving her video testimony and the trial.[31] Although she was deceased, her testimony was admitted into evidence with the other 11 survivors. The *Sepur Zarco* case was shaped by the abuelas' vision for justice, their understanding of the harm that was done to them and their community and their knowledge about what it would take to begin to right those wrongs. The abuelas worked with the plaintiffs' attorneys and the state prosecutor to shape the prosecutorial strategy and provided input for the court's measures to ensure a protective and enabling environment for their participation at trial, and are now leading implementation of the reparations judgment.

UN Women accompanied the abuelas of Sepur Zarco on their path to justice in their criminal case and continues to support their efforts to see the reparations judgment fully implemented. Since 2014 this work has primarily been supported by grants from the UN Peacebuilding Fund, with UN Women leading three projects relating to the *Sepur Zarco* case in partnership with other UN entities and civil society organizations.[32] The most recent round of funding from the Peacebuilding Fund, from 2017 to 2020, focused on supporting a safe and empowering environment for the abuelas and other women in their indigenous communities to lead efforts to bring the *Sepur Zarco* reparations sentence to its full, transformative potential.[33]

Among its achievements, the 2017–2020 project resulted in the establishment of a survivor-led mechanism to monitor the implementation of the reparations sentence by the state. For each of the 16 collective reparations measures included in the *Sepur Zarco* reparations sentence, one of the abuelas was appointed as an 'ambassador', monitoring the implementation thereof through the official state process.[34] The abuelas sit on the monitoring committees, or *mesas de reparaciones* (tables) at the community, municipal and national level. With leadership and guidance from one of the project partners, Mujeres Transformado el Mundo (Women Transforming the World), the abuelas also created a framework for tracking action on the reparation measures with clear, measurable indicators. While there has been progress on some measures, including the opening of a school and health clinic in their community, others still await resolution, including the critical measure of the restitution of ownership of the abuelas' ancestral lands.[35] To recognize their role in the reparations process, the Public Ministry of Guatemala, together with UN Women, presented the abuelas with the Naxjolomi medallion, which in Q'eqchi' means 'the one that leads'.[36]

One of the most important and innovative strategies to ensure a survivor-centred approach in the reparations project was to include the abuelas on the project's steering committee, with one of the abuelas serving as co-president, along with UN Women's country representative.[37] The abuelas' leadership role in the committee ensured that the survivors guided and exercised control over every facet of the project, and that work plans and budgets responded to the realities of ongoing violence and insecurity in their communities. The final independent evaluation of the project recognized the broader transformative impact of this strategy: the fact that there was an indigenous woman survivor as co-president of the steering committee of a UN project was 'an act of power in itself and one of the main results of the project', countering the years of silence and invisibility that the abuelas had endured.[38] One of the key lessons learned from the project was that a survivor-centred approach to *programming* on justice helps to ensure that *outcomes* of that programming are similarly survivor-centred.

Kosovo

Sexual violence was systematically employed in the armed conflicts in the former Yugoslavia.[39] In February 1998 an armed conflict erupted in Kosovo, then a province of Serbia within the former Federal Republic of Yugoslavia, when Belgrade escalated its crackdown against a movement led by ethnic Albanians to establish an independent Kosovo.[40] The conflict culminated in June 1999 with a protected bombing campaign by the North Atlantic Treaty Organization (NATO) against Serbian targets. Over time, allegations of sexual violence before, during and after the conflict emerged.[41]

Nearly a quarter-century after the armed conflict in Kosovo, a culture of shame and silence continues to stigmatize survivors of CRSV. Yet, despite immense social and political constraints, survivors and their allies have begun to turn the tide from impunity to justice. In 2014 the Kosovo Assembly approved a law that gave legal recognition to CRSV survivors as victims of the conflict, and in 2017 a commission, known as the CRSV Commission, was established to verify the identity of survivors of CRSV and provide them with reparations.[42] The Commission became operational in 2018, and as of April 2019 more than 1,000 survivors[43] are receiving a lifetime monthly pension of €230 in recognition of the harm they suffered.[44] Although still falling far short of what is necessary to provide survivors with comprehensive redress, this administrative reparations programme sets Kosovo apart in a world where reparations for sexual violence crimes are exceedingly rare.[45] The advances towards justice for survivors of CRSV are the result of decades of feminist activism from Kosovo's strong women's movement, including women-led victim's associations that provide direct services to survivors, and the Kosovo Women's Network, which has long held accountability for sexual violence as a key demand.[46]

From 2015 to 2018 UN Women's work on accountability for CRSV in Kosovo was primarily funded through a grant from the European Union (UN) for UN Women's global programme on gender-sensitive transitional justice, which included a focus on supporting victims' associations and activists to influence and participate in the planning, development and implementation of transitional justice processes.[47] Following the adoption in Kosovo of the law recognizing the legal status of CRSV survivors and their entitlement to reparations in 2014, UN Women and the Office of the President organized consultations with survivors from October 2015 to January 2016.[48] Throughout the consultations, UN Women and the Office of the President sought to enable a safe and empowering space for survivors to express their concerns and priorities around the establishment of the CRSV Commission. The two-day workshops were thoughtfully designed to include art therapy, stress management and body therapy sessions interspersed with sessions focused on documenting their needs and voices, thereby ensuring that survivors could lead in the reparations design process while also receiving self-care support.[49] During focus group sessions survivors expressed dismay that their participation in justice processes to date had been relegated to retelling their past experiences, and called for meaningful inclusion in the reparations process in future.[50] UN Women's report, *The Conflict Did Not Bring Us Flowers: The Need for Comprehensive Reparations for Survivors of Conflict-Related Sexual Violence in Kosovo*, centred the voices of survivors in the reparations process, and the recommendations contained therein ultimately became the framework for establishing the Commission.

In 2015 Atifete Jahjaga, President of Kosovo, formed a National Council for the Survivors of Wartime Sexual Violence and, with support from UN Women, invited representatives from key government ministries to a three-day meeting with survivors of CRSV and civil society to develop the framework for the CRSV Commission, its application procedure and review process.[51] At the meeting, survivors emphasized that strict confidentiality and anonymity would be essential for their participation in the reparations process. Following the meeting, the law establishing the Commission provided for the 'protection of data of the persons who have survived sexual abuse and rape', and guaranteed that information provided in reparations applications would not be shared with prosecutorial authorities, which had been a key concern of the survivors.[52]

During UN Women's initial research and consultation on reparations in 2015 and 2016 survivors consistently stated that they had few economic opportunities, but that they wished to work and earn money.[53] Understanding that it could take years for the reparations process to become operational and begin to address survivors' economic needs, UN Women saw the need for a project focused on economic empowerment that could build survivors' trust and confidence that the reparations process would also move forward, and demonstrate that the international community cared about their demands for justice. While the right to development and the right to reparations are distinct, development programmes can be beneficial for delivering sustainable and transformative reparations.[54] The Guidance Note of the Secretary-General on Reparations for Conflict-Related Sexual Violence recommends that 'development cooperation should support States' obligation to ensure access to reparations'.[55]

In 2017 UN Women partnered with the Kosovo Women's Network and four victims' associations across Kosovo[56] to provide micro-economic grants to 177 survivors.[57] Interviews with survivors who participated in the micro-grant project showed that the impacts of the micro-grants were beyond expectation.[58] The grants, although small, had

> boosted the self-confidence of the survivors and their acceptance within their families and communities, encouraging them to apply for reparations; gave survivors a place to invest the reparations funds they receive and the financial literacy skills to do so, so that they can use their reparations benefits sustainably.[59]

The outcomes of the project demonstrate the benefits of a holistic approach to access to justice which focuses on survivors' interconnected needs, and the ability of development-focused programming to create an enabling environment for survivors of CRSV to claim their rights vis-à-vis duty-bearers.

Justice Processes Provide Redress while Upholding the Dignity, Wellbeing and Agency of Survivors

Having explored how UN Women has supported survivors of CRSV to participate in and lead justice efforts, this section focuses on the other side of the equation: the obligation of states to protect, respect and fulfil human rights, including the rights of survivors of CRSV to access justice.[60] For most CRSV survivors, the mere fact that a justice process exists does not mean that they will be able access it. Many transitional justice processes have failed adequately to reflect the extent of CRSV and to provide redress to survivors.[61] In some instances, the mandate or work of the justice mechanism or process does not include the types of crimes and human rights violations they experienced, including economic, social and cultural rights violations that are often linked with their experiences of sexual violence.[62] In other scenarios, justice institutions lack the technical capacity to successfully investigate or prosecute CRSV in accordance with international standards.[63] Frequently, however, survivors are deterred from accessing justice by social and cultural barriers, as well as concerns, often well founded, about their physical safety and mental health.[64] The treaty body for the CEDAW Convention, the Committee on the Elimination of Discrimination against Women (CEDAW Committee), notes that, in conflict and post-conflict settings, '[e]xisting justice systems may often be more likely to violate women's rights than to protect them and this can deter victims from seeking justice'.[65]

The CEDAW Committee recommends that states parties ensure that substantive aspects of transitional justice mechanisms guarantee women's access to justice, by mandating transitional justice mechanisms to address all gender-based violations. Furthermore, the Committee calls on states parties to institute proactive measures to facilitate and encourage women's full collaboration and involvement in transitional justice mechanisms, such as protecting their identity during public hearings.[66] The recommendations of the CEDAW Committee, although aimed at protecting the rights of women, are also relevant to all CRSV survivors, regardless of their gender. UN guidance on transitional justice similarly recommends 'special measures to ensure that women receive adequate redress for conflict-related violations, that women can fully participate in these processes and that their rights and perspectives are adequately addressed'.[67]

In guidance specifically geared at reparations for CRSV, the UN recommends special measures including adequate information about the justice process through accessible means in all areas where sexual violence has occurred; confidentiality at all stages of the process; measures to account for the special responsibilities that women have, including unpaid care work; and access to health services, including psychological support.[68] Such measures must be closely tailored to the specific context, in close consultation with survivors of CRSV.

In Guatemala and Kosovo, UN Women's survivor-centred approach included working directly with duty-bearers to strengthen their capacity to hold perpetrators of CRSV to account, and working with survivors to identify and advocate for proactive measures to create a safe and dignified environment for their participation, and then supporting the state to implement those measures.

Guatemala

In Guatemala, UN Women's support to the justice system, including the Office of the Public Prosecutor and the judiciary, was built on a relatively strong foundation. The UN-sponsored International Commission Against Impunity in Guatemala had been working in the country since 2007 to strengthen its legal institutions to respond to organized crime and corruption, which had, in general, enhanced Guatemala's ability to prosecute other complex cases.[69] Still, the Guatemalan justice system had never before applied international law in a case of CRSV. To ensure that the abuelas of Sepur Zarco stood the strongest possible chance to see a conviction result from their case, UN Women supported a peer-to-peer mentoring programme for the Office of the Public Prosecutor, bringing seasoned international criminal prosecutors to Guatemala to work with the local prosecutors to develop their legal strategy for the case.[70] This was complemented by other technical support to judges and prosecutors provided by UN entities including the Office of the High Commissioner for Human Rights (OHCHR) and the United Nations Development Programme.[71]

Through its grant from the UN Peacebuilding Fund that ran from 2014 to 2016, UN Women also partnered with a group of civil society organizations, the Alliance to Break the Silence and Impunity,[72] which had been supporting the abuelas and other indigenous women on their journey to justice since the early 2000s. UN Women supported the Alliance to sustain its multidisciplinary work with the abuelas, developing a legal strategy and advocacy campaign, and providing the abuelas with psychosocial support which was essential to their ability to take their case forward safely. UN Women then leveraged its relationship with state institutions to facilitate exchanges between the abuelas and the Alliance to the State Prosecutor, conveying the international importance of this case, helping to ensure that the case would be heard.[73] Later, the abuelas organized themselves in the collective 'Jalok U', which means 'change' in Q'eqchi', and became joint plaintiffs in the case.[74]

In the *Sepur Zarco* case, the state had an obligation to provide redress to the abuelas, and in the process the state also had an obligation to protect their safety and wellbeing. Ultimately, the Guatemalan Supreme Court did so,[75] and many of the innovative measures adopted in the court proceedings were developed and promoted by the abuelas themselves through the Alliance. One of the most important measures was the use of previously recorded video testimonies from the abuelas tendered as witness statements in court. This alleviated the need for the women to take the stand and recount their stories, which would have risked further harm to their wellbeing.[76] As Judge Yasmin Barrios handed down the verdict in the case, she noted that the tribunal's judgment was based primarily on the individual testimonies of the women survivors.[77] The abuelas' testimonies, conducted and shared in a way that safeguarded their mental health and dignity, captivated a national and international audience, placing the abuelas at the centre of the trial, 'challenging the notion that war crimes tribunals necessarily focus on the defendant(s) to the detriment of victims'.[78]

Kosovo

During UN Women's consultations with CRSV survivors in 2015 and 2016, in addition to demands for reparations, survivors voiced anticipation for criminal accountability for perpetrators of CRSV. More than three-quarters of focus group participants wanted to see sexual violence offenders prosecuted.[79] The desire for criminal accountability has been met with serious obstacles, including Kosovo's complex legal situation since the end of the conflict. The UN Interim Administration in Kosovo (UNMIK), and then subsequently the EU's rule of law mission, EULEX, were responsible for prosecuting war crimes cases in Kosovo from 1999 to 2018.[80] In December 2018 EULEX completed its mandate and handed 900 case files relating to war crimes over to the local Special Prosecutor of the Republic of Kosovo, having not yet successfully reached a conviction for CRSV.[81] Despite many challenges, as of December 2020 the Special Prosecution Office in Kosovo and the Kosovo Police War Crimes Investigation Unit were working on 50 cases of CRSV, an increase from 29 in 2017 and zero in 2016.[82] In a historic step towards accountability, in July 2021 a Kosovar court reached its first conviction ever for CRSV.[83]

As in Guatemala, UN Women has supported a mentoring programme for Kosovo's national authorities with prosecutors and lawyers with international criminal expertise, boosting the confidence and capacity of national prosecutors and investigators to take on cases of CRSV.[84] UN Women has also supported the development of national policies to advance justice for survivors of CRSV, including in an action plan for the implementation of UN Security Council Resolution 1325 (2000) on women, peace and security with Kosovo's Agency for Gender Equality, and a draft action plan on access to justice for victims of sexual violence during the war with the Ministry of Justice and EULEX.[85] UN Women's technical support to Kosovo's authorities has also been matched with infrastructural support to ensure that survivors encounter a safe and empowering environment on their path to the criminal justice system. Through UN Women's work with Kosovo's victim's associations, it came to light that one of the most significant obstacles for survivors in the justice system was the lack of private interview space in investigators' and prosecutors' offices. Survivors were reluctant to come forward, knowing that their confidentiality could immediately be compromised. In response, UN Women supported the establishment of 'friendly interview rooms' within the Special Prosecution Office and the Police War Crimes Investigation Unit for survivors of CRSV and other vulnerable witnesses. These interview rooms have greatly boosted the confidence of survivors of CRSV to share evidence and testimonies with the criminal justice system, thereby helping a number of cases to move forward.

Justice for Survivors Contributes to the Long-Term Goal of Transforming Gender Inequality

A survivor-centred approach to justice for CRSV empowers rights-holders and enables duty-bearers to uphold obligations around justice, safety and security. This section examines how a survivor-centred approach can also contribute to the transformation of societies. Examples of UN Women's experiences in Guatemala and Kosovo demonstrate that a survivor-centred approach is particularly effective at galvanizing social change.

For the individual survivor, it can be a transformative experience to have one's rights and humanity recognized by the state, often for the first time. UN Women's experience in Guatemala and Kosovo also demonstrates that the *process* of survivor-centred programming (i.e. having the abuelas of Sepur Zarco participate in a project steering committee) begins to create an alternative narrative to victimhood, repositioning survivors as agents and leaders, long before a final verdict is rendered, or a single reparations measure is implemented. On a larger scale, the visibility of the most marginalized members of the community being recognized as rights-holders and as leaders sends a message to the rest of the population about who is deserving of rights and respect. Particularly in the case of women survivors, this also sends a clear message about the role of women in society, breaking gender stereotypes about women in leadership. By chipping away at gender inequality, survivor-centred justice processes and programmes contribute to conflict prevention, as there is a direct relationship between gender inequality and conflict.[86]

Guatemala

In Guatemala, the final independent evaluation of the UN Peacebuilding Fund's 2017–2020 project on reparations found that 'the investment in Q'eqchi' women's leadership generated profound and irreversible transformations in the status of women, which included a self-recognition as global, national and community leaders and, their role in advancing gender justice and transformative reparations'.[87] The abuelas have become an unstoppable force for peace and justice, despite enormous social and political push-back. They continue to stand up against gender-based violence, including domestic violence, in their community. They also lead an indigenous women's protection network across three territories of Guatemala, monitoring threats and attacks against indigenous women human rights defenders.[88]

The transformation, however, extends far beyond the abuelas and their immediate communities. Social change was part of a deliberate strategy: UN Women sought to use a survivor-centred approach to help to shift the narrative in Guatemala from victimhood and exclusion to agency and leadership for the indigenous peoples of Guatemala and Guatemalan women. For example, when it became clear that Guatemala's Supreme Court would hear the *Sepur Zarco* case, UN Women informed the Court of the international interest in the case and suggested broadcasting the trial publicly. UN Women also discreetly provided arguments for the trial to be held in the Court's largest and grandest room in keeping with the public and solemn nature of the trial that was necessary to garner national and international attention to spark social transformation. Of course, this attention also aligned with the wishes of the abuelas. Paula Barrios of Mujeres Transformado el Mundo affirmed that '[t]he Grandmothers have always stated that they are taking this path to justice not only for them, but to ensure that other women do not live through what they had to'.[89]

Among the most visible transformative results of the *Sepur Zarco* case, the abuelas have motivated other survivors of sexual and gender-based violence to seek justice.[90] Emma Molina Theissen was 21 years old when she was detained, tortured and raped by soldiers in 1981, and in an interview acknowledged that she was inspired by the *Sepur Zarco* case to speak out:

> Learning about the Sepur Zarco case changed my heart, because they suffered the same thing I did. They suffered for much longer than I did, and they had the courage and the strength to testify in court … I thought, if they could do it, so could I, and that changed me completely.[91]

UN Women has worked to sustain the movement towards justice sparked by the *Sepur Zarco* case by supporting cases like Thiessen's, and linking these new cases explicitly to the same feminist cause.[92] The final independent evaluation for the UN Peacebuilding Fund project on reparations described how the project partners had organized meetings between the abuelas and other survivors of sexual violence, noting that the other survivors 'recognized that the encounters they had with the surviving Q'eqchi' women of Sepur Zarco filled them with strength, courage and desire to continue fighting for justice'.[93]

UN Women is continuing to support the abuelas to bring their message to the world. In October 2019 the Special Representative of the Secretary-General on Sexual Violence in Conflict, Pramila Patten, invited Demecia Yat, one of the abuelas of Sepur Zarco, to speak at the UN during the tenth anniversary commemoration of UN Security Council Resolution 1888 (2009) on sexual violence in conflict. In 2022 UN Women published a report with the War Crimes Research Office at American University Washington College of Law which documents the survivor-centred approach taken by all who contributed to the *Sepur Zarco* case, so that the experiences and lessons learned by the abuelas and their supporters can be shared more widely, thus continuing the cycle of transformation on a global scale.[94]

Kosovo

In Kosovo, as in Guatemala, many survivors of CRSV have undergone a personal transformation as a result of having their harm and suffering recognized by the government, and by becoming agents and leaders in the fight for justice. One survivor shared:

> Throughout the years we have been bearing a guilt that is not ours. We have been bearing a shame that is not ours. We have been neglected. … Now, after the support by the institutions, our life is slightly different. Organizations have helped us in recognizing our suffering, but what mostly helped us is the support of each other. We have been our own voice, giving tens of interviews, which were very challenging, but we found the courage.[95]

Unlike in Guatemala, where survivors of sexual violence like the abuelas of Sepur Zarco and Emma Molina Theissen are increasingly visible in society, in Kosovo, at the time of writing, only three survivors of CRSV have publicly acknowledged the harm they experienced during the conflict due to stigma and fear of reprisal. Too often, survivors' desire for confidentiality is misconstrued for an unwillingness to participate or lead.[96] UN Women has continued to work with survivors to identify creative ways that they can lead the conversation about addressing the violations they have experienced, while still concealing their identifies. For example, in November 2018 UN Women hosted an art exhibition entitled 'The Colours of Our Souls' featuring anonymous artwork created by survivors, illustrating their hopes and needs by using art as a call to break down the stigma of sexual violence in their communities.[97]

UN Women has also created opportunities for justice practitioners in the Western Balkans to learn from each other's experiences, supporting the cross-fertilization of survivor-centred approaches to spark broader transformation across the region. In June 2016 UN Women, OHCHR and the International Organization for Migration co-hosted a two-day workshop on reparations for CRSV in the Western Balkans, with representatives from civil society, ministries and government agencies from Bosnia and Herzegovina,[98] Croatia, Kosovo and Serbia attending. Participants developed a set of recommendations, taking into consideration the common legacy of war, the culture of impunity and past missteps in the region, with a number of recommendations focused on restoring survivors' agency and addressing survivors' multiple needs. The workshop report, *Reparations for Conflict-Related Sexual Violence: Lessons from the Western Balkans*, emphasized that

> [i]ndeed, to realize their transformative potential, reparations, and other transitional justice mechanisms, must be part of a long-term agenda of institutional reform and development anchored in changing the future, as well as addressing the past. In this regard, reparations must recognize and respond to the fact that women's empowerment and gender equality hold the greatest potential for both sustainable peace and development.[99]

Conclusion

UN Women's experiences in Guatemala and Kosovo with survivor-centred programming on access to justice demonstrate how survivors of CRSV, the state and all of society stand to benefit when a survivor-centred approach is put into practice. In both contexts, UN Women sought to centre the rights and aspirations of survivors in the programming process, and by aiming to have survivors realize those rights and aspirations as outcomes of programming. In both cases, this was achieved by working with survivors, civil society, the state and the international community, including other UN entities, to enable a safe and empowering space for survivors to exercise their rights to meaningful participation, consultation and leadership. In both cases, UN Women also added value by leveraging its role as a member of the UN family, to connect women's organizations and survivors of CRSV to those in power in government and the judiciary, and to bring national and international attention to the leadership and agency of survivors demanding justice for themselves and their communities.

This chapter has highlighted many examples of good practice emanating from UN Women's experiences in Guatemala and Kosovo. However, it is important to recognize that both experiences were not without their challenges and shortcomings. Acknowledging that survivor-centred approaches take many forms and can evolve, UN Women continues to work hand-in-hand with survivors to constantly develop improved and more adapted approaches. There also remain serious obstacles to justice for CRSV survivors in both contexts. In Guatemala, a conservative environment continues to threaten progress made on women's rights, and to crack down on the independence of the judiciary. In 2019 the government of Guatemala did not renew the mandate of the International Commission against Impunity in Guatemala,[100] and today judges, prosecutors and human rights defenders operate in fear of their lives. All the progress made in the *Sepur Zarco* case and implementation of its reparations sentence must be viewed in this climate of extreme pushback on equality and accountability. In Kosovo, the reparations process has been flawed by its inability to adequately reach CRSV survivors from non-majority ethnic communities.[101] More can also be done to provide survivors with psychosocial support as they move through the criminal justice process.

In both Guatemala and Kosovo, although CRSV is now beginning to be addressed, other gender-based harms related to the conflicts have largely gone unacknowledged in justice processes, such as the gendered impact of enforced disappearances or displacement. One lesson learned from UN Women's programming on gender-sensitive transitional justice is that '[t]o be effective, sustainable, and transformative, transitional justice cannot exclusively focus on the prosecution of sexual and gender-based crimes but address the full range of harms including social, economic, civil and political rights'.[102] Sexual violence does not occur in a vacuum, it takes place in the context of systemic gender inequality, alongside other forms of gender-based violence. Attempts to address CRSV in a silo, without consideration for its root causes and links to other forms of gender oppression, will be insufficient to prevent future violations.

This chapter has shown that a survivor-centred approach is an effective and efficient way of pursuing justice for all parties involved, including for the UN, for its programming in support of peace, human rights and development. The final paragraphs of the chapter are devoted to sharing a few of the authors' ideas on how UN entities, and other similar or related institutions can apply, or be encouraged to apply, a more consistent a survivor-centred approach to justice. First, as this chapter demonstrates, UN entities have much to learn from their own past experience. Although this chapter focused on examples of UN Women's survivor-centred approach to justice-related programming to address CRSV, other entities of the UN could review and identify equally promising examples and important lessons learned from their work on survivor-centred justice. UN Women can also continue the process of self-reflection, comprehensively analysing lessons learned from survivor-centred justice programming in other contexts, including Colombia, Mali, Nepal and Tunisia, among other countries. The conclusions drawn from these examples and lessons across the UN system could then be incorporated in future policy guidance from the UN on topics including transitional justice and rule of law, to ensure more consistent application of a survivor-centred approach. This is also in keeping with the commitment of the organization to leave no one behind and put human rights principles into action.

Second, member states could do more to hold UN entities to account for implementing a survivor-centred approach. Member states that are donors to UN programmes on justice and rule of law could create an expectation that recipients of their funds integrate a survivor-centred approach, including through the participation of survivors in decision-making on programme design, management, monitoring and evaluation, while ensuring their safety and wellbeing. Member states participating in intergovernmental bodies of the UN, such as the Security Council, the General Assembly and the Human Rights Council, could also incorporate survivor-centred approaches into their working methods; for example, by inviting survivors to provide briefings, with careful attention to having appropriate safety and security measures in place. Furthermore, member states can also ensure that their outcome documents call for survivor-centred approaches in the mandates establishing or renewing peace operations or investigations and monitoring mechanisms. Finally, the most important thing that member states can do to effectively implement a survivor-centred approach is to ensure the non-repetition of sexual and gender-based violence by advancing gender equality.

Third, survivors, civil society and human rights defenders should be encouraged to use the full strength of their voice to call on the UN to ensure that the rights, needs and aspirations of survivors be at the centre of its work to enhance access to justice. A robust survivor-centred approach should inevitably become a feedback loop for the organization: the more consistently a survivor-centred approach is applied, the more survivors will stand up for their rights and demand that they be at the centre of the UN's work in support of access to justice. These demands will bring the organization closer to its original purpose, which as enshrined in the Charter of the United Nations states that the organization was created to 'reaffirm faith in fundamental human rights, in the dignity and worth of the human person',[103] and this forms a pivotal part of a survivor-centred approach to justice.

Notes

1 The authors wish to thank Adriana Quiñones, Ana Grace Cabrera and Germán Vega Cortés for their invaluable inputs to this chapter. The views shared in this chapter are solely those of the authors and do not represent the views of UN Women, and any errors are their own. The authors are indebted to the survivors of conflict-related sexual violence in Kosovo, Guatemala and around the world, who courageously broke their silence and continue to fight for justice.

2 UN Security Council Resolution 2467, 23 April 2019, para. 16, 'encourages Member States to adopt a survivor-centred approach in preventing and responding to sexual violence in conflict and post-conflict situations'.

3 UN Action against Sexual Violence in Conflict, a network of 21 UN entities working on CRSV, including UN Women, is at the time of writing engaged in a research project to develop a comprehensive definition of the term 'survivor-centred approach'.

4 All references to Kosovo in this chapter are understood to be in reference to Security Council Resolution 1244, 10 June 1999.

5 The two contexts highlighted in this chapter, Kosovo and Guatemala, are illustrative of the organization's broader efforts. Globally, UN Women is committed to a survivor-approach to programming, advocacy and policymaking, particularly on access to justice for CRSV. Other excellent examples of UN Women's work in this area can be found in contexts as diverse as Colombia, the Central African Republic and Nepal, among many others.

6 General Assembly Resolution 64/289, 2 July 2010.

7 United Nations Entity for Gender Equality and the Empowerment of Women: Strategic Plan 2022–2025 (UN Women document UNW/2021/6), 12 July 2021.

8 Ibid.

9 Ibid, para. 96.

10 *Guidance Note of the Secretary-General: United Nations Approach to Transitional Justice* (New York: United Nations, 2010), p. 2.

11 See, for example, *Report of the Secretary-General on Conflict-Related Sexual Violence*, Security Council document S/2020/487), 3 June 2020, para. 3. 'A survivor-centred, rights-based response aims to create a safe and participatory environment, including through contextualized solutions that build resilience and address the diverse experiences of all survivors.'

12 See, for example, United Nations, *UN Emphasizes Importance of a Survivor-Centred Approach towards Victims of ISIL Abuses*, 27 June 2019, available at https://iraq.unfpa.org/en/news/un-emphasizes-importance-survivor-centred-approach-towards-victims-isil-abuses.

13 L. Davis, 'Strengthening Participation and Accountability in Peace and Transitional Justice: Dusting off the Law Books on Gender Persecution', *Northwestern Journal of Human Rights*, 20(1), 2021, p. 2323.

14 *Report of the Special Rapporteur on the promotion of truth, justice, reparation and guarantees of non-recurrence* (Human Rights Council document A/HRC/34/62), 27 December 2016, para. 5.

15 A state has an obligation to provide reparations for acts or omissions that can be attributed to it and that violate its obligations under international human rights law or international humanitarian law. Where appropriate, and in accordance with domestic law, the term 'victim' also includes the immediate family or dependants of the direct victim. *Basic Principles and Guidelines on the Right to a Remedy and Reparation for Victims of Gross Violations of International Human Rights Law and Serious Violations of International Humanitarian Law (General Assembly document A/RES/60/147), 21 March 2006, para. 8; Guidance Note of the Secretary-General on Reparations for Conflict-Related Sexual Violence* (New York: United Nations, 2015), p. 4.

16 Universal Declaration of Human Rights, Article 21; International Covenant on Civil and Political Rights, Article 25.

17 Convention on the Elimination of All Forms of Discrimination against Women, Article 7.

18 The Human Rights Based Approach to Development Cooperation Towards a Common Understanding Among UN Agencies (New York: United Nations Development Group, 2003).

19 *Guidance Note of the Secretary-General: United Nations Approach to Transitional Justice*, para. 5. 'Transitional justice mechanisms must thus provide for special measures to ensure that women receive adequate redress for conflict-related violations, that women can fully participate in these processes and that their rights and perspectives are adequately addressed.'

20 A training module series developed by UN Women and the International Center for Transitional Justice explores many of the challenges women face in accessing transitional justice mechanisms, and potential solutions. International Center for Transitional Justice and UN Women, *Gender and Transitional Justice: A Training Module Series*, available at https://www.ictj.org/multimedia/interactive/gender-and-transitional-justice-training-module-series.

21 *Guidance Note of the Secretary-General: United Nations Approach to Transitional Justice*, para. 6. 'National consultations, conducted with the explicit inclusion of victims and other traditionally excluded groups, are particularly effective in allowing them to share their priorities for achieving sustainable peace and accountability through appropriate transitional justice mechanisms.'

22 L. Mellado, E. Kenney and H. Adil, *Women's Meaningful Participation in Transitional Justice: Advancing Gender Equality and Building Sustaining Peace* (New York: UNDP and UN Women, 2022).

23 See, for example, K. Adams, *Principles for Global Action: Preventing and Addressing Stigma Associated with Conflict-Related Sexual Violence* (London: United Kingdom Foreign and Commonwealth Office, 2017).

24 UN Women, *Sepur Zarco Case: The Guatemalan Women Who Rose for Justice in a War-Torn Nation*, 19 October 2018, available at https://www.unwomen.org/en/news/stories/2018/10/feature-sepur-zarco-case.

25 Ibid.

26 S. SáCouto, A.F. Ouoba and C. Martin, *Documenting Good Practice on Accountability for Conflict-Related Sexual Violence: The Sepur Zarco Case* (New York: UN Women and American University Washington College of Law, 2022), p. 4; and S. Beaudoin, 'Sepur Zarco Trial to Start in February', *International Justice Monitor*, 17 November 2015, available at https://www.ijmonitor.org/2015/11/sepur-zarco-trial-to-start-in-february/.

27 UN Women, *Sepur Zarco Case: The Guatemalan Women Who Rose for Justice in a War-Torn Nation*, 19 October 2018, available at https://www.unwomen.org/en/news/stories/2018/10/feature-sepur-zarco-case

28 SáCouto *et al.*, *Documenting Good Practice on Accountability for Conflict-Related Sexual Violence*; and J.M. Burt, 'Military Officers Convicted in Landmark Sepur Zarco Sexual Violence Case', *International Justice Monitor*, 4 March 2016, available at https://www.ijmonitor.org/2016/03/military-officers-convicted-in-landmark-sepur-zarco-sexual-violence-case/.

29 *Changing the Face of Justice: Keys to the Strategic Litigation of the Sepur Zarco Case* (Guatemala: Impunity Watch and the Alliance to Break the Silence and Impunity, 2017), p. 4.

30 J.M. Burt, 'Gender Justice in Post-Conflict Guatemala: The Sepur Zarco Sexual Slavery and Sexual Violence Trial', *Critical Studies*, 4, 2019, p. 77.

31 Ibid.; the deceased victim was Magdalena Pop.

32 The UN partners on the UN Peacebuilding Fund projects were the United Nations Development Programme (UNDP), the United Nations Population Fund (UNFPA), and the United Nations Office of the High Commissioner for Human Rights (OHCHR) and the Food and Agriculture Organization of the United Nations (FAO). The United Nations World Food Programme (WFP) also received funding indirectly as an implementing partner to UN Women for one project. *Thematic Review: PBF-Supported Projects on Transitional Justice* (New York: Secretary-General's Peacebuilding Fund, 2020).

33 The 2017–2020 UN Peacebuilding Fund project was implemented with OHCHR, FAO, WPF and eight civil society organizations: Alianza Rompiendo el Silencio y la Impunidad, compuesta por la Colectiva Jalok U'; Estudios Comunitarios y Apoyo Psicosocial (ECAP); Unión Nacional de Mujeres Guatemaltecas (UNAMG); Mujeres Transformando el Mundo (MTM); Organización de Mujeres Retornadas Mamá Maquín; Red Centroamericana de Mujeres Rurales, Indígenas y Campesinas (RECMURIC); Action Aid; Asociación para el Desarrollo Rural Integral (ADRI); and Fundación Guillermo Toriello (FGT).

34 Office of the High Commissioner for Human Rights, *Workshop Report: Strategic Litigation for Sexual and Gender-Based Violence: Lessons Learned* (Geneva: Office of the High Commissioner for Human Rights, 2019), p. 14.

35 UN Women, *Sepur Zarco Case: The Guatemalan Women Who Rose for Justice in a War-Torn Nation*, 19 October 2018, available at https://www.unwomen.org/en/news/stories/2018/10/feature-sepur-zarco-case.

36 Ibid.

37 Demecia Yat served as co-president of the project steering committee, with UN Women Country Representative Adriana Quinoñes.

38 At the time of publication, the final independent evaluation had not yet been made public. Other documentation relating to this project is available at Multi-Partner Trust Fund Office Gateway, *PBF/IRF-194: Realizing the transformational effect of the Sepur Zarco reparation sentence to break the continuum of conflict and post-conflict related sexual and other forms of violence against women*, available at https://mptf.undp.org/factsheet/project/00108092.

39 N. Lamoreux, *Conference Report: Reparations for Conflict-Related Sexual Violence: Lessons from the Western Balkans* (Jahorina-Sarajevo: UN Women, 2016), p. 6.

40 S. Hobbs, *The Conflict Did Not Bring Us Flowers: The Need for Comprehensive Reparations for Survivors of Conflict-Related Sexual Violence in Kosovo* (Pristina: UN Women, 2019), p. 11.

41 Ibid., p. 2.

42 UN Women, 'In Kosovo, Legal Recognition of War-Time Sexual Violence Survivors after 18 years', 19 October 2017, available at https://www.unwomen.org/en/news/stories/2017/10/feature-kosovo-legal-recognition-of-war-time-sexual-violence-survivors.

43 This figure is according to UN Women records.

44 War veterans in Kosovo are also eligible for a monthly pension of €230.

45 '[R]epurations remain the justice intervention that survivors seek the most but receive the least.' *Report of the Secretary-General on Conflict-Related Sexual Violence* (Security Council document S/2020/487), 3 June 2020, para. 13.

46 See, for example, Kosova Women's Network, 'Forget Flowers: Women Call for Justice for War-Raped Women', 3 March 2012, available at https://womensnetwork.org/forget-flowers-women-call-for-justice-for-war-raped-women-on-8-march-mar-03-2012/.

47 H. Myrttinen and N. Popovic, *'We Were Like Caged Birds, This Gave Us Wings to Fly': A Review of UN Women Programming on Gender-Sensitive Transitional Justice* (New York: UN Women, 2019).

48 Approximately 70 survivors participated in consultations. Hobbs, *The Conflict Did Not Bring Us Flowers*, pp. 13–14.

49 Ibid., p. 14.

50 Ibid., p. 37.

51 Amnesty International, 'Wounds that Burn our Souls': Compensation for Kosovo's Wartime Rape Survivors, but Still No Justice (London: Amnesty International, 2017), pp. 42–43.

52 Ibid., fn. 229.

53 S. Hobbs, 'Bees of Change', in *The Exponential Impact of Micro-Grants for Survivors of Conflict-Related Sexual Violence in Kosovo* (Pristina: UN Women, 2018), p.8.

54 *Guidance Note of the Secretary-General on Reparations for Conflict-Related Sexual Violence* (New York: United Nations, 2014), p. 9.

55 Ibid., pp. 9–10.

56 The organizations were the Kosova Centre for Torture Victims, Medica Kosova, Medica Gjakova and the Center for the Promotion of Women's Rights; and Hobbs, 'Bees of Change', p. 8.

57 There were 176 women and one man participating in the project. *Report of the Working Group on Transitional Justice and SDG16+: On Solid Ground: Building Sustainable Peace and Development After Massive Human Rights Violations* (New York: International Center for Transitional Justice, 2019), p. 14.

58 Hobbs, 'Bees of Change'.

59 Ibid., p. 19.

60 The right to access justice is enshrined in a number of human rights conventions, including the Universal Declaration on Human Rights (Article 8) and the International Covenant on Civil and Political Rights (Article 14). Women's right to access justice is specifically addressed in General Recommendation no. 33 of the CEDAW Committee.

61 Examples include the Timor-Leste Commission for Reception, Truth and Reconciliation, which recognized that 'cases of both sexual and non-sexual violence experienced by women were under-reported'. *Chega! The Final Report of the Timor-Leste Commission for Reception, Truth and Reconciliation* (Timor-Leste: Commission for Reception, Truth and Reconciliation, 2005), chap. 1, para. 210.

62 'Transitional justice mechanisms have not succeeded in fully addressing the gendered impact of conflict and in taking into account the interdependence and interrelatedness of all human rights violations which have occurred during conflict. For most women, post-conflict justice priorities should not be limited to ending violations of civil and political rights but should include violations of all rights including economic, social and cultural rights.' *General Recommendation no. 30 on Women in Conflict Prevention, Conflict and Post-Conflict Situations* (Committee on the Elimination of Discrimination against Women document CEDAW/C/GC/30), 18 October 2013, para 76.

63 See, for example, S. Ribeiro and D. van der Straten Ponthoz, *International Protocol on the Documentation and Investigation of Sexual Violence in Conflict* (London: United Kingdom Foreign & Commonwealth Office, 2017), pp. 85–102.

64 The Liberia, Sierra Leone and Timor-Leste truth commission reports each highlighted the stigma associated with sexual violence as a factor, which inhibited survivors from speaking about these violations. See Priscilla Hayner, *Unspeakable Truths: Transitional Justice and the Challenge of Truth Commissions* (New York: Routledge, 2011), p .86.

65 *General Recommendation no. 30 on Women in Conflict Prevention, Conflict and Post-Conflict Situations* (Committee on the Elimination of Discrimination against Women document CEDAW/C/GC/30), 18 October 2013, para. 74.

66 Ibid., paras 81b and 81f.

67 Guidance Note of the Secretary-General: United Nations Approach to Transitional Justice, p .5.

68 Guidance Note of the Secretary-General: Reparations for Conflict-Related Sexual Violence, p. 10.

69 Burt, 'Gender Justice in Post-Conflict Guatemala', p. 75; and SáCouto *et al., Documenting Good Practice on Accountability for Conflict-Related Sexual Violence*, pp. 34–38.

70 This work was undertaken through UN Women's partnerships with Justice Rapid Response and Partners in Justice International to support accountability mechanisms worldwide with the gender expertise necessary to fulfil their mandates.

71 *Workshop Report: Strategic Litigation for Sexual and Gender-Based Violence: Lessons Learned*, p. 9.

72 The Alliance to Break the Silence and Impunity is comprised of three organizations: Community Studies and Psychological Action Team, Mujeres Transformado El Mundo (Women Transforming the World) and the National Union of Guatemalan Women.

73 UN Women, Reparación Transformadora: El Caso Sepur Zarco, 3 April 2019, available at https://www.youtube.com/watch?v=wtjnUfvUDXE.

74 *Workshop Report*, p. 3; and Burt, 'Gender Justice in Post-Conflict Guatemala', p.76.

75 Burt, 'Gender Justice in Post-Conflict Guatemala', p. 72.

76 SáCouto *et al., Documenting Good Practice on Accountability for Conflict-Related Sexual Violence*, pp. 61–64.

77 Burt, 'Gender Justice in Post-Conflict Guatemala', p. 87.

78 Ibid., p. 72.

79 Hobbs, *The Conflict Did Not Bring Us Flowers*; and Hobbs, 'Bees of Change', p. 43.

80 P. Gopalan, 'Conflict-Related Sexual Violence in Kosovo: Gendering Justice Through Transformative Reparations', in S. Mouthaan and O. Jurasz (eds), *Gender and War: International and Transitional Justice Perspectives* (Cambridge: Intersentia, 2019), p. 290.

81 For more information on the shortcomings of UNMIK and EULEX, see 'Wounds that Burn our Souls'.

82 These figures are according to UN Women records.

83 *Report of the Secretary-General on Women and Peace and Security* (Security Council document S/2021/827), 27 September 2021, para. 66.

84 This work was undertaken in partnership with Partners in Justice International and Justice Rapid Response.

85 'Wounds that Burn our Souls', fn. 129.

86 *Report of the Secretary-General on Women and Peace and Security* (Security Council document S/2018/900), 9 October 2018, para. 7.

87 At the time of writing, the final independent evaluation had not yet been made public. Other documentation relating to this project is available at Multi-Partner Trust Fund Office Gateway, *PBF/IRF-194: Realizing the transformational effect of the Sepur Zarco reparation sentence to break the continuum of conflict and post-conflict related sexual and other forms of violence against women*, available at https://mptf.undp.org/factsheet/project/00108092.

88 *PBF/IRF-194 Semi-Annual Project Progress Report: June 2020* (United Nations Peacebuilding Fund: 2020), p. 9, available at https://mptf.undp.org/factsheet/project/00108092.

89 UN Women, 'Sepur Zarco Case: The Guatemalan Women Who Rose for Justice in a War-Torn Nation', 19 October 2018, available at https://www.unwomen.org/en/news/stories/2018/10/feature-sepur-zarco-case.

90 *Report of the Working Group on Transitional Justice and SDG16+: On Solid Ground*, p. 14.

91 Burt, 'Gender Justice in Post-Conflict Guatemala', p. 95.

92 UN Women, *Final Evaluation of Project 00108092- PBF/IRF194*, 23 November 2020, 52 (see fn. 81).

93 Ibid.

94 SáCouto *et al., Documenting Good Practice on Accountability for Conflict-Related Sexual Violence.*

95 *Koha: For the Survivors* (Pristina: UN Women, 2018), pp. 4–5.

96 Gopalan, 'Conflict-Related Sexual Violence in Kosovo', pp. 304–305.

97 UN Women, 'Exhibition Portraying Life as They Would Love It to Be: Created by Survivors of Conflict-Related Sexual Violence', 22 November 2018, available at https://eca.unwomen.org/en/news/stories/2018/11/news-exhibition-portraying-life-as-they-would-love-it-to-be.

98 Including representatives from the Republic of Bosnia-Herzegovina, Republika Srpska and Brcko District, all autonomous regions within the Federation of Bosnia and Herzegovina.

99 Lamoreux, *Conference Report: Reparations for Conflict-Related Sexual Violence*, p. 17.

100 S. Menchu, 'Guatemala Not Renewing Mandate of U.N. Anti-Corruption Body', Reuters, 31 August 2018.

101 Gopalan, 'Conflict-Related Sexual Violence in Kosovo', pp. 301–302; Hobbs, *The Conflict Did Not Bring Us Flowers*, p. 31.

102 Myrttinen and Popovic, *'We Were Like Caged Birds*', p. 36.

103 *Charter of the United Nations*, 26 June 1945, Preamble.

References

Burt, Jo-Marie (2019) 'Gender Justice in Post-Conflict Guatemala: The Sepur Zarco Sexual Slavery and Sexual Violence Trial', *Critical Studies*, vol. 4, p. 77.

Davis, Lisa (2021) 'Strengthening Participation and Accountability in Peace and Transitional Justice: Dusting off the Law Books on Gender Persecution', *Northwestern Journal of Human Rights*, vol. 20, no. 1, p. 2323.

Gopalan, Priya (2019) 'Conflict-Related Sexual Violence in Kosovo: Gendering Justice Through Transformative Reparations', in Solange Mouthaan and Olga Jurasz (eds), *Gender and War: International and Transitional Justice Perspectives*. Cambridge: Intersentia.

Hayner, Priscilla (2011) *Unspeakable Truths: Transitional Justice and the Challenge of Truth Commissions*. New York: Routledge.

Mellado, Lorena, Kenney, Emily and Adil, Hariwa Negisa (2022) *Women's Meaningful Participation in Transitional Justice: Advancing Gender Equality and Building Sustaining Peace.* New York: UNDP and UN Women.

SáCouto, Susana Ouoba, Ford, Alysson and Martin, Claudia (2022) *Documenting Good Practice on Accountability for Conflict-Related Sexual Violence: The Sepur Zarco Case.* New York: UN Women and American University Washington College of Law.

Reports and other Web-Based Documents

Adams, Kate (2017) *Principles for Global Action: Preventing and Addressing Stigma Associated with Conflict-Related Sexual Violence.* London: United Kingdom Foreign and Commonwealth Office.

Amnesty International (2017) *Wounds that Burn our Souls': Compensation for Kosovo's Wartime Rape Survivors, but Still No Justice*London: Amnesty International.

Beaudoin, Sophie (2015) 'Sepur Zarco Trial to Start in February', *International Justice Monitor*, 17 November. Available at https://www.ijmonitor.org/2015/11/sepur-zarco-trial-to-start-in-february/.

Burt, Jo-Marie (2016) 'Military Officers Convicted in Landmark Sepur Zarco Sexual Violence Case', *International Justice Monitor*, 4 March. Available at https://www.ijmonitor.org/2016/03/military-officers-convicted-in-landmark-sepur-zarco-sexual-violence-case/.

Changing the Face of Justice: Keys to the Strategic Litigation of the Sepur Zarco Case (2017) Guatemala: Impunity Watch and the Alliance to Break the Silence and Impunity.

Chega! The Final Report of the Timor-Leste Commission for Reception, Truth and Reconciliation (2005) Timor-Leste: Commission for Reception, Truth and Reconciliation.

Ferro Ribeiro, Sara and van der Straten Ponthoz, Danaé (2017) *International Protocol on the Documentation and Investigation of Sexual Violence in Conflict.* London: United Kingdom Foreign & Commonwealth Office.

Guidance Note of the Secretary-General: United Nations Approach to Transitional Justice (2010). New York: United Nations.

Guidance Note of the Secretary-General on Reparations for Conflict-Related Sexual Violence (2014). New York: United Nations.

Hobbs, Siobhan (2018) *Bees of Change: The Exponential Impact of Micro-Grants for Survivors of Conflict-Related Sexual Violence in Kosovo.* Pristina: UN Women.

Hobbs, Siobhan (2019) *The Conflict Did Not Bring Us Flowers: The Need for Comprehensive Reparations for Survivors of Conflict-Related Sexual Violence in Kosovo.* Pristina: UN Women.

International Center for Transitional Justice and UN Women (n.d.) *Gender and Transitional Justice: A Training Module Series.* Available at https://www.ictj.org/multimedia/interactive/gender-and-transitional-justice-training-module-series.

Koha: For the Survivors (2018). Pristina: UN Women.

Kosova Women's Network (2012) 'Forget Flowers: Women Call for Justice for War-Raped Women', 3 March. Available at https://womensnetwork.org/forget-flowers-women-call-for-justice-for-war-raped-women-on-8-march-mar-03-2012/.

Lamoreux, Natasha (2016) *Conference Report: Reparations for Conflict-Related Sexual Violence: Lessons from the Western Balkans.* Jahorina-Sarajevo: UN Women.

Myrttinen, Henri and Popovic, Nicola (2019) *'We Were Like Caged Birds, This Gave Us Wings to Fly': A Review of UN Women Programming on Gender-Sensitive Transitional Justice.* New York: UN Women.

Office of the High Commissioner for Human Rights (2019) *Workshop Report: Strategic Litigation for Sexual and Gender-Based Violence: Lessons Learned.* Geneva: Office of the High Commissioner for Human Rights.

Report of the Secretary-General on Conflict-Related Sexual Violence (Security Council document S/2020/487), 3 June2020.

Report of the Secretary-General on Women and Peace and Security (Security Council document S/2018/900), 9 October2018.

Report of the Secretary-General on Women and Peace and Security (Security Council document S/2021/827), 27 September2021.

Report of the Special Rapporteur on the promotion of truth, justice, reparation and guarantees of non-recurrence (Human Rights Council document A/HRC/34/62), 27 December 2016.

Report of the Working Group on Transitional Justice and SDG16+: On Solid Ground: Building Sustainable Peace and Development After Massive Human Rights Violations (2019) New York: International Center for Transitional Justice.

The Human Rights Based Approach to Development Cooperation Towards a Common Understanding Among UN Agencies (2003). New York: United Nations Development Group.

Thematic Review: PBF-Supported Projects on Transitional Justice (2020). New York: Secretary-General's Peacebuilding Fund.

United Nations (2019) *UN Emphasizes Importance of a Survivor-Centred Approach towards Victims of ISIL Abuses*, 27 June. Available at https://iraq.unfpa.org/en/news/un-emphasizes-importance-survivor-centred-approach-towards-victims-isil-abuses.

United Nations Entity for Gender Equality and the Empowerment of Women: Strategic Plan 2022–2025 (UN Women document UNW/2021/6), 12 July2021.

United Nations Multi-Partner Trust Fund Office (n.d.) *PBF/IRF-194: Realizing the transformational effect of the Sepur Zarco reparation sentence to break the continuum of conflict and post-conflict related sexual and other forms of violence against women.* Available at https://mptf.undp.org/factsheet/project/00108092.

UN Women (2017) 'In Kosovo, Legal Recognition of War-Time Sexual Violence Survivors after 18 Years', 19 October. Available at https://www.unwomen.org/en/news/stories/2017/10/feature-kosovo-legal-recognition-of-war-time-sexual-violence-survivors.

UN Women (2018) *Sepur Zarco Case: The Guatemalan Women Who Rose for Justice in a War-Torn Nation*, 19 October. Available at https://www.unwomen.org/en/news/stories/2018/10/feature-sepur-zarco-case.

UN Women (2018) 'Exhibition Portraying Life as They Would Love It To Be: Created by Survivors of Conflict-Related Sexual Violence', 22 November. Available at https://eca.unwomen.org/en/news/stories/2018/11/news-exhibition-portraying-life-as-they-would-love-it-to-be.

UN Women (2019) *Reparación Transformadora: El Caso Sepur Zarco*, 3 April. Available at https://www.youtube.com/watch?v=wtjnUfvUDXE.

UN Women, *Final Evaluation of Project 00108092- PBF/IRF194*, 23 November 2020.

Statutes and Conventions

Basic Principles and Guidelines on the Right to a Remedy and Reparation for Victims of Gross Violations of International Human Rights Law and Serious Violations of International Humanitarian Law (General Assembly document A/RES/60/147), 21 March 2006.

Charter of the United Nations, 26 June 1945.

Convention on the Elimination of All Forms of Discrimination against Women.

General Assembly Resolution 64/289, 2 July 2010.

General Recommendation no. 30 on Women in Conflict Prevention, Conflict and Post-Conflict Situations (Committee on the Elimination of Discrimination against Women document CEDAW/C/GC/30), 18 October 2013.

International Covenant on Civil and Political Rights.

Security Council Resolution 2467, 23 April 2019.

Universal Declaration of Human Rights.

8 The Survivor-Centred Justice Dimensions of the African Union Transitional Justice Policy

Assessing South Africa's Transition

Tim Murithi

Introduction

This chapter will consider how notions of survivor-centred justice can be integrated into regional post-conflict peace and justice interventions by assessing its dimensions in the African Union Transitional Justice Policy (AUTJP). In February 2019 the AU Assembly of Heads of State and Government formally adopted its Policy, which includes a broad range of interventions designed to address the atrocities and violations of the past. The chapter will interrogate whether survivor-centred justice processes as defined in the AUTJP, based on the inclusion of alternative forms of justice, can help to confront impunity and ensure accountability, while also contributing towards the restoration of human dignity, by addressing the social, economic and cultural violations of oppressive regimes in Africa. In interrogating the victim-perpetrator dichotomy, the chapter assesses how 'victims and perpetrators in civil wars often trade places in ongoing cycles of violence … no one is wholly innocent or guilty'.[1] Given this context, the chapter will investigate how victims, perpetrators and beneficiaries can actively be incorporated into an accountability, redress and reconciliation framework which will promote political, social and economic justice in order to create the necessary conditions for more cohesive political communities centred on the needs of all survivors. In particular, the chapter will draw on Mahmood Mamdani's critique of the individualization of criminal justice for mass atrocities, based on the recognition that these violations are fuelled by group grievances and that personalizing crimes tends to conceal the role of constituencies that agitate for these demands, thus creating the conditions for violence.[2] In attempting to move beyond the dominant emphasis on criminal judicial interventions as the method of choice to address past violations, the chapter will make recommendations on how to more effectively articulate and identify key entry points for engaging with a survivor-centred justice approach which is a crucial dimension of the AUTJP.

DOI: 10.4324/9781003212409-12

Situating Transitional Justice

Transitional justice strives to address challenges that emerge from historical violations and affect countries as they strive to transition from war or authoritarian rule to fair, inclusive and democratic societies.[3] More often than not such societies are emerging from a past of brutality, exploitation and victimization. In this context, transitional justice does not seek to replace criminal justice, rather it strives to promote 'a deeper, richer and broader vision of justice which seeks to confront perpetrators, address the needs of victims, and start a process of reconciliation and transformation towards a more just and humane society'.[4]

The broadly accepted purpose of a process of transitional justice is to establish a framework to undo the continuing effects of the past. It is also necessary not to lose sight of the fact that transitional justice is just that – a 'transitional process' – and it should not be viewed as a permanent solution to addressing the atrocities of the past. It is rather a transient process that will have to give way to the rule of law and the restoration of a constitutional order that will manage and resolve the social, political and economic tensions within society. The institutional vehicles through which transitional justice is implemented, bodies such as truth commissions and special courts, are temporary and time-bound institutions and should not be considered as a permanent solution.

The idea of transitional justice emerged from the legal sphere owing to a primary concern to ensure that perpetrators of human rights violations were held accountable for their crimes and punished, ideally through a court of law and in accordance with international standards.[5] The originators and custodians of these 'international standards', however, are less discernible and remain unspecified in the field of transitional justice, even within the United Nations's framing of the field. The notions that initially animated transitional justice drew heavily on legalistic doctrines of 'the duty/right to punish' and the unitary role and function of prosecutions in the context of human rights violations.[6]

The reality of implementing transitional justice through an exclusively prosecutorial framework, as was the case in Latin America and the Balkans, was soon confronted by a proliferation of social, economic and political contradictions, which undermined the narrow focus of transitional justice norms inspired by legal precedents. For example, when confronted with situations in which the perpetrator may also be a former victim, such as child soldiers who were abducted and subsequently became war-makers and violators of human rights, the knee-jerk prosecutorial approach is to punish the most recent crime perpetrated. In this particular case, the historical violations committed against the perpetrator go unpunished, and consequently a condition of injustice and moral contradiction prevails. The legal field remains ambivalent about addressing these moral conundrums, and prefers to cast aside such questions in favour of a narrow-minded commitment towards ensuring that the duty to punish is dogmatically pursued above all else. Take, for example, a senior Lord's Resistance Army (LRA) commander, Brigadier Dominic Ongwen, who was abducted in 1999 by the LRA when he was a ten-year-old child living in northern Uganda. Ongwen was a victim of the LRA militia, but subsequently went on to command its ranks. As a member of the command team of the LRA, Ongwen was therefore personally culpable for the human rights violations that the militia perpetrated against innocent children whom he subsequently abducted. Therefore, Ongwen stands accused of being a perpetrator of human rights violations, yet his historical grievances for the harm done to him as a child also are valid and can be said to be subject to redress and accountability. Ultimately, the Ugandan government of Yoweri Museveni decided to send Ongwen to the International Criminal Court (ICC) to face charges for his most recent atrocities. However, the situation exposed the limits of a tool narrowly focused on a normative judicial approach to transitional justice.

The criminal prosecution approach to transitional justice is also generally unable to effectively provide redress for societal violations and economic crimes which historical victims have endured, because these effects are less visible to the eye and are much more complex to quantify in terms of the specific transgressions which have been perpetrated against victims. Moreover, in situations in which a particular ethnic or racial group has benefited from the economic exploitation of another party, culpability extends across society from the political leaders who implemented the policies in the first place to the constituents who voted or supported them. In effect, 'political violence requires more than just criminal agency; it also needs a *political constituency*'.[7] Therefore, as Mamdani observes, 'by individualizing the crime and the violence, the demand for criminal justice obscures the issues that feed group grievances and hides the constituencies that mobilize around group demands'.[8] In such a context it is much more difficult to pinpoint the violators who should be prosecuted for economic crimes. For example, in the South African context,

> by highlighting amnesty for perpetrators in exchange for full disclosure, the Truth and Reconciliation Commission *concealed the constituency that supported apartheid as a political project* … neither the political project nor its constituency – the beneficiaries of apartheid – was examined by the commission.[9]

As Mamdani observes,

> [t]he TRC made two key decisions with respect to defining the legal category of victims. First, the TRC determined that victims had to be individuals. Africans as a whole could not be victims, nor could particular communities, groups of employees, cohorts of students and so on. To reach this determination was to ignore precisely what was distinctive

> about apartheid that it was a system based on group oppression. Second, the TRC defined the suffering of these victims narrowly, focusing on violations of their 'bodily integrity'. This distinction, too, was problematic in a context where the vast majority of the population suffered economic dispossession. The violence of apartheid did not target bodily integrity so much as land, labour and livelihoods.[10]

Following on from this illustration, it is evident that processes that are adopted to promote redress should include a broad range of interventions which directly engage the victims, perpetrators and beneficiaries in processes that are focused on crafting political solutions for all survivors centred on the promise of social justice, which in effect is a critique of the punishment model of transitional justice.

Elements of a Survivor-Centred Justice Approach in the African Union Transitional Justice Policy

Between 2010 and 2019 the AU became a pioneering regional organization in terms of developing a specific policy relating to transitional justice. In November 2018 the AU Extraordinary Summit of Heads of State and Government in Kigali, Rwanda, formally approved the AUTJP. In February 2019 the AUTJP was formally adopted by the AU Assembly of Heads of State and Government in Addis Ababa, Ethiopia. The purpose of the Policy is to encourage member states to broaden their understanding of justice beyond retributive justice to encompass restorative and transformative measures found in traditional African justice systems and African shared values.[11] In keeping with a broader conception of survivor-centred justice, the AUTJP notes that 'apart from the actions that remedy the wrongs done, justice additionally entails the availability of fair institutional, social and economic systems of governance and inclusive development'."[12] On this basis, the AUTJP anticipates Mamdani's appeal for an approach to survivor-centred social justice through political reforms to forge an inclusive community. Indeed, the AUTJP states that 'transitional justice is first and foremost a *political* rather than a technical process'[13] that is geared towards enhancing 'nation building and, where necessary, comprehensive state reforms as a means of addressing the root causes of conflict'.[14]

The AUTJP recommends that member states enacting transitional justice measures incorporate economic and social rights and encourages states to design reparations programmes that can address the structural nature of economic and social rights violations and that non-state actors and beneficiaries should be encouraged to participate in such programmes.[15] The efforts by the AU to push the boundaries of the way in which transitional justice has been conceived, beyond civic and political rights, to include social and economic rights, rectifies an oversight which was internalized by the dominant legal framework that defined the field, despite the articulation of the need for moral, social and economic restoration and reparation. The political and socio-economic dimension of transitional justice processes is now emerging as a key driver of sustainable transformation for societies that have experienced historical violations.

The AUTJP recommends the promotion of

> reconciliation as a profound process which entails finding a way to live that permits a vision of the future, the rebuilding of relationships, coming to terms with the past acts and enemies, and involves societies in a long-term process of deep change.[16]

The AUTJP is also groundbreaking in terms of incorporating as a policy document a commitment to addressing trauma and woundedness, an issue that is often overlooked in the mistaken belief that it will remain so. Specifically, the AUTJP advocates for the importance of coming 'to terms with the traumas of slavery, colonialism, apartheid, systemic repression and civil wars' as a necessary precursor to 'achieving sustainable peace, justice, reconciliation, social cohesion and healing'.[17] The psychosocial dimension of peacebuilding is often underplayed and the AUTJP seeks to rectify this omission.

Incorporating a Survivor-Centred Justice Approach in the Context of Post-Conflict Peacebuilding: The Case of South Africa

Africa's experiences have demonstrated that transitional justice processes are operationalized predominantly in post-conflict situations, in which it is imperative to pursue a survivor-centred social justice approach to peacebuilding. In effect, there is a norm-convergence between the pursuit of peace and the requirements of justice. This means that the norms that guide the pursuit of peacebuilding, the healing of relationships and the restoration of human dignity, are mutually reinforcing with those of pursuing social justice. Peacemaking, or peacebuilding, is future-oriented in the sense that it is striving to prevent violence that could recur and cause the death of yet more innocent civilians if conditions in the country remain unchanged. International prosecutorial criminal justice by definition is concerned with the prosecution of human right violations that have already transpired through the application of due process, while upholding certain legal criteria and issuing a judgment for past transgressions. Consequently, there is a tension between these two processes, and trying to undertake them in tandem can occasionally generate a moral, legal and political conundrum. As discussed above, in assigning individual responsibility for mass atrocities in war situations, leaders of factions or military organizations usually conceal the role of the constituents to whom they are responsive, and who play an active role in agitating for the group demands which created the framework for mass atrocities to occur.

Essentially, the notion of justice remains a contested concept.[18] In fact, there are multiple dimensions to justice. Retributive justice seeks to ensure prosecution followed by punishment for crimes or atrocities committed.[19] Restorative justice strives to promote societal harmony through a quasi-judicial process of truth telling, acknowledgement, remorse, reparations, forgiveness, healing and reconciliation.[20] Retributive or punitive justice is generally administered by a state-sanctioned legal institution or through the remit of international law and targets the individual. Restorative justice draws on a range of mechanisms including state commissions and other societal reconciliation institutions to reconfigure the relationship between victims and perpetrators.

Both retributive and restorative justice have a central concern with preventing the impunity of perpetrators who have committed atrocities. Retributive justice, however, has a distorting effect on the transformation of societies because it targets individuals who summarily receive a punitive sentence which paradoxically absolves the wider political community for its role in sustaining and supporting the system that led to the perpetration of atrocities in the first place. By contrast, the impact of restorative social justice is more expansive as it seeks to engage victims, perpetrators and bystanders in a series of interpersonal and inter-group engagements and interactions designed socially and politically to transform the war-affected society of all survivors.

The experiences in South Africa demonstrated that the debate over whether a retributive or restorative approach to justice should be deployed in the aftermath or on the conclusion of a war has not been resolved definitively. As Mamdani observes, 'the great achievement of the anti-apartheid movement was to understand that the violence of apartheid was political' and it therefore sought 'a political rather than a criminal solution for it'.[21] This was achieved through the forum for negotiating a peaceful transition to democracy known as the Convention for a Democratic South Africa which emerged from a recognition that there was no victor in South Africa and that 'there were enemies who might become adversaries, if only they were enabled to participate together in the same political order'.[22] Mamdani is, however, unequivocal in criticizing the South African Truth and Reconciliation Commission (TRC), which by borrowing from the ideology of criminal tribunals sought to identify a 'handful of apartheid's collaborators' which in effect 'undermined the deracialization of society by focusing on individual perpetrators in the state while silencing discussion of apartheid's beneficiaries in society'.[23] Mamdani further notes that 'a criminal approach would have sought to separate apartheid's perpetrators from its victims and punish the perpetrators while producing justice for the victims'.[24] Mamdani argues that 'this would not have furthered the goal of political reform, which is what South Africa badly needs: the creation of a democratic state in which all could participate, regardless of race'.[25] Furthermore, Mamdani observes that

> by taking a political approach, South Africans reconfigured perpetrators and victims – alongside beneficiaries and bystanders – as something

> altogether new: survivors. All groups were survivors of apartheid, with a place at the table after the violence. … the post-apartheid political system was informed by the assumption that yesterday's victims and yesterday's perpetrators have no choice but to live in the same state and that they have the capacity to do so because their political identities can change – in particular, that they have the capacity to forge the new identity of the survivor.[26]

The applicability of this survivor-centred social justice model in other situations across Africa and around the world is evident. In particular, the demands of a survivor-centred social justice process with its emphasis on the transformation of political identities, which entails the dimension of a reconfiguration of the political system, as well as the collective societal psychological transformation which can lay the foundations for more inclusive communities, means that this approach has to be carefully designed in a manner that contributes to the healing processes in war-affected societies. In the case of the Darfur crisis in Sudan as well as in the conflict in northern Uganda, individuals and leaders who have been accused of planning, financing, instigating and perpetrating atrocities against citizens of another group, all in the name of civil war, can be investigated by the ICC if the respective country is a state party to the ICC or if the issue is referred to the Court by the UN Security Council. In the Darfur and northern Uganda contexts, these individuals and leaders were drawn from political constituencies which were asserting group demands, and therefore their prosecution cannot be divorced from a focused and deliberate engagement with their wider communities in the process of political transformation and post-conflict peacebuilding. A punitive approach to justice cannot deal with the grievances that often underpin structural violence, identity conflict and the economic marginalization of the majority of people in war-affected countries and thus establish a sustainable basis for peace.[27] It will, however, in a minimalist posture, only prosecute the so-called key individuals who were perceived to have had the greatest responsibility for committing atrocities.

The fact that South Africa adopted its own unique path towards survivor-centred social justice distinguishes it as a norm-setter, despite the incomplete nature of the project which is evident in the widespread poverty and inequality that still afflicts the society. The model that South Africa adopted is constantly being analysed and scrutinized for its important insights even though the country, like other countries around the world, has not yet addressed all the challenges emanating from its past. In effect, South Africa's response to its situation advanced important survivor-centred social justice insights. As Mamdani notes, 'South Africa's political rebirth has been partial … tribal identity has remained an obstacle to political equality … but even partial rebirth is something'.[28] He states that 'the response to political violence in South Africa was not separation – it was not ethnic cleansing, as in North America and Europe … it was a reframing of political identity so that formerly opposed identities could live together in the new political community'.[29]

Tunisia and Liberia placed greater emphasis on adopting and implementing a restorative survivor-centred justice model, in the two countries' respective post-conflict peacebuilding processes, rather than adhering to the prosecutorial fundamentalism which was being championed by external actors. A more nuanced approach would suggest that there is a time and a place for prosecution and, in the context of a civil war if one does not factor in the role played by the political constituency, this will generate skewed and partial social justice outcomes. In addition, the post-conflict context can be viewed as a point in time when tensions within a country tend to be uncharacteristically high and any attempt to prosecute individuals and leaders can often continue the 'war by other means', and indeed is sometimes seen as a deliberate attempt to do so, by targeting the main individual protagonists to a conflict, who were in effect acting in response to the demands of a particular constituency. Effectively what is called for in these situations is a period of time in which the belligerents can pursue a survivor-centred social justice approach premised on deep and sustained political negotiations to reconfigure the governance and structure of the state in order to create an inclusive political order.

Insights from Alternative Forms of Justice: A Cultural Approach to the Survivor-Centred Approach

It is worthwhile asking whether survivor-centred justice processes as defined in the AUTJP, based on the inclusion of alternative forms of justice, can help to confront impunity and ensure accountability, while also contributing to the restoration of human dignity, by pursuing political reform and addressing the social, economic and cultural violations of oppressive regimes in Africa.

In contrast to other transitional justice processes in Latin America and the Balkans, for example, African states have also experimented with culturally informed processes to address the violations of the past. Due to the limitations of internationally imposed ideas of transitional justice, there was a need to draw on Africa's knowledge systems and its traditions and culture of jurisprudence to articulate and document indigenous norms of transitional justice. There have always been customary rules, social sanctions and ethical precepts to regulate African societies. While each society has its own specific approach to dealing with social problems, some common themes emerge across societies. In the majority of African communities, the individual is not considered a separate, autonomous entity but always part of a larger collective of human beings.[30] Family groupings give way to the formation of clan communities and then ethnic nations. These groupings have a responsibility to maintain social harmony and an inclusive communal order. Due to the importance of maintaining harmony, peaceful approaches to resolving disputes are generally preferred to more confrontational and belligerent strategies, though these are also occasionally utilized. Most African societies have developed rich, cultural norms of survivor-centred restorative justice as well as reconciliation for preserving harmony, making and building peace and maintaining this peace by cultivating group solidarity and avoiding aggression and violence.[31]

Some of these practices have been mobilized by African states in transitional justice processes. For example, Rwanda's *gacaca* courts and Uganda's *mato oput* reconciliation framework operationalized indigenous norms of survivor-centred restorative justice. In particular, the Acholi community in northern Uganda has resisted efforts to implement across the board prosecutions for perpetrators involved in the regional conflict, and relied extensively on the use of a culture- and tradition-based survivor-centred justice process known as *mato oput* to frame an exchange between victims and perpetrators during the crisis. This illustrates that the perceived norm-divergence between peace and justice is based on an artificially constructed false dichotomy between the pursuit of peace and the administration of justice. An extensive treatment of these approaches is beyond the scope of this chapter, but as the seminal 2012 book by Dolan *et al.* entitled *When Law Meets Reality: Forging African Transitional Justice* illustrates, the utilization of indigenous norms of survivor-centred restorative justice was a significant innovation that challenged the way in which transitional justice was predominantly conceived and understood. There have been criticisms of such inclusions, which have often included the suggestion that these cultural processes do not live up to international standards.[32] However, the converse has in fact become more evident, in that African states have demonstrated that the esoteric and elusive notion of an arbitrary 'international standard' or norm should not constrain countries that are attempting to address the violations of the past in their own specific context.

Some African conceptions of the individual, and their role and place in society, can provide an alternative normative framework for establishing more harmonious political and economic relations at the local, national, continental and even global level.[33] Through ubiqitous African emphasis on the value of social harmony and non-adversarial dispute resolution, there are lessons that can be learned and applied to contemporary conflict situations. It is necessary to question the notion of a universal conception of justice that can be advanced by a 'world court', such as the ICC. This universalizing tendency is often driven by a civilizing and modernizing imperative, which self-evidently marginalizes the Other's conception of justice. It regrettably assumes that there is only one way of conceptualizing justice, which is erroneous at best and coercive and alienating at worst. Instead, we need to embrace the idea that notions of survivor-centred justice can be locally specific and culturally defined. If cultural forms of survivor-centred justice can achieve this in a way that does not rely exclusively on a prosecutorial imperative, then it is vital to draw lessons from such approaches. As discussed above, African norms of survivor-centred justice emphasize communal harmony over the general tendency within mainstream notions of justice to prioritize individual culpability. The key point is that Africa is innovating when it comes to transitional justice norms and consequently providing normative examples of how countries can draw on their cultural practices to address the violations of the past.

Conclusion

Africa in this sense has challenged the artificial normative strictures of the global discourse of transitional justice and advanced its own home-grown norms to dealing with the violations of the past. Africa's experimentation with a broad range of norms and practices has reaffirmed the interface between justice, peacebuilding and reconciliation. Several countries are emerging from conflict and the challenge of peacebuilding is immediately confronted by the demands for justice for the victims of human rights atrocities. Traditionally, the pursuit of justice in international relations was considered detrimental to achieving peace and reconciliation, which are inherently political processes.

From its predominantly prosecutorial origins in the mid-1990s transitional justice has confronted a range of societal, economic and political pressures that have precipitated a more expansive framing and understanding of its normative parameters. A significant number of these pressures emerged from processes that were unfolding on the African continent, which placed the continent at the forefront of experimentation with norms of transitional justice. The normative pressures on the prosecutorial remit of transitional justice were exacerbated by the demands to address the needs of all survivors through social justice interventions. Transitional justice is now faced with a broad range of challenges pursuing societal transformation through political reform so as to restore inter-group trust and promote reconciliation in deeply divided communities. The calls for reparations and restitution have demanded new approaches to operationalizing transitional justice, which are linked to the peacebuilding and development fields.[34] The requirement of reforming institutions has also compelled transitional justice to expand its parameters to begin to address issues of constitutionalism and democratic governance.

Africa's experiences have demonstrated that traditional notions of transitional justice needed to be rethought and reframed. Specifically, in order to address the real concerns of survivors of past violations effectively, transitional justice norms had to be expanded beyond their narrow civil and political focus to include socio-economic and psycho-social issues.

Culture gives distinctiveness to a particular society's way of doing things. There is a need to draw on Africa's knowledge systems, its traditions and culture of jurisprudence to articulate and document indigenous norms of transitional justice. However, such an activity has to be informed by the fact that Africa is not a homogenous entity and within its societies there is a vast array of different approaches to dealing with the issues of peace and justice.

Africa's experiences have also evoked the need to scale up transitional justice processes from their country-specific focus towards a normative shift based on a regionalized approach to dealing with the past. Despite the growing acknowledgment of regional conflicts, regional reconciliation has *not* been the norm. Africa will continue to innovate on the development of transitional justice norms, due to the fact that a number of countries on the continent will be emerging from conflict in the next decade and beyond. By extension, Africa will continue to be a thought-leader, norm-setter and norm entrepreneur in terms of transitional justice processes and institutions and the perplexing challenge of addressing the violations of the past. In effect, this chapter argued that the notion of transitional justice is today much more expansive in terms of what is being practised on the ground, due in part to the influence of norms and practices that were operationalized and implemented in Africa.

Notes

1 M. Mamdani, *Neither Settler Nor Native: The Making and Unmaking of Permanent Minorities* (Johannesburg: Wits University Press, 2021), p. 193.
2 Ibid., p. 16.
3 T. Murithi (ed.), *The Politics of Transitional Justice in the Great Lakes Region of Africa* (Johannesburg: Jacana Media, 2016).
4 A. Boraine, 'Transitional Justice', in Charles Villa-Vicencio and Erik Doxtader (eds), *Pieces of the Puzzle: Keywords on Reconciliation and Transitional Justice* (Cape Town: Institute for Justice and Reconciliation, 2004), p. 67.
5 L. Balasco, 'The Transitions of Transitional Justice: Mapping the Waves from Promise to and Practice', *Journal of Human Rights*, 12, 2013, pp. 198–216; and H. Binningsbo, 'Armed Conflict and Post-Conflict Justice, 1946–2006: A Dataset', *Journal of Peace Research*, 2012, pp. 731–740.
6 Binningsbo, 'Armed Conflict and Post-Conflict Justice, 1946–2006'.
7 Mamdani, *Neither Settler Nor Native*, p. 194; emphasis added.
8 Ibid., p. 16.
9 Ibid.; emphasis added.
10 Ibid., p. 183.
11 African Union, *Transitional Justice Policy* (Addis Ababa: African Union, 2019), available at https://au.int/sites/default/files/documents/36541-doc-au_tj_policy_eng_web.pdf (accessed 25 October 2024).
12 Ibid., para. 17.
13 Ibid., para. 25; emphasis added.
14 Ibid., para. 10(ii).
15 Ibid., paras 17–19.
16 Ibid., paras 17–19.
17 Ibid., para. 2.
18 N. Grono and A. O'Brien, 'Justice in Conflict? The ICC and Peace Processes', in Nicholas Waddell and Clark P (eds), *Courting Conflict: Justice, Peace and the ICC in Africa* (London: Royal African Society, 2008).
19 C. Villa-Vicencio and E. Doxtader (eds), *Pieces of the Puzzle: Keywords on Reconciliation and Transitional Justice* (Cape Town: Institute for Justice and Reconciliation, 2004).
20 T. Murithi, 'The Role of Security Sector Reform in Dealing with the Past', *Politorbis*, 50(3), 2010, p. 67.

21 Mamdani, *Neither Settler Nor Native*, p. 16.
22 Ibid., p. 349.
23 Ibid., p. 348.
24 Ibid., p. 16.
25 Ibid., p. 17.
26 Ibid., p. 195.
27 E. Asaala and N. Diker, 'Truth-seeking in Kenya: Assessing the Effectiveness of the Truth, Justice and Reconciliation Commission of Kenya', *Africa Nazarene University Law Journal*, 1(2), 2013.
28 Mamdani, *Neither Settler Nor Native*, p. 195.
29 Ibid.
30 M. Okello *et al., Where Law Meets Reality: Forging African Transitional Justice* (Nairobi: Fahamu, 2012).
31 C. Ake, 'Rethinking African Democracy', *Journal of Democracy*, 2(1), 1999, pp. 32–44.
32 Okello et al., *Where Law Meets Reality.*
33 N. Wa Thiongo, *Moving the Centre: The Struggle for Cultural Freedoms* (Nairobi: East African Educational Publishers, 1993), p. 61.
34 T. Murithi, *The Ethics of Peacebuilding* (Edinburgh: Edinburgh University Press, 2009).

References

Ake, C. (1991) 'Rethinking African Democracy', *Journal of Democracy*, vol. 2, no. 1, pp. 32–44.

Arthur, P. (2009) 'How Transitions Reshaped Human Rights: A Conceptual History of Transitional Justice', *Human Rights Quarterly*, vol. 31, pp. 321–367.

Asaala, E. and Diker, N. (2013) 'Truth-seeking in Kenya: Assessing the Effectiveness of the Truth, Justice and Reconciliation Commission of Kenya', *Africa Nazarene University Law Journal*, vol. 1, no. 2.

Balasco, L. (2013) 'The Transitions of Transitional Justice: Mapping the Waves from Promise to Practice', *Journal of Human Rights*, vol. 12, pp. 198–216.

Binningsbo, H. (2012) 'Armed Conflict and Post-Conflict Justice, 1946–2006: A Dataset', *Journal of Peace Research*, pp. 731–740.

Boraine, A.L. (2004) 'Transitional Justice', in Charles Villa-Vicencio and Erik Doxtader (eds), *Pieces of the Puzzle: Keywords on Reconciliation and Transitional Justice.* Cape Town: Institute for Justice and Reconciliation.

Brown, S. and Sriram. C.L. (2012) 'The Big Fish Won't Fry Themselves: Criminal Accountability for Post-Election Violence in Kenya', *African Affairs*, vol. 111, no. 443, pp. 244–260.

Du Toit, F. (2013) 'A Double-Edged Sword', in Ernst Conradie (ed.), *Reconciliation: A Guiding Vision for South Africa?*Johannesburg: EFSA.

Grono, N, and O'Brien, A. (2008) 'Justice in Conflict? The ICC and Peace Processes', in Nicholas Waddell and Phil Clark (eds), *Courting Conflict: Justice, Peace and the ICC in Africa.* London: Royal African Society.

McCargo, D. (2015) 'Transitional Justice and its Discontents', *Journal of Democracy*, vol. 26, no. 2, April, pp. 5–20.

Murithi, T. (2009) *The Ethics of Peacebuilding*. Edinburgh: Edinburgh University Press.

Murithi, T. (2010) 'The Role of Security Sector Reform in Dealing with the Past', *Politorbis*, vol. 50, no. 3, pp. 65–70.

Murithi, T. and McClain, L.O. (2014) 'Regional Reconciliation in Africa', *Policy Recommendations for Cross-Border Transitional Justice*, Policy Brief no. 14. Cape Town: Institute for Justice and Reconciliation.

Sigsworth, R. and Valji, N. (2012) 'Continuities of Violence Against Women and the Limitations of Transitional Justice: The Case of South Africa', in S. Buckley-Zistel and R. Stanley (eds), *Gender in Transitional Justice*, Basingstoke: Palgrave Macmillan.

Sisson, J. (2010) 'A Conceptual Framework for Dealing with the Past', *Politorbis*, vol. 50, p. 12.

Wallensteen, P. (2012) 'Regional Peacebuilding: A New Challenge', *New Routes: A Journal of Peace Research and Action*, vol. 17, p. 20.

'Wa Thiongo, N. (1993) *Moving the Centre: The Struggle for Cultural Freedoms.* Nairobi: East African Educational Publishers.

Reports and other Web-Based Documents

African Union (2019) *Transitional Justice Policy.* Addis Ababa: African Union. Available at https://au.int/sites/default/files/documents/36541-doc-au_tj_policy_eng_web.pdf (accessed 25 October 2024).

International Criminal Court (2003) *The Prosecutor v. Dominic Ongwen.* Available at http://www.icc-cpi.int/en_menus/icc/situations (accessed 28 January 2020).

Kaldor, M. (2013) *New and Old Wars: Organised Violence in a Global Era.* Hoboken, NJ: Wiley.

Karamoja Cluster Project. Available at https://www.facebook.com/pg/karamojaclusterproject/about/?ref=page_internal (accessed 20 January 2020).

Lome Peace Agreement between Government of Sierra Leone and Revolutionary United Front, 7 July1999.

Murithi, T. (ed.) (2016) *The Politics of Transitional Justice in the Great Lakes Region of Africa.* Johannesburg: Jacana Media.

Okello, M.*et al.* (2012) *Where Law Meets Reality: Forging African Transitional Justice.* Nairobi: Fahamu.

United Nations (2004) *The Rule of Law and Transitional Justice in Conflict and Post-Conflict Societies*, Report of the Secretary-General, S/2004/616.

United Nations General Assembly (2005) 'Basic principles and guidelines on the right to remedy and reparation for victims of gross violations of international human rights law and serious violations of international humanitarian law', A/RES/60/147, New York.

Villa-Vicencio, C. and Doxtader, E. (eds) (2004) *Pieces of the Puzzle: Keywords on Reconciliation and Transitional Justice.* Cape Town: Institute for Justice and Reconciliation.

Part IV

Future Prospects for Survivors

9 Male Survivors of Violence and Truth Telling Processes

A Quest for Justice in Mt Elgon, Kenya

Elias O. Opongo

Introduction

Getting male survivors of violence (MSV) to tell their stories of violation in a truth telling process can be a daunting task. This process is often clouded by the gendered perceptions of the characterization of violence, cultural expectations of male resilience and lack of a clear methodology of accessing and encouraging MSV to participate in the process. This study examines the methodology, strategy and sociocultural implications that played into the truth telling process in Mt Elgon, Kenya, in the post-conflict reconstruction. In 2008, following the outbreak of post-election violence over disputed election results that left more than 1,500 people dead, the Kenyan government established the Truth, Justice and Reconciliation Commission (TJRC). The TJRC was instituted with the mandate to investigate acts of gross human rights violations and other historical injustices in Kenya that were committed between 12 December 1963 and 28 February 2008. In its many rounds of public hearings in different parts of the country, it was evident that the TJRC was confronted with the difficult challenge of getting survivors of violence and perpetrators turned victims and survivors to tell their stories. The fear, trauma and embarrassment from these humiliating experiences of violence made it difficult for the TJRC to draw out information from the survivors and perpetrators of violence. This task was even more difficult when it came to male survivors, as is the case in Mt Elgon region.

The chapter is based on a field study conducted in Kopsiro, Cheptais, Kapsokwony, Sasur, Chwele and Bungoma in the wider Mt Elgon region in Kenya. The study applied a phenomenological approach that detailed the lived experiences of the respondents, especially in describing the details of their experiences of violence. The study asserts that in order to attain reconciliation and social healing it is imperative to help the MSV to confront the past while engaging with other survivors, non-survivors and perpetrators. This common sense of being survivors forms bonds of solidarity based on justice and understanding geared towards the restoration of broken relationships, reparations and social healing.

Competition for land and subsequent conflicts between different ethnic groups and clans that live in the Mt Elgon region led to the formation of the

DOI: 10.4324/9781003212409-14

SLDF, a militia group that committed gross human rights violations while purporting to defend their land. The Sabaot is one of the three main ethnic groups in the region, the other two being the Bukusu and the Iteso. The Sabaot Land Defence Force (SDLF) took control of the Mt Elgon region, instituted laws and committed acts of violence against men and women. Men in particular were the targets, especially if they were suspected of being government informers or opponents of the militia group. It was alleged that the militia had committed serious violations of international humanitarian law, including castration, maiming and murder.[1]

It took a lot of effort on the part of the TJRC staff to get the MSV to come forward to tell their stories. Most of the male survivors had been castrated, and in the eyes of the community they had 'lost their manhood', and had to live with the sociocultural humiliation of devalued masculinity. As a result most MSV refused to give their testimonies to the TJRC for fear of public humiliation. Subsequently, the TJRC had to arrange for sessions to be held in places where the male survivors could give their testimonies in private.

The study demonstrates that it is vital to have a clear methodological strategy for truth telling processes, not only in accessing the MSV, but also in getting the society concerned to recognize the social/cultural vulnerabilities of the MSVs in post-conflict reconstruction. The MSV have claimed justice, which includes reparations and healing, as well as commitment to peace-building. The MSV have struggled to make the transition from 'victims of violence', confined to the paralysis of the impact of violence, to 'survivors of violence', committed to social change with strong claims for justice and peaceful coexistence.

The first part of this chapter focuses on contextual analysis and conceptualization of truth telling process and implications for the Mt Elgon conflict. The second part examines the research methodology and key findings from the study, while highlighting pertinent social justice issues around the protection of MSV in post-conflict settings.

Contextual Analysis of Protracted Land Conflicts in Mt Elgon

The conflict in the Mt Elgon region is related to the land question, which is an emotive issue in Kenya. Mt Elgon is located in Bungoma County in the western part of the Kenya and is largely inhabited by the Sabaot, Bukusu and Iteso communities.[2] Other ethnic minorities from different parts of the country come to farm the fertile land along the slopes of the mountain. A study carried out by the Conflict Sensitivity Consortium[3] notes that by 1957 there was already land-related conflict among the Mosop elders who were divided on the way the land should be parcelled up by the colonial administration. In 1920s and 1930s many Sabaots living in the Trans-Nzoia district were displaced by the British colonial government who appropriated their land for settler farmers. The Sabaot in 1932 presented their grievances to the colonial government's Kenya Land Commission, which promised to investigate the land disputes, but this was never solved. In 1968 the five-year-old independent Kenyan government wrongly addressed the Sabaot land dispute by reducing the available land at Chepkitale to an already growing population and designating part of the land as a game reserve. Some of the inhabitants relocated to settle in the forest reserve. Other displaced families settled at Chepyuk. In 1971 the government came up with a resettlement programme that would address displacements in the two locations. This was intended primarily for the Mosop (Ndorobo) and Soy clans of the dominant Sabaot community. According to Simiyu,[4] from its inception the settlement programme was derailed by claims and counterclaims of state favouritism and corruption by both clans, leading to a cycle of allocations, annulments and evictions. This led to disputes and conflicts. Tension thus arose 'between the intended owners and the existing inhabitants'.[5] This resettlement programme was referred to as Chepyuk I.

The government later decided to evict everyone from the settlement schemes and in 1989 carried a second resettlement programme known as Chepyuk II. This attempt failed and many people from Chepkitale attempted twice (in 1979 and 1988) to return to Chepkitale but were repulsed by the police since part of their land had now been designated as a game reserve. In another dramatic twist, the late President Daniel Arap Moi in 1993 annulled the entire Chepyuk settlement and initiated a new settlement scheme, Chepyuk III. However, by this time the population had increased and a generation of families had lived on the same land. Given the controversies around the process, Chepyuk III was never implemented and the issue remained unresolved for a long time. In the wake of 2002 general election that brought an end to the Kenya African National Union's 40-year rule the issue of resettlement was rife again.

Tensions over land control increased and immediately after the 2002 general election the SLDF was formed to defend the land of the Sabaot people against perceived intruders. The SLDF began to recruit youth to join the militia group. In 2005, during the constitutional referendum, the debate around land and resettlement was one of the major topics. In 2005 Chepyuk III land resettlement was implemented but the process was, however, marred by irregularities. This situation engendered discontentment and exacerbated intra-communal tensions and conflicts, which took a more violent turn in 2006 after the finalization of the land allocation process. One of the outcomes of the allocation process required some members of the Soy clan, who had already settled, to vacate their land and others to give up part of their land for subdivision and allocation to other families from the Mosop clan and a section of the Soy clan. This did not augur well with some of the Soy clan members. The SDLF became more lethal, attacking civilians and police, extorting money from civilians and committing rape and other human rights violations. It was the activities of this militia that were to greatly define the conflict in Mt Elgon.[6]

While the question of land allocation in the third phase of the resettlement programme was the immediate trigger for the conflict, a critical analysis of the conflict situation in Mt Elgon also points to historical injustices related to colonial disinheritance of the Sabaot communal lands and to competition over scarce land resources in the post-colonial era. This was induced, in part, by unequitable distribution and access patterns, but also demographics, as the root causes of intra- and inter-community tensions and conflict escalation in Mt Elgon. Simiyu also suggests that there were some pre-existing conditions that interacted with these root causes to configure a landscape of conflict in Mt Elgon.[7] Persistent politicization of the land question and local political dynamics merely helped to exacerbate the worsening situation in Mt Elgon making it one of the most violent conflicts in post-independent Kenya.

Despite the outbreak of violent conflict in Mt Elgon in 2006, the response of the government was largely insufficient and often uncoordinated. The SLDF continued to wreak terror on the communities in Mt Elgon until the election period in December 2007. Given that 2007 was an election year and that the government did not want to lose favour with the electorate, minimum action was taken against the SLDF.[8] The results of the 2007 general election were disputed by the opposition party, the Orange Democratic Movement, leading to violence that resulted in death of over 1,500 people in the country and the displacement of more than 700,000 people.[9] The SLDF seized the opportunity during the post-election violence of 2007–2008 to become even more brutal. During this time the SLDF was alleged to have killed, maimed, raped and tortured hundreds of people. The militia harassed and beat people; it also extorted money and confiscated property within targeted locations especially in Kopsiro and Cheptais.[10] On the ending of the post-election violence and the conclusion of the power sharing deal between the then incumbent President Mwai Kibaki and opposition leader Raila Odinga in February 2008, it was time for the government to act.

In March 2008 the Kenya Defence Force (KDF) Operation Okoa Maisha ('Save Lives') was launched in Mt Elgon to stem the tide of violence that had overwhelmed the police. This led to the defeat of SLDF militia and the restoration of calm and order in the region. Although the army achieved tremendous success in its war against the SLDF militia and killed its top commanders including the militia's leader, Wycliffe Matakuei, it left behind traces of gross human rights violations and other injustices in Mt Elgon.[11] The atrocities that were committed by the army did not only undermine the confidence of the local residents who had joined the army, but also exacerbated the feeling within the community that it was being persecuted by the state,[12] which jeopardized the prospects for sustainable peace in the region. Human Rights Watch released a report accusing the army of killing and torturing people during its campaign to root out the SLDF and restore peace, claims that have been since confirmed by the TJRC. Men suspected to be members or sympathizers of the SDLF were either tortured or killed by the army.[13] In its 2015 report, the TJRC confirmed that security agents had committed serious human rights violations in Mt Elgon that had led to deaths and displacements.[14] Sociopolitical tensions still exist in Mt Elgon and in 2018 conflict erupted again when the SLDF re-emerged with brutal force against the population leading the government to declare a night to dawn curfew in certain locations.

Conceptualizing Truth Telling Process in Mt Elgon

In many conflict situations both men and women are often tortured, killed or abused. In most cases, women and children tend to be the main victims of violence and subsequent consequences of conflict.[15] However, armed conflict also carries the risk of sexual violence against men and boys. Furthermore, sexual violence such as rape, sexual enslavement, castration, sexual humiliation, forced incest and forced rape against men and boys is a pervasive feature in armed conflicts worldwide. While acknowledging the immense suffering of women and children in conflict and war situations, it is important to note that men are more likely to be killed or wounded as a result of fighting, to become the victims of forced recruitment, forced disappearance and extrajudicial killing.[16] Men have also become survivors of different forms of violence, including sexual violence, during military operations against the civilian population but also in detention or in the context of forced conscription. Thus, the experiences on the ground do not always correspond to the stereotypical gender roles and expectations imposed by society.

The case of Mt Elgon reveals that grave violations were perpetrated against male victims and indeed the statements taken by the TJRC in 2013 in Mt Elgon include many cases of men who suffered at the hands of the SLDF and later became victims of the KDF's infamous Operation Okoa Maisha. This is a clear indicator that there can be gendered differential experiences in conflict that can help to change the perceived narrative of men as perpetrators and women as victims into appreciation of the fact that during armed conflict men and women suffer differently and indeed uniquely. Getting MSV to tell their stories of human rights violations ought to be conceptualized within the larger framework of truth telling and peacebuilding in post-conflict contexts.

The truth telling process by MSV served to transform men from victims to survivors. The fact that they were able to narrate their experiences of violence within the context of truth telling aimed at reconciling broken communities suggests that these survivors became peacebuilders. Their stories were not told in the context of the desire for revenge, but instead the desire for healing through the truth telling process. Had they chosen to be victims, they would not have realized the wide horizon of social change before them, and instead they would have remained inactive agents. Hence, the larger framework of transitional justice provided a positive platform for bringing together the community to acknowledge individual and communal suffering and to find ways of moving forward together.

Truth telling strategies of transitional justice through official truth commissions were mainstreamed and the recommendations and guidelines for the truth commissions were developed by Priscilla Hayner and published in collaboration with the International Centre for Transitional Justice.[17] It is hoped that truth commissions will provide a judicial balance for post-conflict societies. However, the assumed beneficial effects of truth telling processes have been questioned in the recent peacebuilding literature.[18] For example, a comprehensive overview of research on the effects of transitional justice[19] assert that there is insufficient evidence to support the proponents' claims that truth telling processes can lead to reconciliation or some sort of psychological healing; furthermore, there is a lack of evidence to support sceptics' claims that truth telling undermines progress towards these goals. In the same vein, Mendeloff claims that 'the literature on transitional justice and post-conflict peace building has, surprisingly with very few exceptions, failed to ask whether truth telling has any salutary or harmful effects for the people involved'.[20]

The opposite causal logic operates as well, implying that if truth telling is not applied, the benefits of a sense of justice and psychological healing will not be reaped and the desire for vengeance will increase, leading to a heightened risk of conflict and war. There are a number of potential benefits of truth telling, depending on the transparency and efficiency of the process, the manner of accompaniment of the victims and the implementation of the recommendations of the commission. The underlying assumption in much of the peacebuilding and transitional justice literature, as well as in the political rhetoric, is that truth telling is cathartic or healing and will thereby advance peacebuilding and reconciliation.[21] Hence, the general causal mechanism through which truth telling is assumed to prevent renewed war is that it may offer victims a sense of justice or psychological healing, which decreases any desire for vengeance and so increases the potential for sustainable peace.[22]

The TJRC in Kenya collected 42,465 statements and 1,828 memoranda from individuals, different groups and communities across the whole country, at the time the highest number of such records to be collected by an international truth commission. The TJRC had structured methodologies of collecting information in four phases, namely statement taking, research and investigations, hearings and report writing.[23] The Commission identified sexual and gender-based violence (SGBV) as a special category. The TJRC Act distinguished SGBV as crimes against humanity.[24]

Likewise, the United Nations (UN) defines what it terms 'conflict-related sexual violence' as referring to 'rape, sexual slavery, forced prostitution, forced pregnancy, forced abortion, enforced sterilization, forced marriage, and any other form of sexual violence of comparable gravity perpetrated against women, men, girls or boys that is directly or indirectly linked to a conflict'.[25] The Rome Statutes that guides the International Criminal Court (ICC) in its definition of SGBV includes the mutilation of sexual organs, that is 'permanent disfigurement or permanently disabling or removing a sexual organ or appendage under circumstances that are not medically justified'.[26]

The TJRC recruited individuals with experience in handling SGBV cases and gave them special training. The training was meant to ensure that SGBV victims and witnesses 'were treated with dignity, utmost sensitivity and respect'.[27] The TJRC underscored that '[s]exual and gender-based violence is a crime that intimately impacts the victim both physically and psychologically. It uses the victim's own sexual anatomy to dominate, suppress and control'.[28] The Commission offered psychosocial services to survivors of sexual violence through counselling and health care support; encouraged the observance of cultural sensitivity; ensured that victims of SGBV were interviewed by persons of the same sex; insisted on being attentive to victims' emotional behaviour and response; and underscored that 'because of the nature of the violation, victims/victims may withhold information for a number of reasons, including because of fear, shame or embarrassment'.[29]

The TJRC offered to interview female survivors of sexual violence in private in order to encourage them to come forward. However, no similar arrangements were made for male survivors. Perhaps it was assumed that women were more vulnerable to SGBV violations than men. However, the Commission noted that 'sexual and gender-based violence against male victims is even more under-reported and under-investigated compared to sexual and gender-based violence against women'.[30] The Commission received over 1,100 statements from adult survivors of SGBV. Of these 103 were given by men. However, taken together the statements and memoranda totalled 2,646 women and 346 men.[31] The Commission noted that

> [w]hile some men actually testified about their ordeal with sodomy, many more women spoke about the sexual and gender-based violence that their sons or husbands went through, reinforcing the existing view that sexually violated men find it extremely stigmatizing to report and talk about the violations.[32]

The TJRC also noted that male residents in Mt Elgon were targeted during the violent attacks from 2006–2008. Many male victims had their genitals mutilated or castrated. As a result these victims were too embarrassed to come forward and give their testimonies during the TJRC hearings. The majority of these victims faced victimization by society owing to their experiences.

Research Methodology

The research was carried out intermittently over a period of six years between 2014 and 2019 in Kopsiro, Cheptais, Kapsokwony, Sasur, Chwele and Bungoma. The locations were chosen because they were the epicentre of the crimes committed by the SLDF militias. The research was interrupted owing to security concerns, the periodic eruption of violence and difficulty in accessing some of the respondents.

The secondary data was collected through documentation gleaned from institutions, civil society groups, journals, newspapers and books. The primary data was put together from in-depth face to face interviews, focus group discussions and observational analysis drawn from the researchers' encounters and experiences in the field. The researchers worked with research assistants to collect data. The researchers had various interactive forums within and outside the Mt Elgon region, particularly in Nairobi. Data collection was not restricted to the duration of physical field visits. Even during the data analysis period, the researchers continued to seek clarification on certain issues from the data emerging from various people who had an interest and a stake in the study. This greatly improved the content and enriched to a greater extent the findings of this study.

A total of 88 respondents aged between 26 to 75 years were interviewed, either personally, in focus group discussions or through telephone communication. Most of those interviewed had in one way or another participated in the truth telling processes initiated by the TJRC. Other institutions and groups were also interviewed, such as non-governmental organizations (NGOs), religious institutions that offered psychosocial support programmes and informal sociocultural activities to the victims, service providers who gave assistance to the victims of violence, community leaders and the general public.

The study applied a phenomenological approach, namely a qualitative descriptive study that has as its important tenet a description of the lived experiences of the respondents, particularly their experiences of violence. This methodological approach was helpful in conducting in-depth interrogations and interviews on the forms of violence perpetrated against the MSV, the impact that this had on them and their experiences. The main purpose of the phenomenological approach is to carry out a critical analysis of the specific cases of violence in Mt Elgon, the suffering that MSV endured and their experiences of the truth telling process by the TJRC. In the social sphere this translates into gathering deep information and perceptions through inductive, qualitative methods such as interviews and discussions.[33] In accordance with the phenomenological requirements, this study did not entail any hypotheses or preconditions. Instead, research questions guided the study and drew critical conclusions that highlighted experiences of MSV. The study had a small sample size of 88 respondents, which according to the phenomenological requirements, allows the qualitative research to test effectively the strength of inferences, illustrate discrepancies, identify issues and draw attention to different situations.[34]

In addition, efforts were made throughout the research period to identify disconfirming (negative) cases[35] in order to ensure data redundancy and saturation, thus leading to a high level of empirical confidence. To do this, the researchers engaged in a repeated triangulation of data for additional information, which was obtained from several participants in order to deliver a satisfactory mark of rigour. This sampling strategy helped to support the emerging theorizing and juxtaposition of data for comparison and development of a sequence that attempts a critical recovery of history in line with key components of the phenomenological approach. The sequence of events that had unfolded since the violations and the truth telling processes were taken into consideration. This was an important strategy since it allowed data from respondents to offer an insight deemed to be atypical (negative case) in the context of what was being theorized, thereby challenging collective assumptions that are founded on social constructions, such as men are perpetrators and women are victims. In this case, the victims – men – became survivors with the deliberate intention of driving peacebuilding and a reconciliation agenda within the framework of transitional justice.

Conducting a study on mens' experiences of violence, trauma, truth telling and reconciliation in a post-conflict peacebuilding setting requires fundamental ethical considerations and careful methodological design. The study went through institutional rigour for approval, acquiring ethical approvals from both the university and government. A 'do no harm' approach was paramount in this research given the vulnerability of the MSV. The research was conscious of the possibility of re-traumatization and subsequently consulted psychologists and social workers on how best to approach the MSV. The gatekeepers were equally helpful in identifying individuals who were sufficiently socially and psychologically stable to narrate their survival of violence. The researchers also took care to acquire the prior consent of the respondents as well as observing their anonymity and confidentiality throughout the research, and in the data analysis and presentation.

Data analysis was organized in themes that followed a set mind-map in tandem with emerging themes within the sociocultural context of the MSV in Mt Elgon. The themes are both collective and individual, thus allowing for the critical analysis on how individual narratives gradually form part of the communal narratives. In this largely patriarchal society, the social narratives of the people found their outlet in the individual life situations and realities that emerged from the male survivors.

The thematic analysis of data relied on systematic processes common to the grounded theory's methodological approach. However, because of purposive sampling limitations, this research was not purely based on grounded theory. The analysis process was achieved by operational techniques and research strategies that include the use of both field and personal journals, and thematic logs in the form of a structured interview schedule during focus group discussions and individual interviews. Operational techniques such as negative case analysis, the constant comparison of data, member checking and peer reviews were also employed since these do not in any way contradict the phenomenological approach to research.

Narratives of Male Survivors of Violence

This section explains the empirical results of the data analysis as outlined in the research design. The presentation, analysis and interpretation of the data is in keeping with the research objectives and the presentation is based on the inferential statistics used in the analysis of the data. As indicated in the research objective, this study sought to highlight the nature and impact of violence on MSV in Mt Elgon. A majority (88%) of the male survivors who were interviewed reported that they had experienced physical injuries inflicted on them by either the SLDF militia or the KDF, or both. This was mainly because these men were suspected accomplices of either side of the conflict.

The narratives of torture and sexual humiliation of male survivors were summarized by a medical practitioner from a district hospital who observed that during the military operation 90% of the victims were civilians, the majority of whom bore physical injuries such as the cutting off of ears, legs or hands or bodily scars from being whipped, stabbed or tortured. The MSV were also humiliated by being forced to carry out certain acts, such as being undressed in public; forced to have sex with their own daughters, mothers or grandmothers; being mutilated by other men, for example, cutting their ears, mouths or hands; and forced to kill their close relatives. These traumatic experiences instilled a perpetual sense of guilt in the persons that were forced to carry out these acts.

When asked whether or not the male victims went to hospital, the medical practitioner said that generally they never did but on few occasions some did. The fear of going to hospital was mainly associated with the fact that most people had taken oaths not to narrate any incidences of physical violence or militia activities to anyone. This view was supported by service providers, religious groups and NGOs. There were threats from the militia against any betrayers, particularly men. Hence, anyone going to hospital to seek treatment for their injuries was likely to be under pressure to reveal the cause of injury. Moreover, cultural beliefs that men were supposed to be strong and should therefore not be seen as going to hospital, compelled some to use traditional herbs for treatment. The fact that people had been forced by the militia to commit violent acts against their own relatives meant that it was difficult for many people to reveal the perpetrators of violence. The militia had also threatened any NGOs offering humanitarian assistance to the people, and as such most NGOs left the country, thereby limiting the humanitarian assistance available to the population.

In explaining the violence experienced by the community, a human rights activist in Bungoma, asserted that:

> The KDF operation dubbed Okoa Maisha [Save Lives] started on 10 March 2008. According to the United Nations records, 4,892 men were arrested between 10 March and 11 June 2008, and when the curfew was imposed 1,200 were arrested. The army conducted arbitrary arrests – some people were tortured, others castrated. So you will hear people refer to the castrated men as 'those who have lost their manhood'. The army killed many people; 128 people disappeared and we do not know

> whether they were killed or are still alive. The violence perpetrated on the men was really extreme. In fact most castrated men do not want to talk about it. No NGOs or media bodies were allowed in the area during the military operations. There were so many cases of unreported human rights violations.

One of the community leaders stated that:

> Immediately the military set foot in Mt Elgon they completely took over control of our region, and this was the time that violence against men was at its highest. Men were indiscriminately assaulted, whether perpetrators or not. Additionally, any organizations working within the community were expelled and nobody was allowed to do any kind of activity during this period.

The arbitrary nature of the violence perpetrated against civilians was a major issue of concern. Civilians found themselves caught up between the militia and the government armed forces. A participant at a focus group discussion in Chwele exclaimed, 'You won't believe this! The policemen who were supposed to protect the community were the ones who caused our husbands' greatest suffering'. She added that one of the male survivors they had talked to told them that the reason why the latter responded with violence was because they wanted to defend themselves. The woman further elaborated that men felt humiliated by the police especially given that some policemen had sexual affairs with the wives of the men who had escaped the violence. In some cases these women were forcefully married to these policemen and had children together, making it difficult for the men to claim back their wives on their return home.

There were several cases of arbitrary detention of MSV in Mt Elgon. At least 44% of male interviewees reported having been detained either by the police or the army. According to one human rights activist from Cheptais:

> There were so many people who were detained in Mt Elgon. When the operation started, most young men were arrested and detained. The soldiers were literally sweeping this place and indiscriminately arresting young men, torturing and detaining them; we still need answers for the conduct of the soldiers. I mean we cannot have these atrocities go unquestioned. If the TJRC failed to bear any fruit, there must be some mechanisms to bring the culprits to book.

Apart from physical injury, the loss and destruction of property remained the most prevalent form of injustice that most MSV experienced in Mt Elgon. All the MSV who were interviewed reported to have lost property during the conflict. Property ranged from land and farm produce to homes and household items. In addition, most men were forced to remit some money to

SLDF as fines, and as such cases of extortion specifically targeting men were rampant. Failure to pay up led either to destruction of property, such as homesteads, or the removal of things such as household items and livestock. For instance, one survivor from Chepyuk reported having lost all his donkeys as well as agricultural produce.

The destruction of property had a serious negative impact on the population: families were broken up, people were displaced and many were reduced to abject poverty. This situation led to serious social disharmony, and according to one community leader from Cheptais, 'the negative effect of the conflict was largely the cause of many social ills such as early pregnancies, early marriages and a high rate of school dropouts in the Mt Elgon region'. One male survivor from Kipsis who lost all his property explained that:

> They came and tied us up, they beat up my sons and threatened to kill us all, they then asked for Ks. 30,000 ($300) which we gave and they drove off with my cattle. I thought it was all over but a few days later they came back again and luckily we managed to escape, but they then torched our houses, my whole homestead was torched and now I do not have a home.

Another male survivor from Kiptii, one of the villages in Mt Elgon, reported having lost all his property to the SLDF. He claimed that his case was politically motivated because at the time he wanted to become a councillor. The SLDF had warned him not to apply for any political or government position, otherwise he would face punishment and a fine of Ks. 100,000 ($1,000). In his narration he observed that:

> The SDLF came the following day after warning me against vying for any political seat. They drove off all my cattle. Later they torched my house and as a result I had to run way. I was then arrested by the KDF, beaten and detained for some time and as a result of the torture I suffered terrible injuries to my limbs. I have not yet recovered.

A human rights activist in Bungoma observed,

> Already between 2003–2005 there were clear signs that a major conflict could erupt. There were young people conducting military combat training. Families were forced to give their young men to the SDLF. If a parent refused to give away their son to the militia group they had to pay Ks. 50,000 ($500), if not someone in the family would be killed. Many schoolchildren had to join.

He added that the SDLF imposed taxes on the people. Usually men were targeted. People had to pay according to their financial capacity. Failure to pay the taxes meant death. For example, one of the judges of the high court was told he had to pay Ks. 100,000 ($1,000) per month. He had to flee the area. At a focus group discussion exclusively for men in Chwele, one of the male community leaders confirmed that he went to school with some of the SDLF members and that he knew them very well. He added that the SDLF were promised many things by the politicians and their sponsors, but were later shortchanged.

Sexual and psychological violence were other forms of violence that were reported by the MSV. Of 37 MSV that were interviewed, 11 of them reported having been castrated; 19 affirmed that they had been sexually assaulted, for instance through the insertion of hard objects into their anus or by having parts of their reproductive organs chopped off; and six indicated that they had been forced to have sex with close family members such as their daughters, mothers or neighbours. Meanwhile, 12 out of the 37 interviewees reported having suffered psychological torture or trauma resulting from abuse. However, further interrogation indicated that this number increased significantly if the victims were sensitized to understand manifestations of trauma or other psychological impacts. While the MSV do not talk about their traumatic experiences or perhaps are not able to identify them, it was evident that their statements and narratives about their experiences of violence were clear indications of the psychological effect thereof on them. For instance, one male survivor from Chongeiyo, one of the villages in Mt Elgon, stated that:

> When I recall how they raped my wife and how they killed my own son, I still feel so traumatized. Remembering that incident is always very painful to me, sometimes I can't even sleep and I get nightmares. She comes to my dreams so vividly. I feel lost sometimes.

Of those who pointed out that they were survivors of psychological torture, the following two selected statements were echoed by different male survivors:

> Losing all those members of my family is very painful, I was psychologically affected and I have gone for counselling twice, but I still feel I need to continue with counselling since it is still very hard for me. I did not know about the psychological impact that I had suffered until some people from one of the NGOs came and offered some counselling to us. That is when I realized that the torture I had gone through during the detention, and the news about the death of my wife had a serious psychological impact on me.

Findings from this study indicate that all 37 MSV interviewed indicated that they had suffered more than one of the abovementioned forms of violation. The following statement from an interviewee from Chesikaki village highlights some of the violations that MSV endured:

> I was beaten badly by the SLDF; they accused me of being a traitor and warned me of dire consequences if I were ever to speak to government officials or forces. Unfortunately, I was later to fall into the hands of the KDF soldiers during the operation; I was again badly beaten. I was later detained for three months without any cause, nor was I charged for any crime. I was held captive in several different places, but during this time my wife ran away and as such I lost my family. I lost many things including my job as a security guard. Since my release, my life has never been the same again and the situation is really very hard for me.

This was not an isolated case since the narrative of violations of MSV portrayed a web of injustices that they went through. One male survivor from Chebuek village summed this up when he stated that:

> We lost a lot, what we lost we cannot recover. Imagine losing a family and your loved ones; how are you going to recover your family back again? I do not think there is any way. It is not possible.

To a large extent men found it difficult to narrate their stories of sexual violations largely due to cultural perceptions of masculinity. The TJRC allowed men who had been affected by violence to choose whether they wanted to give their testimonies in public or in private. This allowed the MSV who were suffering from stigma and shame to come forward and tell their stories in private and confidential statement-taking sessions. However, it still took a lot of counselling and preparation for some of the men to come forward. The shame of narrating a traumatic experience was a difficult one to digest. For example, a man from Chepkube posed the following question:

> How do you expect a man to come forward and say that he was castrated? It is very difficult, some cannot speak about it, and only a very few can have the courage to openly speak about something like that.

Similarly, the TJRC noted that:

> There is shame in reporting the act as they [the male victims of SGBV] are made to feel that they are somehow to blame for what happened to them. In a society that promotes the male norm as being macho, male victims feel and are made to feel emasculated by sexual violence.[36]

One community leader from Cheptais asserted that:

> We as the Sabaot people are part of the Kalenjin and our cultural practices are strong. As a man therefore there are things that people should not know about you. For instance, private family issues and even personal challenges should be kept within you or within a small group of

> people that you really trust. So, telling the men to come forward and reveal everything about what they know and saw or went through especially when it touches on their private lives is indeed very difficult.

In contrast, one respondent was quite blunt in telling his story of castration. He saw it as a means to getting the community to talk about healing and reconciliation:

> I was castrated, I am not a man anymore and I was not afraid to say so to the TJRC when they came. I believe my experience will be a good indicator that we need healing and reconciliation in this community.

This particular interviewee joined other MSV who had committed themselves to mobilizing the community for peace through dialogue, resolution of family disputes over land and support for families that were experiencing hardship as a result of the conflict.

A human rights activist from Bungoma asserted that:

> A few men came forward to tell their stories of torture at a meeting we organized between the victims and perpetrators. The Free Pentecostal Church and the Catholic Justice and Peace Commission have been instrumental in encouraging men to come forward and support peacebuilding initiatives by male survivors of violence.

Indeed, there are quite a number of men who went against all the odds to narrate their stories especially during confidential sessions. These male survivors committed themselves to peacebuilding efforts, to persuading young people not to join militia groups and instead dedicate their lives to uniting the divided community.

The research findings show that in conflict and post-conflict settings the term 'masculinity' can fall into two distinct categories: one is the social construction based on male power and dominance over those perceived to be weaker or enemies, whether male or female. In this case, masculinity is expressed through violent subjugation of the other, often through humiliating acts such as rape, sodomy, genital mutilation or murder. The second category is the sociocultural construction of the male figure as strong, dominant, protective and able to endure pain and suffering. In conflict settings these two categories sometimes overlap, particularly given that offence, self-defence and male toleration of hardship and pain all tend towards patriarchy and dominance.

In many post-conflict truth telling processes masculinity emasculates male vulnerability to violence and draws less attention to assisting MSV. In other words, socialized masculinity tends to camouflage male experiences of violence. This is mainly due to stigmatization of male experiences of SGBV that make them afraid of the social stigma associated with diminishing their manhood or maleness. As a result male victimization in SGBV tends to marginalize male narratives and subsequently does not put into place the necessary responses to assist the MSV.

The case of Mt Elgon demonstrated that the truth telling process was part of the larger agenda of healing and reconciliation. A number of male survivors were working with NGOs, religious institutions and community-based organizations in drawing attention to the need for healing past wounds. Their efforts were mainly focused on community dialogue around their experiences of past violence, support for those who had been badly affected, especially building houses for the old and poor, providing medical care to people who had been affected by the violence, integration of former soldiers into the community through acceptance-awareness programmes that allowed community members to positively receive those who had returned; and human rights awareness programmes, among others. Thus, the intersection between victimhood, survival and direct engagement with peacebuilding activities drew together a progressive metamorphosis of positive social change. However, the underlying complexities of the conflict still remain, and there is a need for continuous support of the peacebuilding efforts in the region.

Conclusion

Truth telling among MSV can be a difficult process given the sociocultural expectations of indomitable masculinity. Creative approaches to getting men to come forward and narrate their experiences of violence ought to be an integral part of transitional justice mechanisms. The findings from this study indicate that men largely formed a great part of the history of violence in Mt Elgon and that they have been, in a very unique way, involved from the start of the conflict, and along the bitter journey involved in the truth telling process. Uniquely, the same men who are at the centre of the conflict appear to have suffered systematic alienation during the process due to the reasons discussed above. The cultural and socio-economic demands, the historical circumstances and other factors largely pushed men out of the mainstream peacebuilding strategies. However, MSV, as demonstrated in this study, summoned up the courage not only to participate in truth telling processes, but also to become proactive agents of peacebuilding efforts.

While truth telling may not always in itself be sufficient to bring about healing it plays a pivotal role in the healing process. The findings of this study show that men as much as women are susceptible to the effects of violence. Truth telling in Mt Elgon led to a revelation of grave human rights violations, historical injustices, human rights abuses and other deep-seated cleavages around land resources and tenure, social order and exclusion, as well as political intolerance. The nationalization of the conflict in Mt Elgon is a clear indicator of the fluidity of conflict and how quickly it became a national and, indeed, an international crisis. Mt Elgon therefore typifies the dilemma that plagues most African countries today. Through the TJRC the state has in some way acknowledged the plight of the people of Mt Elgon. However, despite this acknowledgement there is still a lot that needs to be done to improve the conditions of the survivors of violence.

This study has affirmed the importance of truth telling during the process of transitional justice. While MSV have indicated that not only was it necessary to narrate their stories, it was also important to be able to do so, but they have raised concerns about the amount of pressure that was exerted on them to expose their moments of vulnerability. However, men's agency in actively participating in conflict resolution mechanisms, especially in persuading young people not to engage in violence, has contributed to the overall peacebuilding efforts in the region. It is important to compare the strategies of peacebuilding applied by MSV in comparison to those of women survivors of violence. While the experiences of violence between the two genders may vary, the ultimate concern is how different actors in the society can contribute to the peacebuilding efforts aimed at social cohesion.

Notes

1 Human Rights Watch, *All the Men Are Gone: War Crimes in Kenya's Mt. Elgon Conflict*, 2008, available at https://www.hrw.org/report/2008/07/27/all-men-have-gone/war-crimes-kenyas-mt-elgon-conflict.

2 The Sabaot community is a sub-tribe of the Kalenjin which largely inhabits Kenya's Rift Valley Region. It is composed of six sub-ethnic groups which include the Kony, Bok, Bongomek, Sabiny/Sebei, Somek and the Chepkitale/Mosop: see L. Forsberg *et al.*, 'Facing Mt. Elgon', *Mid-Term Evaluation of the Peace and Rights Programme* (Kitale: FPFK, 2012); and A, Amugune, *Mt. Elgon Violence*, 2008, available at http://www.marsgroupkenya.org. Broadly, they are categorized into two depending on the location of their stay. Thus, the Soy live on the slopes of the mountain and the Mosop live in the highland region of the mountain; see C. Medard, *Indigenous Land Claims in Kenya: A Case Study of Chebyuk, Mount Elgon District*, 2006, available at www.hsrcpress.ac.za. The Sabaot is the only Kalenjin sub-tribe that belongs to Bungoma County formerly part of the western province. The Sabaot community forms the larger population in Mt Elgon. The Bukusu community is part of the larger Luhya community of western Kenya and forms the second largest population in Mt Elgon. Finally, the Iteso community belongs to the Nilotic Cluster. Iteso is the minority community in Mt Elgon although there is a larger population of Iteso community in neighbouring Uganda.

3 Conflict Sensitivity Consortium, *Embracing the Practice of Conflict Sensitive Approaches: An Analysis of the Kenyan Context* (Nairobi: Conflict Sensitivity Consortium, 2010).

4 R.R. Simiyu, *Militarization of Resource Conflicts: The Case of Land-Based Conflict in the Mount Elgon Region of Western Kenya* (Pretoria: Institute for Security Studies, 2011).

5 Ibid.

6 Ibid.

7 Ibid.

8 Médecins Sans Frontières, *Mount Elgon: Does Anybody Care? MSF Takes Stock After One Year in the Heart of the Crisis in Mount Elgon*, 2008, available at http://www.lekari-bezhranic.cz/cz/downloads/MSF_MtElgon_May2008.pdf.

9 J. Klopp and P. Kamung, 'Violence and Elections: Will Kenya Collapse?' *World Policy Journal*, 24, 2008.
10 Simiyu, *Militarization of Resource Conflicts.*
11 Human Rights Watch, *Kenya: Army and Rebel Militia Commit War Crimes in Mt. Elgon*, 2008, available at http://www.reliefweb.int/rw/rwb.nsf/db900sid/ASAZ7DDCD5opendocument.
12 Simiyu, *Militarization of Resource Conflicts.*
13 Human Rights Watch, *All the Men Are Gone.*
14 Truth, Justice and Reconciliation Commission, *Report of the Truth, Justice and Reconciliation Commission*, 2015, p. 7, available at www.tjrckenya.org.
15 H. Ryanga, *Women and Conflict in Mt. Elgon, Kenya: Rape as a Weapon of War* (thesis, University of Nairobi, 2015).
16 D. Bloomfield, T. Barnes L. and Huyse (eds) (2003), *Reconciliation after Violent Conflict: A Handbook* (Stockholm: International Institute for Democracy and Electoral Assistance, 2003); see also P.B. Hayner, *Unspeakable Truths: Transitional Justice and the Challenge of Truth Commissions* (New York: Routledge, 2010).
17 P.B. Hayner, *Negotiating Justice: Guidance for Mediators* (Geneva: HD Centre for Humanitarian Dialogue, 2009).
18 M.B. Hirsch, M. MacKenzie and M. Sesay, 'Measuring the Impacts of Truth and Reconciliation Commissions: Placing the Global "Success" of TRCs in Local Perspective', *Cooperation and Conflict*, 47(3), 2012, pp. 386–403.
19 O.N. Thomas, J. Ron and R. Paris (*The Effects of Transitional Justice Mechanisms: A Summary of Empirical Research Findings and Implications for Analysts and Practitioners* (Ottawa, ON: Centre for International Policy Studies, 2008), p. 4.
20 D. Mendeloff, 'Trauma and Vengeance: Assessing the Psychological and Emotional Effects of Post-conflict Justice', *Human Rights Quarterly*, 31, 2009, pp. 592–623.
21 E.O. Opongo, 'Amani Mashinani Conflict Transformation Model: Bishop Korir's Legacy on Peace and Reconciliation', *The Journal of Social Encounters*, 4(1), 2020, pp. 9–21.
22 M.C. Okello, 'Afterward: Elevating Transitional Local Justice or Crystallizing Global Governance', in Rosalind Shaw and Lars Waldorf (eds), *Localizing Transitional Justice: Interventions and Priorities after Mass Violence* (Stanford, CA: Stanford University Press, 2010), pp. 275–284; see also K. Brouneus, 'Truth-Telling as Talking Cure? Insecurity and Re-traumatization the Rwandan Gacaca Courts', *Security Dialogue*, 39(1), 2008, pp. 55–76.
23 Truth, Justice and Reconciliation Commission, *Report.*
24 Ibid.
25 United Nations, *Handbook for Field Missions on Preventing and Responding to Conflict-Related Sexual Violence* (Geneva: United Nations, 2020).
26 Rome Statute of the International Criminal Court, available at https://www.icc-cpi.int/sites/default/files/RS-Eng.pdf.
27 Truth, Justice and Reconciliation Commission, *Report*, pp. 712–713.
28 Ibid., p. 707.
29 Ibid., pp. 712–713.
30 Ibid.
31 The Kenya Transitional Justice Network, *Summary: Truth Justice and Reconciliation Report* (Nairobi: KTJN, 2013).
32 Truth, Justice and Reconciliation Commission, *Report*, p. 714.
33 S. Lester, *An Introduction to Phenomenological Research* (Taunton: Stan Lester Developments, 1999), available at http://www.sld.demon.co.uk/resmethy.pdf.
34 Ibid.
35 M.B. Miles and A.M. Huberman, *Qualitative Data Analysis: An Expanded Sourcebook* (Thousand Oaks, CA: SAGE Publications), 1994.
36 Truth, Justice and Reconciliation Commission, *Report*, p. 760.

References

Amugune, A. (2008) *Mt. Elgon Violence.* Available at http://www.marsgroupkenya.org.

Bloomfield, D., Barnes, T. and Huyse, L. (eds) (2003) *Reconciliation after Violent Conflict: A Handbook.* Stockholm: International Institute for Democracy and Electoral Assistance.

Brouneus, K. (2008) 'Truth-Telling as Talking Cure? Insecurity and Re-traumatization: The Rwandan Gacaca Courts', *Security Dialogue*, vol. 39, no. 1, pp. 55–76.

Brouneus, K. (2010) 'The Trauma of Truth Telling: Effects of Witnessing in the Rwandan Gacaca Courts on Psychological Health', *Journal of Conflict Resolution*, vol. 54, no. 3, pp. 408–437.

Conflict Sensitivity Consortium (2010) *Embracing the Practice of Conflict Sensitive Approaches: An Analysis of the Kenyan Context.* Nairobi: Conflict Sensitivity Consortium.

Crotty, M. (1998) *The Foundations of Social Research: Meaning and Perspective in the Research Process.* London: SAGE Publications.

Forsberg, L.*et al.* (2012) 'Facing Mt. Elgon', *Mid-Term Evaluation of the Peace and Rights Programme.* Kitale: FPFK.

Hayner, P.B. (2009) *Negotiating Justice: Guidance for Mediators.* Geneva: HD Centre for Humanitarian Dialogue.

Hayner, P.B. (2010) *Unspeakable Truths: Transitional Justice and the Challenge of Truth Commissions.* New York: Routledge.

Hirsch, M.B, MacKenzie, M. and Sesay, M. (2012) 'Measuring the Impacts of Truth and Reconciliation Commissions: Placing the Global 'Success' of TRCs in Local Perspective', *Cooperation and Conflict*, vol. 47, no. 3, pp. 386–403.

Imbuye, B.D. (2016) *Intra-Ethnic Relations among the Sabot of Mt. Elgon, Kenya 1945–2010*, thesis. Nairobi: School of Humanities and Social Sciences, Kenyatta University.

Lester, S. (1999) *An Introduction to Phenomenological Research.* Taunton: Stan Lester Developments.

Medard, C. (2006) *Indigenous Land Claims in Kenya: A Case Study of Chebyuk, Mount Elgon District.* Available at www.hsrcpress.ac.za.

Mendeloff, D. (2009) 'Trauma and Vengeance: Assessing the Psychological and Emotional Effects of Post-conflict Justice', *Human Rights Quarterly*, vol. 31, pp. 592–623.

Miles, M.B. andHuberman, A.M. (1994) *Qualitative Data Analysis: An Expanded Sourcebook.* Thousand Oaks, CA: SAGE Publications.

Okello, M.C. (2010) 'Afterward: Elevating Transitional Local Justice or Crystallizing Global Governance', in Rosalind Shaw and Lars Waldorf (eds), *Localizing Transitional Justice: Interventions and Priorities after Mass Violence.* Stanford, CA: Stanford University Press, pp. 275–284.

Opongo, E.O. (2020) 'Amani Mashinani Conflict Transformation Model: Bishop Korir's Legacy on Peace and Reconciliation', *The Journal of Social Encounters*, vol. 4, no. 1, pp. 9–21.

Ryanga, H. (2015) *Women and Conflict in Mt. Elgon, Kenya: Rape as a Weapon of War.* Lambert Academic Publishing.

Simiyu, R.R. (2011) *Militianisation of Resource Conflicts: The Case of Land-Based Conflict in the Mount Elgon Region of Western Kenya.* Pretoria: Institute for Security Studies.

The Kenya Transitional Justice Network (2013) *Summary: Truth Justice and Reconciliation Report*. Nairobi: KTJN.

Thomas, O.N., Ron, J. and Paris, R. (2008) *The Effects of Transitional Justice Mechanisms: A Summary of Empirical Research Findings and Implications for Analysts and Practitioners.* Ottawa, ON: Centre for International Policy Studies.

Truth and Reconciliation Commission (2004) *Witness to Truth: Report of the Sierra Leone Truth & Reconciliation Commission*, vol. 1. Accra: Graphic Packaging Press.

United Nations (2020) *Handbook for Field Missions on Preventing and Responding to Conflict-Related Sexual Violence.* Geneva: United Nations.

Web-based Documents

Human Rights Watch (2008) *Kenya: Army and Rebel Militia Commit War Crimes in Mt. Elgon*. Available at http://www.reliefweb.int/rw/rwb.nsf/db900sid/ASAZ7DDCD5opendocument.

Human Rights Watch (2008) *All the Men Are Gone: War Crimes in Kenya's Mt. Elgon Conflict*. Available at https://www.hrw.org/report/2008/07/27/all-men-have-gone/war-crimes-kenyas-mt-elgon-conflict.

Médecins Sans Frontières (2008) *Mount Elgon: Does Anybody Care? MSF Takes Stock After One Year in the Heart of the Crisis in Mount Elgon*. Available at http://www.lekari-bez-hranic.cz/cz/downloads/MSF_MtElgon_May2008.pdf.

Rome Statute of the International Criminal Court. Available at https://www.icc-cpi.int/sites/default/files/RS-Eng.pdf.

Thomas, O.N., Ron, J. and Paris, R. (2008) *Does Transitional Justice Work? Perspectives from Empirical Social Science Version*. Available at http://ssrn.com/abstract=1302084.

Truth, Justice and Reconciliation Commission (2015) *Report of the Truth, Justice and Reconciliation Commission*. Available at www.tjrckenya.org.

10 Disruptive Technology

An Enabler to Support the Rehabilitation of Survivors in Post-Conflict Societies

Kuben David and Anusharani Sewchurran

Introduction

The shift from a conflict to a post-conflict situation is often predicated on the short-term pragmatism of reducing violence and instability in war-torn spaces.[1] In order to do this, deals are brokered with the top tier of opposing forces, and in some cases blanket amnesties are issued.[2] As such, the question of justice is subsumed by the maintenance of peace in the affected geographical region. Post-conflict justice must be cast within a cohesive human rights agenda which includes global, local and individual trajectories.[3] In this larger conception of post-conflict rehabilitation and peace, notions of survivor-centred[4] justice may take on a broader complexion in order to address in part structural violence and resultant omissions and invisibilities. In this chapter we argue for the merits of building a safe digital space for survivors that can respond relationally, with immediacy, and address social justice issues. Simultaneously, care must be taken to avoid rumination[5] and protraction,[6] often the unfortunate by-products of post-conflict truth commissions organized by state bureaucracies.[7]

The chapter begins with a survey of related research dealing with survivor-centred digital and communication-based interventions. The review of innovative ideas stemming from African, Asian and South American countries also includes delineations for this chapter, further outlining the conceptual field used. An important conceptual aspect is the typology of justice which incorporates notions of truth and considers cognitive labour and pluralism of voice.[8] The chapter concludes with a summary of how such a safe digital space for survivors might work and considers areas for possible future study.

Contexts of Conflict

Naimark maintains that when genocide and war take place in contemporary society, sovereign states have a responsibility to protect their citizens.[9] During the post-conflict period violence and strife do not necessarily abate. Thus, the international community has a moral and civic obligation to step in to prevent mass atrocity crimes from occurring because conflict-ridden societies are

DOI: 10.4324/9781003212409-15

characterized by high rates of displacement, damaged infrastructure and weak or absent institutions. These states are more vulnerable to disease, and may under some conditions provide fertile ground for other ills such as international arms trafficking, transnational crime and terrorist networks during both the conflict and post-conflict phases.[10] Patrick supports Kurlantzick's argument that the situation is exacerbated when refugees attempt to return to their countries of origin, as the survivors of any conflict are naturally prone to the fallout resulting from the perpetration of mass atrocity crimes.[11]

In 2017 and 2018 fighting between predominantly Muslim Seleka rebels, anti-balaka militias, and other armed groups in the central, north-western, and eastern parts of the Central African Republic forced thousands to flee their homes. Armed groups killed civilians, raped and sexually assaulted women and girls, attacked displacement camps, recruited and used children as soldiers, burned down villages and took civilians hostage. Regrettably, access to justice for the serious crimes committed remained difficult or impossible for many people. In 2017 renewed violence, including reported rape, murder and arson triggered an exodus of Rohingya, a Muslim ethnic minority group in Myanmar's Rakhine State. Myanmar's security forces claimed that they were undertaking a campaign to reinstate stability in the country's western region; however, the Rohingya fled their homes fearing persecution, thereby fuelling a historic migration crisis. Obtaining justice to alleviate the problem presents itself as a complex dialogue to engage and enforce. However, Kurlantzick argues that the grim prospects for refugees in host countries notwithstanding, particularly in the case of the Rohingya, repatriation to Myanmar is even worse due to the possible repercussions that could lead to the outbreak of genocide.[12]

Furthermore, according to a 2019 Human Rights Watch report,[13] in that year the total number of internally displaced people (IDPs), based on UN figures, reached over 642,800, and the number of refugees totalled 574,600, the highest number since 2014. Conditions for IDPs and refugees, most of whom were housed in camps, remained harsh. Many IDPs had little or no access to humanitarian assistance. Persons with disabilities at displacement camps faced difficulties in accessing sanitation, food and medical assistance. Armed conflict and organized violence had a profound psychological effect on the victims who experienced it, exacerbating the already intensely traumatic conditions. From a psychosocial viewpoint, altering those stressful conditions is likely to improve people's mental health, while also fostering their inherent capacity to recover given adequate social support and the passing of time from the lingering effects of exposure to war-related violence and loss.[14] Although developed countries have increased the level of humanitarian assistance and protection afforded to IDPs and advocacy groups continue to pressure for more assistance, innovative solutions need to be found and devised that can help to alleviate the complexities and challenges that emerge in these situations for conflict victims and post-conflict survivors.

Interestingly, with the advancement of global technological innovations, Friedman *et al.* purport that information systems and interaction design have a critical solution-driven role to play in addressing these post-conflict socio-political challenges.[15] This argument could hold much merit by taking into account the rapid and disruptive nature of technology. Considering the innovative problem-solving successes that arise due to technological disruptions, a similar model could be initiated or piloted for the rehabilitation and resurgence of conflict victims and post-conflict survivors to manage and survive the harsh conditions that they experience. This chapter closely considers research on the use of ICTs in conflict and post-conflict societies. We explore in particular the impact of technological advances on the rehabilitative process of post-conflict survivors. Thus, the key focus is on how ICTs may assist in the rehabilitation of post-conflict survivors.

Survey of Peacebuilding Efforts and ICTs

Call and Cousens explain that during the 1990s peacebuilding in conflict societies became rather expansive, driven by growing awareness of the complexities of post-conflict transitions and the multiple needs of post-conflict societies.[16] However, the literature shows that ICTs have been used in post-conflict situations, chiefly in the field of medicine. Woodward et al. describe how e-health innovations were successfully deployed by health workers in conflict zones such as Liberia, the West Bank, Gaza, Sierra Leone and Somaliland.[17] Sjölund et al. examined the use of internet-based psychiatric therapy for asylum seekers who were also survivors of torture,[18] while Wagner et al. described the complexities of internet-based interventions for post-traumatic stress disorder.[19] The medicalized approach to internet-based rehabilitation is recognized as being effective. However, it is also important to explore other possibilities in case post-conflict survivors limit themselves to deficit or damage-centred frameworks.[20]

Digital Disruption and its Potentiality

During the Arab Spring uprisings pro-democracy protesters made use of technology to build extensive networks, create social capital and organize political action at an unprecedented speed and scale. As a result, virtual networks materialized in the streets. Digital media became the tool that allowed social movements to reach formerly unachievable goals. This eventually led to initiatives such as widely circulated PDF documents via the digital platform packed with information on how to undertake and achieve a successful protest. In relation to this chapter, the Arab Spring comparison is a good example to kick-off further initiatives. The advancement of technology can only enhance and innovate the ideation further.

Looking at the use of technology as an enabler for conflict victims and post-conflict survivors, Andreopoulou explains that ICTs have been adopted in several areas of our lives and work.[21] The global lockdown of countries and societies during the COVID-19 pandemic in 2020 showed how technology can offer convenience and connectivity in our lives through the use of FaceTime and WhatsApp video calls, Zoom, Skype, Webex and Google Meet solutions. Comparably, a similar model could be considered as an enabler for the rehabilitation for conflict victims and post-conflict survivors.

However, before undertaking action on a pilot project, we must bear in mind that in conflict situations and wars basic infrastructure is destroyed, and the delivery of core services such as health care and education are disrupted. Even everyday routines associated with making a living are disrupted. Brinkerhoff has shown that restoring and creating service delivery capacity and initiating economic recovery are central to governance reconstruction agendas, whereby effective basic services depend on more than government, while the functions and capacities of the private sector and civil society are also critical.[22] Existing research shows that because the media plays an important role in modern society, as was demonstrated during the Arab Spring uprisings, the media also can play a role in post-conflict societies, in both the private and public sectors. In recent years technological advances have had an impact on the way in which media content is distributed. An example of a private (innovative) intervention is Google's pilot Rural Community Project. The approach involved beaming[23] the internet to rural areas from high-altitude helium-filled balloons floating 20 kilometres above sea level in the stratosphere for 100 days at a time, ensuring that internet access was conveniently accessible for the masses. The technology and the approach was trialled in New Zealand, Sri Lanka and Puerto Rico. Later it was used to provide internet access to regions in central Kenya.[24]

Facebook, now called Meta, developed its Free Basics internet access platform that was tailored for users in developing markets and conflict regions such as the Democratic Republic of the Congo (DRC), Myanmar, Sudan, Côte d'Ivoire and Bolivia. The mobile app offers users free access to the internet, thereby providing insightful content to keep users informed about current affairs. However, in Myanmar, where Facebook was flooded with hate speech in the wake of the Burmese government's ethnic cleansing of Rohingya Muslims, the Free Basics program was eventually cancelled in August 2017. Facebook clarified that Myanmar's state-owned telecommunications provider Myanmar Posts and Telecommunications cooperated with the Myanmar government to shut down access to all free services, including Free Basics in September 2017.[25] Consequently, according to an article published online by the British Broadcasting Company on 7 December 2021,[26] Rohingya refugees in the USA and the United Kingdom sued Facebook for US $150 billion on the grounds that the technology company allowed hate speech against Rohingya Muslims to be disseminated on its online platform. However, Facebook has not denied that it could have taken measures to prevent hate speech from appearing on its online platform. Facebook claimed that it had taken action to prevent harmful information from appearing on its platform in order to 'keep people safe'. Both initiatives from these private technology giants demonstrate some merit for workable solutions to support wireless connections in order to allow people to access online content via smart devices in conflict zones.

Although McKell argues that the media serves as a key mechanism in the process of peacebuilding and reconciliation, the way that the media depicts identity, history and justice can be problematic for a post-conflict society.[27] Post-conflict societies are often left in a weak position after the cessation of hostilities. The process of peace and rebuilding does take much time and effort. However, parallel to this, victims need more support during this transition. The media can be an effective tool to build relationships and alter perspectives and behaviour, especially when the media content is distributed digitally to provide a user-friendly experience and reach a mass audience. The user can easily form a strong relationship with the digital device and content which allows them to access the content at their own free will and at their own pace.

Currently, the United Nations High Commissioner for Refugees (UNHCR) has prioritized mental health for conflict victims and post-conflict survivors, particularly those living in refugee camps, by offering virtual counselling for people in quarantine or isolation. In Kenya's UNHCR Kakuma Refugee Camp, refugees are offered yoga classes.[28] Orphan refugees credit yoga in helping them to overcome the trauma of growing up in a refugee camp without parents and finding peace in their lives. A refugee named Rita who arrived at a camp when she was 17 years old is now a qualified yoga instructor. She described the trauma that she had experienced being in a refugee camp for many years, but also confirmed that the practice of yoga strengthened her mentally, spiritually and emotionally, and that she now finds peace through yoga. During the COVID-19 pandemic she used technology to continue teaching yoga to other refugees in the camp. With the use of a smartphone, she teaches yoga via videolink on Facebook and Zoom. She also offered small socially distanced classes via the same approach. Although free helplines are available for refugees to deal with mental health issues, access is limited due to the number of refugees increasing to almost 200 000 in that particular camp. Lynn Waithera Karanja, a counselling psychologist working at the refugee camp, confirms that there are too many refugees to be advocated for and helped especially when it comes to mental health and psychosocial issues. This poses a challenge in providing the delicate rehabilitation approach in order to help conflict victims and post-conflict survivors. However, the effectiveness of similar approaches is demonstrated in the implementation and evaluation of the Clinical Care for Sexual Assault Survivors (CCSAS) with multimedia training tools initiated by the International Rescue Committee (IRC) and UNHCR. The initiative was developed to assist sexual assault survivors in refugee camps. This presents an opportunity to introduce a wide subject content using the same approach. If the digital tool proves effective for helping sexual assault survivors, other inceptions could be rolled out to tackle survivors' mental health and psychosocial issues too.

The Role of Spirituality

Isgandarova emphasizes that ethnic cleansing or genocide always involves violence because people do not leave their homes willingly.[29] They leave if they are forced out, sometimes in the most brutal fashion, and hunger, disease and enforced displacement claim many lives. The method of ethnic cleansing includes coerced departure, harassment to induce departure, cultural cleansing and the taking of payment for expulsion. Ethnic cleansing is closely related to war, because many ethnic cleansing events have taken place during armed conflicts or during the chaotic transition from war to peace, leaving many innocent people in harm's way, suffering from intense emotional and psychological trauma. Call and Cousens argue that in recent years international military forces and civilian agencies have worked hard to improve their cooperation in post-conflict states to maintain security in order to prevent and alleviate harsh conditions.[30] However, maintaining security and peacekeeping efforts does not alleviate the obvious mental deviation suffered by conflict victims and post-conflict survivors. Miller and Rasmussen maintain that trauma-focused advocates believe that ameliorating symptoms of war-related trauma will not only improve mental health but will also enable people to cope more effectively with ongoing environmental stressors.[31] Isgandarova refers to similar studies where spirituality played an important role for Azerbaijani women who were victims of genocide in dealing with war-related trauma. Empirical evidence on the positive role of spirituality, particularly for female survivors of ethnic violence, suggests that spiritual and religious support contributes to the resilience of conflict victims and post-conflict survivors, and may help professionals to contribute towards reducing the experience of depressive and post-traumatic stress for trauma survivors.[32]

The argument that spirituality helps survivors to overcome tragedy and acts as a buffer in the relationship between trauma and resulting emotional problems or mental illness is echoed by Reinert and Bloomingdale.[33] Although conflict victims and post-conflict survivors are instinctively resilient, there is still a paramount need for distinct approaches in supporting and enhancing their instinctive resilience, especially if there is a risk of 'reverse development'[34] during the peace development phase. Perhaps the distribution of spiritual and religious content in an engaging interactive multimedia format through digital platforms, and access to spiritual and religious counsellors or counselling through the use of technologically connected devices affirms a rationale for the exploration of this study to expand further solutions to alleviate the source of trauma for conflict victims and post-conflict survivors.

Davies indicates that there must be an attempt to bring together people of traditionally opposing sides to share perceptions, experiences and emotions in order to gain an understanding and viewpoint from opposing sides in order to move forward in the healing process.[35] Davies further suggests that the question is how far can new learning be spread to others, and while nobody says that such experiences are an easy panacea, there should be consensus that it is at least a starting point. Davies's suggestion is relevant to this study because he reinforces the idea that different approaches need to be attempted to determine whether an ideation can succeed or not. Perhaps the implementation of technological platforms as a means to access stimulating rehabilitative content, from a Human Computer Interaction (HCI)[36] perspective, if executed appropriately could result in effective rehabilitation outcomes for conflict victims and post-conflict survivors. Findings from this study suggest that the multimedia training approach appeared useful, as it was positively associated with improvements in HCP respect for patient rights, knowledge, confidence and clinical practice. Findings also suggested that other agencies working in humanitarian settings could use the CCSAS training tool to build the capacity of health care professionals to offer improved quality clinical care for sexual assault survivors.[37] Therefore, the distribution of stimulating content aligned to the needs of conflict victims and post-conflict survivors (spiritual content among other relevant content), via digital platforms such as cost-effective tablets and mobile phones, could offer a convenient, worthwhile and stabilizing outcome for conflict victims and post-conflict victims.

Demonstrating the potency of utilizing technology in circumstances challenging such inequalities, Hussain and Howard affirm similar approaches in conflict situations, with particular emphasis on the events of the Arab Spring.[38] In December 2010 and early 2011 massive public demonstrations demanding political reform erupted in the north Africa and parts of the Middle East. Citizens from Tunis, Cairo, Sanaa, Aman, Casablanca, Damascus, Tripoli and many other cities in the region took to the streets to call for change. The most consistent narratives from civil society leaders in Arab countries regarding the Arab Spring have underscored that the internet, mobile phones and social media such as Facebook and Twitter (now known as X) had an effect on to the eventual outcome.

For our purposes, using CSHMA and participatory visual methodologies, survivors from post-conflict spaces may be able to promote relational communication which in turn could encourage participation and lower social barriers. This could be achieved by sharing personal narratives in closed groups online, with the possibility of external mediation. Narratives have matured in the human sciences, especially after Bourdieu's work on contemporary stories.[39] Other theorists such as Ellis became significant in developing applications of narrative rationality which contest invisibility emerging in post-conflict spaces.[40] In addition, digital connectivity creates access to global human rights discourses. As Laclau and Mouffe argue, 'only when citizens have the idea of what they call the 'democratic imaginary' that inequalities of all kinds will be challenged'.[41] In this chapter we argue that digital networks have the potential to create the democratic imaginary where post-conflict survivors may negotiate their past trauma in order to move forward.

The Problematics of Peacekeeping

As cohorts of peacekeeping forces move through conflict zones to negotiate peace and restore some sort of stability, several problematics emerge for the long term. While these forces bring aid to displaced communities in desperate need for it, there remains some deficiencies when it comes to addressing gender, time and agency (voice). Ryan therefore differentiates between peacekeeping and peacebuilding, whereby the former attempts to 'build bridges between warriors' and the latter attempts to 'build bridges between ordinary people'.[42] This speaks to the important gaps emerging in the pursuit of peacekeeping.

Gender

Women, who often experience the worst effects of conflict, are generally excluded from peace negotiations.[43] This is perhaps why women in post-conflict spaces tend to favour 'restitutive justice more than retributive justice'.[44] Gender is implicated in the larger fabric of nationhood, where widows 'are treated as the social embodiment of the nation, and are expected to advance at the same pace as the state institutions which are created in their name, but which are primarily pursuing a national political agenda'.[45] In the practice of peacekeeping, the gendered individual is magnified in different ways as the collective in order to build an imagined nation,[46] and in the process the individual becomes subsumed in the broader peacekeeping project. Foucault described power as relational.[47] Relational power manifests itself where some accounts of collective violence may be 'hidden behind more dominant historical contents that are hierarchically superior'.[48] Given that all voices are not equal post-conflict, it is important to allow for the multiplicity of voices[49] to engage relationally as opposed to hierarchically. This means that interventions and communication for post-conflict survivors need not be persistently mediated by journalists, psychologists and experts in peacekeeping.

Time

It was interesting to note in the literature the amount of time that peacekeepers spent with ordinary people. Researchers spent as little as one-day seminars and two-week-long workshops to sessions numbering between six and 11 over a period of one to two months, respectively.[50]

The work included a mix of psycho-educational lectures, large and small group discussions, individual and group counselling. It is clear from these accounts that the sessions were greatly valued, where participants talked of feeling 'rehumanised'.[51] However, Liebling *et al.* reflected on the inadequacies of the amount of time afforded for this process:

Survivors had to travel for long distances to access the service, with poverty restricting regular access. Although a survivor could rarely choose the gender of the counsellor, they voiced universal appreciation of a listening ear and the availability of professional advice. Group counselling tended to be offered after individual counselling. This was often greatly valued since it gave survivors comfort to realise that their experiences had been shared. It also served to decrease isolation, as participants met others who then provided mutual social support.[52]Brahimi makes an important point for external peacekeeping forces, indicating that their presence (although vital) is temporary and care must be taken to entrench peacekeeping efforts in local values .[53]

Agency (Voice)

Here Couldry's conceptualization of voice beyond sonic and even political resonances is useful as it implies a measure of self-determination, which is perhaps the key element that post-conflict survivors are trying to wrest back in reconstituting their identity.[54] Foucault's hierarchical superiority reveals the amplification of some voices as they relate to power, and so peace negotiations tend to be reserved for those who 'speak the language of the "liberal club"'.[55] While this results in exclusions, it also opens the way for peacebuilding workers to create alternative spaces to accommodate ordinary discourses around building life through and after conflict.

Exploring Social Justice

Post-conflict situations typically involve the promotion of peace and transitional justice. Transitional justice refers to both legal and social justice. Galtung defined positive peace as the effort of countering structural violence perpetrated against a community.[56] Therefore, while legal justice may not be easily achieved, Galtung's idea of positive peace balances the pursuit of social justice which Kabwete describes as 'memory, truth, healing, human rights protection, reparation, and reconciliation, to name a few'.[57] Lederach indicates that attention to positive peace is a justice gap as socio-economic needs are critical to long-term stability: 'we need to reorient our peacebuilding framework toward the development of support infrastructures that enhance our capacity to adapt and respond to relational needs rather than being defined and driven by events and agreements'.[58]

Apart from structural aspects, long-term attention to the inner psyche of post-conflict survivors is essential. In psychoanalytic theory, it is argued that external traumatic events can overwhelm the individual and can cause enduring affectation if there is no possibility of finding conscious expression for it.[59] McCann and Perlman argue for 'seven psychological need areas' in the case of post-conflict trauma, namely 'frame of reference, safety, dependency/trust of self and others, power, esteem, intimacy, and independence'.[60]

The past must be continually negotiated in order to shift the experiential and existential, to rework memories' contextual meaning and attempt to create a shared humanity where post-conflict survivors make sense of the meaninglessness of man-made atrocities.[61]

Lambourne offers a comprehensive typology of justice for the post-conflict setting. In this chapter our concern lies with social justice[62] and symbolic justice.[63] Hence, the focus is on working through

- identity (inclusivity, interdependence, common humanity and values, respect and autonomy);
- validation (of pain and suffering); and
- mercy (forgiveness and letting go, identification with the pain of the other, rituals of healing and joint sorrow, releasing the past and it pain).[64]

Notions of Truth and Healing

The notion of truth is activated in post-conflict societies as a means of promoting reconciliation and peace. In the context of truth commissions, Kriesberg lists the dimensions of reconciliation as the shared truth about the past, justice, remorse and security or a sense of cohesion.[65] There are subtle yet important differences between 'forensic truth and personal or narrative truth, and restorative truth'.[66] While these are interconnected, notions about the past are always contested as ideologies of violence are delegitimized in the negotiation for reconciliation and peace.[67] Truth, bearing witness to and acknowledging suffering are important precursors to healing.

> [Post-conflict] survivors desperately want to have the truth of what was done to them be established and their suffering acknowledged. Acknowledgement, especially when it is empathic, is healing. When the world (other groups, one's society, other countries, and the international community) acknowledge and condemn victimization of a group of people, this says that such violence is unacceptable. It tells survivors that the moral order is being reinstated and helps them feel safer.[68]

However, Browning states that authenticity is more important than factual accuracy.[69] To be able freely to negotiate and narrate one's own story without external mediation is a key factor in healing.

Restoring Self in Digital Communities of Practice

Conflict and its attendant levels of violence obliterate the very sense of self. So much of the work done in post-conflict societies focuses on rebuilding, restoring and reconstituting a sense of self. It was noted by Schulz that in Uganda both researchers and peacekeeping forces paid little attention to survivors of male sexual violence perpetrated in conflict spaces, as women were in the majority when it came to experiencing sexual violence.[70] Schulz makes a case for inclusion as a type of 'micro level justice' whereby men were brought into the safe spaces for story telling so that others could bear witness to their experiences.[71] It is interesting to note that when survivors know that others have also suffered as they have, it reduces their sense of isolation and victimization, and increases their levels of confidence.

Safe spaces, groups and communities of practice become an effective response to post-conflict resilience, especially when individual survivors may be discounted by the peacekeeping or state-level processes. While writing has been used as a means to promote healing, it has limitations in terms of reach. The media has played a role in creating the platforms through which these communities of practice can operate. In some cases such as Rwanda, traditional radio was a useful way to offer a generic survivor story created out of many narratives in the form of a radio play.[72]

Social Media Platforms

Social media is also another vehicle that can be used to create communities of post-conflict survivor practice. Such platforms can accommodate text, images, video or voice and this is very helpful to reflect the multitude of survivor voices. Edwards *et al.* showcase interesting uses of social media to amplify refugee voices:

Sarah sees social media as powerful tool … for giving voice to survivors and their stories and removing their dependency on traditional media to tell survivor stories publicly: 'I want survivors to tell their story in the way they want to'. From this perspective, social media was a way of wresting back representational control from journalists, who did not work sensitively with survivors.[73]Vardeman-Winter *et al.* assert that the 'Survivor-to-Survivor Communication Mode' creates a 'micro-environment' that is more responsive to crisis.[74] This depends on developing social capital among participants. While Durkheim is attributed to the origin of the concept, Putnam took the theory further, whereby 'social capital refers to connections among individuals-social networks and the norms of reciprocity and trustworthiness that arise from them'.[75] Within this definition binding capital refers to that which connects a group while bridging capital connects across groups.

Survivor-to-survivor communication focuses on harnessing the gains achieved through post-crisis therapy, where survivors (peers) are encouraged to share personal narratives as a means of collaborative recovery. The attempt is to foster bonding, bridging and linking which is the 'main engine for long-term recovery'[76] and in the process a network is created. Vardeman-Winter *et al.* refers to these groups as therapeutic communities, which are often defined by geographical proximity.[77] The three stages of recovery include sharing personal narratives, social network and community building. Vardeman-Winter et al. offer the method of community concept mapping as a means of moving the same processes to the digital network so as to enable the growth of 'socio-technical communities' via bonding, bridging and linking techniques.[78]

Digital Privacy

The overarching principle of privacy is critical when it comes to post-conflict survivors such as Esperande Bigirimana,[79] who maintains that speaking out can have a terrible cost. Reports of ensuing threats, kidnapping and even murder have routinely occurred after survivors spoke publicly about their trauma.[80] Social media (in particular Facebook) presents challenges when it comes to issues around privacy. This is the main motivation for mediated closed digital networks, where survivors' privacy is maintained at all times.

There is a fine balancing that occurs between telling one's story as a means of healing and creating a collective memory for the atrocities that occurred. Here the chapter borrows from archiving and heritage work in order to theorize the best possible way of achieving both goals.[81]

Borrowing from Archiving and Heritage: Introducing a Flexible Living Archive

The literature on the politics of archiving has grown causing some authors to reflect on how the processes of archiving in the context of reconciliation can cause further trauma as a result of exclusions, absences and contrary ideological perspectives.[82] Political manipulation also plays a gatekeeping role post-conflict, and may influence inclusion criteria. Gilliland argues that if archiving is seen as a human rights concern rather than a preservation activity, it could lead to more inclusive archiving processes:

> The UNESCO Universal Declaration on Archives recognized the 'the vital necessity of archives for supporting business efficiency, accountability and transparency, for protecting citizens rights, for establishing individual and collective memory, for understanding the past, and for documenting the present to guide future actions'.[83]

One method to offset bureaucratic archiving which can be alienating, is to consider the place of arts-based methods, in particular fictional narratives as a means of creating a dialogic negotiation with the past. Gilliland lists these methods as

> records-related activities; conversations and reciprocal storytelling; interviews with key informants; photography and personal journaling. These have been coupled with visits to archives and other records offices

and repositories, as well as to cemeteries, memorials, and other sites of important events.[84]

A similar method has been used by people working with refugees, who created 'aesthetic expressions performed online and offline' that create a sort of documentation of diasporic refugee voices.[85] These poems and stories captured online and sometimes performed offline reflect authorship, ownership and agency and are a critical aspect of post-conflict healing. Caswell refers to this as 'community archives discourses' and lists five important principles to note for our purpose: 'participation, shared stewardship, multiplicity, archival activism, and reflexivity'.[86] These kinds of community discourses have the potential to counter-balance and contest official archival discourses and create critical sites of visibility and healing.

A Digital Post-Conflict Community of Practice

Digital collaborative approaches are suggested as a means of developing artistic kinds of products (digital storytelling and the living archive) to promote inclusion, healing and agency. The goal is to foster non-hierarchical relationships that create an overall sense of community. Special attention will be paid to generating values of belonging, inclusion, participation, recognition, legitimacy, shared values, co-operation and belief.

The arts have always been the frontrunner to innovative methodologies. Lee asserts that the arts can generate social capital and foster intergroup social cohesion.[87] This is achieved through the use of 'participatory and collaborative arts, high-level interactions, authentic personal interactions, informal settings and non-hierarchical relationships'.[88] Bawa highlights the importance of continuity, emphasizing the process rather than the outcome: 'it is taken to mean the continuous development of a society that progressively builds broad social purpose and action towards the intensification of its human rights and social justice agendas'.[89]

We propose a flexible living archive as a digital collaborative method, whereby post-conflict survivors can meet online, communicate with each other relationally, share information and practise empathic communication. A flexible living archive is one that is not overly bureaucratic and not defined too rigidly. It creates a repository for personal narratives and is flexible in ordering these narratives. It should be able to house text, images, voice and video. While it serves as a repository, it must also contain dynamic activities which bring the community together to foster participation, interaction and collaboration. It may also serve as an information site. The community creating and using this flexible archival space may choose whether it should be an open or closed site. In addition, the community can decide which platforms may be used in tandem with this one. This need not be an exclusive decision as communication and information may be mediated via multiple platforms. This decision also depends on the kind of budget received for such a rehabilitation project.

With the exception of UNESCO and global or regional human rights organizations, public institutions such as universities can also serve as suitable partners to host flexible living archives for post-conflict survivors. Promoting human rights is a legitimate part of nation building[90] and in their role as public institutions universities could easily support such endeavours. Universities' community engagement is rapidly growing into a compulsory aspect, alongside research and teaching, as its core business.[91] The complexity and principles surrounding ethics and privacy is familiar to researchers, and international organizations looking to fund such endeavours could start by looking to universities within the region or continent as technical hosts as a starting point. Given that the interaction would occur digitally, funding organizers could include other institutions to partner with facilitating the online exchanges. In addition, this endeavour could be both inter-institutional and intra-institutional.

In post-conflict societies, generally institutions such as universities often lack capacity and are in the process of rebuilding after mass conflict or violence. In such cases, regional community blocs would need to be developed so that a range of regional partners come together to host flexible living archives for post-conflict survivors. These networks can exist outside of the conflict zone, and may supply resources such as data and smart devices, which could be shared.

A Snapshot of How Such a Partnership Could be Activated

Funding sources	*Human rights organizations/NGOs and non-profit organizations*	*University infrastructure*	*University expertise*	*Community interest groups*
Source and provide funding and equipment	Management of online site	University hosts site on its server	Facilitators from various disciplines such as Psychology, Clinical medicine, Performance Studies	Community members could be screened to facilitate
	Content development and management; healing and rehabilitation	Digital literacy	Facilitation may address health related issues, and mental health issues.	Generate micro-funding for relational needs as they arise

Ideally, partnerships may be formed across different types of institutions and organizations, as empathic volunteers appear. While the infrastructure would need to be resourced and must be closely managed, the inclusion of facilitators may be more flexible so that they can share their skills and empathy without too much bureaucracy.

Phase 1

The table below elaborates the content showing justice domains as they relate to values and specific exercises for the introductory building phase of the site. One of the findings in the literature was that post-conflict survivors want to be heard. They want to tell their story in a safe space. Although peacekeepers devoted time to this kind of work, it was insufficient. It is envisaged that the flexible living archive will be developed over the course of a year, divided up into four phases each lasting three months. The external facilitator(s) is of paramount importance to set the tone and drive the weekly engagements. As stated earlier, one challenge facing post-conflict rehabilitation was the lack of direct contact with a facilitator which could lead to poor motivation and despondency on the part of post-conflict survivors. External facilitators may also lend the idea of transnational or even global witnessing to post-conflict survivor's experiences.

Phase 1 focuses on introductory aspects such as participation, connecting and familiarizing oneself with the digital space. Phase 2 deals more intensely with validation, narratives of pain and empathic responses. Phase 3 deals with forgiveness and letting go. Phase 4 deals with growth and upskilling.

Domains of Justice Condensed into Units of Activity for Phase 1

Symbolic justice	*Session 1* *1 hr and 15 minutes*	*Session 2* *45 minutes*
Introduction	Introduction, ice-breaker exercises; some ground rules related to empathic listening, in appropriate responses	Introduce the key ideas for the next ten weeks; look for co-facilitators from the group; address relational needs
Common values	Generate a common prayer (articulating a wish for all) – a ritual to start each session	Collate and complete communal prayer; address relational needs
Inclusiveness	Introduce the fairy tales, e.g. *Little Red Riding Hood*; introduce Todorov and Propp's equilibrium, disturbance, new equilibrium	Creative session: Start developing the plot for a children's story. What will be the equilibrium, disturbance, new equilibrium? Address relational needs
Empathy	Continue with the many versions of *Little Red Riding Hood*; introduce protagonist, villain, helper	In your children's story, who is the protagonist, villain, and helper? Address relational needs
Common humanity	*Hansel and Gretel* or a local children's story; start to categorize and identify what moved the action in the story in each version	In your children's story, what moves the action? Address relational needs

Symbolic justice	*Session 1* *1 hr and 15 minutes*	*Session 2* *45 minutes*
Identity	*Cinderella* or a local children's story; start to categorize and identify the main characters and their roles	In your children's story, who are the main characters? What are their roles? How would the story change if you gave a minor character a big role? Address relational needs
Accepting other's identity	*Snow White* or a local children's story; categorize and identify what moved the action in the story in each version	In your children's story, how could you change the story? What action could you change? Address relational needs
Mutual acceptance and respect	*Sleeping Beauty* or a local children's story; categorize and identify the main characters and their roles.	In your children's story, what would happen if you gave all the important characters small roles and all the small characters major roles? Address relational needs
Belonging	*The Three Little Pigs*	Compare the three versions of *The Three Little Pigs.* Which ending do you prefer? Why? Address relational needs
Autonomy	Start to think of writing (telling) your own story	What would be the plot of your story? Who is the main character? Address relational needs
Evaluation	Commentary on the sessions thus far	Commentary on the sessions thus far

It is likely that a more detailed manual may be useful; however, in phase 1 participants begin by jointly developing a prayer or list of hopes that is collated and read out before each session begins. This is not meant to be overtly religious, but can be viewed as an expression of the groups' collective hopes and wishes and to act as a bridging tool for the group. In addition the exercise is meant to simulate a recurring ritual created by the group. Participants are then introduced to children's fairy tales through which they can get to know the architecture and universal characterizations in narratives. It is hoped that in the safe space of children's stories, participants can start to see the potential for multiple versions of an event, and may re-envision their own narratives.[92]

Although these methods have thus far only been tested in practice, Benmayor argues that narrative and digital story telling has the tremendous potential to create visibility of that which was invisible.[93] Benmayor posits that this process of creating visibility is profoundly transformative as it creates space for empathic listening and shared understandings of similar experiences.[94] A key finding in the literature was that post-conflict survivors want to be heard, they want their experiences to be witnessed, and they want to tell their stories in a safe space. The entry point of children's fairy tales could create safe spaces for stories to be told from multiple perspectives. It is hoped that in this environment empathic listening may unfold as part of the healing process.

According to this timetable, participants meet twice a week. Essentially, similar content is covered and discussed over both days. The rationale behind holding two sessions on two different days is to accommodate participants who may miss one session, thus allowing them not to feel left out.

These sessions may be held live on platforms such as Microsoft Teams or Zoom, which allows for closed groups and may be accessed on smartphones with connectivity. These sessions may also be on other social media platforms, but facilitators have to weigh up privacy issues and connectivity. Platforms such as Moodle (used by universities for teaching purposes) can also be used as repositories for non-live interaction.[95] Here communication can occur via live platforms, but all videos, images and text may be saved to a Moodle site as a repository for participants to look at when possible if they have issues with connectivity.[96]

The slot for *relational needs* occurs once a week, during which participants may raise personal needs such as medical advice, or input on a particular problem they are experiencing. While this may not necessarily relate to healing or trauma, facilitators can address these issues by linking to relevant expertise either in the universe or community context. It is envisaged that through community links micro funding could be raised in the event that participants have minor needs.[97] As participants hear about each other's needs, and are able to lend their support, this creates greater cohesion, a sense of belonging and a tremendous sense of capacity.

Phase 2

Phase 1 is an introductory phase designed to create a cohesive online supportive community. In phase 2, participants' individual stories will be dealt with more intensely. Here the focus will be on empathic listening as a key mechanism of healing. Participants will be able to narrate their stories live, and also upload their textual accounts. The method of photovoice and video can be utilized effectively here. In phase 2, considerable time will be given to listening and responding to and collecting narratives of pain. The overarching themes listed under symbolic justice may apply with facilitators highlighting these themes as participants narrate their stories. The photovoice method can help to encapsulate narratives and could form thematic galleries for members to reflect on outside of the discussion. Participants can decide if they wish for this to be included in a living archive (which will form part of the digital repository).

Phase 3

In phase 3, the focus will be on forgiveness and letting go. Here participants will use the skills learned thus far to disrupt their narratives of pain (to the extent they are able to) and develop new equilibriums (again to the extent they are able to). Facilitators will actively encourage participants to rewrite their stories as a means of re-envisaging the future and recasting action and behaviours. Rewriting by no means equates to writing over. This is not an attempt to forget the atrocities of the past. It is an attempt to imagine new ways of being. As a means of remembering and honouring victims of conflict (participants' family members and friends), Crenshaw's method of creating frames to hold such names in our consciousness is powerful. Crenshaw's #sayhername campaign was an attempt to bring to light and bear witness to the invisible yet routine violent tragedies of African American women.[98] At the end of her lecture Crenshaw does a roll call saying, 'join us in saying these names [of victims who were killed] as loud as you can, randomly, disorderly. Let's create a cacophony of sound to represent our intention to … bear witness to them.'[99]

Crenshaw's method may be mirrored, it may be translated to text and images, and even video. It is important that these remembrances, along with participants' narratives, are saved as part of the living archive, and participants can decide whether this may be included in a long-term repository.

Phase 4

In phase 4, the focus will be on growth. Participants will be asked to list their needs in terms of training as it relates to sustaining the group activity without facilitators. Facilitators will take these requests back to their home institutions to see what may be possible. In phase 4, training needs could be addressed. While facilitators will be on hand, the dynamic of the group should shift to becoming an independent online community. Independence is important as a means of self-determination. Participants will need to decide how continuously to intensify social justice agendas in their communities.

As facilitator manuals for each phase are developed, it is important to include a range of prompts and exercises, in addition to a range of platforms that could be used.

Future Study

In the nexus of post-conflict survivor safe spaces and digital potentiality, there is scope to develop praxis on post-conflict digital spaces as sites of education around citizenship and further agency. There is also bridging work to be done with the fields of archiving and human rights, particularly in post-conflict spaces. This work could activate funding to set up the transnational digital sites proposed in this chapter. The technical solutions to intermittent connectivity and the lack of access to technological devices are an important part of creating digital communities of practise. There are many manuals available for therapeutic work with post-conflict survivors. These manuals need to be adapted for the digital space, including developing digitally specific interventions and activities. In addition, manuals must be translated into local languages, if possible in voice and text, and ideally ought to be open-access. Finally, linking survival and resilience as a powerful means of resistance in the broader contexts of post-conflict and crisis, would create the potential for larger communities of practise and support.[100]

Conclusion

Post-conflict societies are troubled with the memory of conflict and the fear of tenuous stability. In this chapter we explore the contexts of conflict spaces and innovations that have been used thus far to assist in post-conflict rehabilitation. We consider how to enable post-conflict survivors to use digital technology, specifically CSHMA.

We distinguish between peacekeeping and peacebuilding, the latter relating more to notions of social justice, which is our primary source of interest. Digital disruptors are then considered for their practical value in spaces with compromised infrastructure and diminished resources. These differing states of infrastructure create huge barriers for digital uptake and usage. Therefore, we argue for regional community-based blocs of support, where digital networks can be set up, while not located in the post-conflict zone itself.

CSHMA facilitates the pursuit of social justice agendas such as common humanity, respect and validation. Thus, gender, time and agency are key qualifiers towards achieving social justice. Post-conflict rehabilitation focuses on e-health and psychiatric therapy. We found that time, (empathic) listening and witnessing are key factors in the rehumanizing process in post-conflict zones. One problem to emerge was that there was not enough time for peacekeepers to engage in this type of post-conflict rehabilitation.

Hence, digital communities of practise are offered as a means of creating flexible living archives where post-conflict survivors can attend to the restoration of self, using digital contexts, over a longer period. The infrastructure of these digital spaces requires support in terms of funding, training and human resources, such as empathic facilitators.

As a means of operationalizing a flexible, digital living archive for post-conflict survivors, a snapshot of feasible partners is suggested, and thereafter a summary of the four different phases is given. Phase 1 is outlined in greater detail, with the idea of full facilitator manuals being generated once a specific post-conflict community has been identified for rehabilitation. We conclude, based on the available evidence, that the use of ICTs, specifically CSHMA tools and online participatory methodologies may function as sites of ideological contestation where survivors of post-conflict conditions may contest (to the extent they can) and negotiate moving on from a problematic past.

Notes

1 W. Lambourne, *Post-Conflict Peacebuilding: Meeting Human Needs for Justice and Reconciliation*, (Washington, DC: United States Institute of Peace, 2004). Available at http://www.genocideresearchhub.org.rw/document/post-conflict-peacebuilding-meeting-human-needs-justice-reconciliation/.

2 Ibid.

3 A. Betts, 'Should Approaches to Post-Conflict Justice and Reconciliation be Determined Globally, Nationally or Locally?' *The European Journal of Development Research, 17*(4), 2005, pp. 735–752.

4 Women surviving conflict were traditionally described as victims, borrowing from legal definitions, perhaps due to the normalization of sexual violence perpetrated against women in such regions. This began to be contested as the term victim carried the baggage of passivity, helplessness and other deficit connotations. Feminists argued that this fixed the individual's identity to the violation, while the term survivor suggested a more hopeful, empowered description, one that better encapsulates the agency of women in post-conflict societies. We use the term 'survivor' as we believe it is a better signifier for the heroic struggles of women in post-conflict societies which looks to the future with hope.

5 Rumination refers to the trauma emerging from telling the truth about the experience of violence; see K. Brounéus, 'The Trauma of Truth Telling: Effects of Witnessing in the Rwandan Gacaca Courts on Psychological Health', Journal of Conflict Resolution, 54(3), 2010, p. 426.

6 Ibid,; p. 427. Protraction refers to the repeated processing of trauma, often occurring as a result of traditional post-conflict interventions such as truth commissions requiring multiple accounts of victims experiences.

7 Ibid., pp. 408–437.

8 L. Edwards, F. Philip and Y. Gerrard, 'Communicating Feminist Politics? The Double-Edged Sword of Using Social Media in a Feminist Organisation', *Feminist Media Studies*, 20(5), 2020, pp. 605–622.

9 N.M. Naimark, 'Srebrenica in the History of Genocide: A Prologue', *In Memories of Mass Repression* (New York: Routledge, 2017).

10 S. Patrick, 'Weak States and Global Threats: Assessing Evidence of Spillovers', *Center for Global Development Working Paper*, no. 73, 2006.

11 Ibid.

12 J. Kurlantzick, 'Rohingya Refugees Risk Going Back to Another Genocide in Myanmar', *World Politics Review*, 2019, available at https://www.worldpoliticsreview.com/articles/28219/rohingya-refugees-risk-going-back-to-another-genocide-in-myanmar.

13 Available at https://www.hrw.org/world-report/2019.

14 T.S. Betancourt and T. Williams, 'Building an Evidence Base on Mental Health Interventions for Children Affected by Armed Conflict', *Intervention*, 2008.

15 B. Friedman, L.P. Nathan, M. Lake, N.C. Grey, T.T. Nilsen, R.F. Utter, E.J. Utter, M. Ring and Z. Kahn, '*Multi-lifespan Information System Design in the Aftermath of Genocide: An Early-Stage Report from Rwanda*', 28th Annual CHI Conference on Human Factors in Computing Systems, Conference Proceedings and Extended Abstracts, Atlanta, GA, 2010.

16 C.T. Call and E.M. Cousens, 'Ending Wars and Building Peace: International Responses to War-Torn Societies', *International Studies Perspectives*, 9(1), 2008, pp. 1–21.

17 A. Woodward, M. Fyfe, J. Handuleh, P. Patel, B. Godman, A. Leather and A. Finlayson, 'Diffusion of E-health Innovations in 'Post-Conflict' Settings: A Qualitative Study on the Personal Experiences of Health Workers', *Human Resources for Health*, 12(1), 2014, pp. 1–10.

18 B.H. Sjölund, M. Kastrup, E. Montgomery and A.L. Persson, 'Rehabilitating Torture Survivors', *J Rehabil Med.*, 41(9), 2019, pp. 689–696.

19 B. Wagner and A. Maercker, 'Internet-based Intervention for Posttraumatic Stress Disorder', *Internet Use in the Aftermath of Trauma* (Amsterdam: IOS Press, 2010, pp. 255–267.

20 D. Calderon, 'Moving from Damage-Centered Research through Unsettling Reflexivity', *Anthropology & Education Quarterly*, 47(1), 2016, pp. 5–24.

21 Z. Andreopoulou, E. Stiakakis and M. Vlachopoulou, 'Green ICT Applications towards the Achievement of Sustainable Development', In *E-innovation for Sustainable Development of Rural Resources during Global Economic Crisis* (Hershey, PA: IGI Global. 2014), pp. 11–21.

22 D.W. Brinkerhoff, 'Rebuilding Governance in Failed States and Post-Conflict Societies: Core Concepts and Cross-cutting Themes', *Public Administration and Development: The International Journal of Management Research and Practice*, 25(1), 2005, pp. 3–14.

23 This refers to the directional flow of particles or radiation.

24 M. Reynolds, 'Facebook and Google's Race to Connect the World Is Heating Up', *WIRED*, 2008, available at https://www.wired.co.uk/article/google-project-loon-balloon-facebook-aquila-internet-africa.

25 T. Hatmaker, 'Facebook's Free Basics Program Ended Quietly in Myanmar Last Year', *Techcrunch*, 2018, available at https://techcrunch.com/2018/05/01/facebook-free-basics-ending-myanmar-internet-org/#:~:text=Facebook%20confirmed%20to%20TechCrunch%20that,2016%20launch%20in%20the%20country.

26 See https://www.bbc.com/news/world-asia-59558090.

27 K.L. McKell, 'How Civil Society Organizations (CSOs) Use Media for Peacebuilding in Post-Conflict Societies', unpublished master's thesis, Aristotle University of Thessaloniki, 2020, available at http://ikee.lib.auth.gr/record/319287/files/GRI-2020-27361.pdf.

28 S. Otieno, 'Finding Wellbeing through Yoga at a Kenyan Refugee Camp' (UNHCR, 2020), available at https://www.unhcr.org/news/stories/2020/10/5f7ebb6c4/finding-wellbeing-yoga-kenyan-refugee-camp.html.

29 N. Isgandarova, 'What the Spiritual Caregiver Should Know While Dealing with Survivors of Ethnic Violence', *Khazar Journal of Humanities and Social Science*, 14(3), 2011.

30 Call and Cousens, 'Ending Wars and Building Peace'.

31 K.E. Miller and A. Rasmussen, 'War Exposure, Daily Stressors, and Mental Health in Conflict and Post-conflict Settings: Bridging the Divide between Trauma-Focused and Psychosocial Frameworks', *Social Science & Medicine*, 70 (1), 2010, pp. 7–16.

32 K.M. Connor, J.R. Davidson and L.C. Lee 'Spirituality, Resilience, and Anger in Survivors of Violent Trauma: A Community Survey', *Journal of Traumatic Stress*, 16(5), 2003, pp. 487–494.

33 D.F. Reinert and J.R. Bloomingdale, 'Spiritual Maturity and Mental Health: Implications for Counseling', *Counseling and Values, 43*(3), 1999, pp. 211–223.

34 Erasing the gains of development during the peace-making phase in a post-conflict society, resulting in more violent warfare.

35 L. Davies, 'Teaching about Conflict through Citizenship Education', *International Journal of Citizenship and Teacher Education*, 1(2), 2005, pp. 17–34.

36 Human-computer interaction studies the design and use of computer technology, focused on the interfaces between people and computers. Researchers in the field of HCI observe the ways in which humans interact with computers and design technologies that let humans interact with computers in novel ways.

37 J.R. Smith, L.S. Ho, A. Langston, N. Mankani, A. Shivshanker and D. Perera, 'Clinical Care for Sexual Assault Survivors Multimedia Training: A Mixed-

Methods Study of Effect on Healthcare Providers' Attitudes, Knowledge, Confidence, and Practice in Humanitarian Settings', *Conflict and Health*, 7(1), 2013, pp. 1–10.

38 M.M. Hussain and P.N. Howard, *Democracy's Fourth Wave? Digital Media and the Arab Spring* (London: Oxford University Press, 2013).

39 P. Bourdieu, 'Making the Economic Habitus: Algerian Workers Revisited', *Ethnography*, 1(1), 2000, pp. 17–41.

40 C. Ellis, *The Ethnographic I: A Methodological Novel about Autoethnography*, vol. 13 (Walnut Creek, CA: Rowman Altamira, 2004).

41 E. Laclau and C. Mouffe, *Hegemony and State Socialism: Towards a Radical Democratic Politics* (London and New York: Verso Books, 1985).

42 Ryan quoted in W. Lambourne, *Post-Conflict Peacebuilding: Meeting Human Needs for Justice and Reconciliation* (Washington, DC: United States Institute of Peace, 2004), available at http://www.genocideresearchhub.org.rw/document/post-conflict-peacebuilding-meeting-human-needs-justice-reconciliation/.

43 H. Nabukeera-Musoke, 'Transitional Justice and Gender in Uganda: Making Peace, Failing Women during the Peace Negotiation Process', *African Journal on Conflict Resolution*, 9(2), 2009.

44 Ngendahayo quoted in Lambourne, *Post-Conflict Peacebuilding.*

45 B. Hamber and R.A. Wilson, 'Symbolic Closure Through Memory, Reparation and Revenge in Post-conflict Societies', *Journal of Human Rights*, 1(1), 2002, pp. 35–53.

46 Ibid.

47 R. Kevers, P. Rober, I. Derluyn and L. De Haene, 'Remembering Collective Violence: Broadening the Notion of Traumatic Memory in Post-conflict Rehabilitation', *Culture, Medicine, and Psychiatry*, 40(4), 2016, pp. 620–640.

48 Ibid.

49 Ibid.

50 E. Staub, 'Promoting Reconciliation after Genocide and Mass Killing in Rwanda—and other Post-conflict Settings: Understanding the Roots of Violence, Healing, Shared History, and General Principles', *The Social Psychology of Intergroup Reconciliation*, 2008, pp. 395–422.

51 Ibid.

52 H. Liebling, L. Davidson, G.F. Akello and G. Ochola, 'The Experiences of Survivors and Trauma Counselling Service Providers in Northern Uganda: Implications for Mental Health Policy and Legislation', *International Journal of Law and Psychiatry, 49*, 2016, pp. 84–92.

53 S. Yusuf and J. Woodham, 'A Human Rights Agenda for Social Change', *Frontiers of Legal Research, 1*(2), pp. 1–20.

54 N. Couldry, *Why Voice Matters: Culture and Politics after Neoliberalism* (SAGE Publications, 2010).

55 A.M. Watson, 'Resilience is its Own Resistance: The Place of Children in Post-conflict Settlement', *Critical Studies on Security*, 3(1), 2015, pp. 47–61.

56 Lambourne, *Post-Conflict Peacebuilding.*

57 C.M. Kabwete, 'Towards Justice and Reconciliation In Post-conflict Countries: Meaningful Concepts and Possible Realities', *African Journal on Conflict Resolution*, 18(1), 2018, pp. 65–91.

58 Lambourne, *Post-Conflict Peacebuilding.*

59 K. Saha and M. De Choudhury, 'Modeling Stress with Social Media Around Incidents of Gun Violence on College Campuses', *Proceedings of the ACM on Human-Computer Interaction*, 1(CSCW), 2017, pp.1–27.

60 Ibid.

61 Kevers *et al.* 'Remembering Collective Violence', pp. 620–640.

62 Social justice is concerned with achieving equity.

63 Symbolic justice is concerned with acknowledging injustices that have occurred.
64 These concepts are abridged from Lambourne, *Post-Conflict Peacebuilding*.
65 Kabwete, 'Towards Justice and Reconciliation in Post-conflict Countries', pp. 65–91.
66 Ibid.
67 Ibid.
68 Staub, 'Promoting Reconciliation after Genocide and Mass Killing in Rwanda', pp. 395–422.
69 Ibid.
70 P. Schulz, 'To Me, Justice Means to be in a Group': Survivors' Groups as a Pathway to Justice in Northern Uganda', *Journal of Human Rights Practice*, 11 (1), 2019, pp. 171–189.
71 Ibid.
72 Staub, 'Promoting Reconciliation after Genocide and Mass Killing in Rwanda', pp. 395–422.
73 L. Edwards, F. Philip and Y. Gerrard, 'Communicating Feminist Politics? The Double-Edged Sword of Using Social Media in a Feminist Organisation', *Feminist Media Studies*, 20(5), 2020, pp. 605–622.
74 J. Vardeman-Winter, R. Lyn and R. Sharma, 'Survivor-to-Survivor Communication Model: How Organizations Can Use Post-disaster Interviewing to Facilitate Grassroots Crisis Communication', 2014.
75 R.D. Putnam, *Bowling Alone: The Collapse and Revival of American Community* (New York: Touchstone Books/Simon and Schuster, 2000).
76 Vardeman-Winter *et al.*, 'Survivor-to-Survivor Communication Model'.
77 Ibid.
78 Ibid.
79 OCHA, 'Putting the Individual First: The Importance of Survivor-Centred Approaches when Responding to Sexual Violence in Conflict', 2020, available at https://reliefweb.int/report/world/putting-individual-first-importance-survivor-centred-approaches-when-responding-sexual.
80 Ibid.
81 J.D. Giblin, 'Post-conflict Heritage: Symbolic Healing and Cultural Renewal', *International Journal of Heritage Studies*, 20(5), 2014, pp. 500–518.
82 A.J. Gilliland, 'Moving Past: Probing the Agency and Affect of Recordkeeping in Individual and Community Lives in Post-conflict Croatia', *Archival Science*, 14(3), 2014, pp. 249–274.
83 Ibid.
84 Ibid.
85 M. Godin and G. Doná, '"Refugee Voices," New Social Media and Politics of Representation: Young Congolese in the Diaspora and Beyond', *Refuge: Canada's Journal on Refugees*, 32(1), 2016, pp. 60–71.
86 M. Caswell, 'Toward a Survivor-Centered Approach to Human Rights Archives: Lessons from Community-Based Archives', *Archival Science*, 14(3–4), 2014, pp. 307–322. Special Double Issue on Human Rights Archives.
87 D. Lee, 'How the Arts Generate Social Capital to Foster Intergroup Social Cohesion', *The Journal of Arts Management, Law, and Society*, 43, 2013, pp. 4–17.
88 Ibid.
89 C.J. Ballantine, M.J. Chapman, K. Erwin and G. Maré (eds), *Living Together, Living Apart?: Social Cohesion in a Future South Africa* (Pietermaritzburg: University of KwaZulu-Natal Press, 2017).
90 S. Yusuf and J. Woodham, 'A Human Rights Agenda for Social Change', *Frontiers of Legal Research*, 1(2), 2013, pp. 1–20.
91 N. Poku, 'Community Engagement at UKZN: Current Practices, Future Directions' (Seminar Respondent: University of KwaZulu Natal Vice-

Chancellor), December 2020, available at https://ndabaonline.ukzn.ac.za/UkzndabaStory/Vol8-Issue57/Community%20Engagement%20at%20UKZN%20Examined%20during%20Webinar/ (accessed 26 October 2024).

92 A. Sewchurran and F. Pannach, 'Negotiating the Possibilities Digital Humanities Offers Media and Cultural Studies for Crisis Curriculum Adjustments in the Time of COVID-19 (KwaZulu Natal: Alternation African Scholarship Book Series, 2020), pp. 48–75.

93 R. Benmayor, 'Digital Testimonies as a Signature Pedagogy for Latin Studies', *Equity and Excellence in Education*, 5(3), 2012, pp. 507–524.

94 Ibid.

95 Moodle is an online teaching and content management platform. The Moodle platform provides for the uploading of articles, notes, discussion threads and video files, and may accommodate a large number of users. Unlike the synchronous platforms, Moodle may be used asynchronously and is more cost-effective in terms of data usage, hence it could be useful in the event of infrastructure collapse.

96 The idea of Google's helium balloon pilot can be explored in the case of diminished infrastructure which may in turn affect connectivity.

97 This approach has been very successful in the Ezakhaleni Informal Settlement, north of Durban, KwaZulu-Natal, South Africa. Mirco-funding was generated via the university and other community structures to fund things such as repairs to housing where inclement weather has cause roofs to blow off, food parcels for very poor and elderly residents of Ezakhaleni, and books for children whose parents cannot afford reading material. Mirco-funding was extremely important during the level five lockdown imposed as a result of the COVID-19 pandemic.

98 K. Crenshaw, 'The Urgency of Intersectionality', TED Talk, 2016, available at https://www.ted.com/talks/kimberle_crenshaw_the_urgency_of_intersectionality/transcript?language=en.

99 Ibid.

100 A.M. Watson, 'Resilience is its Own Resistance: The Place of Children in Post-conflict Settlement', *Critical Studies on Security*, 3(1), 2015, pp. 47–61.

References

Andreopoulou, Z., Stiakakis, E. and Vlachopoulou, M. (2014) 'Green ICT Applications towards the Achievement of Sustainable Development', in *E-innovation for Sustainable Development of Rural Resources during the Global Economic Crisis*. Hershey, PA: IGI Global, pp. 11–21.

Ballantine, C.J., Chapman, M.J., Erwin, K. and Maré, G. (eds) (2017) *Living Together, Living Apart?: Social Cohesion in a Future South Africa*. Pietermaritzburg: University of KwaZulu-Natal Press.

Benmayor, R. (2012) 'Digital Testimonies as a Signature Pedagogy for Latin Studies', *Equity and Excellence in Education*, vol. 45, no. 3, pp. 507–524.

Betancourt, T.S. and Williams, T. (2008) 'Building an Evidence Base on Mental Health Interventions for Children Affected by Armed Conflict', *Intervention*.

Betts, A. (2005) 'Should Approaches to Post-conflict Justice and Reconciliation be Determined Globally, Nationally or Locally?' *The European Journal of Development Research*, vol. 17, no. 4, pp. 735–752.

Bourdieu, P. (2000) 'Making the Economic Habitus: Algerian Workers Revisited', *Ethnography*, vol. 1, no. 1, pp. 17–41.

Brinkerhoff, D.W. (2005) 'Rebuilding Governance in Failed States and Post-conflict Societies: Core Concepts and Cross-cutting Themes', *Public Administration and*

Development: The International Journal of Management Research and Practice, vol. 25, no. 1, pp. 3–14.

Brounéus, K. (2010) 'The Trauma of Truth Telling: Effects of Witnessing in the Rwandan Gacaca Courts on Psychological Health', *Journal of Conflict Resolution*, vol. 54, no. 3, pp. 408–437.

Calderon, D. (2016) 'Moving from Damage-Centered Research through Unsettling Reflexivity', *Anthropology & Education Quarterly*, vol. 47, no. 1, pp. 5–24.

Call, C.T. and Cousens, E.M. (2008) 'Ending Wars and Building Peace: International Responses to War-Torn Societies', *International Studies Perspectives*, vol. 9, no. 1, pp. 1–21.

Caswell, M. (2014) 'Toward a Survivor-Centered Approach to Human Rights Archives: Lessons from Community-Based Archives', *Archival Science*, 14, nos 3–4, pp. 307–322. Special Double Issue on Human Rights Archives.

Connor, K.M., Davidson, J.R. and Lee, L.C. (2003) 'Spirituality, Resilience, and Anger in Survivors of Violent Trauma: A Community Survey', *Journal of Traumatic Stress*, vol. 16, no. 5, pp. 487–494.

Couldry, N. (2010) *Why Voice Matters: Culture and Politics after Neoliberalism*. London: SAGE Publications.

Davies, L. (2005) 'Teaching about Conflict through Citizenship Education', *International Journal of Citizenship and Teacher Education*, vol. 1, no. 2, pp. 17–34.

Duane F.R. and Bloomingdale, J.R. (2000) 'Spiritual Experience, Religious Orientation, and Self-Reported Behavior', *The International Journal for the Psychology of Religion*, vol. 10, no. 3, pp. 173–180.

Edwards, L., Philip, F. and Gerrard, Y. (2020) 'Communicating Feminist Politics? The Double-Edged Sword of Using Social Media in a Feminist Organisation', *Feminist Media Studies*, vol. 20, no. 5, pp. 605–622.

Ellis, C. (2004) *The Ethnographic I: A Methodological Novel about Autoethnography*, vol. 13. Walnut Creek, CA: Rowman Altamira.

Friedman, B., Nathan, L.P., Lake, M., Grey, N.C., Nilsen, T.T., Utter, R.F., Utter, E. J., Ring, M. and Kahn, Z. (2010) '*Multi-lifespan Information System Design in the Aftermath of Genocide: An Early-Stage Report from Rwanda*', 28th Annual CHI Conference on Human Factors in Computing Systems, Conference Proceedings and Extended Abstracts, Atlanta, GA.

Giblin, J.D. (2014) 'Post-conflict Heritage: Symbolic Healing and Cultural Renewal', *International Journal of Heritage Studies*, vol. 20, no. 5, pp. 500–518.

Gilliland, A.J. (2014) 'Moving Past: Probing the Agency and Affect of Recordkeeping in Individual and Community Lives in Post-conflict Croatia', *Archival Science*, vol. 14, no. 3, pp. 249–274.

Godin, M. and Doná, G. (2016) '"Refugee Voices," New Social Media and Politics of Representation: Young Congolese in the Diaspora and Beyond', *Refuge: Canada's Journal on Refugees*, vol. 32, no. 1, pp. 60–71.

Hamber, B. and Wilson, R.A. (2002) 'Symbolic Closure through Memory, Reparation and Revenge in Post-conflict Societies', *Journal of Human Rights*, vol. 1, no. 1, pp. 35–53.

Hussain, M.M. and Howard, P.N. (2013) *Democracy's fourth wave? Digital Media and the Arab Spring*. London: Oxford University Press.

Isgandarova, N. (2011) 'What the Spiritual Caregiver Should Know while Dealing with Survivors of Ethnic Violence', *Khazar Journal of Humanities and Social Science*, vol. 14, no. 3.

Kabwete, C.M. (2018) 'Towards Justice and Reconciliation in Post-conflict Countries: Meaningful Concepts and Possible Realities', *African Journal on Conflict Resolution*, vol. 18, no. 1, pp. 65–91.

Kevers, R., Rober, P., Derluyn, I. and De Haene, L. (2016) 'Remembering Collective Violence: Broadening the Notion of Traumatic Memory in Post-conflict Rehabilitation', *Culture, Medicine, and Psychiatry*, vol. 40, no. 4, pp. 620–640.

Laclau, E. and Mouffe, C. (1985) Hegemony and State Socialism: Towards a Radical Democratic Politics. London and New York: Verso.

Lee, D. (2013) 'How the Arts Generate Social Capital to Foster Intergroup Social Cohesion', *The Journal Of Arts Management, Law, And Society*, vol. 43, pp. 4–17.

Liebling, H., Davidson, L., Akello, G.F. and Ochola, G. (2016) 'The Experiences of Survivors and Trauma Counselling Service Providers in Northern Uganda: Implications for Mental Health Policy and Legislation', *International Journal of Law and Psychiatry*, vol. 49, pp. 84–92.

Manzi, Y. (2013) *Jean Paul Sartre: Existential 'Freedom' and the Political*. Thesis, E-International Relations, pp. 3–9. Available at https://www.e-ir.info/2013/01/23/jean-paul-sartre-existential-freedom-and-the-political/.

Miller, K.E. and Rasmussen, A. (2010) ,War Exposure, Daily Stressors, and Mental Health in Conflict and Post-conflict Settings: Bridging the Divide between Trauma-Focused and Psychosocial Frameworks', *Social Science & Medicine*, vol. 70, no. 1, pp. 7–16.

Moreno-Ger, P., Burgos, D., Martínez-Ortiz, I., Sierra, J.L. and Fernández-Manjón, B. (2008) 'Educational Game Design for Online Education', *Computers in Human Behavior*, vol. 24, no. 6, pp. 2530–2540.

Nabukeera-Musoke, H. (2009) 'Transitional Justice and Gender in Uganda: Making Peace, Failing Women during the Peace Negotiation Process', *African Journal on Conflict Resolution*, vol. 9, no. 2.

Naimark, N.M. (2017) 'Srebrenica in the History of Genocide: A Prologue', in *Memories of Mass Repression*. New York: Routledge.

Patrick, S. (2006) 'Weak States and Global Threats: Assessing Evidence of Spillovers', Center for Global Development, Working Paper 73.

Poku, N. (2020) 'Community Engagement at UKZN: Current Practices, Future Directions' (Seminar Respondent: University of KwaZulu Natal Vice-Chancellor), December, available at https://ndabaonline.ukzn.ac.za/UkzndabaStory/Vol8-Issue57/Community%20Engagement%20at%20UKZN%20Examined%20during%20Webinar/ (accessed 26 October 2024).

Putnam, R.D. (2000) *Bowling Alone: The Collapse and Revival of American Community*. New York: Touchstone Books/Simon and Schuster.

Reinert, D.F. and Bloomingdale, J.R. (1999) 'Spiritual Maturity and Mental Health: Implications for Counseling', *Counseling and Values*, vol. 43, no. 3, pp. 211–223.

Saha, K. and De Choudhury, M. (2017) 'Modeling Stress with Social Media around Incidents of Gun Violence on College Campuses', *Proceedings of the ACM on Human-Computer Interaction*, vol. 1 (CSCW), pp. 1–27.

Schmid, E. and Cohen, J. (2014) 'The New Digital Age: Reshaping the Future of Peoples, Nations and Business', *VIKALPA*, vol. 29, no. 3.

Schulz, P. (2019) '"To Me, Justice Means to be in a Group": Survivors' Groups as a Pathway to Justice in Northern Uganda', *Journal of Human Rights Practice*, vol. 11, no. 1, pp. 171–189.

Sewchurran, A. and Pannach, F. (2020) 'Negotiating the Possibilities Digital Humanities Offers Media and Cultural Studies for Crisis Curriculum Adjustments in the

Time of COVID-19', KwaZulu Natal: Alternation African Scholarship Book Series, pp. 48–75.

Sjölund, B.H., Kastrup, M., Montgomery, E. and Persson, A.L. (2009) 'Rehabilitating Torture Survivors', *J Rehabil Med.*, vol. 41, no. 9, pp. 689–696.

Smith, J.R., Ho, L.S., Langston, A., Mankani, N., Shivshanker, A. and Perera, D. (2013) 'Clinical Care for Sexual Assault Survivors Multimedia Training: A Mixed-Methods Study of Effect on Healthcare Providers' Attitudes, Knowledge, Confidence, and Practice in Humanitarian Settings', *Conflict and Health*, vol. 7, no. 1, pp. 1–10.

Staub, E. (2008) 'Promoting Reconciliation after Genocide and Mass Killing in Rwanda—and Other Post Conflict Settings: Understanding the Roots of Violence, Healing, Shared History, and General Principles', in A. Nadler, T.E. Malloy and J. D. Fisher (eds), *The Social Psychology of Intergroup Reconciliation*, New York: Oxford University Press, pp. 395–422.

Vardeman-Winter, J., Lyn, R. and Sharma, R. (2014) 'Survivor-to-Survivor Communication Model: How Organizations Can Use Post-Disaster Interviewing to Facilitate Grassroots Crisis Communication'. Paper presented to the Public Relations Division, AEJMC, Montreal.

Wagner, B. and Maercker, A. (2010) 'Internet-based Intervention for Posttraumatic Stress Disorder', *Internet Use in the Aftermath of Trauma*. Amsterdam: IOS Press, pp. 255–267.

Watson, A.M. (2015) 'Resilience is its Own Resistance: The Place of Children in Post-conflict Settlement', *Critical Studies on Security*, vol. 3, no. 1, pp. 47–61.

Yusuf, S. and Woodham, J. (2013) 'A Human Rights Agenda for Social Change', *Frontiers of Legal Research*, vol. 1, no. 2, pp. 1–20.

Web-based Documents

Crenshaw, K. (2016) 'The Urgency of Intersectionality', *TED Talk*. Available at https://www.ted.com/talks/kimberle_crenshaw_the_urgency_of_intersectionality/transcript?language=en.

Hatmaker, T. (2018) 'Facebook's Free Basics Program Ended Quietly in Myanmar Last Year', *Techcrunch*. Available at https://techcrunch.com/2018/05/01/facebook-free-basics-ending-myanmar-internet-org/#:~:text=Facebook%20confirmed%20to%20TechCrunch%20that,2016%20launch%20in%20the%20country https://www.hrw.org/world-report/2019.

Kurlantzick, J. (2019) 'Rohingya Refugees Risk Going Back to Another Genocide in Myanmar', *World Politics Review*. Available at https://www.worldpoliticsreview.com/articles/28219/rohingya-refugees-risk-going-back-to-another-genocide-in-myanmar.

Lambourne, W. (2004) 'Post-Conflict Peacebuilding: Meeting Human Needs for Justice and Reconciliation', *United States Institute of Peace*. Available at http://www.genocideresearchhub.org.rw/document/post-conflict-peacebuilding-meeting-human-needs-justice-reconciliation/.

McKell, K.L. (2020) *How Civil Society Organizations (CSOs) Use Media for Peacebuilding in Post-Conflict Societies*. Unpublished master's thesis, Aristotle University of Thessaloniki. Available at http://ikee.lib.auth.gr/record/319287/files/GRI-2020-27361.pdf.

OCHA (2020) *Putting the Individual First: The Importance of Survivor-Centred Approaches when Responding to Sexual Violence in Conflict*. Available at https://

reliefweb.int/report/world/putting-individual-first-importance-survivor-centred-approaches-when-responding-sexual.

Otieno, S. (2020) 'Finding Wellbeing through Yoga at a Kenyan Refugee Camp', UNHCR. Available at https://www.unhcr.org/news/stories/2020/10/5f7ebb6c4/finding-wellbeing-yoga-kenyan-refugee-camp.html.

Reynolds, M. (2018) 'Facebook and Google's Race to Connect the World Is Heating Up', *WIRED.* Available at https://www.wired.co.uk/article/google-project-loon-balloon-facebook-aquila-internet-africa.

Sørensen, B. (1998) 'Women and Post-conflict Reconstruction: Issues and Sources (no. 3), WSP Occasional Paper, *ECONSTOR*. Available at https://www.econstor.eu/handle/10419/148841.

Conclusion

Ingrid Roestenburg-Morgan and Tim Murithi

Introduction

This book has dealt exclusively with 'survivors' as a distinct category within the framework of transitional justice as well as the commonly derived 'survivor-centred approach'. Through the views expressed by various authors from the international community the reader has been exposed to the various efforts geared towards justice for survivors, which have been undertaken by instrumental transitional justice institutions, mechanisms and organizations all contributing to justice for survivors within the transitional justice landscape.

Underlying the main objective of highlighting justice for survivors this volume has also sought to provide global perspectives on the definition of survivors. This is because the term survivor currently remains subjective and miscellaneous, albeit that it is commonly and popularly employed by legal and international scholars, practitioners and institutions. Ancillary to this is the understanding and implementation of a survivor-centred approach, which is also highly subjective and is less concretized in practice and academic circles. Weaved throughout this book, therefore, is a focus on various definitions and understandings of a survivor and of a survivor-centred approach.

Summary of the Chapters and Findings

Part I

Part I of this book is dedicated to the efforts of the International Criminal Court (ICC) in relation to survivors of mass atrocities. In Chapters 1, 2 and 3, we witnessed how the ICC as a pivotal transitional justice actor administers justice for survivors. An underlying objective is whether the ICC adheres to the rights that should naturally accrue to survivors such as the right to justice, reparations and the right to truth. Central to this investigation is an examination of the ICC's victim participation programme that has been an innovative and groundbreaking development within international criminal

DOI: 10.4324/9781003212409-16

law as well as a focus on its impact on and value to survivors of mass atrocities. This part of the book delves more deeply into the concerted efforts made on behalf of survivors at the ICC that include the work of the Trust Fund for Victims and relatedly reparations for victims and survivors. Finally, while the ICC has provided a more central space for victims within the criminal justice process, it has done so based on the legal category and basis of what constitutes a 'victim' and not a 'survivor'. Ultimately, the question that arises is whether a legally bereft category such as that of the 'survivor' would enable 'survivors' to be entitled to the same rights and privileges that victims as a legal category are entitled to more generally and at the ICC. This question is explored in more detail in this part of the book. An analysis of a survivor-centred approach and its application at the ICC is also included.

In Chapter 1 Pena focuses extensively on victim participation at the ICC and shows how ideally victim and survivor participation should be administered at the Court. She pays specific attention to a holistic form of victim participation, which takes into account grassroots and community needs. In practice, however, Pena purports that the Court has fallen short of facilitating truly meaningful and engaging victim and survivor participation based on three main aspects from the perspectives of victims and survivors, namely access to justice, the participatory experience and the outcomes of the judicial process. In terms of the latter identified criteria victims and survivors are limited by the selected crimes designated for prosecution as well as the scope of the case. Other barriers include less than optimal legal representation for survivors and delayed convictions. Further limitations include the right to tender evidence and the right to question witnesses, which limits their ability to participate effectively and as a result to access meaningful justice. Furthermore, survivors' material and psychological needs are only partially addressed by the Court. While Pena takes note of the ICC's value to survivors she highlights the multiple barriers that prevent meaningful participation for victims and survivors of mass atrocities. She recommends that the ICC should question the impact of its work in terms of meeting victims' justice needs by questioning the decision-making on the scope of cases ensuring adequate consultations, improving staff and officials' understanding of the local context, and linking participation to complementary initiatives in order to address survivors' needs in a more holistic manner.

As was reiterated earlier, one of the ways that the ICC provides an avenue to justice for survivors is through the work of the Trust Fund for Victims, a topic that is covered in Chapter 2. The chapter highlights some of the criticisms that compromise effective justice being accorded to survivors of mass atrocities based on the way in which individuals are excluded from the definition of a 'victim' under the ICC's legal framework. Throughout the chapter substantial case law is drawn upon in order to demonstrate how exclusion from victim status prevents survivors from attaining justice since they may not legally be classified as victims. With this in mind, Ingber argues that if we consider restorative justice as a process of settling the present, then the inclusion of Article 79 of the Rome Statute may nevertheless provide an avenue to justice for survivors of mass atrocities even when the individual is not legally classified as a victim. Under Article 79 the ICC may order that money collected through fines or forfeiture is transferred to the Trust Fund for Victims and may be used for the benefit of victims of crimes and their families. As Ingber suggests, although the Trust Fund was established by the Rome Statute, its dual mandate enables it to incorporate victim-survivors into its assistance mandate and this has enabled the Trust Fund to shift some of the language of legal victimhood through the discursive construction of the victim-survivor to allow the survivor to appear in situation-based reparative processes. This enables survivors to have at least a limited voice in the justice process by subsuming them in the reparations system through the use of the term victim-survivor. Such an acknowledgement can help survivors restore their dignity since reparation measures focus on the empowerment of the victim and the survivor by aiming to place the latter in a better position than before the conflict took place.

Chapter 3 focuses on the definition of the terms 'survivor' and 'survivor-centred approach' as they are currently understood and conceptualized within transitional justice settings and by the international community. Roestenburg-Morgan in this chapter suggests that a transitional justice actor such as the ICC, which currently leans more towards a victim-centred approach, should also actively seek to recognize survivors as a distinct category in a similar manner comparable to the rights and privileges that victims are accorded. This is because the ICC as a leading transitional justice actor owes allegiance to all individuals recovering from mass atrocities and therefore to those who identify as survivors. As a result the ICC should be more assertive in coining a legal definition of the term survivor in order to facilitate adherence and to give credence to a survivor-centred approach, thereby constituting the foundational underpinnings of the approach. This is important to provide survivors with legal standing, which will enable them to access their rights more freely and readily under the legal framework of the ICC. In sum, the power and value of the ICC to contribute to survivors' rights can be groundbreaking and empowering in a similar fashion to victims' rights at the ICC. However, this can only be achieved by ensuring that relevant legal recognition is accorded to survivors so that their dignity is respected and upheld in all their dealings with and participation at the Court.

Part II

Local, informal and traditional/customary justice mechanisms are highlighted in Chapters 4 and 5, which constitute Part II of this book, in order to assist the reader in understanding the nature of some of these mechanisms, their interaction with formal justice and their contribution to achieving justice for survivors recovering from mass atrocities. Chapter 4 outlines how traditional healing ceremonies can be of value and use to survivors in transitional societies. The basic premise in this chapter follows the argument that if healing ceremonies can be instrumental in innovative community efforts at peacebuilding, then they can surely be integrated into deliberately formulated transitional justice processes. As this chapter demonstrates there are many potential benefits of traditional healing ceremonies in survivor communities recovering from mass conflict. Some of the advantages include a therapeutic function for survivors, reintegration of survivors into the community, reconciliation through decreasing distrust within survivor communities and healing with regard to mental health issues.

However, there are also drawbacks, namely the creation and perpetuation of inequality and patriarchy and gender discrimination. Given these drawbacks Odhiambo argues that with the appropriate modifications these ceremonies can be used within transitional justice settings. The African Union Transitional Justice Policy (AUTJP) recognizes the efficacy of healing ceremonies and purports that they can be adapted and used alongside other formal mechanisms to address justice, peace, accountability, social cohesion, reconciliation and healing. Odhiambo calls for African states to recognize the value of these ceremonies to promote healing for survivors and to use them in a way that is consistent with the demands of transitional justice.

In Chapter 5 Adam focuses on local justice mechanisms that already exist in Sudan and which are available through customary law. They may be a possible avenue to justice for victims and survivors of mass atrocities in Darfur. Local justice mechanisms such as *judiyya* and the town and rural courts are highlighted in this chapter, demonstrating the traditional and cultural linkages in enabling justice for victims and survivors in Darfur. Judiyya is a traditional mediation and arbitration system which, as Adam notes, can be modified in post-conflict settings to become part of a larger transitional justice mechanism capable of dealing with the gravity and scale of the crimes committed in the region. Adam suggests that judiyya is similar to other indigenous, traditional or local justice mechanisms in Africa, and that it has a restorative justice purview; moreover, this is important for achieving justice in the Sudanese context. However, he cautions against romanticizing the function of local justice mechanisms in their entirety. In his view they require modification to ensure that they are able to meet international fair trial standards. The chapter therefore highlights the hidden value and untapped potential of local, customary or indigenous systems of justice that could provide an amenable and legitimate solution to Sudan in a similar fashion to the way in which other local justice mechanisms such as the Gacaca courts functioned in Rwanda. However, Adam notes that it is essential to modify such mechanisms in view of due process and human rights standards.

Thus, while Odhiambo and Adam recognize the value of local/traditional/customary/ alternative justice mechanisms, they both highlight the need to ensure that such mechanisms receive modification and enhancement to meet the demands of transitional justice in recovering societies. If they are to be utilized or relied upon then they should be modified in a way in which the rights of the survivor are placed centre stage in accordance with fair justice standards and due process of the law. This would mean that any drawbacks that give way to discrimination or unfairness against survivors should be mitigated according to international and transitional justice standards.

Part III

In Part III comprising Chapters 6, 7 and 8, emphasis is placed on the advocacy efforts made on behalf of survivors by international civil society organizations such as the Denis Mukwege Foundation together with initiatives initiated by continental and international institutions such as the AU and UN Women, respectively, to showcase the impact of advocacy on behalf of survivors. Through these efforts the reader is exposed to the impact that non-governmental organizations (NGOs) and international institutions have on the promotion and execution of survivors rights in transitional societies. Chapter 6 explores the dynamics of social movement theory to show how survivors through collective information gathering and the formation of networks can influence decision-making and justice processes. Laxminarayan and Fernandes Thomaz argue that in order for survivors to achieve meaningful justice there must be a survivor-centred approach in place within transitional justice processes to ensure that the objectives of transitional justice are met. Such an approach would mean that survivors gain autonomy and decision-making over the justice processes that affect them. The authors suggest that this can be achieved through the conduit of civic mobilization to make effective demands for justice. They consider civil society comprising NGOs, social movements and collective behaviours as pivotal in strengthening the voice of survivors within transitional justice. They argue that the participation of survivors through these avenues will enhance survivors' agency, ensure their equal participation in transitional justice processes and accord them recognition and validation in the relevant society concerned. Survivor networks are therefore important in placing survivors in leadership roles, which helps them to assert a public voice through meaningful participation and this in turn leads to meaningful transitional justice. Through practical examples of what constitutes meaningful participation an explorative approach was used as a practical framework to assist survivor networks in functioning effectively to contribute to or support the development of the rule of law and transitional justice.

Through the lens of two employees of UN Women Chapter 7 provides useful information for civil society practitioners on how to place survivors centre stage in post-conflict justice processes. Through the use of the examples of Kosovo and Guatemala where UN Women has been engaged Kenney and Kelmendi demonstrate that through an innovative survivor-centred approach UN Women has made significant strides in supporting survivors by ensuring strong programming on justice to address conflict-related sexual violence (CSVR) in both Kosovo and Guatemala. In Kosovo the authors show how survivors played a leading role in developing and implementing a reparations programme to tackle CSVR, and are now working with investigators and prosecutors to pursue criminal cases against perpetrators. In Guatemala they show how a group of indigenous survivors of CRSV won a groundbreaking conviction in the *Sepur Zarco* case of two former military officers convicted of rape and sexual slavery, and a wide-ranging reparations judgment. The survivors are now leading efforts to ensure the implementation of the reparations judgment. Through its programming efforts UN Women has provided support to survivors, governments and justice institutions in both the aforementioned contexts in order to make a greater impact in dealing with the root causes of CSVR and to bring attention to the plight of survivors of CSVR. According to both authors, despite the success of UN Women's efforts there still remain challenges which UN Women need to improve on to ensure for a consistent survivor-centred approach to justice. This includes analysing lessons learned from other transitional contexts. Furthermore, because UN member states are donors to UN programmes they should ensure that UN entities integrate a survivor-centred approach in their decision-making and vice versa; member states themselves should be include survivor-centred approaches in their working methods in order to empower survivors.

In other related advocacy efforts aimed at justice for survivors Murithi assesses and delves into notions of survivor-centred justice as viewed from the perspective of the AUTJP largely embodied and drawing inspiration from Mahmood Mamdani's views on survivors in post-conflict or transitional societies. Based on the continental and regional advocacy efforts of the AU through its transitional policy Murithi explores whether alternative forms of justice can contribute to accountability and uplift the dignity of survivors in post-conflict African societies. According to Murithi, this question must be examined in light of the transient processes, which are consistent with transitions. As the term 'transition' suggests. Murithi maintains that processes to shift societies from chaos to peace must be designed solely as a temporary process and not as a permanent solution. This is why alternative forms of justice may be more suitable for dealing with issues of mass violence rather than criminal justice processes or prosecutions because the crimes committed are difficult to quantify, and culpability is more widespread. Murithi's view is consistent with that of Mamdani, who highlights the difficulties of using or relying fully on prosecutions for a broad range of interventions, ideally political ones, which directly engage survivors comprising victims, perpetrators and beneficiaries. In a similar vein, the AUTJP states that transitional justice should primarily be viewed as a political process geared towards nation building and addressing the root causes of violence. The chapter further uses the South African transition to demonstrate the complexities of post-conflict societies and to advocate for alternative forms of justice as a solution based on the AUTJP, in order to address the real economic and social concerns of survivors. The regional efforts of the AUTJP are geared at supporting survivors through community-led transitional justice efforts as well as transformative initiatives, which are African and/or locally led. Although in its infancy stage the Policy's aim is to provide for the needs of needs of survivors of sexual and gender-based violence to ensure that they are able to access the appropriate medical, protective and psycho-social services as well as ensuring that survivors are able to obtain successful reparative justice.

Part IV

The final section of this volume, Part IV (Chapters 9 and 10) is dedicated to the future prospects for survivors. Here the practical findings of research and the means to support peacebuilding and atrocity prevention are showcased. This includes technological advances that support a digital solution that allows survivors to access an online community of support that could re-establish their dignity and nurture their psychosocial needs. Additionally, optimizing justice for survivors for future purposes should include establishing clearer understandings of the categorical determination of survivors as well as challenging the existing stereotypes and myths characterizing the 'survivor category'. Current understandings of who comprises a 'survivor' limit effective responses by transitional justice processes owing to the existence of myths or stereotypes that have been determined subjectively.

This is evidenced in Chapter 9, which is an innovative study into male survivors of violence (MSV) in the post-conflict setting of Mt Elgon region in western Kenya. Through the use of a phenomenological approach, this chapter details the lived experiences of interviewees and shows that in order for MSV to attain reconciliation and healing in transitional societies, it is imperative that they have the opportunity to confront the past by having a safe space, which will facilitate truth telling. In this chapter most of those interviewed participated in truth telling processes facilitated by the Truth Justice and Reconciliation Commission (TJRC) which was established by the Kenyan government after the electoral violence. The chapter therefore delves into the lived experiences of MSV in Mt Egon revealing intimate experiences of both the violence they encountered and the shortcomings of the transitional justice processes that were in place at that particular time.

The chapter shows through the empirical research conducted that men, like women, can become the targets of sexual violence during conflict. While they do not meet the stereotypical gender role that assumes that women and children are the main targets, men have in fact been subjected to similar kinds of severe violence. During conflicts men are usually perceived as the perpetrators of violence, while women are typically victims and survivors. This has been demonstrated through the Kenyan TJRC that offered women an opportunity to come forward to relate their stories, while efforts were seldom made to encourage MSV to come forward to narrate their experiences.

Through the interviews conducted the narrative of male survivors are brought forward to show that men's agency in actively participating in conflict resolution mechanisms is limited in comparison to female survivors. The study undertaken in this chapter is innovative for future research on male survivors because it reveals that socialized masculinity camouflages male experiences of violence and is important for further future research under transitional justice. It further demonstrates the importance of truth telling for peacebuilding which if ignored can lead to a heightened risk of conflict and war, thereby highlighting the nexus between peacebuilding and atrocity prevention. As the author of this chapter, Opongo, reveals, truth telling can offer victims and survivors a sense of justice, which lessens the desire for vengeance and increases the potential for sustainable peace contributing to the peacebuilding and atrocity prevention nexus.

In keeping with peacebuilding and atrocity prevention the final chapter of this book explores various technological innovations and advancements, which have been used in post-conflict societies in order to support the rehabilitation of survivors and contribute to peacebuilding. David and Sewchurran focus on the value and relevance of information and communication technologies and more specifically Computer-based Self-help Mutual Aid (CSHMA) for the benefit of survivors including visual methodologies. According to the authors, CSHMA can promote social justice by helping survivors to heal from past traumas since they will be able to share their stories and narratives in closed groups online with the possibility of mediation where necessary. They argue that by building a safe digital space the agency, empowerment and healing of survivors may be better supported.

The authors argue that under transitional justice if legal justice cannot be achieved then it will be necessary for survivors to focus on and pursue social justice which contributes to positive peace. Part of this includes survivors working on their self-awareness, pain and suffering and their healing and forgiveness which for future purposes may be valuable in atrocity prevention, once reconciliation comes into sight. This can be achieved through a flexible living archive as a digital collaborative method whereby post-conflict survivors can meet online and where a repository for personal narratives can be created.

By partnering with regional human rights institutions and universities flexible living archives can be hosted as part of promoting human rights and nation building. Given that in post-conflict societies it is necessary to rebuild infrastructure, including institutions such as universities, the authors suggest that regional partner community blocks should be developed so that a range of regional partners can come together to host flexible living archives for survivors and supply resources such as data and smart devices. In extreme cases where the destruction of infrastructure such as microwave towers takes place, then the idea of putting into operation high-altitude helium-filled balloons floating 20 kilometres above sea level in the stratosphere, can be contemplated. David and Sewchurran also conceive of a plan consisting of four phases with feasible partners to demonstrate the operation of a flexible, digital living archive for post-conflict survivors which speaks to the future of digital technology in rebuilding war-torn societies and in contributing to social healing for the benefit of sustainable peace.

Significant Findings and Relevant Recommendations

A number of significant findings emerged from this volume.

1 **Survivors face obstacles as a result of a lack of legal recognition. The definition of a survivor and a survivor-centred approach requires legal recognition and concretization.**

A common thread running through this book points to the necessity of legal recognition of survivors. A person's identity is a crucial aspect of their dignity, agency and development and the lack of recognition is rooted in inequality and discrimination. The denial of a person's identity can lead to feelings of injustice, lack of respect, lack of self-esteem and humiliation. The legal and political recognition of one's identity can therefore change the way in which individuals perceive and value themselves. Similarly, individuals who identify as survivors require specific recognition of their survivor identity and should not resort to falling under the umbrella of the victim identity when accessing their rights and benefits unless they identify as victims too. Survivors should be in a position to share an equal identity with other legally recognized groups under transitional justice and international law. This is important because as authors such as Pena, Ingber and Roestenburg-Morgan have suggested, survivors may face greater difficulty and participate less meaningfully at the ICC and other transitional justice processes due to a lack of legal recognition or standing. Currently, the definition of a survivor and a survivor-centred approach remains subjective which diminishes a survivor's rights and opportunities to engage meaningfully on various fronts.

Recommendation: It is recommended that available international legal instruments, legal institutions like the ICC, NGOs, continental and international organizations be cognizant of the 'narrative' surrounding survivors as a category or group under transitional justice and aspire to address the issue of their identity in recognition of the wrongs committed against them during conflict and as part of the principle of equality under international law.

2 **While of value to survivors traditional, local or customary justice mechanisms still require modification to fully meet survivors' justice needs as well as international legal standards.**

An analysis of traditional, local or customary mechanisms by Odhiambo, Adam and Murithi reveal that they are of value to post-conflict societies in achieving justice, peace and reconciliation for survivors and society at large. It has been particularly useful in politically divisive societies where unity and reconciliation is necessary and where context-specific demands necessitate a local or community response to justice. For survivors its value can have a cathartic and therapeutic function and provides a meaningful space for truth telling. However, as the authors suggest, such mechanisms need modification taking into account due process and broader transitional justice standards that will ensure the fair and equal participation of all survivors.

Recommendation: It is recommended that traditional, local, alternative or customary justice mechanisms be established on the basis of restorative tenets of justice but that a prosecutorial option supplement or work in tandem with such mechanisms to uphold domestic and international due process standards in order to satisfy a more holistic approach to justice consistent with transitional and international justice standards.

3 **Survivors can increase their agency and empowerment, and showcase and accelerate their struggles by supporting survivor networks and social movements or through strong programming efforts.**

Based on the analysis by Laxminarayan and Fernandes Thomaz, Murithi, as well as Kenney and Kelmendi it has become evident that survivor-led activism supported by the advocacy efforts of NGOs and international organizations such as the United Nations or the AU is valuable in helping survivors to overcome insecurity and stigma to become more empowered and take the lead in their own lives. This is because survivor networks, social movements, programming efforts and policies offer a platform to survivors where there can be a sharing and exchange of information and the ability to advocate for and lobby more powerfully for their individual and collective causes. Survivor networks in particular, present a powerful tool for survivors creating a safe space to organize and raise awareness around survivors' experiences and their realities, including challenging and overcoming stigmas. This ultimately has the ability to foster agency since it creates spaces for survivors to speak out create change, influence policies, and demand justice and accountability.

Recommendation: It is therefore recommended that survivors link their struggles ideally with survivor networks, NGOs and social movements which create and facilitate change, influence policies, and demand justice and accountability for survivors. It is further recommended that NGOs and other international organizations advocating for survivors' support initiatives to promote survivor-centred justice programmes that place the survivor at the centre of their work and efforts.

4 **Gender stereotypes and myths confronting survivors need to be challenged and combated in order to avoid gaps in the determination of the truth.**

Myths and gender stereotypes confronting survivors make it difficult for survivors to speak about their experiences and contribute to truth telling and a record of wrongs committed against them. This creates shame and stigma leading to self-blame. One of the predominant gender stereotypes or myths revealed in Chapter 9 is that men do not get raped and are less likely to be subject to CRSV. Another myth is that women and children do not commit sexual violence during conflict, which leads to the assumption that both women and children can only be classified as survivors but men cannot. Opongo has shown that while there remains a particular focus on women and children the impact of sexual violence and abuse is no less devastating on men. Similarly, women and children can be the perpetrators of violence against men. This needs to be acknowledged under transitional justice in order to dispel these myths and to help survivors to receive the necessary support and space in which to tell their stories and to contribute to their own healing and the wider societal healing.

Recommendation: Transitional justice processes and mechanisms need to dispel myths and gender stereotypes in order to register an accurate record of wrongs committed and to facilitate truth telling. It is thus incumbent upon governments, justice institutions, health care services and organizations engaged both overtly and more generally with survivors to be aware of, expose and guard against such stereotypes and myths.

5 **New technology can support survivors' justice needs and transform the transitional justice landscape, thereby contributing to atrocity prevention and effective peacebuilding.**

Transitional justice practice and scholarship has been slow to deal with the impact of technological and artificial intelligence in supporting survivors' rights and needs in post-conflict societies. David and Swechurran have shown that new technology can offer new ways to support a survivor-centred platform that can assist survivors to heal from past traumas through the sharing of stories and narratives in closed groups online. Such technological resources are innovative and will support work in truth telling, accountability and reparations. Furthermore, these exciting possibilities can lead to initiatives that support the dignity of survivors and further contribute to atrocity prevention and peacebuilding.

Recommendation: It is incumbent upon governments, scholars, public institutions such as universities and transitional justice actors to focus on the possibilities and dilemmas that new digital spaces create for transitional justice practice and research in order to utilize this effectively for the benefit of survivors.

Final Thoughts

In closing, this book has sought to provide both theoretical and practical underpinnings supporting survivors together with an understanding of the implementation of a survivor-centred approach. Through demonstrable experiences this book has shown that there are various pathways or avenues for survivors to access justice apart from criminal justice; first to hold perpetrators to account and second to highlight survivors' individual and collective narratives. These pathways or avenues were shown to exist through advocacy efforts, survivor networks, social movements, online spaces and alternative justice mechanisms. Aside from these alternative pathways to justice, survivors recovering from mass atrocities may still primarily rely on international criminal justice vis-à-vis the ICC which includes its Victim Participation Programme and its Trust Fund for Victims. However, the ICC's work in relation to survivors still requires much more effort and attention to ensure adequate and meaningful justice for this category of actors.

The conclusions drawn from this book highlight that access to justice through both formal and informal means is a key component supporting a strong survivor-centred approach to justice. Particularly in transitional societies there is a need for robust justice systems that are well equipped to deal with and respond to CRSV and other atrocity crimes. It is therefore important for survivors to rely on a multi-pronged approach in accessing justice together with their rights and supporting their dignity in such fragile contexts. Transitional justice mechanisms must therefore be equipped with non-discriminatory legal frameworks, non-patriarchal practices and norms as well as awareness and centrality of rights including adequate support services that will enable instead of impede a survivor's ability to access justice in these contexts.

In essence, justice for survivors is linked to a survivor's own definition of what justice means to them. As this volume has demonstrated, justice for survivors may be linked to retributive justice, restorative justice, truth, dignity, economic empowerment or acknowledgement. Survivor-centred justice should aim to keep the survivor at the centre of justice interventions and find ways to strengthen and empower survivors by enabling them to speak up for themselves and promote their own agency and autonomy. A survivor-centred approach therefore means giving voice to survivors and placing their needs and rights at the forefront of any justice process. A survivor-centred approach is also a pivotal step towards healing, overcoming shame and stigma and moving towards truth and reconciliation in complex societies in order to restore a sense of self (identity) and community. Survivor-centred justice must therefore be viewed as a critical element of transitional justice, which must not be ignored or trivialized if progress is to be made in transforming situations of impunity into situations of peaceful co-existence and simultaneously overcoming disenfranchisement and supporting the empowerment and the dignity of the survivor.

Index

Note: **Bold** page number refer to **tables**.

For Product Safety Concerns and Information please contact our EU representative GPSR@taylorandfrancis.com
Taylor & Francis Verlag GmbH, Kaufingerstraße 24, 80331 München, Germany

www.ingramcontent.com/pod-product-compliance
Lightning Source LLC
LaVergne TN
LVHW021120300926
849160LV00010B/798

* 9 7 8 1 0 3 2 0 7 9 9 5 0 *